THE
ILLUSTRATED
ENCYCLOPEDIA
OF
GENERAL
AVIATION

2nd Edition

THE ILLUSTRATED ENCYCLOPEDIA OF GENERAL AVIATION

2nd Edition

Paul Garrison

TAB BOOKS Inc.
Blue Ridge Summit, PA

SECOND EDITION
FIRST PRINTING

Library of Congress Cataloging-in-Publication Data

Garrison, Paul.
   Illustrated encyclopedia of general aviation / by Paul Garrison. -
- 2nd ed.
     p. cm.
   ISBN 0-8306-8316-X   ISBN 0-8306-3316-2 (pbk.)
   1. Aeronautics–Dictionaries.   2. Private flying–Dictionaries.
I. Title.
TL509.G27   1990
629.13″003–dc20   89-29160
                                      CIP

TAB BOOKS Inc. offers software for sale. For information and a catalog, please contact TAB Software Department, Blue Ridge Summit, PA 17294-0850.

Questions regarding the content of this book should be addressed to:

Reader Inquiry Branch
TAB BOOKS Inc.
Blue Ridge Summit, PA 17294-0214

Acquisition Editor: Jeff Worsinger
Technical Editor: Norval G. Kennedy
Production: Katherine Brown
Book Design: Jaclyn B. Saunders

Cover photograph courtesy of Piper Aircraft Corporation

CONTENTS

Preface

This is a revised and updated version of the *Illustrated Encyclopedia/Dictionary of General Aviation* that was published originally in 1979. This edition not only includes all the still-applicable information that was contained in the original, but also everything that is new at this time. I have retained the mention of aircraft that are no longer in production because many are still available on the used aircraft market.

As before, the names and addresses of all aviation organizations, aviation publications, FAA FSDO/GADO offices, and state aviation departments are listed. Also listed are airframe manufacturers, avionics, engine and equipment manufacturers along with their products, and, where applicable, performance specifications.

One of the most significant changes that has taken place during the past ten years is the extensive use of various types of computers, both in the cockpit and on the ground. With this in mind, computer-related data that are applicable to general aviation have been added.

Also new are the global positioning systems (GPS) for long-range navigation, the gradual installation of microwave landing systems (MLS) at major airports and heliports and the introduction of Loran-C for long-range navigation in the United States and on a limited worldwide basis.

Not included are specifications related strictly to military aviation and to the airlines, though some aircraft data relating to these disciplines are included when it was deemed that such information would be of interest to general aviation pilots.

In order to avoid the frequent repetition of the rather awkward he/she phraseology, I have used *he* throughout and I ask that the many female pilots accept my apology.

Paul Garrison
Santa Fe, New Mexico

List of Illustrations and Tables

A

B

C

D

H

I

J

K

N

O

P

T

A   Absolute (temperature).

A   Alaskan Standard Time.

A   Alpha (phonetic alphabet).

A   Alternate (on instrument approach charts).

A   Altimeter (on radio logs).

A   Arctic air mass.

A   Cleared to the airport (ATC clearance shorthand).

A   Ceiling as reported by an aircraft (in sequence reports).

A   Hail (in sequence reports).

AAA   Antique Aircraft Association.

AAAE   American Association of Airport Executives.

AAC   Alaskan Air Command.

AACA   Alaskan Air Carriers Association.

AAP   Advise if able to proceed.

AAP   Association of Aviation Psychologists.

AAS   Airport advisory service.

AAS   Airport advisory station.

AATM   At all times.

AAWF   Auxiliary aviation weather facility.

AB   Air base.

AB   Airborne.

AB   Continuous automatic transcribed broadcast service (AIM).

ABAC   Association of Balloon and Airship Constructors.

ABCST   Automatic broadcast.

ABD   Aboard.

abeam   In aviation radio phraseology a term used to describe the position of an aircraft relative to a fixed point on the ground, such as: Abeam the tower.

ABM   Abeam.

abort   The act of terminating a takeoff or other planned maneuver, or the command to do so.

absolute altitude   Actual height above terrain in feet agl.

absolute ceiling   The maximum altitude above sea level to which a particular aircraft can climb and then maintain horizontal flight under standard atmospheric conditions.

absolute humidity   The weight of water vapor per unit volume of air.

ABV   Above.

AC   Advisory circular.

AC   Alternating current.

AC   Altocumulus.

AC   Approach control.

ACAS   Automatic collision-avoidance system.

accelerated stall   A high-speed stall caused when excessive g-loads are applied quite rapidly.

accelerate-stop distance   The distance required to accelerate an aircraft from a standing start to a specific speed, usually liftoff speed, and, assuming failure of the critical engine at the instant that speed is reached, to bring the aircraft to a stop, using heavy breaking. The accelerate-stop distance for any aircraft varies drastically depending on runway-surface conditions, wind, temperature and other factors.

acceleration   Increase in velocity or the rate at which such increase takes place.

acceleration error   The error in the reading of the magnetic compass which is caused when the compass card tilts in its mounting as a result of changes in the speed of the aircraft. It is especially noticeable on east or west headings. It turns to the north when the aircraft is accelerating and to the south when decelerating.

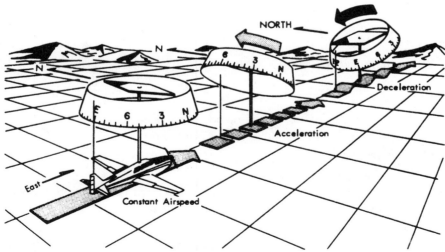

Magnetic compass reading errors due to acceleration or deceleration.

accelerometer   An instrument capable of recording the rate of acceleration. Not usually found in light aircraft.

accident   With relation to aviation the term accident means an occurrence associated with the operation of an aircraft which takes place between the time any person boards the aircraft with the intention of flight until such time when all such persons have disembarked, in which any person suffers death or serious injury as a result of being in or upon that aircraft or by direct contact with the aircraft or anything attached to it. In this context a *fatal injury* is one which results in death within seven days. A *serious injury* means an injury which requires hospitalization for more than 48 hours within seven days from the date on which the injury was received; results in the fracture of any bone other than fingers, toes or nose; involves lacerations which cause severe hemorrhages, nerve muscle or tendon damage; involves injury to an internal organ; or involves second or third-degree burns or any burns affecting more than five percent of the body surface. *Substantial damage* means damage or structural failure which adversely affects the structural strength, performance or flight characteristics of the aircraft and which would normally require major repair or replacement of the affected component. Engine failure limited to an engine, bent fairings or cowling, dented skin, ground damage to rotor or propeller blades, damage to landing gear, wheels, tires, flaps, engine accessories, brakes or wing tips are not considered substantial damage according to FARs.

accuracy landing   *See* SPOT LANDING.

ACDNT   Accident.

ACFT   Aircraft.

ACK   Acknowledge.

acknowledge   A request for verification that the message has been received and understood.

ACLD   Above clouds.

ACPT   Accept.

acrobatics   *See* AEROBATICS.

ACSL   Standing lenticular alticumulus.

active runway   The runway in use under prevailing wind, weather and/or noise-abatement conditions.

ACTV   Active.

Adams Balloon Loft, Inc.   Mike Adams Balloon Loft, manufacturer of a variety of hot-air balloons. (P.O. Box 12168, Atlanta, GA 30355).

ADAP   Airport Development Assistance Fund.

ADC   Air data computer. A digital computer using input from air-data instruments in altitude and speed-control alert functions.

ADF   Automatic direction finder.

ADF approach   A nonprecision instrument approach using a nondirectional beacon, an LF/MF navaid or standard broadcast station as an aid in navigational guidance. (*See also* NONPRECISION APPROACH).

ADI   Attitude director indicator. The visual display associated with flight directors. (*See also* FLIGHT DIRECTORS).

adiabatic lapse rate   The rate at which the temperature of the air changes without any outside source for this change being involved. Temperature increases when air is compressed and it decreases when air rises and expands. When the air is dry this change occurs at a rate of 5.5 degrees F. per 1,000 feet of change in altitude. With moist air, condensing water vapor gives off heat and at the saturation point the lapse rate is three degrees F. per 1,000 feet of increase in altitude.

ADIZ   Air Defense Identification Zone.

ADJ   Adjacent.

adjustable-pitch propeller   A propeller on which the blade angle can be changed on the ground to achieve the most efficient operation for special conditions, such as flight at high altitudes.

ADMA   Aviation Distributors and Manufacturers Association.

ADMIN   Administration.

administrator   The administrator of the Federal Aviation Administration. Also refers to any person to whom he has delegated appropriate authority in a particular situation.

AD Notes   Advisories issued by the FAA, usually as a result of the detection of some type of structural or other defect on an aircraft, after it has been certificated and is in service. Compliance with AD notes within the period of time stated therein is mandatory and the responsibility of the aircraft owner or operator.

ADVC   Advice.

ADVCTN   Advection.

Advanced Navigation, Inc. (ANI)   Manufacturer of the ANI Model 7000 Loran-C navigation system, certified for en route and terminal flight across all of the U.S. including the "Mid-Continent Gap." The company also manufactures a Loran-C simulator including a portable version. (61 Thomas Johnson Drive, Frederick, MD 21701. (301) 695-4040.)

advise intentions   A phrase used by ATC, requesting the pilot to state what he is planning to do.

advisory   Information provided by ground facilities or pilots which is of a nature as to be helpful in assisting pilots in the safe and efficient conduct of a flight; such as weather, airport conditions, traffic, out-of-service navigational facilities, etc.

advisory for light aircraft (AIRMET) An in-flight weather advisory covering weather phenomena of importance to light aircraft and of potential importance to all aircraft; such as moderate icing, wide-spread but moderate turbulence, visibilities less than two miles, ceilings less than 1,000 feet, and winds of 40 or more knots near the surface.

ADVN Advance.

ADVY Advisory.

ADZ Advise.

AEA Aircraft Electronics Association.

AERO Aeronautical or aeronautics.

aerobatics Maneuvers involving abrupt changes in altitude and often resulting in unusual attitudes not used in normal flight. These may include all manner of stunts. Aircraft designed for this type of use must be especially stressed, normally to a minimum of six positive and three negative g. Also referred to as *acrobatics*.

Aero Commander One of the first twin-engine piston aircraft designed specifically for business and corporate use. Designed by the late Ted Smith, it was flown coast to coast with one propeller removed to prove its single-engine reliability. The original manufacturer was bought by Rockwell International (then North American Rockwell), which for several years continued to produce an entire family of Commander aircraft, most based on the original design. Eventually Rockwell sold the Aero Commander and Jet Commander operation to Israel Aircraft Industries, which continued to produce the Jet Commander until it introduced its own business jet, known in the U.S. as Westwind.

aerodrome Airport. A term used by most ICAO member nations.

aerodynamics The forces, such as resistence, pressure, velocity, and others involved in the movement of air or gases around a moving body. Conversely, the branch of dynamics and physics dealing with these forces.

Aero Mechanism A manufacturer of electronic flight instruments including altimeters, altitude encoders, airspeed indicators, altitude alert systems, and cabin pressure indicators. (20327 Nordhoff Street, Chatsworth, CA 91311-6161. (818) 709-2851.)

aeronaut A pilot. The term is used practically exclusively in ballooning.

aeronautical advisory station *See* UNICOM.

aeronautical beacons Displays of stationary or rotating white and/or colored lights indicating an airport, the route leading to an airport or a point from which bearings can be taken to an airport, an outstanding landmark or ground-based hazard.

aeronautical charts   A map developed especially for use in aviation navigation. The U.S. government periodically publishes a variety of such charts and pilots are urged to operate with the latest editions. These charts include 55 Sectionals at a scale of 1:500,000, covering the 48 contiguous United States, Hawaii, Alaska, and portions of the Caribbean, northern Mexico and southern Canada. World Aeronautical Charts called WACs or ONCs are produced at a scale of 1:1,000,000 and are available for every land portion of the free world. There are 57 of those. Then there is one VFR/IFR planning chart covering the 48 contiguous states. In addition there are three jet navigation charts (JNCs) covering all of Northern America. For IFR operations a variety of radio-navigation charts are published, both by the government and by Jeppesen Sanderson. These are low altitude en route charts (government: 28; Jeppesen: 32 for the contiguous states) showing primarily the airways, distances between navaids, VORs, VORTACs, NDBs, LF/MF navaids, airports of importance, MEAs, MRAs, nav and com frequencies and other information applicable to operating within the ATC system. There is also a nearly indefinite number of approach charts picturing and describing the authorized instrument approaches to various airports. Then there are so-called SID and STAR charts showing standard instrument departure and arrival procedures. There are special large-scale charts for each of the TCAs. In addition, many states publish aeronautical charts of the state, some available free of charge, some for a small fee. Charts are available from the U.S. Department of Commerce, National Oceanic and Atmospheric Administration, National Ocean Service, Washington, D.C., or from the charts department of the AOPA (at no increase in price). Charts produced by Jeppesen Sanderson can be ordered on a subscription basis from Jeppesen Sanderson, Inc., 8025 East 40th Avenue, Denver, CO 80207.

aeronautical planning chart   A chart covering the 48 contiguous United States, designed for use in flight planning. Scale: Approximately 70 nm per inch.

Aeronetics   Manufacturer of navigation and flight instrumentation and gyros. (2100 Touhy Avenue, Elk Grove Village, IL 60007. (312) 437-9300.)

Aerosonic Corporation   Manufacturer of encoding altimeters, flight instruments, and related equipment. (1212 North Hercules Avenue, Clearwater, FL 33575-5063. (813) 461-3000.)

Aerospatiale Helicopter Corporation   The U.S. subsidiary of Aerospatiale of France, manufacturers of the family of Aerospatiale Helicopters consisting of the Alouette II and III, Gazelle, Lama, Puma, Dauphin, AStar, Super Puma, and TwinStar. (2701 Forum Drive, Grand Prairie, TX 75053-4005. (214) 641-0000.)

Aerospatiale single-turbine helicopter, the AStar.

Aerospatiale twin-turbine helicopter, the TwinStar.

Aerospatiale twin-turbine helicopter, the Dauphin 2.

Aerospatiale twin-turbine helicopter, the Super Puma.

Aerospatiale Light Single-Turbine Helicopters

		SA315B LAMA	SA319B ALOUETTE 3	SA341G GAZELLE	SA342J GAZELLE	SA350B ECUREUIL	SA350B-1 ECUREUIL	SA350D ASTAR
ENGINE	manufacturer	Turbomeca	Turbomeca	Turbomeca	Turbomeca	Turbomeca	Turbomeca	Lycoming
	model	Artouste	Astazou	Astazou	Astazou	Ariel 1B	Ariel 1D	LTS-101-600A2
	installed hp	858	858	592	858	641	684	615
	takeoff hp	590	592	592	592	529	590	529
	max continuous	542	542	523	592	529	555	529
WEIGHTS lbs	max gross	4300	4960	3970	4190	4300	4850	4300
	external ld.	5290	4960	3970	4190	4650	5400	4630
	empty	2277	2527	2127	2164	2432	2505	2432
	useful load	2023	2433	1843	2026	1868	2345	1868
DIMENSIONS ft	length total	42.4	42.1	39.9	39.3	42.45	42.45	42.6
	fuselage	33.6	33.4	31.9	31.3	35.86	35.86	35.8
	height	10.1	9.8	10.5	10.5	10.3	10.3	10.1
	width	7.8	8.5	6.6	6.6	8.3	8.3	8.3
MAIN ROTOR	diameter ft	36.2	36.2	34.5	34.5	35.07	35.07	35.1
	no of blades	3	3	3	3	3	3	3
FUEL gal	internal	152	152	120	144	137	141	137
	aux.	46	n/a	24	53	126	126	126
SPEEDS kts	V_{ne}	113	119	168	168	147	155	147
	max cruise	103	105	142	142	125	130	125
	economy	102	n/a	125	128	125	119	125
RANGE nm	max	278	340	346	407	378	335	405
SERVICE CEILING ft		17,720	13,125	n/a	14,105	15,600	14,432	13,450
HOVER ft	IGE	16,565	10,170	n/a	11,970	9,670	9,184	8,860
	OGE	15,100	5,574	n/a	9,430	7,380	6,560	5,580

Aerospatiale Light Twin-Turbine Helicopters

		AS355E TWINSTAR	AS355F1 TWINSTAR	AS355F2 TWINSTAR	SA365C1 DAUPHIN II	SA365N DAUPHIN II	SA365N-1 DAUPHIN II	SA366G1 HH-65A
ENGINE	manufacturer	Allison	Allison	Allison	Turbomeca	Turbomeca	Turbomeca	Lycoming
	model	250-C20F	250-C20F	250-C20F	Ariel	Ariel 1C	Ariel 1C1	LTS-101-750A-1
	installed hp	840	840	840	1340	1320	1400	1300
	takeoff hp	640	686	686	1260	1206	1206	1294
	max continuous	640	640	640	1159	1134	1134	n/a
WEIGHTS lbs	gross	4630	5291	5600	7495	8818	9040	8928
	external	5070	5512	5732	7495	8818	9040	8928
	empty	2741	2900	2933	4291	4700	4765	5792
	useful load	1889	2391	2667	3204	4118	4275	2936
DIMENSIONS ft	length total	45	45	45	43.7	44.2	44.88	44.2
	fuselage	35.86	35.86	35.86	36	37.5	38.15	37.5
	height	10.3	10.3	10.3	11.4	13.2	13.02	13.2
	width	8.3	8.3	8.3	10.4	10.5	10.53	10.5
MAIN ROTOR	diameter ft	35.07	35.07	35.07	38.3	39.1	39.17	39.1
	no of blades	3	3	3	4	4	4	4
FUEL gal	internal	190	193	193	169	302	300	291
	aux.	126	126	126	57	47 + 125	47 + 125	n/a
SPEEDS kts	V_{ne}	147	150	150	150	163	160	175
	max cruise	129	124	122	136	153	153	159
	economy	119	113	110	124	140	140	140
RANGE nm	max	414	391	382	246	443	460	410
SERVICE CEILING ft		13,000	13,120	11,152	15,000	15,000	11,810	n/a
HOVER ft	IGE	7,220	7,880	6,560	6,890	2,000	6,890	7,510
	OGE	4,920	6,400	4,920	2,790	2,000	3,610	5,340

Aerospatiale Medium Turbine Helicopters

		SA360C DAUPHIN	SA330J PUMA	AS332C SUPER PUMA	AS332L SUPER PUMA STRETCHED	AS332L-1 SUPER PUMA STRETCHED
ENGINE	MANUFACTURER	Turbomeca (1)	Turbomeca (2)	Turbomeca (2)	Turbomeca (2)	Turbomeca (2)
	model	Astazou XVIIIA	Turmo IVC	Makila	Makila	Makila 1A1
	installed hp	1032	3116	3510	3510	3638
	takeoff hp	872	2988	3370	3370	n/a
	max continuous	805	2524	3028	3028	n/a
WEIGHTS lbs	gross	6615	16,315	18,960	18,960	18,960
	external ld	6615	16,315	20,615	20,615	20,615
	empty	3797	8,358	9,261	9,536	9,745
	useful load	2818	7,957	9,699	9,424	9,215
DIMENSIONS ft	length total	43.4	59.8	61.4	61.4	61.35
	fuselage	36	48.6	51.2	53.3	53.44
	height	11.5	16.9	16.1	16.1	16.14
	width	10.3	9.8	12.8	12.4	12.43
MAIN ROTOR	diameter ft	37.7	49.5	51.1	51.2	51.18
	no of blades	4	4	4	4	4
FUEL gal	internal	169	408	408	544	544
	aux.	57	186	273	262	85 + 159
SPEEDS kts	V_{ne}	170	142	160	160	150
	max cruise	146	139	150	150	144
	economy	133	134	140	140	138
RANGE nm	max	354	296	343	461	470
SERVICE CEILING ft		14,270	15,750	15,092	15,092	15,088
HOVER ft	IGE	8,035	7,545	8,858	8,858	10,168
	OGE	5,740	5,580	6,890	6,890	7,544

Aerosport, Inc. Manufacturer of kits for homebuilt aircraft. (Box 278, Holly Springs, NC 27540. (919) 552-6375)

Aerostar A high-performance piston twin aircraft of the owner-flown class, produced with and without turbocharging. Designed by the late Ted Smith and originally manufactured and marketed by his own company, the manufacturing and marketing rights were subsequently acquired by Piper Aircraft Corporation, which renamed it the *Piper Aerostar,* and continued to produce it for a limited period of time. It seated six and in its time it was the fastest piston twin in production. Many Aerostars are still in operation, maintained by the fiercely loyal members of the Aerostar Owners Association. (Page 13)

Aerostars (Piper)

		600A	601B	601P
ENGINES (2)	manufacturer	Lycoming	Lycoming	Lycoming
	model	IO-540-K1J5	IO-540-S1A5	IO-540-S1A5
	TBO hours	2,000	1,800	1,800
PROPELLERS	type	const.speed, f.f.	const.speed, f.f.	const.speed, f.f.
	number of blades	3	3	3
WEIGHTS lbs	ramp	5,500	6,000	6,000
	takeoff	5,500	6,000	6,000
	landing	5,500	6,000	6,000
	useful load	1,720	1,905	2,015
FUEL U.S. gallons	standard tanks	175	175	175
DIMENSIONS ft	length	34.8	34.8	34.8
	height	12.1	12.1	12.1
	span	34.2	36.7	36.7
CABIN ft	length	12.5	12.5	12.5
	height	4.3	4.3	4.3
	width	3.83	3.83	3.83
WINGS	area ft^2	170	168	178
	loading lb/ft^2	32.4	33.7	33.7
SEATS	number	6	6	6
PRESSURIZATION	psi	n/a	4.25	n/a
TURBOCHARGER	manufacturer	n/a	Rajay	Rajay
	type	n/a	dual automatic	dual automatic
SPEEDS knots	V_{mc}	80	84	80
	V_{xse}	104	100	100
	V_{yse}	113	100	109
STALL knots	approach config.	74	77	77
CRUISE knots	high speed	220	257	257
	economy	200	209	218
RANGE nm	high speed cruise	1,103	1,086	1,063
	economy cruise	1,320	1,271	1,244
RATE OF CLIMB fpm	2 engines	1,800	1,530	1,530
	1 engine	450	254	254
SERVICE CEILING ft	2 engines	21,200	25,000	30,000
	1 engine	6,150	9,300	9,300

The pressurized Piper Aerostar 700P.

Aerostar International, Inc.   Manufacturer of a family of hot-air balloons. (Subsidiary of Raven Industries, 1813 "E" Avenue, P.O. Box 5057, Sioux Falls, SD 57117-5057. (605) 331-3500.)

Aerostat   A hot-air or gas balloon.

aerostation   Same as aerostat.

AF   Air Force.

AFB   Air Force base.

affirmative   In aviation-radio phraseology the term is used to indicate correct or yes.

AFHF   Air Force Historical Foundation.

AFMF   Air Force Museum Foundation.

AFT   After.

AFTN   Afternoon.

ag aviation   Agricultural aviation, such as using aircraft for seeding or pest control.

Ag Cat   A heavy-duty agricultural biplane originally produced by Grumman Aviation and now produced by Schweizer Aircraft Corporation. (Page 14)

agl   Above ground level.

agonic line   The line of zero magnetic variation. In the U.S. it runs approximately southeast from the middle of Lake Superior to Savannah, Georgia.

Agusta Aerospace Corporation   Manufacturer of the Agusta 109A twin-turbine helicopters and of the Siai Marchetti SF 260 TP single-engine turboprop trainer and the SF 600 Canguro high-wing twin-engine piston aircraft. (U.S. office: 3050 Red Lion Road, Philadelphia, PA 19114. (215) 281-1400.) (Pages 15-16)

Ag Wagon   A low-wing agricultural aircraft once manufactured by Cessna Aircraft Company.

AHD   ahead.

The Ag-Cat 450 agricultural aircraft currently being manufactured by Schweizer Aircraft Corporation.

The turbine powered Ag-Cat agricultural aircraft currently being manufactured by Schweizer Aircraft Corporation.

Agusta Twin-Turbine Helicopters

		109A MARK II	AS-61N1 SILVER
ENGINES	manufacturer	Allison (2)	General Electric (2)
	model	250-C20B	CT58-140
	installed hp	840	3000
	takeoff hp	740	2500
	max continuous hp	740	2100
WEIGHTS lbs	gross	5730	21,000
	external	5730	22,500
	empty	3258	12,522
	useful load	2472	8,478
DIMENSIONS ft	total length	42.8	72
	fuselage length	35.1	58.8
	height	10.8	17.2
	width	9.4	20.0
MAIN ROTOR	diameter ft	36.1	62.0
	number of blades	4	5
FUEL gal	usable, standard	146	920
	aux.	n/a	n/a
SPEEDS knots	V_{ne}	168	131
	max cruise	147	121
	economy cruise	126	110
SERVICE CEILING	ft	15,000	12,500
HOVER	IGE	7,900	3,800
	OGE	4,900	500

Agusta Aviation Corporation

Agusta 109A twin-turbine helicopter.

The Siai Marchetti single-engine turboprop.

The Siai Marchetti SF 260 TP single-engine trainer powered by an Allison 250-B17C turbine engine developing 420 shp.

The Siai Marchetti SF 600 twin-turbine aircraft.

AIA   Aerospace Industries Association.

AIAA   American Institute of Aeronautics and Astronautics.

AID   Airport information desk.

aileron   The primary control surface located at the trailing edges of the outer wing panels, which, when moved up or down, causes the airplane in flight to bank. Movement of the control column (wheel, yoke, or stick) to the right raises the right aileron and lowers the left, thus inducing a right bank. Some ailerons are referred to as drooped, meaning that both can be deflected either downward or upward simultaneously (while maintaining their lateral control function), thus adding a small degree of lift during low-speed operation or, conversely, effecting a slight degree of increase in speed during cruise. On some aircraft the function of the ailerons is accomplished by the use of spoilers. For details, *See* SPOILERS.

aileron roll   An aerobatic maneuver in which full aileron deflection causes the airplane to rotate (roll) around its lengthwise axis without a change in heading.

AILS   Automatic instrument landing system.

AIM   Airman's Information Manual.

air   The air we breathe, and which permits us to fly, consists of 78.09 percent nitrogen, 20.95 percent oxygen, plus minute quantities of argon, carbon dioxide, neon, helium, krypton, xenon, ozone and radon, not to mention moisture, dust and a huge variety of chemical pollutants caused by industry, automobiles, aircraft, etc. At sea level the average pressure of a column of air measuring one square inch is about 14.5 pounds, which corresponds to the weight of a comparable column of mercury 29.92 inches high. This then is the origin of our standard altimeter setting.

airborne telephone systems   These systems permit pilot or passengers to contact any number of ground-based stations and from there to be connected to any telephone anywhere in the world. There is no monthly charge. Charges are a fixed fee per (completed) call plus the applicable long-distance rate from the ground station to the party being called. Persons on the ground can contact the aircraft in flight if they know the number assigned to the particular telephone in the aircraft, and the approximate location of the aircraft at the time the call is being placed. Airborne telephone systems are produced by three manufacturers. (Page 18).

airborne weather radar   Radar carried aboard the aircraft and used to detect areas of precipitation, especially in relation to thunderstorms where such areas are indicative of the greatest degree of turbulence. Historically, the radar display has been analog in monochrome (green on black). Recent developments have introduced digital computer technology in airborne radars and most new models are digital, using a computer-generated display, which most pilots find easier to interpret. Latest models are also capable of projecting suggested flight routes on the radar display and can be used to display checklists and a virtually endless variety

Airborne Telephones

MANUFACTURER	MODEL	PRICE	VOLTS	PUSH	DUPLEX	HEADSETS	SOLID	UNITS	lbs	REMARKS
Global-Wulfsberg	WH-6		27.5 VDC		¤	¤	¤	3	8.8	Direct dial
Global-Wulfsberg	WH-10		27.5 VDC		¤	¤	¤	3	8.8	Direct dial buttons in handset
Terra	TD 3000		28 VDC		¤	¤	¤	5	5.8	Direct dial

VOLTS: input
PUSH: push-to-talk
HEADSETS: additional headsets
SOLID: 100% solid state

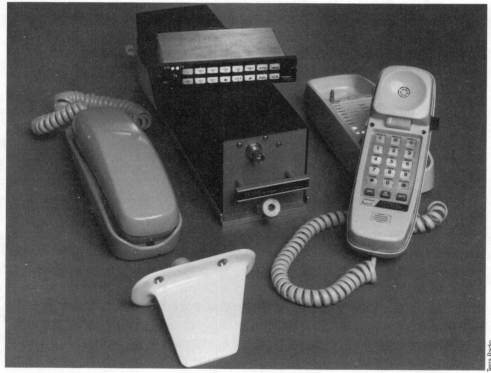

Airborne telephone system.

of data stored in the computer memory and recalled at command by the pilot, producing an alphanumeric readout. (Pages 19-20).

Airbus Industrie of North America   Service and support organization for Airbus
aircraft in North America. (593 Herndon Parkway #350, Herndon, VA 22070.
(703) 834-3400)

Airborne Weather Radar Systems

MANUFACTURER	MODEL	PRICE	VOLTS (D A a)	kw	MHz	RANGE nm (0-50 / 50-100 / 100-200 / 200-300)				Scan°	+/-	ANTENNA (F P)	READOUT (B C E)	SIZES (S I)	STAB+/- (P R)	DISPLAY (D N)	
Bendix/King																	
RDR models	1300	n/a	28	10		¤	¤	¤	¤	60/120	¤	¤	¤	1	30	¤	¤
	1400C	n/a	28	10	9345	¤	¤	¤		60/120	¤	¤	¤	2	30	¤	¤
RDS models	81	13,850	28 26	1	9345	¤	¤	¤	¤	90	¤	¤	¤	3	25	¤	¤
	82	20,355	28 26	1	9345	¤	¤	¤	¤	90	¤	¤	¤	4	25	¤	¤
	84	37,125	28 26	1.3	9345	¤	¤	¤	¤	120	¤	¤	¤	5	30	¤	¤
Collins	WXR-220	n/a	28	5	9345	¤	¤	¤		90	¤	¤	¤	*	**	¤	¤
Collins	WXR-270	n/a	28	5	9345	¤	¤	+		120	¤	¤	¤		**	¤	¤
Collins	WXR-300	n/a	28	5	9345	¤	¤	¤	¤	120	¤	¤	¤			¤	¤ #
Collins	TWR-850	n/a	28 115	5	9340	¤	¤	¤	¤	120	¤	¤	¤		30	¤	¤ #

1 $6^1/_4 \times 6^1/_4 \times 10^7/_8$"
2 $6^1/_4 \times 6^1/_4 \times 10^7/_8$"
3 $4.1 \times 6.25 \times 10.5$"
4 $4.1 \times 6.25 \times 10.5$
5 $4.5 \times 6.4 \times 11.45$"

* pitch corrected
** fully stabilized
\+ to 250 nm
\# turbulence weather radar system

PRICE:		uninstalled
VOLTS	D:	DC;
	A:	AC 400 Hz;
	a:	amps
kw:		Output in kilowatts
MHz:		Frequency, X-band
RANGE nm:		0-50;
		50-100;
		100-200;
		200-300
Scan°:		Scan degrees
+/-:		Antenna tilt
ANTENNA	F:	Flat Plate;
	P:	Parabolic
READOUT	B:	Black and white;
	C:	Color;
	E:	EFIS cathode ray tube
SIZES	S:	Scope;
	I:	Indicators in inches wide/high/deep
STAB+/-:		Stabilization in degrees
DISPLAY	D:	Digital
	N:	Distance and other optional displays

air-cooled engine   Term used primarily in relation to piston engines cooled by outside air passing directly over the cylinders, the heat of which is generally transferred to the air by flat cooling fins or baffles. (Page 20)

aircraft   Any man-made object that flies. Primarily used with reference to fixed-wing aircraft, helicopters, gyroplanes, gliders and sailplanes, hot-air and gas balloons, blimps and dirigibles, but technically also including hang gliders and probably even kites.

aircraft approach category   Categories based on speeds representing $1.3V_{so}$, or on maximum certificated landing weight. Category A covers aircraft of less than 30,000 pounds and speeds of less than 91 knots. Category B: Weight 30,001 to

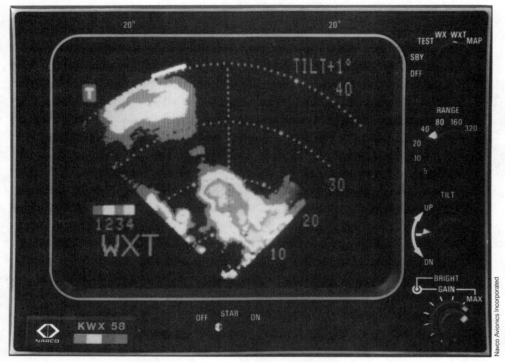

Airborne weather radar display.

Air-cooled piston engine, the Lycoming IO-540.

60,000 pounds; 91 + knots but less than 121 knots. Category C: Weight 60,001 to 150,000 pounds; speeds 121 + knots but less than 141 knots. Category D: Weight 151,000 pounds and up; speed 141 + knots but less than 166 knots. Category E: Speed over 166 knots regardless of the weight of the aircraft.

aircraft classes   In order to establish criteria with relation to wake turbulence and the necessary separation minimums, ATC has classified aircraft as follows: Heavy: Aircraft capable of takeoff weights of 300,000 pounds or more, regardless of the actual takeoff weight during a particular operation. Large: Aircraft with a maximum certificated takeoff weight between 12,500 and 300,000 pounds. Small: Aircraft with a maximum certificated takeoff weight of under 12,500 pounds.

aircraft flight manual   A document issued by the manufacturer which contains certification details, limitations, procedures, performance parameters, and all other data and information needed by the pilot for the safe operation of that aircraft. Also known as *owner's manual*.

Aircraft Instrument and Development, Inc.   Designer and manufacturer of aircraft instruments. (535 South Topeka, Wichita, KS 67202. (316) 265-4271.)

aircraft movement   The phrase refers to takeoffs and landings. Aircraft movements are counted by control towers to establish the amount of traffic being handled. Thus two movements constitute one flight of an aircraft (ARTCCs and FSSs count contacts rather than movements).

aircraft type designators   The letter-number combinations given to all civilian and military aircraft, such as PA-31T-1 which stands for Piper Aircraft Cheyenne I.

Air Defense Identification Zone   An area of airspace over land or water within which proper identification, location, and control of aircraft are required for national security. The zones are principally off the Atlantic, Pacific, and Gulf coasts, along the Mexican border, around Hawaii, and over most of Alaska. There is also a Distant Early Warning Identification Zone (DEWIZ) located primarily over Alaska and parts of northern Canada. As a general rule the filing of IFR or CVFR flight plans is mandatory before entering this airspace. (Page 22)

Air density   The mass of molecules in a given volume of air. This changes with variations in air pressure. (*See* DENSITY ALTITUDE).

Air density error   The error in the presentation of an airspeed indication caused by changes in air density resulting from changes in altitude and barometric pressure. True airspeed (TAS) can be calculated by using a standard aviation computer.

Airfile   Means filing an IFR flight plan while airborne. Rarely used with reference to filing a VFR flight plan from the air.

airfoil   Any surface designed to create lift, either positive or negative, when moving through the air at a given speed. Primarily, wings and control surfaces, though propellers and helicopter rotor blades are also airfoils. (Page 22)

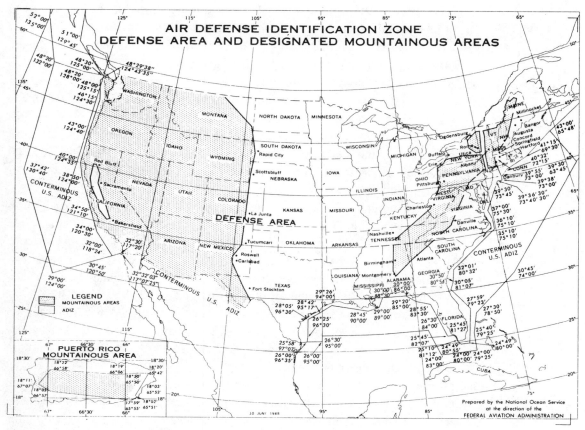

Air Defense Identification Zones (ADIZ).

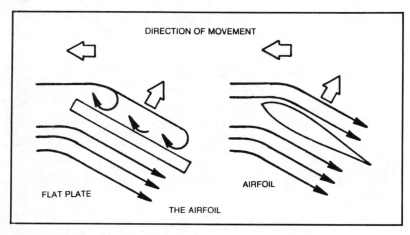

Airfoil movement through air.

airframe   The frame, covering, and components of an aircraft, not including engine, propellers, tires, avionics, and instruments.

airframe manufacturers   Manufacturers of fixed- and rotary-wing aircraft, gliders, balloons, hang gliders, etc. Current airframe, avionics, engine, and equipment manufacturers are listed aphabetically by company names.

Airliner (Beech 1900 and 1300)   A family of regional airliners manufactured by Beech Aircraft Corporation.

Beech 1900 Airliner.

Beech 1300 Airliner.

Airman's Information Manual (AIM)   The operational manual for pilots containing information needed for the planning and conduct of flights in the contiguous U.S. It consists of a basic flight manual, ATC procedures, airport facilities directory, flight operation information, and NOTAMs. It is published periodically by the FAA.

air mass   A large body of air with uniform properties of temperature and moisture content in a horizontal plain.

air mass thunderstorm   Individual thunderstorms, widely separated from other such storms, most often found in mountainous terrain and rarely associated with frontal activity.

AIRMET   *See* ADVISORY FOR LIGHT AIRCRAFT.

air navigation facility   A facility, electronic or visual, that assists the pilot or navigator in determining his position relative to a fixed point or path on the ground.

airplane   Any heavier-than-air craft supported by airflow over the airfoils. Primarily a powered fixed-wing aircraft.

airplane tow   In soaring, the term used for towing a glider off the ground and into the air to any predetermined altitude, using a powered aircraft. It is the most popular means of glider launch in the U.S.

air pocket   A popular but incorrect term for descending currents of air which cause the aircraft to momentarily sink rapidly. The correct term is downdraft.

airport   Any place on land or water designed to be regularly used by aircraft for takeoffs and landings, including associated buildings and facilities.

Airport Development and Assistance Fund (ADAP)   A fund authorized by Congress and administered by the FAA for the purpose of providing financial assistance for the improvement of existing airports and the development of new airports. The funds are available on a matching-fund basis, meaning that states, counties, or municipalities must come up with a given percentage of the total amount needed for the project in order to be eligible for the ADAP funds. These funds are earmarked for work actually affecting the establishment, development, and improvement of the airport as such, and may not be used for terminal buildings or customer-convenience items. While originally designated to be available only to publicly owned airports, there is strong sentiment to use them also to save and improve privately owned public-use airports.

airport advisory area   The area within five statute miles of an uncontrolled airport on which FSS is located. Within this area a pilot on approach should contact the FSS for advisories; or a pilot about to depart should inform the FSS of his intentions. Communication with such FSS is advisable but not mandatory, and its advisories should not be misunderstood as air traffic control clearances, unless prefaced by "ATC clears."

airport advisory service The service provided by FSS personnel operating on an airport without operating control tower for the purpose of advising arriving and departing aircraft on wind direction and velocity, active runway, altimeter setting, traffic, field conditions, standard approach procedures such as left or right traffic patterns and other facts of importance to the pilot. The service is not authorized to give takeoff or landing clearances. Frequency: 123.6 MHz.

airport directory A section of the AIM listing all airports available for civil-aviation use, by states. Another and more convenient listing of all airports, helipads, and seaplane bases is published annually by the AOPA. Another airport directory is published by Jeppesen Sanderson, displaying the runway patterns of each. Also published by Jeppesen Sanderson are detailed diagrams of each airport with a published instrument approach. (Pages 26-27)

airport elevation (field elevation) The listed airport elevation is the highest point of any of the useable runways, given in feet msl.

airport identification beacon (rotating beacon) A beamed, green and white light timed to rotate at six rpm and usually located at or near the control tower. Beacons are operating during hours of darkness and usually (but not always) during hours of daylight when the airport is reporting weather conditions below VFR minimums. Alternating one green and one white light indicates a civil airport. Alternating one green and two white lights indicates a military or combined military-civilian airport.

airport information desk (AID) An unmanned facility located at an airport and designed to facilitate self-briefing by pilots in flight preparation, planning and the filing of flight plans. AIDs are kept supplied with the latest NOTAMs, weather reports, forecasts, flight-plan forms, etc.

airport lighting *See* RUNWAY LIGHTS.

airport radar service area (ARSA) Regulatory airspace surrounding designated airports wherein ATC provides radar vectoring and sequencing on a full-time basis for all IFR and VFR aircraft. The service provided in an ARSA is called ARSA service, which includes: IFR/IFR—standard IFR separation; IFR/VFR—traffic advisories and conflict resolution; and VFR/VFR—traffic advisories and, as appropriate, safety alerts. (Page 28)

airport surface detection equipment (ASDE) Radar which is designed especially to "read" all principal features on the airport surface, including the movements of aircraft and vehicles, presenting the resulting image on a radar display in the control tower for use by ground controllers. Usually found at large and busy airports where part of the airport cannot be seen from the tower, or where, under conditions of restricted visibility, outlying areas cannot be observed by the naked eye.

airport surveillance radar (ASR) A relatively short-range radar used to control traffic in the vicinity of an airport. It provides azimuth and distance information

DENVER (Jeffco)   BJC
5658'. 39°55'N 105°07'W. Lights: REIL
11L. VASI 29R. Activate MALSR 29R,
VASI 11L-118.6 when Twr inop. Mgr:
D.C. Gordon, (303) 466-2314. Fuel:
3,JetA. Ox 1,2. Repairs: MAME.
CAUTION: Birds. Deer. Rwy 11R/29L
clsd ngts. Rwys 11R,20,29R rgt tfc
when Twr op. Accom: All. ATIS 126.25.
APP Denver 126.9. Jeffco TWR CTAF
118.6. GND 121.7. UNICOM 122.95.
290°/12.3 NM-Denver VORTAC.

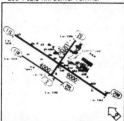

DENVER (Stapleton Int'l)   KDEN
5333'. 39°46'N 104°53'W. TCA II. Lights:
REIL 18.26R. PAPI 18. VASI 8R, 17L, 17R
(3-bar). 26R. CL 17L,35R. TDZ 35R. Mgr:
G. Doughty, (303) 398-3844. Fuel: 3,6,
JetA. Ox 1,3. Repairs: MAME. LLWAS.
Customs on PR. Rwy 7/25 clsd excpt to
DHC-7, BEO-2 & prop acft under 14,500;
VFR days only; rwy clsd when breaking
action poor. T/O rwy 7, land rwy 25 only.
Rwys 17L/R, 35L/R, 8R/26L max GWT
750,000 lbs. Rwy 8L/26R clsd to B747
acft lndg only. Lndg fee (303) 398-2140.
Rwy 18/36 no IFR deps to the south.
Lndg length rwy 8L--6696', rwy 36--
4410'. Accom: All. ATIS 125.6 Arr, 124.45
Dep. TCA Denver App 126.9 (211°-
089°), 119.3 (090°-210°). App 120.2
(N), 120.8 (S). TWR 118.3 (E-W), 119.5
(N-S). GND 121.9. UNICOM 122.95.
155°/1.6 NM-Denver VORTAC.

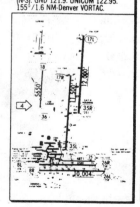

DOVE CREEK   8V6
6975'. 37°46'N 108°53'W.
Mgr: R.A. Anderson, (303) 677-2282.
Hrs. of opn: Unattended. Repairs: AE.
9' chem storage tanks within 50' of
centerline, 600' frm rwy 19 thr.
Accom: L. Traffic CTAF 122.9.
129°/3.4 NM-Dove Creek VORTAC.

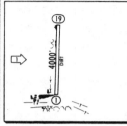

(Downtown-) see FT COLLINS

DURANGO (Animas)   5C00
6690'. 37°12'N 107°52'W. Lights:
LIRL on PR. Mgr: J. Gregg, (303) 247-
4632. Hrs. of opn: Days. Fuel: 3,JetA.
Ox 1. Repairs: MAME. 1' to 3' ditch
along W side of rwy. Overrun rutted,
soft when wet. 200' dropoff 30' E of
thr 1. Accom: L,T.
UNICOM CTAF 122.8.
284°/6.5 NM-Durango VORDME.

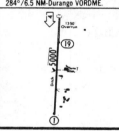

DURANGO (-La Plata Co)   DRO
6685'. 37°09'N 107°45'W. Lights:
Activate HIRL, MALSR 2, REIL 20, VASI
2,20-122.8. Mgr: R. Dent, (303) 247-
8143. Hrs. of opn: Apr-Oct 0600-2200,
Nov-Mar Sun-Thur 0600-2100, Fri-Sat
0600-2200. Fuel: 3,JetA. Ox 1,2. Repairs:
MAME. Accom: All. UNICOM CTAF 122.8.
At field-Durango VORDME.

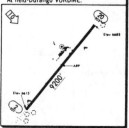

EADS (-Mun)   9V7
4245'. 38°29'N 102°49'W.
Hrs. of opn: Unattended.
First 100' of both rwy ends rough.
Eads Mun Traffic CTAF 122.9.
329°/17.6 NM-Lamar VORTAC.

EAGLE (-Co)   EGE
6538'. 39°39'N 106°55'W. Lights: REIL
25. PAPI 25, visbl only to 6° left of C/L
due to terrain. After 2200 activate MIRL
7/25, PAPI 25-123.6. Mgr: H.K. Hurd,
(303) 328-7311. Hrs. of opn: 0600-
2200. Fuel: 4, JetA. Ox 1,3. Repairs:
MAME. Mountains 3/4 NM N. Rwy 8/26
sharp drop-offs 100' frm both thrs.
Wildlife on apt. Rwy 7 rgt tfc. Accom: All.
Eagle Rdo CTAF 123.6. UNICOM 122.95.
065°/3.7 NM-Snow VORDME.

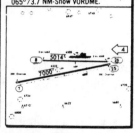

(Easton) see GREELEY

ELLICOTT (Colorado Springs East) C050
6145'. 38°52'N 104°25'W. Mgr: C.
Susemihl, (719) 634-2188. Hrs. of opn:
0800-1600. Fuel: 3,6. Repairs: AE.
Unlimited vehicle access to rwy. Fee for
coml acft. Rwy 35 rgt tfc. Accom: F.
Colorado Springs East Traffic CTAF 122.9.
099°/11.3 NM-Colorado Springs
VORTAC.

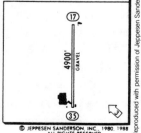

Airport directory page.

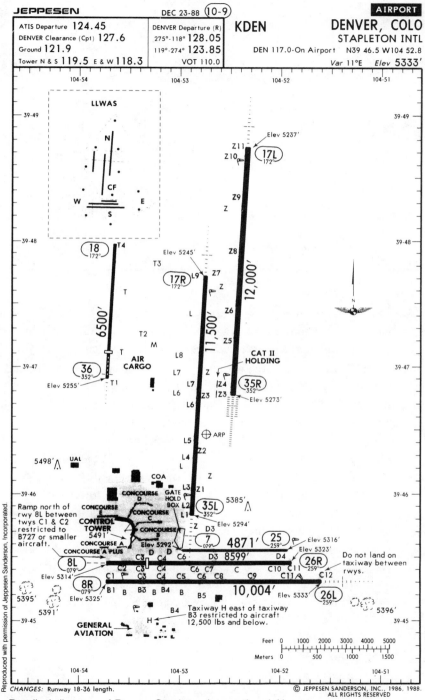

Detailed diagram of Denver Stapleton International Airport.

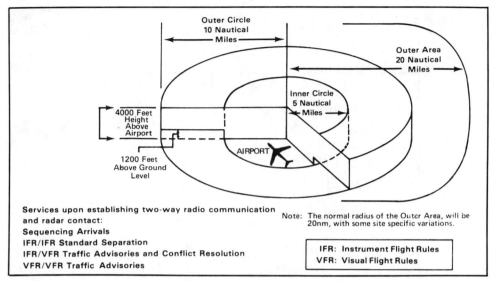

Airport Radar Service Area.

but no altitude information. It can be used for a ground-controlled radar approach (GCA) under appropriate ceiling and visibility conditions. Such an approach is a nonprecision approach as it includes no vertical guidance.

airport traffic area   The area within a radius of five statute miles around an airport with an operating control tower, reaching upward from the ground to (but not including) 3,000 feet agl. Within an airport traffic area all VFR aircraft, whether intending to land or just passing through, must maintain two-way radio contact with the control tower. (Airport traffic areas do not affect IFR traffic). Airport traffic areas are not shown on aeronautical charts. (Page 29)

airport traffic control tower   The central operations facility serving ATC in the airport area. It consists of the tower structure and the tower cab, an IFR room if radar is used (a separate facility in the New York area where the Common IFR Room serves Kennedy International, La Guardia and Newark), and accommodates all equipment needed to signal to or communicate with aircraft. Activities performed by the tower are ground control, tower control, approach and departure control or any portion of those. (Pages 29-30)

airshows   There are quite a few airshows that take place either annually or biannually and are available to the general public, usually for a fee.

Abbotsford International Aviation Exhibition and Air Show is held annually at Abbotsford Airport, Abbotsford, BC, Canada, usually in August. For information call (604) 859-9211.

Aircraft Owners and Pilots Association (AOPA) annual meeting and convention is usually held in October. For information call (301) 695-2052.

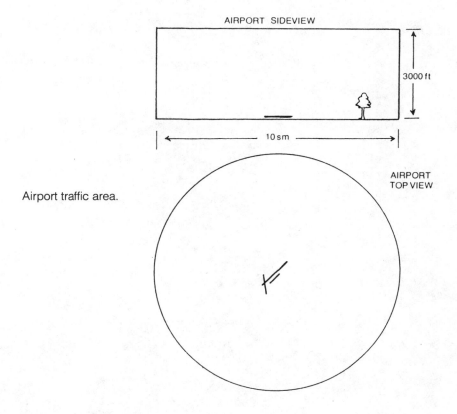

AIRPORT SIDEVIEW

3000 ft

10 sm

AIRPORT
TOP VIEW

Airport traffic area.

Airport control tower interior.

Airport control tower.

Air/Space America biannual air show designed to rival the Paris Air Show, to be held in even-numbered years at Brown Field, San Diego, California. For information call (619) 294-8808.

Albuquerque/Southwest Airlines Airshow takes place annually in mid-June. For information call (505) 247-7469.

Aviation/Space Writers Association (AWA) holds an Annual News Conference usually in either April or May. For information call (614) 221-1900.

Balloon Fiesta is held annually in Albuquerque, NM, beginning the first Saturday in October. For information, call (505) 821-1000.

Dayton International Air Show and Trade Exposition held annually at Dayton International Airport, Vandalia, OH, usually in July. For information, call (513) 898-5901.

Experimental Aircraft Association (EAA) annually conducts a week-long fly-in at Wittman Field in Oshkosh, WI, usually during the first week of August. For information call (414) 426-4800.

Farnborough Air Show held biannually in even-numbered years in September at Farnborough, England. For information contact Society of British Aerospace Companies, Ltd. Telephone, UK: 01 839 3231, US: (212) 752-8400.

Hannover Air Show held biannually in even-numbered years in May or June in Hanover, West Germany. Contact German Aerospace Industries Association. Telephone, Germany: 02 28 33 0011, US: (609) 987-1202.

Helicopter Association International conducts an annual convention and industry exhibition, usually in either January or February. For information call (703) 683-4646.

National Business Aircraft Association (NBAA) holds its annual convention and exhibition usually in either late September or early October. For information call (202) 783-9000.

Paris Air Show is a 10-day event, held biannually in odd-numbered years in Paris, France, usually in early June. For information: 331-4720-6109.

Reading Air Show has been revived and is held annually at Reading Municipal Airport, Reading PA, usually in August. For information call (215) 372-4666.

Reno Air Races held annually in September at Reno Stead Airport in Reno, NV. For information call (702) 826-7500.

Singapore Air Show (Asian Aerospace '90, '92, etc.) is held biannually in even-numbered years, usually in January or February, at Changi International Airport. For information, contact Asian Aerospace Private Ltd., Cahners Exposition Group Pte. Ltd., 1 Maritime Square, No. 12-03 World Trade Center, Singapore 0409. Telephone: 271-1013 or 271-1830.

air traffic pattern   A pattern of flight around the active runway, established to provide safe flow of traffic. Patterns usually consist of a downwind leg, base leg, and

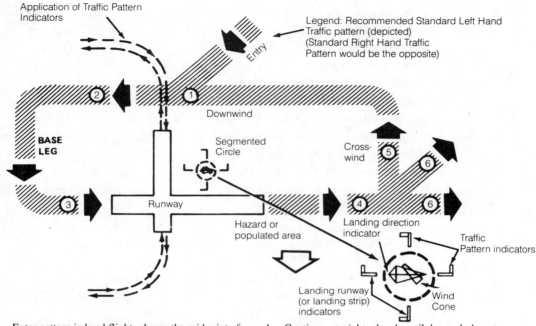

Application of Traffic Pattern Indicators

Legend: Recommended Standard Left Hand Traffic pattern (depicted) (Standard Right Hand Traffic Pattern would be the opposite)

Entry

Downwind

BASE LEG

Segmented Circle

Cross-wind

Runway

Hazard or populated area

Landing direction indicator

Traffic Pattern indicators

Landing runway (or landing strip) indicators

Wind Cone

1. Enter pattern in level flight, abeam the midpoint of the runway, at pattern altitude. (1000' AGL is recommended pattern altitude unless established otherwise.)

2. Maintain pattern altitude until abeam approach end of the landing runway, on downwind leg.

3. Complete turn to final at least ¹/₄ mile from the runway.

4. Continue straight ahead until beyond departure end of runway.

5. If remaining in the traffic pattern, commence turn to crosswind leg beyond the departure end of the runway, within 300 feet of pattern altitude.

6. If departing the traffic patterns, continue straight out, or exit with a 45° left turn beyond the departure end of the runway, after reaching pattern altitude.

Airport traffic pattern.

the final approach, in most instances involving left-hand turns all the way. At some airports right-hand patterns are in effect for some or all runways. At uncontrolled airports the segmented circle provides the pilot with the appropriate information. At controlled airports the tower will often clear pilots for abbreviated base-leg or straight-in approaches.

air route surveillance radar   Long-range radar used primarily by ARTCCs in controlling the en route portions of flight.

air route traffic control center (ARTCC)   A central operations facility in the ATC system in charge of en route operations over a given geographic area, using two-way radio communications and long-range surveillance radar to control IFR traffic. The FAA operates 27 ARTCCs, each of which is divided into a number of sectors with discrete frequencies. ARTCCs are usually simply referred to as *centers*. (Page 33)

Air route traffic control center (ARTCC) interior.

airspace   A term usually used to mean the navigable airspace, for all practical purposes between ground level and 60,000 feet. In the United States the airspace is divided into uncontrolled airspace (airspace in which IFR operations may be conducted without contacting ATC and over which ATC has no jurisdiction), and various types of controlled airspace, affecting all IFR and in some instances VFR operations. For detailed descriptions of the various types of controlled airspace and its effect on aircraft operating in that space, *see:* AIRPORT TRAFFIC AREA; AIRPORT CONTROL ZONE; AIRWAYS; CONTROL AREAS; CONTROL ZONES; CONTINENTAL CONTROL AREA; TERMINAL CONTROL AREA (TCA); TRANSITION AREA; POSITIVE CONTROL AREA; UNCONTROLLED AIRSPACE (Page 34).

airspeed   The speed with which an aircraft is moving with relation to the air around it. Airspeed may be measured and expressed in a variety of ways. Indicated airspeed (IAS) is the speed shown in the cockpit by the airspeed indicator. Calibrated airspeed (CAS) is indicated airspeed corrected for installation and instrument error. True airspeed (TAS) is the calibrated airspeed corrected for air density and temperature differences. It is identical to IAS at sea level under standard atmospheric conditions. At any altitude above sea level the TAS can be determined by using a standard aviation computer.

airspeed indicator   A flight instrument with a cockpit readout which, in terms of knots or mph, shows the difference between pitot pressure and static pressure. On modern aircraft, airspeed indicators are equipped with colored circular bands: The white band indicates the speed range during which flaps may be operated, with the lower end of the arc coinciding with the stalling speed with power off and flaps and gear in landing position. The upper end of the arc represents the maximum speed with the flaps extended. The green band represents the normal operating speed range from stall speed up to the maximum structural cruising speed.

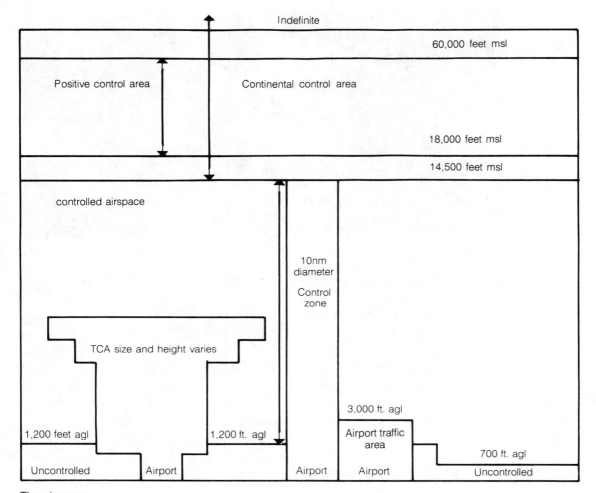

The airspace.

The yellow arc or band is the so-called caution range, covering speeds which should be avoided in turbulent conditions. The red line indicates the never-exceed speed. In addition, on twin-engine aircraft a blue line indicates the best single-engine rate-of-climb speed and a second the red line (in the low-speed area) represents minimum single-engine control speed (V_{mc}).

airstart Restarting an engine in flight.

air traffic control (ATC) The sytem operated by the FAA (and to a limited extent by the military) for the purpose of promoting safe, orderly, and expeditious flow of air traffic. The primary obligation of ATC is to assure safe separation between IFR aircraft in controlled airspace.

air traffic control specialist (controller) An employee of the FAA working in control towers, ARTCCs, and related FAA air traffic control facilities. (Persons manning FSSs are *flight service specialists.*)

air transport rating A pilot's license required of pilots operating airline jets in the position of captain. Also known at *ATR* or *ATP*.

airway Any path within the navigable airspace designated by the FAA as usable for air traffic. Usually airways are associated with ground-based navaids. The airways most used by general aviation are the Victor airways, which extend vertically from 1,200 feet agl up to but not including 18,000 feet msl. Generally they are eight miles wide and are shown on all types of aviation charts. Airways are controlled airspace.

airworthiness directive (AD Notes) Notices issued by the FAA when a certain defect has been discovered during the operation of a certificated aircraft. AD Notes spell out corrective measures and deadlines within which these measures must be accomplished in order to keep the airworthiness certificate in effect. Compliance is mandatory.

AIS aeronautical information service.

Alcor, Inc. Manufacturer of exhaust gas temperature gauges (EGT), cylinder head temperature gauges (CHT), fuel monitoring systems, combustion analysis equipment, and related products. (10130 Jones-Maltsberger, San Antonio, TX 78216-4191. Mail address: P.O. Box 792222, San Antonio, TX 78279-2222. (512) 349-3771.)

alert area Airspace that may accommodate a high degree of (military) pilot training activity or other types of unusual aerial activity. These areas are shown on aeronautical charts to warn non-participating pilots to be extra alert. Activities in these areas are conducted in accordance with the FARs and participating aircraft, as well as those not participating, are responsible for collision avoidance.

alert notice (ALNOT) A message distributed by flight service stations requesting an extensive communication search for an overdue aircraft, unreported aircraft or one that appears to be missing.

ALG Along.

algorithm Any mathematical formula.

Allied-Signal Aerospace Company, Garrett Turbine Engine Division *See* GARRETT TURBINE ENGINE DIVISION.

Allied-Signal Aerospace Company, Electric Power Division (Formerly Bendix Electric and Fluid Power Division) Manufacturers of Bendix generating systems for the Airbus A-310, Bell-Boeing V-22, Bell Helicopter AH-15, Bell Textron LCAC, Boeing E-3, Boeing 737, 747, 757, 767, Marine PHM, KC-135R, British Aerospace BAe-146, deHavilland Dash 8, Fokker F-27, Gates Learjet, General Dynamics F-111, M-1, M-60, Grumman E-2C. EA-6B, EF-111, F-14,

S-2T, Gulfstream FEWSG, GIII, GIV, Lockheed C-130, McDonnell Douglas A-4, F-4, F-15, AH-64, Rockwell B-1, Sikorsky CH-53, SH-3, SH-60, UH-60. (118 Highway 35, Eatontown, NJ 07724. (201) 542-2000.)

Allison Gas Turbine Division   Manufacturer of turbofan, turboshaft, and turboprop aircraft engines and gas turbine industrial engines. The advanced technology 578-DX ultra high-bypass turbofan engine is produced in a joint venture with Pratt & Whitney. (2001 Tibbs Street, Indianapolis, IN 46241. Mailing address: P.O. Box 420, Indianapolis, IN 46206-0420. (317) 242-7000.) (Page 37)

all weather low altitude training route (Olive Branch Routes) (OB Routes) (AWLARs)   Routes used for the training of Air Force and Navy jet pilots in IFR or VFR weather conditions, from the surface to a published altitude. Routes, altitudes, and graphic representations are included in AIM Part 4. When not available, they and their current operational status may be obtained by contacting a nearby Flight Service Station.

ALNOT   Alert notice.

Alouette   A seven-place single-turbine helicopter manufactured by Aerospatiale Helicopters in France.

ALPA   Air Line Pilots Association.

alpha   In aviation radio phraseology the term for A.

alpha-numerics   Data consisting of a combination of letters and figures.

Allison Gas Turbine Division

Allison Enhanced Performance 250-C30S turbine engine.

Allison Gas Turbine Division

Allison 250-C20R turbine engine.

Allison Gas Turbine Division

Allison 250-B17-C turbine engine.

alpha-numeric display   The data blocks representing aircraft in-flight as appearing on the controller's radarscope. These displays are generated by computers or may be manually entered by controllers. They move about the radar scope in physical relation to the actual blip.

ALS   Approach-light system.

ALT   Altitude.

ALTA   Association of Local Transport Air Lines.

alternate airport   An airport chosen by a pilot, filing IFR, as a secondary choice, in the event that the primary destination is below landing minimums at arrival time.

alternator   An electrical device (in recent years having replaced the old-style generator in most aircraft) that is driven by the engine and supplies current to the battery and to all electrical equipment except the ignition system. When a battery is completely drained, an alternator will not recharge it, even if the aircraft is started by hand propping it. In that case the battery must first receive a charge from another source.

altimeter   A flight instrument capable of reading height above sea level (or any other predetermined level), activated by an aneroid barometer measuring atmospheric pressure at the given altitude. This information is transformed into a readout showing feet above sea level (or any level) on a circular dial. The instrument is adjusted to the prevailing barometric pressure by turning a knob on the face of the instrument. It is a part of the pitot-static system.

altimeter   In aviation radio phraseology the term used for altimeter setting, i.e., the prevailing barometric pressure.

altimeter setting   The barometric pressure reading in the small window provided for that purpose on the face of the instrument, as set by the pilot in accordance with information received from a station located in the vicinity of where the aircraft happens to be located (on the ground or in the air) at that particular time.

altitude   The height above sea level, ground level or any other reference plane. The various types of altitude of concern to the pilot are: *Indicated altitude*—the reading shown by the altimeter when the proper altimeter setting has been made; *Pressure altitude*—the altitude above sea level (or any other given level) when the altimeter is set to 29.92; *Density altitude* is the pressure altitude corrected for prevailing temperature conditions; *True altitude*—actual height above mean sea level; *Absolute altitude*—actual altitude above the terrain over which the aircraft is flying. Of the five, those of primary interest to pilots in the every-day operation of the aircraft are: indicated altitude, which he will habitually use when flying below 18,000 feet; pressure altitude is used for all operations above 18,000 feet; and density altitude, which is of primary importance when planning a departure from a high-elevation airport on a warm day. The higher the density altitude, the less efficient is the (non-turbocharged) engine, and at the same time the lifting capability of the airfoil is reduced, resulting often in very long takeoff runs or, in extreme cases, the inability of a heavily loaded aircraft to accomplish liftoff and climbout.

altitude chamber   Pressurized facilities usually operated by the military, in which pilots may (and are encouraged to) experience the effects of oxygen starvation under high-altitude conditions without ever leaving the ground. These exercises are performed under strict supervision. They are quite safe and extremely informative. Pilots interested in participating should contact the nearest Air Force establishment.

altitude encoder   An instrument that either optically or mechanically reads the current altimeter reading and gives this information to the transponder which, in turn, transmits it to ATC. Also referred to as the encoding altimeters or digitizers.

altitude reservation (ALTRV)   A specialized use of the airspace, usually for the mass movement of aircraft, which would be difficult to accomplish otherwise. They must be applied for and are approved by the appropriate FAA facility.

altitude restriction   An altitude or series of altitudes issued in order flown, and which are to be maintained until reaching a specific checkpoint or time. They are usually issued as part of ATC clearances as the result of traffic, terrain or airspace considerations.

Altitude Encoders/Digitizers

MANUFACTURER	MODEL	PRICE	VOLT	D	C	DISPLAY						DIGITIZER				TYPE		ALTITUDE	lbs
						1	2	3	4	5	6	1	2	3	4	1	2		
Bendix/King	KE 127	1,075	14/28	¤								¤				¤		to 20,000'	1
Bendix/King	KEA129	2,585	14/28			¤	¤					¤				¤		to 20,000'	1.9
Bendix/King	KEA130	2,850	14/28			¤	¤					¤				¤		to 35.000'	1.9
Bendix/King	KEA346	8,800	28			¤			¤		¤	¤					¤	to 50,000'	2.9
Terra	AT 3000	n/a	10-32	¤								¤				¤		to 30,000'	0.5
Aero	AM 2030	n/a	11-32	¤								¤		*		¤		to 30,000'	0.5
Mechanism	AM 275C	n/a	11-32		¤						¤							to 50,000'	13oz

* This is an altitude alert system only, digitally displaying the altitude

PRICE:	uninstalled
VOLT:	input VDC
D:	digitizer only
C:	combined altimeter/digitizer
DISPLAY	1: three-pointer
	2:drum pointer
	3:counter drum pointer
	4:counter pointer
	5:pointer dial
	6:digital
DIGITIZER:	1: solid state
	2:optical
	3:contact
	4:magnetic
TYPE	1: pneumatic
	2:servoed

ALTN   Alternate.

altocumulus   A middle cumuliform cloud that forms in a layer or group of small, broken puffs. It may merge with altostratus; distinguished from cirrocumulus by the slightly grey color.

altostratus   A middle stratiform cloud, usually in a thick, solid, greyish layer through which the sun may be vaguely seen.

ALTRV   Altitude reservation.

aluminum overcast   A term humorously describing the so-called crowded-sky situation.

ALWOS   Automated low-cost weather observation station.

ambiguity meter   The TO/FROM indicator in an OBI.

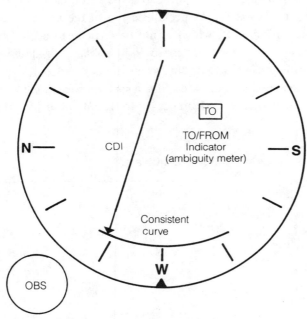

Ambiguity meter, the TO/FROM indicator on an OBI.

AMDT   Amendment.

AME   Aviation medical examiner.

Amecom Division, Litton Industries   Manufacturer of telecommunication and voice communication systems, weatherfax recorders, and a variety of sophisticated aviation equipment. (5115 Calvert Road, College Park, MD 20740-3898. (301) 864-5600)

AMFI   Aviation Maintenance Foundation, Inc.

ammeter   A readout on the instrument panel that indicates the rate at which the battery is being charged by the generator or alternator, in terms of amperes (amps).

amp. Ampere.

ampere A unit used in measuring electrical current, in terms of its strength.

AMS Air mass.

AMT Amount.

anabatic wind Lateral air movement caused by rising air currents.

analog computer A computer that operates with numbers represented by directly measurable quantities, such as voltages or revolutions per minute. Recently most analog computer applications in aircraft have been replaced by digital computers because of their smaller size and weight and vastly greater capacity.

anemometer An instrument for measuring wind speed, frequently of the rotating-cups type, which has cup-shaped scoops on the shaft. The cups are pushed by the wind and rotate around a shaft at a rate that varies with the speed of the wind.

aneroid barometer A device to measure atmospheric pressure by measuring the amount of expansion or contraction of the walls of a sealed hollow disk or diaphragm from which most of the air has been removed. It is the basic mechanism of the standard altimeter.

angle-of-attack The angle at which the chord line of the wing meets the relative wind. It determines the amount of lift developed at any airspeed. (Page 42)

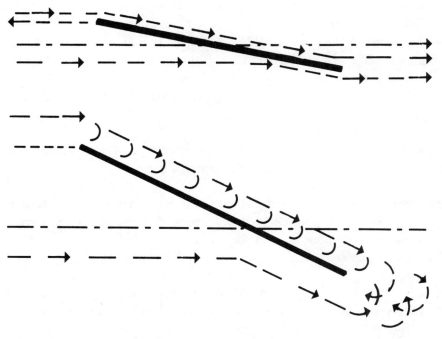

When the angle-of-attack is increased beyond a certain limit, the air breaks away from the surface of the moving object.

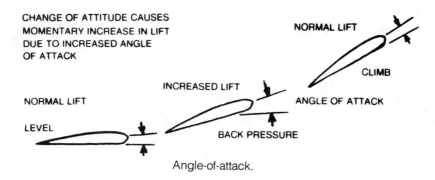

CHANGE OF ATTITUDE CAUSES
MOMENTARY INCREASE IN LIFT
DUE TO INCREASED ANGLE
OF ATTACK

NORMAL LIFT

CLIMB

INCREASED LIFT

NORMAL LIFT

ANGLE OF ATTACK

LEVEL

BACK PRESSURE

Angle-of-attack.

angle-of-attack indicator   A cockpit instrument that senses the angle-of-attack of the aircraft and displays it in the form of a cockpit readout. (Angle-of-attack indicators are manufactured by Conrac Corporation, Humphrey, Inc., Safe Flight Instrument Corporation, Teledyne Avionics).

angle of bank   The angle between the lateral axis of the aircraft and the plane of the earth's surface. Also called, angle of roll.

angle of climb   The angle between the flight path of a climbing aircraft and the horizontal plane.

angle of glide   The vertical angle between the flight path of a descending aircraft and the horizontal plane.

angle of incidence   The angle formed by the longitudinal axis of an aircraft and the chord line of the wing. It is a built-in, usually slightly upward, angle of the wing. Also used in reference to helicopter rotor blades.

angle of pitch   The angle between the longitudinal axis of an aircraft and the horizontal plane.

angle of roll   Angle of bank.

angle of yaw   The acute angle between the longitudinal axis of an aircraft and its flight path as seen from above, such as during a slip.

ANLYS   Analysis.

annual inspection   The complete examination of an aircraft and its systems by a licensed mechanic or repair station. It is required once a year of all aircraft to maintain the airworthiness certificate in force.

ANRA   Air navigation radio aids.

ANT   Antenna.

antenna   A device designed to send or receive radio energy. Its type and shape depend on the type of equipment to be operated in conjunction with a given antenna, and whether airborne or ground-based.

Antenna Specialists Company   Manufacturer of two-way communication antennas for aircraft. (30500 Bruce Industrial Parkway, Cleveland, OH 44139-3996. (216) 439-8400.)

anti-collision device   Collision-avoidance system.

anti-collison light   A rotating red light on an aircraft, required for night and IFR flight. Certain strobe lights may be used in conjunction with or instead of the red rotating light.

anticyclone   A high-pressure area.

anti-icing devices   Devices such as heated wings, pulsating leading edge boots and alcohol systems designed to prevent ice from forming on the propeller, wings, and tail surfaces of an aircraft.

anti-torque rotor   Tail rotor on a helicopter.

anvil cloud   A cumulonimbus cloud with an anvil-like shape at the top; typical of active and dissipating thunderstorms.

AOCI   Airport Operators Council International.

AOE   Airport of entry.

AOPA   Aircraft Owners and Pilots Association.

AP   Small hail (in sequence reports).

APCH   Approach.

apex   The top of an inflated balloon.

apex rope   The rope attached to the top of a balloon which, when pulled, causes a release of the hot air or gas.

API   American Petroleum Institute.

APP CON   Approach control.

appendix   The sleeve at the bottom of a gas balloon through which gas is fed into the balloon.

approach clearance   ATC authorization for a pilot to commence an instrument approach. The clearance includes the type of approach to be executed, plus other pertinent information.

approach control   The ATC facility monitoring and directing traffic approaching an airport where such a facility is in operation.

approach fix   A fix usually associated with electronic navigation aids, marking points along the final approach.

approach gate   A position one mile from the approach fix and usually five miles from the runway threshold. Aircraft are vectored to this point to put them into position for the final touchdown.

approach light system   Lighting that might be installed at an airport to help guide arriving aircraft. (For details *See* RUNWAY-LIGHT SYSTEMS).

approach path   A flight course in the vicinity of an airport, designed to bring aircraft in to safe landings. Usually, approach paths are marked by appropriate navigation aids.

approach plate   The chart depicting an instrument approach.

approach procedures   Published procedures describing the manner in which a precision or nonprecision instrument approach must be flown.

approach speed   The speed at which an approach to a landing is made at a relatively slow rate of descent. It is generally approximately 50 percent above the stalling speed of a given aircraft.

apron   That part of an airport designed for tiedown, fueling, loading, etc.

APRXLY   Approximately.

Archer   A single-engine piston aircraft manufactured by Piper Aircraft Corporation. No longer in production.

arctic air mass   An extremely cold air mass originating in the arctic regions.

area broadcast   A weather broadcast made by FSSs at 15 minutes past the hour, reporting on weather conditions for an area covering approximately 150 miles from the FSS in all directions.

area forecast   A weather forecast for a 12-hour period covering weather conditions to be expected within a region of the U.S. For this purpose the U.S. is divided into 23 regions. The area forecast is issued every six hours.

area navigation (RNAV)   A method of navigating without using the established airway system. RNAV operations require a variety of special on-board instrumentation depending on the type of area navigation to be used. There are five entirely different types of RNAV.

One uses the North American VOR/DME network. The RNAV avionics systems are used to electronically displace VOR/DMEs and VORTACs to locations other than their actual geographical location, thus making it possible to fly directly to such a phantom navaid. The system does not work outside the North American VOR/DME and VORTAC reception area.

Another RNAV system is known as VLF/Omega. It utilizes signals from a network of low-frequency transmitters located in various locations around the globe. This system can be used worldwide. For details, *See* VLF/OMEGA.

A third type is known as INS (inertial guidance system) and it employs on-board gyroscopes or a system of lasers. This system, too, can be used worldwide. For details, *See* INERTIAL NAVIGATION SYSTEM.

The fourth type is known as Loran-C and it uses low-frequency radio signals from a network of Loran stations. It can be used in North America (with some minor geographical restrictions). For details, *See* LORAN-C NAVIGATION.

The fifth is known as global positioning system (GPS) and it uses signals from a number of satellites in stationary orbit for precision navigational guidance. For details, *See* GLOBAL POSITIONING SYSTEM.

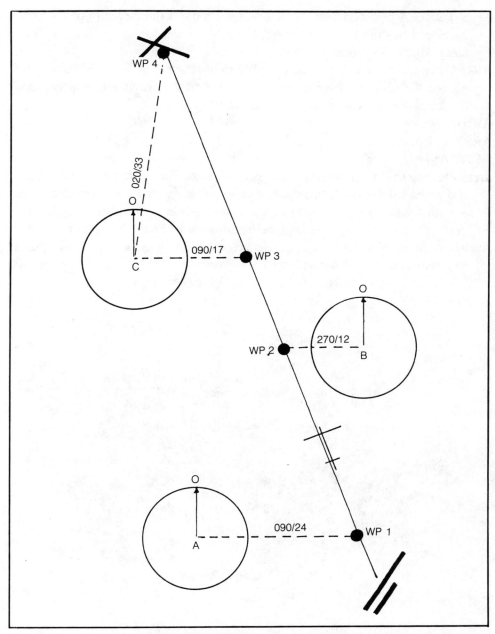

With RNAV equipment the available VORTACs can be moved electronically to more convenient locations, known as waypoints.

Aries T-250 A high-performance single-engine aircraft (no longer in production), developed by Anderson-Greenwood Corporation and briefly marketed by Bellanca Aircraft Corporation.

ARINC Aviation Radio, Inc., an organization that sets a variety of standards for high-performance avionics, especially for equipment designed for the airlines and the top-of-the-line corporate turbine aircraft.

ARND Around.

ARPT Airport.

ARR Arrival; arrive.

arresting system A variety of mechanical means by which aircraft can be stopped and prevented from overrunning the end of the runway. The most prevalent is the arresting cable, a steel cable stretched across the runway (or the deck of an aircraft carrier) designed to engage the arresting hook of military aircraft.

Arriel A family of turbine engines manufactured by Turbomeca in France and used to power a number of Aerospatiale helicopters.

Turbomeca Arriel turbine engine.

arrival time The touchdown time of an arriving aircraft.

ARNAV Systems, Inc. Manufacturer of Loran-C navigation systems, databases, and test equipment and fuel computers. (16100 SW 72nd Avenue, P.O. Box 23939, Portland, OR 97223. (503) 684-1600.)

Arrow A high-performance single-engine retractable-gear piston-engine aircraft manufactured by Piper Aircraft Corporation.

Piper Turbo Arrow IV.

ARSR Air route surveillance radar.

ARTCC Air route traffic control center. Usually simply referred to as *center.* The ATC facility handling en route IFR traffic. There are 27 such centers in the U.S.

articulated rotor Helicopter main rotor with individual flapping, lead-lag, and feathering hinges.

artificial horizon A gyro instrument showing the attitude of the aircraft with reference to pitch and roll as compared to the horizon.

ARTS I, II, III Automated radar terminal system, a system of terminal air traffic control based on sophisticated computer technology and radar. The I, II, and III refer to the degree of automation at a given facility.

Artouste A family of turbine engines manufactured by Turbomeca in France and used to power a number of Aerospatiale helicopters, among other aircraft.

ASDE Airport surface detection equipment.

ASL Above sea level. Usually expressed mean sea level (msl).

aspect ratio The aspect ratio of an aircraft wing is defined as the square of the wing span divided by the wing area.

ASR Airport surveillance radar.

ASRS Aviation Safety Reporting System. A function of NASA.

asymmetrical power The situation existing in a twin-engine aircraft, when one engine is inoperative. This does not include the push-pull type twins such as the Cessna Skymaster, which have one engine located fore and aft.

AStar The single-engine turbine-powered helicopter produced by Aerospatiale Helicopter Division in France.

Astazou A family of turbine engines manufactured by Turbomeca in France and used to power a number of Aerospatiale helicopters, among other aircraft. (Page 48)

Turbomeca Astazou turbine engine.

Astra   A twin fan-jet corporate aircraft developed and manufactured by Israel Aircraft Industries.

Astra Corporation   The company that markets the Astra and Westwind I and II corporate jet aircraft, manufactured by Israel Aircraft Industries. (4 Independence Way, Princeton, NJ 08540.)

Astronautics Corporation of America   Manufacturer of ADIs, VSIs, HSIs, bearing, distance, heading and range indicators, flight director systems, autopilots, CDUs, heads-up displays, air-data computers, and other instruments for general aviation, the airlines, and the military. (4115 N. Teutonia Avenue, Milwaukee, WI 53209-6731. (414) 447-8200.)

Astrotech Corporation   Manufacturer of a family of digital aircraft chronometers. (10201 North 21st Avenue, Phoenix, AZ 85021-1886. (602) 870-3801.)

ATA   Air Transport Association. A powerful trade and lobbying organization representing the airline industry.

ATC   Air traffic control.

ATCA   Air Traffic Control Association.

ATCAA   ATC assigned airspace.

ATC advises   A term used to preface non-control information relayed by ATC to the pilot via a person other than an air traffic controller.

ATC assigned airspace   Airspace defined in terms of lateral and vertical limits for the purpose of separating special-purpose activity (usually military) from other IFR traffic.

ATC clearance   An authorization by ATC with reference to the course and altitude to be flown by an IFR aircraft designed to assure separation between various IFR traffic.

ATC clearance limit   The farthest point to which an IFR aircraft has been cleared and beyond which it may not proceed without having received a further clearance.

ATC clearance shorthand   A convenient means of copying a clearance while it is being issued by ATC. It is non-mandatory and different pilots may use different types of such shorthand.

Suggested ATC clearance shorthand.

Words and Phrases	Shorthand	Words and Phrases	Shorthand
Above	ABV	Direct	DR
Above (Altitudes—Hundreds of feet)	70	Direction (Bound)	
Advise	ADV	Eastbound	EB
After (Passing)	<	Westbound	WB
Airway (Designation)	V26	Northbound	NB
Airport	A	Southbound	SB
Alternate Instructions	( )	Inbound	IB
Altitude 6,000—17,000	60 – 170	Outbound	OB
And	&	DME FIX (Mile)	21
Approach	AP	Each	EA
Approach Control	APC	Enter Control Area	△
At	@	Estimated Time of Arrival	ETA
(ATC) Advises	CA	Expect	EX
(ATC) Clears or Cleared	C	Expect Approach Clearance	EAC
(ATC) Requests	CR	Expect Further Clearancre	EFC
Back Course	BC	Fan Marker	FM
Bearing	BR	Final	F
Before (Reaching, Passing)	>	Flight Level	FL
Below	BLO	Flight Planned Route	FPR
Below (Altitude—Hundreds of Feet)	70	For Further Clearance	FFC
Center	CTR	For Further Headings	FFH
Cleared as Filed	CAF	From	FR
Cleared to Land	L	Heading	HDG
Climb to (Altitude—Hundreds of Feet)	↑70	Hold (Direction)	H-W
Contact	CT	Holding Pattern	⊂⊃
Contact Approach	CAP	ILS Approach	ILS
Contact (Den er) Approach Control	(den	Initial Approach	I
Contact (Denver) Center	(DEN	Intersection	XN
Course	CRS	Join or Intercept Airway/	≥
Cross	X	Jet Route/Track or Course	
Cruise	→	Left Turn After Takeoff	↰
Delay Indefinite	DLI	Locator Outer Marker	LOM
Depart	DP	Maintain or Magnetic	M
Departure Control	DPC	Maintain VFR Conditions on Top	VFR
Descent To (Altitude—Hundreds of Feet)	↓70		

(continued)

Words and Phrases	Shorthand	Words and Phrases	Shorthand
Middle Compass Locator	ML	Standby	STBY
Middle Marker	MM	Straight-in Approach	SI
Nondirectional Beacon Approach	NDB	Surveillance Radar Approach	ASR
Out Of (Leave) Control Area	⬈	Takeoff (Direction)	T→N
Outer Marker	OM	Tower	Z
Over (Station)	OKC	Until	U
On Course	OC	Until Advised (By)	UA
Precision Radar Approach	PAR	Until Further Advised	UFA
Procedure Turn	PT	VIA	VIA
Radar Vecto	RV	Victor (Airway Number)	V14
Radial (080° Radial)	080R	Visual Approach	VA
Remain Well to Left Side	LS	VOR	⊙
Remain Well to Right Side	RS	VORTAC	Ⓣ
Report Crossing	RX	While in Control Area	△
Report Departing	RD		
Report Leaving	RL	**Example**	
Report on Course	R	An example of a clearance written in	
	CRS	shorthand:	
Report Over	RO	C A F M RY HDG RV	
Report Passing	RP	V18 SQ 0700 DPC 120.4	
Report Reaching	RR	Translated it reads: (Aircraft num-	
Report Starting Procedure Turn	RSPT	ber), cleared as filed, maintain run-	
Reverse Course	RC	way heading for radar vector to	
Right Turn After Takeoff	↷	Victor 18, squawk 0700 just before	
Runway (Number)	RY18	departure, departure control fre-	
Squawk	SO	quency—120.4.	

ATC clears   A term used to preface an ATC clearance when it is relayed to the pilot by a person other than an air traffic controller.

ATC Flight Simulator Co.   Manufacturer of a family of non-motion flight simulators for single-engine and twin-engine piston aircraft, and turboprop aircraft with optional color visual displays. (1650 19th Street, Santa Monica, CA 90404. (213) 453-3557.) (Pages 51-53)

ATC instruction   Instructions issued by ATC in order to cause the pilot to take a given action, such as: *Go around* or *Turn right to 180 degrees.*

ATC requests   A term used to preface an ATC request when it is relayed to the pilot by a person other than an air traffic controller.

ATCRBS   Air traffic control radar beacon system.

ATIS   Automatic terminal information service. Recorded information about weather and other conditions at the airport, periodically updated when conditions change. Each such report is prefaced by *Information alpha* (*bravo,* etc.) and the pilot is expected to inform tower, ground or approach control that he has received information alpha (bravo, etc.).

ATC Flight Simulators

Standard configuration Equipment		MODEL 610/710	MODEL 810/820
		desktop*	enclosed cockpit
	ADF	yes	yes
	airspeed indicator	yes	yes
	alternator l/r	no	yes
	altimeter	yes	yes
	ammeter l/r	no	yes
	attitude indicator	yes	yes
	audio panel	no	yes
	circuit breakers	no	yes
	com receiver	yes	yes
	cowl flaps	no	yes
	cylinder head gauge	no	yes
	DME	yes	yes
	door warning lights	no	yes
	engine audio	optional	yes
	EGT	no	dual
	elapsed time	yes	yes
	engine start l/r	no	yes
	flap	no	yes
	flight mode/freeze	no	yes
	fuel crossfeed select	no	yes
	fuel flow l/r	no	yes
	fuel pressure l/r	no	yes
	fuel pump	yes	yes
	fuel quantity	yes	dual
	fuel selector(s)	yes	yes
	gear handle	yes	yes
	gyro pressure gauge	no	yes
	headset jack	optional	yes
	HSI	no	optional
	key	yes	yes
	magnetic compass	yes	yes
	magneto l/r	no	yes
	manifold press. gauge	yes	dual
	marker beacon audio	yes	yes
	nav 1 receiver	yes	yes
	nav 2 receiver	no	yes
	no smoking light	no	yes
	nose trim	yes	yes
	oil gauge	no	yes
	panel light adjustment	no	yes
	parking brake	no	yes
	pitch trim	yes	yes
	pitot heat	no	yes
	plotter scale selector	no	yes
	position reset	no	yes
	RMI indicator	no	yes
	roll trim	no	yes
	rpm l/r	no	yes
	rudder pedals	optional	yes
	seatbelt light	no	yes
	surface deice	no	yes
	throttle	yes	power quadrant
	transponder	yes	yes
	turn coordinator	yes	yes
	VOR indicator	yes	yes
	VSI indicator	yes	yes
	yoke	yes	yes
PRICE basic	1989 $s	$8,845.00	$47,950.00

* Options include a cockpit enclosure and an instructor's station.

ATC single-engine flight simulator with enclosure.

atmosphere   The total mass of air surrounding the earth in layers of varying characteristics. A unit of atmospheric pressure is equal to a column of 29.92 inches of
mercury, also expressed as 1613.2 millibars.

atmospheric pressure   *See* ATMOSPHERE.

atmospherics   Static.

ATC twin-engine flight simulator with copilot position.

ATP   Air transport pilot certificate.

ATR   *See* ATP.

attitude   The position of an aircraft in relation to a given reference, usually the ground, along its longitudinal, lateral, and vertical axes.

attitude indicator   *See* ARTIFICIAL HORIZON.

Audio Selector Panels

MANUFACTURER	MODEL	PRICE	VOLT	INPUT		MARKR		SELECTR				A	S	SIZE			lbs	REMARKS
				T	R	I	S	V	H	P	I			W	H	D		
Bendix/King	KMA 24	1,225	14	¤	¤	¤		¤				¤	¤	6.	1.	6.	1.7	incl. DME, ADF
	/24H	1,225	14	¤	¤	¤		¤	¤	¤	¤	¤	¤	25	3	8	1.7	Helicopter version
Bendix/King	KA 134	635	14/28	¤	¤		¤	¤		¤	¤		¤	6	1	6	.8	Audio panel
	KR 22	480	14/28			¤								3	1	8	.4	Marker beacon recvr
Terra	TMA 230	n/a	14/28	¤	¤		¤	¤		¤	¤		¤	6.3	1.2	5.5	1.05	TM 23 Marker avail.
Aire-Sciences	A-550	425	14	¤	¤		¤	¤					¤					incl. DME, ADF
Aire-Sciences	AM-550	845	14	¤	¤	¤		¤					¤					incl. DME, ADF
Aire-Sciences	AM-660	945	14	¤	¤	¤		¤					¤					incl. DME, ADF TSOd
Mentor	AP-1	530	14/28	¤	¤		¤	¤*		¤			¤	6.4	1.6	7.4	1.45	incl. DME, ADF *add
Mentor	APM-1	796	14/28	¤	¤	¤		¤*		¤			¤	6.4	1.6	7.4	1.5	incl. DME. ADF $21

PRICE:		uninstalled
VOLT:		input
INPUT	T:	transceiver
	R:	receiver
MARKR	I:	built in
	S:	separate
SELECTR	V:	VHF com
	H:	HF com
	P:	PA system
	I:	intercom
A:		auto feature
S:		solid state
SIZE	W:	width, inches
	H:	height, inches
	D:	depth, inches

Audio selector panel with marker beacon indication.

audio selector panel   An avionics device making it simpler for the pilot to select the particular nav or com radio he wants to use at a given time. Audio selector panels are produced by all major avionics manufacturers.

AUTO   Automatic.

automated radar terminal systems   *See* ARTS.

automated altitude reporting The function of a transponder, designated Mode C, which accepts altitude information from the encoding altimeter and/or digitizer, and automatically transmits it to ATC in 100-foot increments.

automatic direction finder (ADF) A cockpit instrument that responds to radio signals from nondirectional beacons (NDB), standard broadcast stations and a variety of other ground-based LF/MF navigation aids, translating this information into a cockpit readout, the needle of which points to the station, thus telling the pilot the position of the nose of the aircraft with relation to the station. (Page 56)

Automatic Direction Finder Systems (ADF)

MANUFACTURER	MODEL	PRICE	VOLT	FREQUENCY	P	R	D	B	SIZE W	H	D	U	lbs	REMARKS
Collins	ADF-650	n/a	14-28	200-1,799	¤		¤	¤	6.25	1.75	10.82	3	5.9	Micro Line Loop-sense antenna
Collins	ADF-462	n/a	28	190-1,799 2179-2185		¤	¤	¤				3	3.7	ProLine II
Bendix/King	KR 87	3,855	14-28	200-1,799	¤		¤	¤	6.31	1.38	11.28	3	9.1	w.KI 227 slaved mag. hdg.indicator $4,020
Bendix/King	KDF 806	8,935	11-33 26VAC	190-1,799	¤	¤	¤	¤	2	5	10	3	9.1	Gold Crown. Indicator unit:2.01x2.25x7.375
Bendix/King	DFS 43	13,315	28	190-1,860	¤	¤	¤	¤				2	5.8	Series III

PRICE:	uninstalled		SIZE W:	width in inches
VOLT:	input VDC		H:	height in inches
FREQUENCY:	frequency range in kHz		D:	depth in inches
P:	panel mounted		U:	number of units
R:	remote mounted			
D:	digital tuning			
B:	BFO			

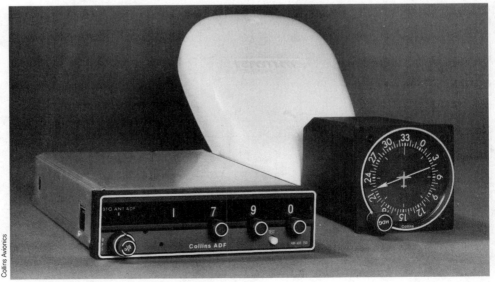

Automatic direction finder (ADF) system.

Collins Avionics

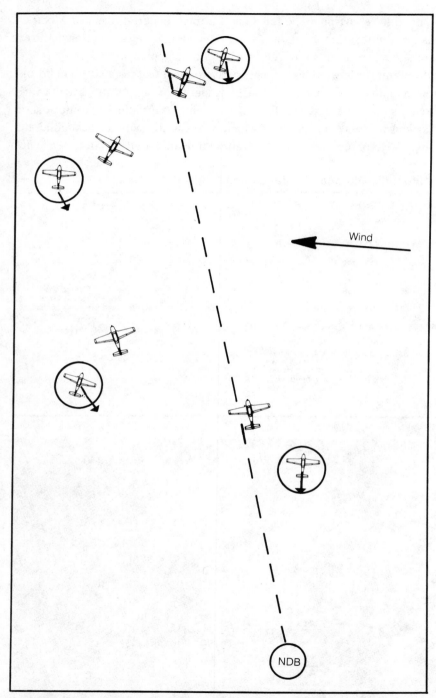

The ADF display when flying from the station and correcting for wind drift.

automatic pilot *See* AUTOPILOT.

automatic terminal information service *See* ATIS.

autopilot A device, usually consisting of gyroscopic, electronic and/or hydraulic elements which operates the flight controls of an airplane. Autopilots come in a wide variety of degrees of sophistication and prices.

Autopilot Systems

MANUFACTURER	MODEL	PRICE	VOLT	GYROS D.A.R	SURFC A.E.R	CNT L.P	C	HDG H.P	ALT H.P	W	RDO V.L	SRV E.P	lbs	REMARKS
S-Tec	40	3,195	14/28	¤	¤	¤		¤ ¤			¤ ¤	¤ ¤	7.1	Single axis
S-Tec	50	5,075	14/28	¤	¤ ¤	¤		¤ ¤		¤	¤ ¤	¤ ¤	10.0	Two axis
S-Tec	60-1	4,975	14/28	¤	¤	¤	¤ ¤		¤ ¤ ¤		¤ ¤	13.2	Single axis
S-Tec	60-2	8,795	14/28	¤	¤ ¤	¤ ¤	¤ ¤ ¤ ¤		¤ ¤	¤ ¤	16.1	Two axis
Century Flt.	I	n/a	14/28	¤ ¤	¤ ¤		¤	¤ ¤		¤	¤	7	Single axis
Century Flt.	IIB	n/a	14/28	¤ ¤	¤		¤	¤ ¤ ¤		¤ ¤ ¤ ¤	9	Single axis
Century Flt.	III	n/a	14/28	¤ ¤	¤ ¤	¤ ¤ ¤ ¤ ¤ ¤		¤ ¤ ¤ ¤	19.5	Two axis
Century Flt.	21	n/a	14/28	¤ ¤	¤		¤	¤ ¤ ¤		¤ ¤ ¤ ¤	12.5	Single axis
Bendix/King	KAP 100	8,320	14/28	¤	¤	¤	¤ ¤ ¤		¤ ¤ ¤	10.93	Single axis, slaved comp.opt.
Bendix/King	KAP 150	13,835	14/28	¤	¤ ¤	¤ ¤ ¤ ¤ ¤		¤ ¤ ¤ ¤	18.05	Two axis, slaved HSI opt.
Bendix/King	KAP150H	21,890	28	¤	¤ ¤	¤ ¤ ¤ ¤ ¤ ¤		¤ ¤ ¤ ¤	18.50	Helicopter version
Bendix/King	KAP 200	22,045	14/28	¤	¤ ¤	¤ ¤ ¤ ¤ ¤ ¤		¤ ¤ ¤ ¤	28.30	Two axis. 3-axis available
Collins	APS-65	n/a	28	¤ ¤	¤ ¤ ¤ ¤ ¤ ¤ ¤ ¤ ¤ ¤ ¤ ¤ ¤ ¤ ¤	30.50	ProLine II
Collins	APS-80	n/a	28	¤ ¤	¤ ¤ ¤ ¤ ¤ ¤ ¤ ¤ ¤ ¤ ¤ ¤ ¤ ¤ ¤	37.9	ProLine II
Collins	APS-85	n/a	28	¤ ¤	¤ ¤ ¤ ¤ ¤ ¤ ¤ ¤ ¤ ¤ ¤ ¤ ¤ ¤ ¤	30.3	ProLine II

*options include altitude preselect and yaw damper.

PRICE:		uninstalled
VOLT:		input
GYROS	D:	directional
	A:	attitude
	R:	rate
SURFC	A:	surface control - ailerons
	E:	surface control - elevators
	R:	surface control - rudder
CNT	L:	lateral control
	P:	pitch control
C:		command turns
HDG	H:	heading hold
	P:	heading preset
ALT	H:	altitude hold
	P:	altitude preset
W:		crosswind correction
RADIO	V:	radio coupling - VOR
	L:	radio coupling - localizer
SRV	E:	electric servo
	P:	pneumatic servo

Autopilot system: S-Tec 50.

S-TEC Corporation

autorotation   The condition caused by engine failure in a helicopter. The gravity pull will cause the rotor blades to rotate and thus to slow the power-off descent. Autorotation can also be achieved by pulling the throttle back to idle power.

auto tow   A means of launching a sailplane, using an automobile to tow the aircraft until it becomes airborne.

AUX   Auxiliary.

AVBL   Available.

AVG   Average.

Avian Balloon Company   Manufacturers of hot-air balloons. (South 3722 Ridgeview Drive, Spokane, WA 99206. (509) 928-6847.)

Avanti   A canard-equipped twin turboprop pusher corporate aircraft manufactured by Rinaldo Piaggio S.p.A. in Italy. *See* PIAGGIO.

Piaggio Avanti twin-turboprop pusher corporate aircraft.

aviation medical examiner   A licensed physician designated by the FAA to perform medical examinations and issue medical certificates.

Aviation Organizations   Listed here are the more prominent aviation organizations in the U.S. For the benefit of international travelers, aviation organizations outside the U.S. are listed under *International Aviation Organizations*. In addition to those listed, there are literally hundreds of local and regional clubs and organizations, which, because of space limitations and their often rather brief life span, could not be included.

Aero Club of Washington, 1133 13th Street, N.W. #620, Washington, DC 20005. (202) 293-5913.

Aeronautical Radio, Inc. (ARINC), 2551 Riva Road, Annapolis, MD 21401. (301) 266-4000.

Aerospace Education Foundation, Inc. 1501 Lee Highway, Arlington, VA 22209. (703) 247-5839.

Aerospace Industries Association of America, Inc. (AIA), 1725 DeSales Street N.W., Washington DC 20036-4473. (202) 429-4600.

Aerospace Medical Association, c/o Rufus R. Hessberg, M.D., Washington National Airport, Washington DC 20001. (703) 892-2240. Annual meetings in May. Monthly publication: *Aviation, Space & Environmental Medicine*.

Airborne Law Enforcement Association, Inc., 500 Newport Center Road, Newport Beach, CA 92660. Bimonthly publication: *Air Beat*.

Aircraft Electronics Association, Inc., P.O. Box 1981, Independence, MO 64055. (816) 373-6565. Annual meetings in May. Monthly publication: *Avionics News*.

Aircraft Mechanics Fraternal Association, 4150 Cypress Road #13, St. Ann, MO 63074. Quarterly publication: *Grapevine*.

Aircraft Owners and Pilots Association (AOPA), 421 Aviation Way, Frederick, MD 21701. (301) 695-2000 (800) 872-2672 Annual meetings in October. Monthly publication: *The AOPA Pilot*. Other publications: *AOPA's Airports USA, AOPA Aviation Fact Card*.

Air Force Association, 1501 Lee Highway, Arlington, VA 22209-1198. (703) 247-5800. Annual meetings in September. Monthly publication: *Air Force Magazine*.

Air Line Pilots Association (ALPA), 1625 Massachusetts Avenue N.W., Washington, DC 20036. (703) 689-2270. Monthly publication: *Air Line Pilot*.

Airport Operators Council International., Inc., 1221 19th Street N.W. #800. (202) 293-8500. Annual meetings in October. Weekly publication: *Airport Highlights*.

Air Traffic Control Association, 2020 North 14th Street, Arlington, VA 22201. (703) 522-5717. Annual meeting in October/November. Monthly publication: *ATCA Bulletin*.

Air Transport Association of America (ATA), 1709 New York Avenue N.W., Washington, DC 20006-5206. (202) 626-4000. Annual meetings in October. Official publication: *Air Transport*.

American Association of Airport Executives (AAAE), 4224 King Street, Alexandria, VA 22302. (703) 824-0500. Annual meetings in May, October, November, December. Bimonthly publication: *Airport Report*.

American Bonanza Society, P.O. Box 12888, Wichita, KS 67277. (316) 945-6913.

American Electronics Association, P.O. Box 10045, 2670 Hanover Street, Palo Alto, CA 94303. (415) 857-9300.

American Institute of Aeronautics & Astronautics, Inc., (AIAA) 370 L'Enfant Promenade, Washington, DC 20024. (202) 646-7400. Annual meetings in February, May. Official Publications: *Aerospace America; AIAA Journal; Journal of Aircraft; Journal of Guidance, Control & Dynamics; Journal of Propulsion & Power; Journal of Spacecraft & Rockets; Journal of Thermophysics & Heat Transfer; Progress in Astronautics & Aeronautics; AIAA Student Journal; AIAA Education Series.*

Association of Aviation Psychologists, Ohio State University, Dept. of Aviation, Box 3022, Columbus, OH 43210-0022. (614) 459-4299. Annual meetings in April.

Association of Balloon & Airship Constructors (ABAC), Box 7, Rosemead, CA 91770. (818) 918-0298. Bimonthly publication: *Aerostation.*

Aviation Distributors & Manufacturers Associations (ADMA), 1900 Arch Street, Philadelphia, PA 19103. (215) 564-3484. Annual meetings in June, November. Official publication: *Aviation Education News.*

Aviation Maintenance Foundation, Inc. (AMFI), Box 2826, Redmond, WA 98073. Official publications: *AMFI Confidential Bulletin; AMFI History; AMFI Job Opportunities Listings; AMFI Statistical Data Service; AMFI Technical Bulletins; Professionalism: A A & P's Guide to the World of Aviation Maintenance.*

Aviation/Space Writers Association (AWA), 17 South High Street, Columbus, OH 43215. (614) 221-1900. Annual meetings in May. Quarterly publication: *AWA News.* Annual publications: *AWA Yearbook & Directory.*

Caribbean Aero Clubs International. (Flying Pirates), 75 Fairway Drive #23W, Miami Springs, FL 33166. (305) 871-3519. Monthly publication: *Caribbean Flyer.*

Civil Air Patrol (CAP), Bldg. 714, Maxwell AFB, AL 36112-5572. (205) 293-6019. Monthly publication: *Civil Air Patrol News.*

Civil Aviation Medical Association, 775 Bank Lane #211, Lake Forest, IL 60045. (312) 234-6330. Quarterly publication: *CAMA Bulletin.*

Confederate Air Force, P.O. Box CAF, Harlingen, TX 78551. (512) 425-1057. Bimonthly publication: *CAF Dispatch.*

Corporate Angel Network, Inc., Westchester County Airport, Bldg. 1, White Plains, NY 10604. (914) 328-1313.

Dayton International Airshow & Trade Exposition, Dayton International Airport, Room 214, Terminal Building, Vandalia, OH 45377. (513) 898-5901. Expositions in July at Dayton International Airport.

Electronic Industries Association, 2001 1st Street N.W., Washington, DC 20006. (202) 457-4900. Annual meetings in April, October. Monthly Publication: *Electronic Market Trends.* Bimonthly publication: *Executive Report.*

Experimental Aircraft Association (EAA), Wittman Field, Oshkosh, WI 54903-3086. (414) 426-4800. Annual meetings July/August. Monthly publications: *Sport Aviation; The Experimenter.*

Flight Safety Foundation, Inc., 5510 Columbia Pike, Arlington, VA 22204-3194. (703) 820-2777. Annual meetings in April, October, December. Bimonthly publications: *Aviation Mechanics Bulletin; Helicopter Safety Bulletin; Human Factors Bulletin; Cabin Crew Safety Bulletin; Air Taxi/Commuter Safety Bulletin; Pilots Safety Exchange; Airport Operators Safety Bulletin.* Monthly Publications: *Flight Safety Digest; Accident Prevention Bulletin; Newsletter.*

Flying Chiropractors Association, 215 Belmont Street, Johnstown, PA 15904. (814) 266-3314.

Flying Physicians Association, 801 Green Bay Road, Lake Bluff, IL 60044.

General Aviation Manufacturers Association (GAMA), 1400 K Street N.W. #801, Washington, DC 20005. (202) 393-1500. Quarterly publication: *Shipment Reports.* Annual publication: *General Aviation Statistical Databook.*

International Air Transport Association (IATA), 1730 K Street N.W., Washington, DC 20006. (202) 822-3929 (Headquarters in Montreal, Canada). Annual meetings in October. Annual publications: *IATA Airport Handling Manual; IATA Air Waybill Handbook; IATA Dangerous Goods Regulations; IATA Live Animals Regulations; IATA Review; IATA Technical Policy Manual; IATA Ticketing Handbook; IATA World Air Transport Statistics.*

International Civil Aviation Organizations (ICAO), Suite 327, 1000 Sherbrooke Street W., Montreal, PQ, Canada H3A 2R2. (514) 285-8219. Monthly publications in English, French, Spanish, quarterly in Russian: *Aircraft Accident Digest; ICAO Bulletin.*

International Comanche Society, P.O. Box 477, Frostproof, FL 33843. (813) 635-5555. Monthly publication: *Comanche Flyer.*

International Council of Aircraft Owners & Pilots Associations (IAOPA), 421 Aviation Way, Frederick, MD 21701. (301) 695-2220.

International Flying Farmers, Box 9124, Wichita, KS 67277. (316) 943-4234. Monthly publication: *International Flying Farmer.*

Lawyer-Pilots Bar Association, 600 Maryland Avenue S.W. #701, Washington, DC 20024. (202) 863-1000. Quarterly publication: *LPBA Journal.*

Lighter-Than-Air Society, Inc. (LTA), 1800 Triplett Blvd., Akron, OH 44306. Bimonthly publication: *Buoyant Flight.*

National Aeronautic Association (NAA), 1763 R Street N.W., Washington, DC 20005. (202) 265-8720. Annual meetings in October. Monthly publication: *National Aeronautics Association Newsletter.* Eight times a year: *For the Record.*

National Agricultural Aviation Association (NAAA), 115 D Street S.E., #103, Washington, DC 20003. (202) 546-5722. Annual meetings in November/December. Publication eight issues annually: *Agricultural Aviation.*

National Air Traffic Controllers Association, 444 N. Capitol Street N.W. #800, Washington, DC 20001. (202) 347-8585.

National Air Transportation Association (NATA), 4226 King Street, Alexandria, VA 22302. (703) 845-9000. Annual meetings in April. Monthly publication: *Air Tran News.* Annual Publications: *Analysis of Airport Rates & Charges; Official NATA Membership Directory; Industry Barometer; Wage & Salary Handbook. Quarterly publication:* General Aviation Operational Profile.

National Association of Flight Instructors (NAFI), P.O. Box 793, Ohio State University Airport, Dublin, OH 43017. (614) 889-6148. Bimonthly publication: *NAFI Foundation Newsletter.*

National Association of Priest Pilots, Box 309, Preston, IA 52069. (319) 689-5161. Annual meetings in July. Bimonthly publication: *NAPP Newsletter.*

National Association of Rocketry, 182 Madison Drive, Elizabeth, PA 15037. (412) 384-6490. Annual meeting in August. Monthly publication: *American Spacemodeling.*

National Association of State Aviation Officials (NASAO), 777 14th Street, N.W. # 717, Washington, DC 20005. (202) 783-0588. Annual meeting in September/October. Monthly publication: *NASAO State Aviation Newsletter.*

National Aviation Hall of Fame, Inc., Dayton Convention & Exhibition Center, Dayton, OH 45402. (513) 226-0800. Annual meeting in July.

National Business Aircraft Association (NBAA), 1200 18th Street, N.W., Washington, DC 20036. (202) 783-9000. Annual meeting in September/October. Monthly publication: *NBAA Business Aircraft Report.* Quarterly Publications: *Business Aviation Management Guide, NBAA For Your Information Reports, NBAA Action Bulletins, NBAA Maintenance Bulletins, NBAA Business Flying.* Also available: *NBAA Guide to Membership Services.*

National EMS Pilots Association, P.O. Box 2354, Pearland, TX 77588. (713) 997-2563. Monthly publication: *Air Net.*

National Safety Council, 444 North Michigan Avenue, Chicago, IL 60611. (312) 527-4800. Annual meeting in October/November. Bimonthly Publication: *Aerospace Newsletter.*

The Ninety-Nines, Inc., Box 59965, Will Rogers World Airport, Oklahoma City, OK 73159. (405) 685-7969. Annual meeting in July/August. Monthly publication: *Ninety-Nine News.*

OX-5 Aviation Pioneers, 207 Dormont Village, 2961 W. Liberty Avenue, Pittsburgh, PA 15216. (412) 341-5650. Bimonthly Publication: *OX-5 News.*

Professional Aviation Maintenance Association (PAMA), 500 N.W. Plaza, St. Ann, MO 63074. (314) 739-2580. Annual meeting in March. Bimonthly Publication: *PAMA News.*

Professional Race Pilots Association, P.O. Box 60084, Stead Airport, 4895 Texas Avenue, Reno, NV 89506. (702) 322-1421. Bimonthly Publication: *Checkered Pylon.*

Seaplane Pilots Association, 421 Aviation Way, Frederick, MD 21701. (301) 695-2082. Quarterly Publication: *Water Flying.* Annual publication: *SPA Seaplane Landing Directory.*

Silver Wings Fraternity, Box 11970, Harrisburg, PA 17108. (717) 232-9525. Annual meeting in October/November. Monthly publication: *Silver Wings Slipstream.*

Soaring Society of America, Inc., P.O. Box E, Hobbs, NM 88241. (505) 392-1177. Monthly publication: *Soaring.*

Society for Computer Simulation, P.O. Box 17900, San Diego, CA 92117. (619) 277-3888. Annual meeting in February. Official publication: *Simulation.*

Society of Automotive Engineers (SAE), 400 Commonwealth Drive, Warrendale, PA 15096-0001. (412) 776-4841. Annual meetings in March, May, October, November. Monthly publication: *Aerospace Engineering.* Also publishes: *Aircraft Materials Specifications, Aerospace Standards, Aerospace Information Reports, Aerospace Recommended Practices, SAE Technical Papers, SAE Conference Proceedings.*

United States Hang Gliding Associations, P.O. Box 66306, Los Angeles, CA 90066. (213) 390-3065. Monthly publication: *Hang Gliding.*

The Wings Club, 52 Vanderbilt Avenue, New York, NY 10017. (212) 867-1770.

Aviation Publications   Listed here are the national and regional aviation publications that are not associated with or published by one or another of the aviation organizations. Those publications can be found under *Aviation Organizations.*

AC Flyer, McGraw-Hill, Inc. 1221 Avenue of the Americas, New York, NY 10020. (212) 512-2528. (Monthly).

Aerospace Canada, 777 Bay Street, Toronto, ON, Canada M5W 1A7. (416) 596-5000. (Bimonthly).

Aerospace Daily, McGraw-Hill, Inc. 1221 Avenue of the Americas, New York, NY 10020. (212) 512-2528. (Monthly).

Aerospace Online, McGraw-Hill, Inc. 1221 Avenue of the Americas, New York, NY 10020. (212) 512-2528. (Monthly).

Ag Pilot International, 405 Main Street, Mount Vernon, WA 98273. (206) 336-9737. (Monthly).

Air Classic, 7950 Deering Avenue, Canoga Park, CA 91304. (818) 887-0550. (Monthly).

Air Combat, 7950 Deering Avenue, Canoga Park, CA 91304. (818) 887-0550. (Bimonthly).

Air Force Times, 6885 Commercial Drive, Springfield, VA 22159. (703) 750-8646. (Weekly).

Airports, McGraw-Hill, Inc. 1221 Avenue of the Americas, New York, NY 10020. (212) 512-2528. (Weekly).

Airport Services Management, 50 S. 9th Street, Minneapolis, MN 55402. (612) 333-0471. (Monthly).

Air Progress, 7950 Deering Avenue, Canoga Park, CA 91304. (818) 887-0550. (Monthly).

Air & Space/Smithsonian, Rm. 3401, National Air & Space Museum, Washington, DC 20560. (Bimonthly).

Air Transport World, 1030 15th Street, N.W. #420, Washington, DC 20005. (202) 659-8500. (Monthly).

Armed Forces Journal, 1414 22nd Street, N.W. #104, Washington, DC 20037. (202) 296-0450. (Monthly).

Aviation Consumer, 75 Holly Hill Lane, Box 2626, Greenwich, CT 06836-2626. (Semimonthly).

Aviation Daily, McGraw-Hill, Inc. 1221 Avenue of the Americas, New York, NY 10020. (212) 512-2528. (Daily).

Aviation International News, P.O. Box 277, Midland Park. NJ 07432. (201) 444-5075. (Bimonthly and daily at the HAI, NBAA, and other aviation conventions).

Aviation Safety, 75 Holly Hill Lane, Box 2626, Greenwich, CT 06836-2626. (Monthly).

Aviation/USA, P.O. Box 2029, Tuscaloosa, AL 35403. (800) 633-5953. (Weekly).

Aviation Week and Space Technology, 1221 Avenue of the Americas, New York, NY 10020. (212) 512-2528. (Weekly).

Business Aviation, McGraw-Hill, Inc. 1221 Avenue of the Americas, New York, NY 10020. (212) 512-2528. (Weekly).

Business & Commercial Aviation, McGraw-Hill, Inc. 1221 Avenue of the Americas, New York, NY 10020. (212) 512-2528. Editorial offices, Westchester County Airport, White Plains, NY.

Canadian Aviation, 777 Bay Street, Toronto, ON, Canada M5W 1A7. (416) 596-5791. (Monthly).

Flyer, P.O. Box 98786, Tacoma, WA 98498-0786. (206) 588-1743. (Semimonthly).

Flying, 1515 Broadway, New York, NY 10036. (212) 719-6950. (Monthly).

General Aviation News, 4949 Westgrove Drive, Dallas, TX 75248. (214) 248-0928. (Biweekly).

Homebuilt Aircraft, 16200 Ventura Blvd. #201, Encino, CA 91436. (818) 986-8400. (Bimonthly).

International Aviation Mechanics Journal, P.O. Box 36, Riverton, WY 82501. (307) 856-1582. (Monthly).

Jane's All the World's Aircraft, 238 City Road, London, England EC1V 2PU. Phone: 01 251-9281.

Kit Planes, P.O. Box 6050, Mission Viejo, CA 92690. (714) 240-6001. (Monthly).

Light Plane Maintenance, 111 East Putnam Avenue, Riverside, CT 06878. (203) 637-5900. (Semimonthly).

Pacific Flyer Aviation News, 3355 Mission Avenue, Oceanside, CA 92054. (619) 439-4466. (Monthly).

Pilot, 88 Burlington Road, New Malden, Surrey, England KT3 4NT. Phone: 01 949-3462. (Monthly).

Plane & Pilot, 16200 Ventura Blvd. #201, Encino, CA 91436. (818) 986-8400. (Monthly).

Private Pilot, P.O. Box 6050, Mission Viejo, CA 92690. (714) 240-6001. (Monthly).

Regional Aviation Weekly, McGraw-Hill, Inc. 1221 Avenue of the Americas, New York, NY 10020. (212) 512-2528. (Weekly).

Skydiving Magazine, P.O. Box 1520, Deland, FL 32721. (904) 736-9779. (Monthly).

Soviet Aeronautics, 150 Fifth Avenue, New York, NY 10011. (212) 924-3950. (Quarterly, in English).

Sport Flyer, Box 98786, Tacoma, WA 98498-0786. (206) 588-1743. (Monthly).

Sport Pilot Ultralight, 7950 Deering Avenue, Canoga Park, CA 91304. (818) 887-0550. (Quarterly).

Trade-A-Plane, 410 West 4th Street, Crossville, TN 38555. (615) 484-5137.

Travel Weekly, McGraw-Hill, Inc. 1221 Avenue of the Americas, New York, NY 10020. (212) 512-2528. (Weekly).

Ultralight Flying, P.O. Box 6009, Chattanooga, TN 37401. (615) 629-5375. (Monthly).

World Aviation Directory, McGraw-Hill, Inc. 1221 Avenue of the Americas, New York, NY 10020. (212) 512-2528. Editorial offices: 1156 15th Street N.W., Washington, DC 20005. (202) 822-4600. (Semiannual, March, September).

aviation weather service   The service is provided by the National Weather Service and the FAA, which collect and disseminate pertinent weather information.

avionics   A catch-all phrase for communication, navigation, and related instrumentation in an aircraft.

avionics management systems   Highly sophisticated electronic instrumentation that collects a variety of navigation data automatically and feeds them into a computer that, in turn, controls the flight director and autopilot systems.

Avions Marcel Dassault-Breguet   A major aircraft manufacturing company in France, partly government owned. Manufacturers of the line of Falcon Jet aircraft.

AvStar   A computer/calculator designed specifically to deal with the basic aviation functions. Manufactured by Jeppesen Sanderson. (Page 66)

AW   Winds aloft forecast.

AWA   Aviation/Space Writers Association.

AWLAR   All weather low altitude training route.

AX   A designation by the Federation Aeronautique Internationale (FAI) referring to various categories of balloons.

axes   Plural of axis.

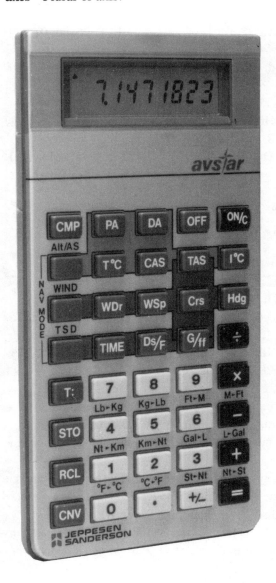

The AvStar flight computer from Jeppesen Sanderson.

axis   The theoretical line extending through the center of gravity of an airplane along the longitudinal, lateral and vertical planes.

azimuth   Bearing, as measured clockwise from the true or magnetic north (except in celestial navigation.)

Aztec   A twin piston engine aircraft manufactured by Piper Aircraft Corporation, but no longer in production.

B Balloon ceiling (weather reports only).

B Beginning of precipitation, followed by time in minutes. (Weather reports only).

B Bravo in the phonetic alphabet.

B Ceiling as measured by a balloon (in sequence reports).

B Scheduled weather broadcast.

back course The reverse side of a localizer. A back course approach is a nonprecision approach along the back course of a localizer.

back course approach *See* BACK COURSE.

backing Wind shifting in a counter-clockwise direction, to the left of the direction from which it was blowing before (the opposite of veering).

bail out Jumping out of an aircraft with or without (preferably with) a parachute.

Baker Electronics, Inc. Manufacturer of audio amplifiers, multistation intercom systems and related aircraft equipment. (1734 Northgate Boulevard, Sarasota, FL 33580. (813) 355-7625.)

balance The stability of an airplane achieved when the four forces, thrust, drag, lift, and weight (gravity) act to produce steady flight.

balanced field length The distance within which a jet aircraft can accelerate to V_1 and then either stop or accelerate to a safe climb speed (V_2) and clear a height of 35 feet on one engine.

ballast Weight, usually bags of sand, carried aloft in gas in balloons as a means of maintaining altitude by jettisoning ballast.

Balloon Federation of America (BFA) National organization of sport balloonists.

balloon license License issued by the FAA to properly trained balloon pilots.

Balloon Works Manufacturer of hot-air balloons. (Rhine Aerodrome, RFD 2, Statesville, NC 28667).

bank To tilt an airplane by means of the ailerons, causing it to turn while rolling either right or left along its longitudinal axis.

bar A unit of pressure equal to 29.531 inches of mercury at 32 degrees F. (0 degrees C.) at 45 degrees latitude.

barnstorming   An activity of pilots who used to fly into small communities and take passengers up for short rides for a fee. Barnstorming, prevalent in the 1920s and 30s, has virtually vanished from the aviation scene.

barometer   An instrument for measuring atmospheric pressure. Mercurial barometers measure the effect of atmospheric pressure on a column of mercury. Aneroid barometers detect pressure changes in the partial vacuum of a hollow disc.

barometric pressure   Atmospheric pressure measured by a barometer.

barometric tendency   The net change in barometric pressure during the last three hours before the observation; given in station reports as + or – a given number of tenth of millibars.

Baron   A six- or eight-seat high-performance piston twin manufactured by Beech Aircraft Corporation.

barrel roll   An aerobatic maneuver in which the aircraft, while maintaining its original heading, rolls in a complete circle, all points of which are equidistant from an imaginary line extending forward from the starting point.

base leg   A part of the airport traffic pattern. A flight path at right angles to the runway, following the downwind leg and followed by the final approach.

basic operating weight   The weight of the aircraft including fuel and equipment necessary for flight and also including the mandatory minimum crew.

basket   The gondola of a balloon, regardless of the material of which it is made.

B & D Instruments, Inc.   Manufacturer of air data computers, passenger compartment display systems, TAS computers. (209 West Main Street, Valley Center, KS 67147. (316) 755-1223.)

BC   Back course.

BC   Beginning climb.

BCKG   Backing.

BCM   Become.

BCN   Beacon.

BCST   Broadcast.

BCSTN   Broadcast station.

BD   Blowing dust (in sequence reports).

BD   Beginning descent.

BDR   Border.

beacon   A fixed reference point in aviation navigation. It may be visual, such as the rotating beacon at an airport, or it may be electronic such as nondirectional homing beacons, outer markers, etc.

bearing   The horizontal direction of an aircraft to any point, usually measured clockwise in 360 degrees relative to true or magnetic north. When navigating with VORs the term bearing is usually used with reference to the direction *to* the station, while the direction *from* the station is referred to as the radial.

Beaufort scale   A convenient scale for roughly indicating wind velocity in terms of a simple number (1 through 12) plus a descriptive word (calm through hurricane).

Becker Flugfunkwerk GmbH   Manufacturer of avionics equipment. (D757 Baden-Baden, West Germany).

Bede   A family of kit-built single-seat aircraft ranging from several piston models to the BD-5 jet aircraft. At this writing (Spring 1989) the ever enterprising Jim Bede claims to be developing the BD-10J kit-built supersonic single-engine jet. The aircraft will have a maximum takeoff weight of 2,400 pounds, carrying 300 gallons of fuel. Top speed is predicted to be Mach 1.4 with a range of 2,300 nm at a cruise altitude of 45,000 feet. Price is estimated at $160,000 without engine or avionics. The aircraft will be pressurized and engines under consideration are the General Electric 2,900-pound-thrust CJ10 turbojet and the Pratt & Whitney JT12 3,300-pound-thrust turbojet.

Jim Bede's BD-5 jets in a demonstration flight at the Reading Air Show.

Beech Aircraft Corporation   A subsidiary of Raytheon Corporation. Manufacturer of aircraft from single-engine models through turboprops and a jet. (9709 East Central, Wichita, KS 67201 (316) 681-7111.) (Pages 72-76)

Beechcraft   An aircraft manufactured by Beech Aircraft Corporation.

Beech Single-Engine Piston Aircraft

		BONANZA F33A	BONANZA A36	BONANZA B36TC
ENGINES	manufacturer	Continental	Continental	Continental
	model	IO-529-BB	IO-550-B	TSIO-520-UB
	rating	285 hp	300 hp	300
PROPELLER	diameter in./blades	84/3	80/3	78/3
WEIGHTS (lbs)	max ramp	3,412	3,663	3,866
	takeoff	3,400	3,650	3,850
	landing	3,400	3,650	3,850
	empty	2,237	2,266	2,410
	useful load	1,175	1,397	1,456
WING	area sq.ft.	181	181	188.1
	loading lbs/sq.ft.	18.8	20.2	20.5
	span ft.in	33.6	33.6	37.10
FUSELAGE	length ft.in	26.8	27.6	27.6
	height ft.in	8.3	8.7	8.7
CABIN	length ft.in	10.1	12.7	12.7
	width in.	3.6	3.6	3.6
	height in.	4.2	4.2	4.2
FUEL	U.S. gallons	74	74	102
SPEED	maximum knots	182	184	213
	operating knots	168	174	188
RANGE	194 gal. max nm	889	903	984
RATE OF CLIMB		1,157 fpm	1,208 fpm	1,053
SERVICE CEILING ft.		17,858	18,500	25,000+
STALL	clean knots	64	68	65
	dirty knots	51	59	57
TAKEOFF	ground run	1,000 ft.	1,182 ft.	1,156 ft.
	50-ft. obstacle	1,740 ft.	2,100 ft.	2,364 ft.
LANDING	ground roll	760 ft.	920 ft.	976 ft.
	50-ft. obstacle	1,300 ft.	1,450 ft.	1,692 ft.
STANDARD EQUIPMENT:		KX 155 package: com transceiver nav receiver VOR/LOC, ADF, DME transponder	KX 155-09 com transceiver nav receiver VOR/LOC	KX 155-09 com transceiver nav receiver VOR/LOC

Beech Twin-Engine Piston Aircraft

		BARON 58
ENGINES	manufacturer	Continental (2)
	model	IO-550-C
	rating	300 hp each
WEIGHTS (lbs)	max ramp	5,524
	takeoff	5,500
	landing	5,400
	empty	3,481
	useful load	2,043
WING	area sq.ft.	199.2
	loading lbs/sq.ft.	27.6
	span ft.in	37.10
FUSELAGE	length ft.in	29.10
	height ft.in	9.9
CABIN	length ft.in	12.7
	width in.	3.6
	height in.	4.2
FUEL	standard U.S. gallons	136
	option 1 U.S. gallons	166
	option 2 U.S. gallons	194
SERVICE CEILING	2 engines	20,688 ft.
	1 engine	7,284 ft.
SPEED	maximum knots	208
	operating knots	192
RANGE	194 gal. max nm	1,275
RATE OF CLIMB	2 engines	1,735 fpm
	1 engine	390 fpm
STALL	clean knots	84
	dirty knots	75
TAKEOFF	ground run	1,400 ft.
	50-ft. obstacle	2,300 ft.
LANDING	ground roll	1,425
	50-ft. obstacle	2,450
STANDARD EQUIPMENT:		KX 155-09 720/200-channel com transceiver/nav receiver KI 208 VOR/LOC KR 87 ADF KI 227 indicator

Beech Twin-Turboprop Aircraft

		KING AIR C90A	SUPER KING AIR B200	SUPER KING AIR 300	KING AIR EXEC LINER
ENGINES	manufacturer	Pratt & Whitney	Pratt & Whitney	Pratt & Whitney	Pratt & Whitney
	model	PT6A-21	PT6A-42	PT6A-60A	PT6A-65B
	rating	550 shp each	850 shp each	1,050 shp each	1,100 shp each
PROPELLER	diameter in./blades	$93^3/_8$/3	98.5/3	105/4	109.5/4
WEIGHTS (lbs)	max ramp lbs.	10,160	12,590	14,100	16,710
	takeoff lbs.	10,100	12,500	14,000	16,600
	landing lbs.	9,600	12,500	14,000	16,100
	zero fuel lbs.		11,000	11,500	14,000
	empty lbs.	6,580	8,060	8,490	9,940[*]
	useful load lbs.	3,580	4,530	5,610	6,770
WING	area sq.ft.	293.94	303.0	303.0	303.0
	loading lbs/sq.ft.	34.4	41.3	46.2	54.8
	span ft.in	50.3	54.6	54.6	54.5
FUSELAGE	length ft.in	35.6	43.9	43.10	57.9
	height ft.in	14.3	15	14.4	14.9
CABIN	length in.	152	200	200	408.5
	width in.	52	52	52	54
	height in.	57	57	57	57
FUEL	pounds	2,472.8	3,644.8	3,611.3	4,468.9
SPEED	maximum knots	247	294	317	283
	operating knots	242	289	311	271
RANGE	full fuel max nm	1,277	1,974	1,959	1,590
RATE OF CLIMB	2 engines fpm	2,003	2,450	2,844	2,980
	1 engine fpm	554	740	867	850
SERVICE CEILING	2 engines ft.	28,900+	35,000+	35,000+	25,000+
	1 engine ft.	14,260	21,900	22,878	18,100
STALL	clean knots	88	99	n/a	104
	dirty knots	78	75	n/a	88
TAKEOFF	ground run ft.	1,885	1,856	1,350	2,220
	50-ft. obstacle ft.	2,078	2,579	1,992	3,350
LANDING	ground roll ft.	1,036	1,760	1,686	1,530
	50-ft. obstacle ft.	2,087	2,845	2,907	2,560
STANDARD EQUIPMENT:		Collins	Collins	Collins	Collins Pro Line
		com transceiver	com transceiver	com transceiver	com transceiver
		nav receiver	nav receiver	nav receiver	nav receiver
		VOR/LOC/GLS/MKR	VOR/LOC/GLS/MKR	VOR/LOC/GLS/MKR	VOR/LOC/GLS/MKR
		ADF, DME, RMI	ADF, DME, RMI	ADF, DME, RMI	ADF, DME, RMI
		ADI, HSI	ADI, HSI	ADI, HSI	ADI, HSI
		Autopilot	Autopilot	Autopilot	Autopilot
		Weather radar	Weather radar	Weather radar	Weather radar
		transponder	transponder	transponder	transponder
					Radar altimeter

[*] Basic operating weight

Beech Starship 1

		STARSHIP 1
ENGINES	manufacturer	Pratt & Whitney (2)
	model	PT6A-67A
	TBO hours	3,000
	rating	1200 shp flat rated
PROPELLERS	diameter in inches	104
	number of blades	5
	type	hydraulic, full feathering
WEIGHTS lbs.	max ramp	14,360
	max takeoff	14,250
	max landing	13,538
	max zero fuel	12,050
	empty	9,511
	useful load	4,649
	max payload	2,339
FUEL lbs	usable	3,752
WINGS	area sq.ft.	280.88
	loading lb/sq.ft.	49.8
	span ft.	54.40
	loading lbs/sq.ft.	49.8
CANARD WING	span in cruise ft.	21.77
	span, landing ft.	25.55
FUSELAGE	length ft.in	46.1
	height ft.	13
COCKPIT	height in.	58.18
	width in.	67
CABIN	length in.	253.5
	width in.	66
	height in.	63.5
PRESSURIZATION	psi	8.4
SPEED	max cruise, kts.	336
V_{mo}	KIAS	270
V_a	KIAS	175
V_{mca}	KIAS	101
RANGE	max power, nm	1,670
	long range, nm	1,920
RATE OF CLIMB	2 engines fpm	3,250
	1 engine fpm	911
TAKEOFF DISTANCE	50 ft.obst. ft.	3,380
LANDING DISTANCE	50 ft.obst. ft.	2,675
SERVICE CEILING	2 engines ft.	41,000
	1 engine ft.	19,000
EQUIPPED PRICE	1989 $s	$3,886,700
STANDARD EQUIPMENT	Collins	com transceivers (2)
		nav receivers (2)
		ADF, DME
		transponders (2)
		radio altimeter
		weather radar
		EFIS multicolor displays
		flight director
		long-range nav system
		autopilot
		Integrated flight management system
		turbulence detection Doppler radar
		automatic anti-icing activated without pilot action
		real-time fault annunciation & diagnostics

* In this aircraft this is the key factor, not the stall speed.

Beech Turbofan Beechjet

		BEECHJET
ENGINES	manufacturer	Pratt & Whitney (2)
	model	JT15D-5
WEIGHTS (lbs)	max ramp	15,850
	takeoff	15,780
	landing	14,220
	zero fuel	12,470
	basic operating	10,115
	max payload	2,355
	full fuel payload	831
WING	area sq.ft.	241.40
	loading lbs/sq.ft.	64.4
	span ft.in	43.6
FUSELAGE	length ft.in	48.5
	height ft.in	13.9
CABIN	length ft.in	19.6
	width in.	59
	height in.	57
PRESSURE	to 24,000 feet	sea level
	at 41,000 feet	6,400 ft.
FUEL	U.S. gallons	731.8
SERVICE CEILING	2 engines	41,000 ft.
	1 engine	25,500 ft.
SPEED	maximum knots	461
	operating knots	320
RANGE	max nm	1,930
RATE OF CLIMB	2 engines	3.960 fpm
	1 engine	1,110 fpm
STALL	clean knots	105
	dirty knots	87
TAKEOFF	field length ft.	3,950
LANDING	distance ft.	2,830
STANDARD EQUIPMENT:		ADI, HSI, RMI, DME, Marker Beacon, Angle of Attack Indicator Radio Altimeter, Autopilot

Beech Starship 1.

Beech Aircraft Corporation

Beechjet.

Collins Avionics

Beech Aircraft Starship panel with 100 percent Collins Pro Line avionics.

Bellanca Aircraft Corporation Manufacturer of sport and high-performance single-engine aircraft. The company is no longer in business but because many of the aircraft are still in operation, a performance comparison chart is included.

Bellanca Aircraft (no longer in production)

		CITABRIA 115 7ECA	DECATHLON FP 8KCAB	SUPER VIKING 10-30A	TURBO VIKING 17-31ATC	ARIES T-250
ENGINE	manufacturer	Lycoming	Lycoming	Lycoming	Lycoming	Lycoming
	model	O-235-K2C	AEIO-320-E2B	IO-520-K	TIO-540-S1AD	O-540-A4D5
	rating hp	115	150	300	350	350
PROPELLER	pitch	fixed	fixed	variable	variable	variable
	blades	2	2	2	3	2
LANDING GEAR		fixed, tail	fixed, tail	retrct,tricycl	retrct,tricycl	retrct,tricycl
SEATS		2	2	4	4	4
TAKEOFF	ground roll ft	340	630	510	510	n/a
	50 ft. obst.ft	716	1,180	750	750	n/a
LANDING	50 ft. obst.ft	890	1,450	1,420	1,420	n/a
RATE OF CLIMB fpm		725	1,000	1,210	1,170	1,240
SPEEDS	max, knots	109	128	181	193	187
	75% knots	107	119	176	193	181
	55% knots	96	105	170	144	174
	V_x knots	50	56	65	65	n/a
	V_y knots	65	66	96	96	n/a
STALL	clean knots	36	37	63	63	63
	dirty knots	n/a	n/a	56	56	56
RANGE	75% nm	319	468	826	666	990
	55% nm	528	540	930	695	1,170
FUEL	usable pounds	210	240	408	408	456
	flow 75% pph	48	52	96	95	84
	flow 55% pph	30	41	71	70	72
WEIGHTS	ramp lbs	1,650	1,800	3,325	3,325	3,150
	takeoff lbs	1,650	1,800	3,325	3,325	3,150
	landing lbs	1,650	1,800	3,325	3,325	3,150
	zero fuel lbs	1,067	1,260	2,185	2,372	1,850
	useful load	583	540	1,140	1,053	1,300
WING	area sq.ft.	n/a	n/a	n/a	n/a	170
	load lb/sq.ft	10	10.6	20.6	20.6	18.5
	span ft.	33.4	32	34.2	34.2	31.4
FUSELAGE	length ft.	22.7	22.9	26.3	26.3	26.2
	height ft.	7.7	7.7	7.3	7.3	8.6
TURBO CHARGER					dual Rajay	

Bell Helicopter Textron, Inc. Manufacturer of civilian and military helicopters. (P.O. Box 482, Fort Worth, TX 76101. (817) 280-8417.) (Pages 78-81)

belly landing An emergency or forced landing made without extending the landing gear. Belly landings are often made inadvertently. Usually damage, except to the propeller, is light. A proficient pilot, flying an aircraft with a two-bladed propeller and making an intentional gear-up landing, can stop the prop in a horizontal position, thus avoiding such damage.

Bell Helicopter Textron Light Single-Turbine Helicopters

	JETRANGER III 206B	LONGRANGER II 206L-1	LONGRANGER III 206L-3
ENGINE manufacturer	Allison	Allison	Allison
model	250-C20J	250-C288	250-C30P
hp	420	500	650
WEIGHT basic operating	1646	2216	2223
useful load	1554	1934	1927
CARGO HOOK capable lbs	1500	2000	2000
LENGTH rotors turning	39.1	42.5	42.52
fuselage	31.2	33.2	33.2
height	9.3	10.3	10.3
width	6.0	7.4	7.4
MAIN ROTOR blades	2	2	2
diameter	33.3	37.0	37.0
SEATS	4	6	6
CREW required	1	1	1
SPEED V_{ne} knots	122	130	130
max cruise kts	118	114	112
economy kts	118	108	112
RANGE max nm	378	294	325
RATE OF CLIMB fpm	1280	1340	1320
SERVICE CEILING ft.	13,500	17,700	20,000
HOVER IGE ft.	12,800	12,400	16,500
OGE ft.	8800	5300	5400
PRICE 1988 $s	$495,000	$760,000	$760,000

Bell Helicopter Textron Light Twin-Turbine Helicopters

	BELL 222	BELL 222B	BELL 222UT
ENGINE manufacturer	Lycoming	Lycoming	Lycoming
model	LTS-101-650C-3	LTS-101-750C-1	LTS-101-750C-1
hp	1240	925	1470
WEIGHT basic operating	4918	4929	4903
useful load	2932	3321	3347
CARGO HOOK capable lbs	2500	2800	2800
LENGTH rotors turning	47.5	50.3	49.9
fuselage	41.0	42.9	42.6
height	11.0	11.211.5	
width	11.3	11.3	11.3
MAIN ROTOR blades	2	2	2
diameter	39.8	42.0	42.0
SEATS	7	7	7
CREW required	1	1	1
SPEED V_{ne} knots	150	150	150
max cruise kts	147	139	136
economy kts	134	134	135
RANGE max nm	329	300	378
RATE OF CLIMB fpm	1580	1460	1460
SERVICE CEILING ft.	12,800	15,800	15,800
HOVER IGE ft.	4200*	7100*	7100*
OGE ft.	4600	6400	6400
PRICE 1988 $s	n/a	n/a	$1,835,000

* WAT Limit

Bell Helicopter Textron Medium Single-Turbine Helicopters

	BELL 205A-1	BELL 214B/B-1
ENGINE manufacturer	Lycoming	Lycoming
model	T5313B	T5508D
hp	1400	2930
WEIGHT basic operating	5313	7760
useful load	4187	6040 (B) 4740 (B-1)
CARGO HOOK capable lbs	5000	8000
LENGTH rotors turning	57.1	60.76
fuselage	44.4	45.17
height	12.3	15.0
width	9.0	9.42
MAIN ROTOR blades	2	2
diameter	48.0	50.0
SEATS	14	14
CREW required	1	1
SPEED V_{ne} knots	128	140
max cruise kts	110	134
economy kts	107	134
RANGE max nm	270	175
RATE OF CLIMB fpm	1700	1910
SERVICE CEILING ft.	12.700	16,000
HOVER IGE ft.	10,400	15,000
OGE ft.	6004	10,500

Bell Helicopter Textron Medium Twin-Turbine Helicopters

	BELL 212	BELL 214ST	BELL 412	BELL 412SP
ENGINE manufacturer	Pratt & Whitney	General Electric	Pratt & Whitney	Pratt & Whitney
model	PT6T-38	CT7-2A	PT6T-38	PT6T-38
hp	1800	3250	1800	1800
WEIGHT basic operating	5997	9521	5575	6495
useful load	5203	7727	5575	5405
CARGO HOOK capable lbs	5000	7900	4500	4500
LENGTH rotors turning	57.27	62.17	56.2	56.2
fuselage	42.39	49.08	46.0	46.0
height	12.85	15.58	10.8	10.8
width	9.37	10.78	9.4	9.4
MAIN ROTOR blades	2	2	4	4
diameter	48.0	52.0	46.0	46.0
SEATS	14	18	14	14
CREW required	1	2	1	1
SPEED V_{ne} knots	100	130	140	140
max cruise kts	100	140	130	130
economy kts	100	140	125	125
RANGE max nm	224	450	234	364
RATE OF CLIMB fpm	1420	1780	1350	1350
SERVICE CEILING ft.	12,900	10,000	16,500	16,500
HOVER IGE ft.	4900	6500	6800	1400
OGE ft.	N/C	1000	N/C	N/C
PRICE 1988 $s	$3,085,000 VFR	$5,915,000	n/a	$3,340,000 VFR
	$3,330,000 IFR			$3,515,000 IFR

Bell 47 helicopter.

Bell Helicopter Textron 212 twin-turbine helicopter.

Bell Helicopter Textron 214ST twin-turbine helicopter.

Bell Helicopter Textron 412 twin-turbine helicopter.

Bell Helicopter Textron 412SP twin-turbine helicopter.

Bell Helicopter Textron 222UT twin-turbine helicopter in utility configuration.

below minimums   Weather conditions below the minimums in terms of ceiling and/or visibility, as prescribed by the FARs for a particular type of activity such as landing, takeoff, VFR, or IFR.

Bendix Avionics Division   *See* BENDIX/KING GENERAL AVIATION AVIONICS DIVISION.

Bendix Electric and Fluid Power Division   *See* ALLIED-SIGNAL AEROSPACE COMPANY, ELECTRIC POWER DIVISION.

Bendix Flight Systems Division   *See* BENDIX/KING GENERAL AVIATION AVIONICS DIVISION.

Bendix/King General Aviation Electronics Division   Manufacturer of a full line of avionics for general aviation ranging from simple navcom systems to weather radar and complete flight management systems. (400 North Rogers Road, Olathe, KS 66062. (913) 782-0400)

Bendix Instruments and Life Support Division   Manufacturer of encoding altimeters. (P.O. Box 4508, Davenport, IA 52808.)

Bernoulli's principle   The basic theory in describing lift: As velocity of a fluid (air) increases, the pressure decreases.

best angle of climb   The combination of airspeed and power that enables an airplane to gain maximum altitude over the shortest distance. Also called *steepest angle of climb*.

best rate of climb   The combination of airspeed and power that produces maximum gain in altitude within a given period of time. The best rate of climb produces a somewhat shallower climb angle than does the best angle of climb.

BFA   Balloon Federation of America.

BFDK   Before dark.

BFR   Biennial flight review.

BFR   Before.

BFO   Beat frequency oscillator.

BGN   Begin; began.

BHND   Behind.

BHP   Brake horsepower.

binary   The information storage and manipulation system used by digital computers. It consists entirely of zeros (0) and ones (1) that can represent such meanings as yes/no, up/down, right/wrong, etc., or in combination they represent numbers:

00000 = 0	00111 = 7	01110 = 14
00001 = 1	01000 = 8	01111 = 15
00010 = 2	01001 = 9	10000 = 16
00011 = 3	01010 = 10	
00100 = 4	01011 = 11	
00101 = 5	01100 = 12	
00110 = 6	01101 = 13	

BINOVC Breaks in the overcast.

bird Slang for airplane.

birdman Prior to World War I, the common term for flyers.

bit The smallest possible unit of information used by computers. One bit determines the difference between 0 and 1 representing yes or no, right or wrong, etc.

biz jet Business jet aircraft.

B.K.M. Company Manufacturer and designer of aircraft components and modification systems. (P.O. Box 7001, Dallas, TX 75209. (214) 350-8955.)

BL Between layers.

black box Aviation jargon for any piece of avionics equipment.

blade Part of a propeller. Propellers may have two or more blades. Each blade is, in fact, an airfoil, twisted lengthwise to compensate for the increasing distance from the hub.

blade angle The angle of the propeller blade relative to the plane of rotation. It is generally measured at a point three quarters of the distance from the hub. On fixed-pitch propellers the angle is constant. Variable-pitch propellers can be increased or decreased by the pilot during flight.

blade coning The upward bending of helicopter rotor blades when they are in the process of producing lift.

blast fence A barrier erected on airports near the takeoff positions to divert or dissipate jet or propeller blast.

blast valve The valve on the burner of a hot-air balloon with which the pilot can regulate the amount of heat directed into the balloon.

BLDG Building.

blimp A non-rigid airship using gas for lift.

Goodyear blimp at Reading Air Show.

blind flying   Flying by instruments alone.

blind speed   The rate of closing or departure of a target relative to the radar antenna at which cancellation of the primary radar target by moving target indicator circuits (MTI) causes reduction or complete loss of the signal.

blind spot   Areas from which radio or radar transmissions cannot be received. Also portions of an airport invisible from the tower.

blind zone   *See* BLIND SPOT.

blip   The reflected or transponder-augmented echo from an aircraft or other object and seen on the radar scope as a spot of light. It indicates the position of the object relative to the location of the radar scope.

BLN   Balloon.

BLO   Below.

blower   A portable fan equipped with a small gasoline motor, used by balloonists to force air into the balloon as the first step toward inflation of a hot-air balloon.

Blower used to initially inflate a hot-air balloon.

blower   Mechanically-driven supercharger.

BLZD   Blizzard.

BMEP   Brake mean effective pressure.

BMEWS   Ballistic missile early warning system.

BN   Blowing sand (in sequence reports.)

BNDRY   Boundary.

BNTH   Beneath.

Boeing Helicopters   Formerly Boeing Vertol Company, manufacturer of the twin-engine twin-rotor Boeing 234 and 260 heavy-duty helicopters. (P.O. Box 16858, Philadelphia, PA 19142. (215) 522-3751.) (Pages 86-87)

Boeing Helicopters

		234 LR	234 UT	234 MLR	360
ENGINE	manufacturer	Lycoming (20	Lycoming (2)	Lycoming (2)	Lycoming
	type	AL5512	AL5512	AL5512	AL5512
SHP	takeoff (5 minutes)	4,075	4,075	4,075	n/a
	max continuous	2,975	2,975	2,975	3,436
	max OEI (30 minutes)	4,355	4,355	4,355	n/a
WEIGHTS lbs	max internal gross	48,500	42,000	42,000	31,000
	max gross w. ext.load	51,000	51,000	51,000	n/a
	empty	25,900	21,600	24,500	n/a
	basic operating	27,100	22,050	25,700	n/a
	max external load	28,000	28,000	28,000	20,000
PASSENGERS	max number	44	0	44	n/a
ATTENDANTS	optional	1	0	3	n/a
ROTOR (2)	diameter, ft.	60	60	60	49.75
	number of blades	4	4	4	4
MEASURES	overall length ft.	99	99	99	n/a
	overall height ft/in	18/7.8	18/7.8	18/7.8	n/a
	fuselage length ft/in	52/1	52/1	52/1	51
	cabin length ft.	n/a	n/a	n/a	26
	height in.	n/a	n/a	n/a	71.4
	width in.	n/a	n/a	n/a	75.5
FUEL CAPACITY U.S. gallons		2,100	978	2,100	824
PERFORMANCE V_{ne} knots		150	140	150	200*
	max cruise knots	145	140	145	180
	econ.cruise knots	135	130	135	n/a
	range (44 pax) nm	540		395	n/a
HOVER	OGE ft.	2,700	11,500	2,700	n/a
SERVICE CEILING ft.		15,000	15,000	15,000	n/a
	OEI ft.	1,400	4,700	1,400	n/a

* Preliminary.

Boeing Helicopters' 234 twin-rotor helicopter.

Boeing Helicopters' 360 twin-rotor helicopter.

Boeing of Canada, Ltd., de Havilland Division Manufacturers of the Dash 8 series of turboprop aircraft used by regional airlines and as corporate aircraft. (Garratt Boulevard, Downsview, Ontario, Canada M3K 1Y5. (416) 633-7310.) (Page 88)

Bonanza A family of high-performance single-engine aircraft manufactured by Beech Aircraft Corporation. (Pages 88-89)

Boeing of Canada, de Havilland Division Aircraft

	DASH 7 Series 150	DASH 8 Series 100	DASH 8 Series 300	DASH 8 Series 400 *
ENGINES manufacturer	Pratt & Whitney (4)	Pratt & Whitney (2)	Pratt & Whitney (2)	n/a
model	PT6A-50	PW120A	PW123	n/a
PROPELLER manfacturer	Hamilton Standard	Hamilton Standard	Hamilton Standard	n/a
model/blades	24 PF-305/4	14SF-7/4	14SF-15/4	n/a
WEIGHT max takeoff	47,000 lbs	34,500 lbs	41,100 lbs	n/a
max landing	45,000 lbs	33,900 lbs	40,000 lbs	n/a
zero fuel	39,000 lbs	31,000 lbs	37,200 lbs	n/a
empty	27,620 lbs	22,000 lbs	24,700 lbs	n/a
WING area	860 sq.ft.	585 sq.ft.	605 sq.ft.	n/a
span	93 ft.	85 ft.	90 ft.	n/a
LENGTH/HEIGHT	80'6"/26'2"	73'/24'7"	84'3"/24'7"	n/a
CABIN L/W/H	39'6"/8'6.2"/6'1"	30'/8'2"/6'2"	41'4"/8'2"/6'2"	n/a
seats	50-54	36-40	50-56	under 100
pressure psi	4.26	5.5	5.5	n/a
FUEL standard US gal	1,493	835	835	n/a
optional US gal	2,626	1,506	1,506	n/a
SPEED maximum knots	228	265	286	330 approx
RANGE w. reserve nm	1,100	1,085	890	500 +
FIELD LENGTH takeoff	3,000 ft.	3,150 ft.	3,675 ft.	n/a
landing	3,150 ft.	2,979 ft.	3,642 ft.	n/a

* Expected to enter service in the early 1990s.

Boeing Canada de Havilland Dash 8.

Boeing Canada de Havilland Dash 8-300.

Beechcraft Bonanza V35B.

Beechcraft Bonanza F33A.

Beechcraft Bonanza A36.

boost pump An electric fuel pump used to force increased fuel pressure during engine start.

boundary lights *See* RUNWAY LIGHTS.

BOVC Base of overcast.

BOW Basic operating weight.

BPT Beginning procedure turn.

BRAF Braking action fair.

BRAG Braking action good.

brain bag Aviation jargon for the case in which the pilot carries his charts, computers, plotters, and other necessary paraphernalia.

brake horsepower (BHP) The usable horsepower delivered to the propeller shaft. The amount of energy remaining after the actual horsepower developed by the engine is reduced by the friction of moving parts and the amount dissipated by other engine-driven systems.

brake mean effective pressure The average of effective combustion pressures acting upon the crankshaft.

braking action The term used to describe the condition of a runway, usually in winter weather when snow and/or ice are present, affecting the ability of a landing aircraft to use its brakes in order to come to a full stop.

BRAN Braking action nil.

BRAP Braking action poor.

Brave An agricultural piston-engine aircraft once manufactured by Piper Aircraft Corporation. No longer in production.

bravo In aviation phraseology the term used for the letter B.

breaks in the overcast Cloud conditions in which the cloud cover obscures 90 or more percent of the sky, but less than 100 percent.

Brelonix, Inc. Manufacturer of HF transceivers, antennas, and antenna couplers. (1425 10th Avenue, Seattle, WA 98119. (206) 282-7352.)

BRF Brief.

BRG Bearing.

briefing Information given the pilot with reference to weather, NOTAMs, and anything else required for the planning of a proposed flight.

Brittain Industries, Inc. Manufacturer of flight control systems. (3266 North Sheridan Road, Tulsa, OK 74115. (918) 836-7701.)

British Aerospace, Inc. Manufacturer of the BAe 800 corporate jet aircraft. The aircraft, in its various incarnations was over the years the Hawker Siddeley 125, the Beech 125 and after being re-engined with Garrett turbofans, the Beech 125-731. (P.O. Box 35, Stevenage, Hertfordshire SG1 2DG England. Phone 07072-68123. U.S. office: P.O. Box 17414, Washington Dulles International Airport, Washington, DC 20041-0414. (703) 478-9420.) (Pages 91-92)

BRK Break.

BRKN Broken.

broadcast A transmission of information requiring no acknowledgment by the pilot.

broken cloud *See* BROKEN OVERCAST.

broken overcast Cloud cover that obscures the sky by between 60 and 90 percent.

British Aerospace Aircraft

		BAe 800
ENGINES (2)	manufacturer	Garrett
	model	TFE 731-5
	thrust each lbs.	4,300
WEIGHTS	ramp, lbs.	27,520
	takeoff lbs.	27,400
	landing lbs.	23,350
	zero fuel lbs.	18,000
	operating lbs.	15,500
	payload lbs	2,500
FUEL	maximum lbs.	10,000
CABIN	height	5'9"
	length	21'4"
	width	6'0"
RANGE	nautical miles	2,913*
CRUISE SPEED	knots	441**
BALANCED FIELD LENGTH ft.		5,325**

* with six passengers & baggage, NBAA VFR reserves
** with fuel for 2,913 nautical miles

British Aerospace Incorporated

BAe 800 twin turbofan.

BAe 800 instrument panel with Collins Pro Line avionics.

Brooklands Aircraft Co. Ltd.   Designer and manufacturer of the Optica slow-flying air-to-ground twin-tail observation aircraft, powered by a piston-engine driving a pusher propeller. (Old Sarum Airfield, Salisbury, Wilts, England SP4 6BN. Phone 0722 21812. U.S. phone: (202) 626-1600.)

BS   Standard broadcast station.

BS   Blowing snow (in sequence reports.)

BSFC   Basic specific fuel consumption.

BTN   Between.

BTR   Better.

BTU   British thermal unit. A unit used to measure heat output.

bucket   The gondola of a balloon.

buck the weather   A term used to describe flying into or through rough weather or to proceed despite adverse weather conditions.

buffet   The shudder of an airframe caused by disturbed airflow set up by some part of the aircraft.

buffeting   *See* BUFFET.

bulkhead A piece of the structure of an aircraft; a more or less circular section of aluminum or other rigid material to which the side panels are attached.

Bulkheads for a homebuilt aircraft.

burble point The angle-of-attack that results in air separation above the wing. Also called the critical or stalling angle-of-attack. At this angle-of-attack the wing loses its lift capability.

burbling The separation of the airflow from an airfoil, especially its upper surface, causing loss of lift and increased drag.

burner The heater carried aloft in a hot-air balloon. (Page 94)

bus bar A section of the instrument panel containing electrical switches and circuit breakers or fuses.

bush pilot A pilot operating in thinly or unpopulated areas, such as Alaska or Central or South America.

Business Aviation *See* AVIATION PUBLICATIONS.

business aviation The use of aircraft in the pursuit of business.

Business Liner (Cessna 402) A cabin-size piston twin, manufactured by Cessna Aircraft Company. No longer in production. (Page 95)

Buys Ballot's law Refers to the fact that if a person in the Northern Hemisphere stands with his back to the wind, his left hand will point to the area of low pressure.

Burner blowing flames into a hot-air balloon.

Cessna 402 Business Liner.

BVR, Inc. Manufacturer of a series of high-performance course-deviation indicators (CDI) for use with signals provided by VOR, Loran-C, inertial guidance, and Omega navigation systems, priced at $525 in 1989 $s. (5459 Eleventh Street, Rockford, IL 61125. (815) 874-2471.)

BVR's course deviation indicator (CDI).

BY   Blowing spray (in sequence reports.)

BYD   Beyond.

byte   Eight bits of information as used by computers. Each letter, digit, or symbol can be represented by one byte. Computer memories are identified by their storage capacity in terms of the number of bytes, where one K byte represents 1024 bytes and one M byte represents 1024 K bytes or 1,048,576 bytes.

C Calm (on sequence reports.)

C. Celsius.

C. Centigrade.

C Charlie in the phonetic alphabet.

C Circling approach (on approach charts.)

C Control tower.

C Central standard time.

C Continental air mass.

CAA Civil Aviation Administration, the forerunner to the FAA.

CAB Civil Aeronautics Board, the government agency that used to supervise airline activity before deregulation. The agency was terminated because its function was eliminated by deregulation.

CADIZ Canadian Air Defense Identification Zone.

CAF Cleared as filed.

caging mechanism A device that locks a gyro or compass into a desired position, controlled by a knob on the instrument face. Gyros should be uncaged only in straight and level flight or on the ground.

calculator A mechanical or electronic instrument capable of making mathematical calculations. Small electronic pocket calculators should not be used in the cockpit while navigating with the ADF, as they tend to confuse the ADF readout.

calibrated airspeed (CAS) Indicated airspeed corrected for instrument and installation error.

call sign The name, numbers and letters identifying an aircraft or a ground station, such as "Bonanza Three Two Six Eight Hotel," or "Santa Fe Radio."

call-up The initial voice contact between an aircraft and a facility, using the call sign of the aircraft or station being called and that of the caller, such as: "Santa Fe Radio, Bonanza Three Two Six Eight Hotel, over."

calm The absence of wind with speeds of more than 3 knots.

camber The curvature of a wing or other airfoil, measured from the leading to the trailing edge.

Cameron Balloons U.S. Affiliated with *Cameron Balloons Ltd.,* manufacturer of hot-air balloons. (P.O. Box 3672, Ann Arbor, MI 48106. (313) 426-5525).

Camp Systems, Inc. Operator of computerized aircraft maintenance programs, operations manuals, and specifications. (Long Island MacArthur Airport, Ronkonkoma, NY 11779. (516) 588-3200.)

Canadair, Ltd. A Canadian airframe manufacturer, divided into a number of divisions serving a variety of purposes. The Challenger Division is the producer of the Challenger family of aircraft. The CL-215 Division manufactures the CL-215 and CL-215T amphibian aircraft designed specifically for fire fighting and maritime patrol. The Surveillance Systems Division produces the CL-289 surveillance drone system and the CL-227 Sentinel, which is a small rotary-winged remote-piloted vehicle system. The military Aircraft Division provides support for the Canadian Forces. The Manufacturing Division manufactures components used in the Airbus A330/340 and the Boeing 767 airliners and for military aircraft manufactured by Lockheed and McDonnell Douglas. (P.O. Box 6087, Station A, Montreal PQ, Canada H3C 3G9. (514) 744-1511.) *See* CHALLENGER. (Pages 99-101)

Canadair Challenger Aircraft

		CHALLENGER 601	CHALLENGER 601-3A
ENGINES (2)	manufacturer	General Electric	General Electric
	model	CF34-1A turbofan	CF34-1A turbofan
	thrust max lb	9,140	9,220
	" continuous	8,650	8,729
FUSELAGE	length	68'5"	68'5"
	height	20'8"	20'8"
WING	span	64'4"	64'4"
	area	450 ft^2	450 ft^2
CABIN	length	28'3"	28'3"
	width	8'2"	8'2"
	height	6'1"	6'1"
WEIGHTS lbs	ramp	43,250	43,250
	takeoff	43,100	43,100
	landing	36,000	36,000
	zero fuel	29,500	29,500
	empty	19,950	20,485
	basic operat'g	24,585	24,685
	max payload	4,915	4,815
	w.full fuel	2,000	1,900
FUEL	max usable lb	16,665	16,665
SPEEDS kts	hi speed crse	459	476
	normal cruise	442	459
	long range	424	424
RANGE nm	w.reserve	3,440	3,430
MAX OPERATING ALTITUDE ft.		41,000	41,000
CEILING	single engine	24,000	27,000
BALANCED FIELD LENGTH ft.		5,400	5,500
LANDING	avge dist. ft.	3,550	3,300

Avionics offered are Sperry SPZ 8000 flight director and
Collins ProLine II navcom systems.
Options include Sperry LSS lighting sensor system,
Primus 650 or 870 color radar,
several flight management systems,
Honeywell Laseref inertial guidance system

Canadair Regional Jet

		REGIONAL JET
ENGINES (2)	manufacturer	General Electric
	model	CF34-3A
	thrust, max lb	9,220
	" continuous	8,729
FUSELAGE	length	88'5"
	height	20'8"
WING	span	70'4"
	area	520 ft^2
CABIN	length	48'3"
	width	8'2"
	height	6'1"
	pressure pse	7.8
WEIGHTS lbs	ramp	47,500
	takeoff	47,250
	landing	44,500
	zero fuel	42,000
	empty	28,808
	basic operating	29,730
	max payload	12,270
	payload, full fuel	8,390
FUEL	usable lbs	9,380
SPEEDS kts	high speed cruise	459
	long range cruise	424
RANGE nm	with reserve	982
OPERATING CEILING	max ft.	37,000
FIELD LENGTH	takeoff	5,200
	landing	5,050

Note: This aircraft, introduced late in 1988, is, in fact,
a considerably stretched Challenger and can therefore be
expected to be used as a corporate aircraft in addition to
its regional airline use.

Canadair Fire Fighter Amphibian

		CL-215	CL-215T
ENGINES (2)	manufacturer	Pratt & Whitney	Pratt & Whitney
	model	R-2800 series	PW123AF
	rating	2,100 bhp	2,380 shp
FUSELAGE	length	65'0.2"	65'0.2"
	height	29'5.5"	29'5.5"
WING	span	93'10"	93'10"
CABIN	length	30'9.5"	30'9.5"
	height	6'3"	6'3"
	width	7'10"	7'10"
WEIGHTS lbs	takeoff	43,500	43,850
	max pre-scooping	33,500	
	max after scooping	43,500	46,000
	max payload	12,000	13,500
WATER CAPACITY	U.S. gallons	1,410	1,620
FUEL	usable lbs	9,360	10,250
SPEEDS	max cruise kts	164	192
	stall w.15° flaps	78	80
TAKEOFF	land ft.	2,320	2,500
	water ft.	2,620	2,420
LANDING	land ft.	2,520	2,500
	water ft. .	2,740	2,750
SCOOPING DISTANCE	safe clearance height	3,940	4,100
RATE OF CLIMB	fpm	1,000	1,220

Canadair Challenger twin-turbofan wide-body corporate jet.

Canadair Regional Jet.

Canadair CL-215 Fire Fighter Amphibian.

Canadian Marconi Company, Avionics Division Manufacturer of VLF/Omega and GPS long-range navigation systems, MLS systems and integrated navigation management systems. (2442 Trenton Avenue, Montreal, Quebec, Canada H3P 1Y9. (514) 341-7630.)

Canadian Marconi's CMA-771 ''Alpha'' omega navigation system.

CAP   Civil Air Patrol.

Caproni Vizzola   An Italian manufacturer of high-performance sailplanes. (Milano, Italy.)

Caravan I, II   Single- and multi-engine turboprop aircraft manufactured by Cessna Aircraft Company.

carburetion   The act of mixing fuel and air to the proportion necessary for combustion in a piston-engine aircraft.

carburetor   The device that measures the flow of air and fuel to a piston engine.

carburetor heat system   A small heating unit located near the carburetor throat and controlled by a plunger, lever or other device on the instrument panel. It is used to melt ice accumulations in the carburetor. It should be turned full on at the first sign of carburetor-ice buildup causing a certain degree of power reduction. When the carburetor-heat system is turned on, it causes an enriching effect on the mixture and the mixture should therefore be appropriately leaned.

carburetor ice   Ice forming in the carburetor.

carburetor icing   The formation of ice in the throat of the carburetor when moist air, expanding while passing through it, cools quickly due to the vaporization of fuel and the moisture condenses as frost or ice. It initially reduces the power output and, if not stopped, might cause the engine to quit.

Cessna Caravan I.

Cardinal   A family of exceptionally comfortable single-engine aircraft with excellent visibility because of the recessed high wing. The aircraft were manufactured by Cessna Aircraft Company but are no longer in production.

cardinal altitudes   Specific altitudes or flight levels to be used by aircraft when operating under certain conditions or in given directions. Cardinal altitudes for

VFR aircraft flying in an easterly direction (0 to 179°) are odd thousands plus 500 feet, starting at 3,000 feet agl. For VFR aircraft flying in an westerly direction (180 to 359°) they are even thousands plus 500 feet, starting at 3,000 feet agl. For IFR aircraft in uncontrolled airspace the cardinal altitudes are odd or even thousands depending on easterly or westerly direction of flight, also starting at 3,000 feet agl.

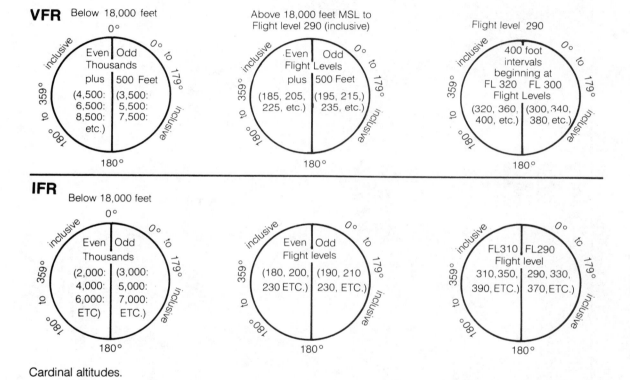

Cardinal altitudes.

cardinal heading Any of the four major compass headings: north, south, east, west.

Carter Engineering Co. Inc. Manufacturer of headsets, helmets, microphones, and accessories. (232 South Glasgow Avenue, Inglewood, CA 90301. (213) 649-0111.)

CAS Calibrated airspeed.

CAS Collision avoidance system.

CASA Aircraft USA, Inc. Subsidiary of Construcciones Aeronauticas, S.A., manufacturer of the CASA C-212, 212-300 and CN-235 aircraft. (C.A.S.A. Rey Francisco, 4, 28008 Madrid, Spain. Phone: 1 247-2500. U.S. address: 14102 Sullyfield Circle #200, Chantilly, VA 22021. (703) 378-2272.) (Pages 104-105)

Casa Twin-Turbine Aircraft

		C212-300	CN235
ENGINES	manufacturer	Garrett (2)	General Electric (2)
	model	TPE 331-10R	CT7-9C
	takeoff power shp	900	1,870
	max continuous shp	900	1,750
PROPELLERS	manufacturer	Dowty Rotol	Hamilton Standard
	model	n/a	14 RF-21
	number of blades	4	4
	diameter	n/a	132 inches
WEIGHTS lbs	max ramp	n/a	31,857
	max takeoff	16,976	31,746
	max landing	15,424	31,305
	zero fuel	n/a	29,983
	max payload cargo version	n/a	11,023
	max payload passenger version	n/a	9,260
FUEL U.S. gallons	inboard tank	190.2	1,393
	outboard tank	79.3	n/a
DIMENSIONS	length	53'2"	70'2.5"
	height	21'8"	26'9.8"
	span	66'11"	847.8"
CABIN	length	23'8"	32'9"
	height	5'11"	6'2"
	width	6'10"	7'7"
SPEEDS kts	max cruise	191	244
SERVICE CEILING	2 engines ft	26,000	25,000
	1 engine ft	11,100	15,300
TAKEOFF	field length ft	2,680	4,300
LANDING	distance ft	1,703	4,300
STANDARD EQUIPMENT	vhf com (Collins)	¤	¤
	vhf nav (Collins)	¤	¤
	ADF (Collins)	¤	¤
	DME (Collins)	¤	¤
	transponder (Collins)	¤	¤
	radar altimeter (Collins)	¤	¤
	weather radar (Collins)	¤	¤
	ELT (Dorne Margolin)	¤	¤
	flight contr.system (Collins)		¤
	VOR/ILS/MB (Collins)		¤
	flight director (Collins)		¤
	autopilot (Collins)		¤
	electro-mechanical instruments (Collins)	¤	
	cockpit voice recorder (Fairchild)	¤	¤
	flight data recorder (Fairchild)	¤	

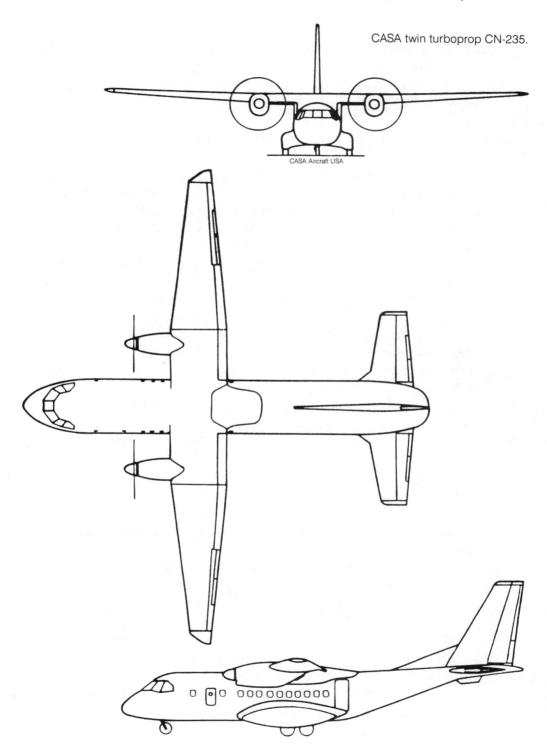

CASA twin turboprop CN-235.

CASA Aircraft USA

Castleberry Instruments and Avionics, Inc.   A subsidiary of B.F. Goodrich Aerospace and Defense Division. Manufacturer of gyroscopes and electronic equipment for navigation and flight control systems. (817 Dessau Road, Austin, TX 78753. (512) 251-3441.)

CAT   Category landing.

CAT   Clear-air turbulence.

Category I landing   The standard ILS landing requiring a ceiling of 200 feet and a half mile visibility at airports equipped with a full ILS.

Category II landing   The low-minimum approach system using modified ILS ground equipment and appropriate cockpit instrumentation, permitting landings when the ceiling is down to 100 feet and visibility is at least 1,200 feet along the runway (Runway Visual Range.) Pilots must be especially qualified to fly CAT II approaches.

Category III landing   A landing in zero-zero conditions, not authorized in the U.S. for civil aircraft except in test situations.

caution area   Airspace within certain geographic limits in which military activities are conducted that are not hazardous but are of interest to non-participating pilots. Caution areas are designated on charts by the letter C.

caution range   The range of airspeeds within which an aircraft should not be operated under conditions of other than smooth air. It is indicated on the face of the airspeed indicator by a yellow arc.

CAVU   Ceiling and visibility unlimited. Technically clear or scattered clouds and visibilities of better than 10 miles.

CB   Citizens band radio. A range of frequencies reserved for use by the average citizen. A favorite piece of equipment among truckers.

CDI   Course deviation indicator.

ceiling   The altitude of the lowest layer of broken or overcast clouds not classified as thin or partial obscuration.

ceiling   The highest altitude a specific aircraft can reach under standard atmospheric conditions.

celestial navigation   The determination of the geographic position of an aircraft, using stars as reference points. Today, it is rarely used in aviation.

Celsius   A temperature scale in which 0° represents the melting point of ice and conversely the freezing point of water and 100° the boiling point of water, both at sea level. Celsius is equal to degrees Fahrenheit − 32 / 9 * 5. The algorithm for converting Celsius (C.) to Fahrenheit (F.) is: C. * 9 / 5 + 32 = F.

center   Air route traffic control center.

center area   The geographical limits of the air space controlled by a given ARTCC.

centerline   The line, either actually visible or imaginary, running along the longitudinal center of a runway. The term is used also in relation to radio ranges, airways, and aircraft fuselages.

centerline thrust   The thrust produced by both engines of a twin-engine aircraft with a puller engine in front and a pusher engine in back, such as the Cessna Skymaster.

center of gravity (CG)   The point at which the moments in all direction are zero. The geometric center of balance.

Centigrade   *See* CELSIUS.

centimeter   ¹/₁₀₀ meter. *See* CONVERSION CHARTS.

centralized control system   A computerized electronic system permitting the pilot to control all his avionics equipment through one central control panel.

centrifugal force   The reaction of a body against a force causing it to move in a curved path, caused by inertia.

Centurion   A family of high-performance single-engine aircraft that used to be manufactured by Cessna Aircraft Company. The top of the line was the pressurized Centurion, representing the first successful use of pressurization in a single-engine aircraft.

Cessna Centurion.

Century Flight Systems, Inc.   Manufacturer of the family of Century flight control systems. (P.O. Box 610, Municipal Airport, Mineral Wells, TX 76067. (817) 325-2517).

Century I, II, III, IV, 21, 31, 41, 2000   A family of flight-control systems, manufactured by Century Flight Systems, Inc.

Century 2000 flight director system.

certificate   A document, generally issued by the FAA, certifying that a pilot, mechanic, aircraft, new design or other person or piece of equipment meets the standards set down for him, her, or it.

certification   The process of obtaining a certificate. Most frequently used with reference to new types of aircraft.

Cessna Aircraft Company   Manufacturer of the Citation family of corporate jets and the Caravan turboprops. Cessna used to manufacture a full line of general aviation aircraft, ranging from the Cessna 150 (152) two-place single-engine trainer to piston twins, like the Golden Eagle and the popular 310, up to the Citations. None of the piston-engine aircraft are still being manufactured but because huge numbers of them are still in the used aircraft feet, specification tables for the more popular models are once more included. (P.O. Box 7704, Wichita, KS 67277. (316) 946-6000.) (Pages 109-113)

CFIT   Controlled flight into terrain.

CFN   Confine.

CG   Center of gravity.

Cessna Citations

		CITATION II	CITATION III	CITATION V[#]
ENGINE	manufacturer	Pratt & Whitney	Garrett	Pratt & Whitney
	model	JT15D-44	TFE 731-3B-100S	JT15D-5A
	thrust lbs	2,500	3,650	2,900
WEIGHTS lbs	ramp	13,500	22,200	16,100
	takeoff	13,300	22,000	15,900
	basic operat'g	7,801	12,196	9,284
	landing	12,700	20,000	15,200
	zero fuel	11,000	15,300	11,200
	empty	7,416	11,811	8,899
	useful load	5,699	10,004	6,816
	payload	3,199	3,104	1,916
FUEL lbs	usable	5,008	7,384	5,820
FUSELAGE ft.	length	47.2	55.5	48.9
	height	15.0	16.8	15.0
	wing span	52.2	53.5	52.2
CABIN ft.	height	4.8	5.83	4.8
	width	4.9	5.67	4.9
	seats, number	7 to 10	7 to 11	8 to 15
PRESSURE	psi	8.7	9.3	8.9
BAGGAGE lbs	external	550	700	850
SPEEDS	cruise kts.	385	473	427
	V_{mo} KIAS	262[*]	305-366[*]	261[*]
	V_{mo} KIAS		336-278[**]	292[**]
	M_{mo} Mach	.705[***]	.851[****]	.755[*****]
CEILING	certified ft.	43,000	51,000	45,000
RATE OF CLIMB	2 engines fpm	3,370	3,699	3,650
	1 engine fpm	1,057	805	1,180
RANGE nm	max	1,594	2,525	1,920
BALANCED FIELD LENGTH ft.		2,990	5,180	3,160
LANDING	max ldg.weight	2,270	2,900	2,920
STALL kts.	max ldg.weight	82	97	87
FUEL FLOW pph	typical cruise	804	1,241	n/a

[#] Preliminary data
[*] Sea level to 30,500 feet for the II and to 8,000 feet for the III and V.
[**] 8,000 feet to 36,500 feet for the III and 8,000 feet to 28,900 feet for the V.
[***] 30,500 feet and above
[****] 36,524 feet and above
[*****] 28,900 feet and above

Cessna Caravans

		CARAVAN I	CARAVAN I SUPER CARGOMASTER	CARAVAN II
ENGINE	manufacturer	Pratt & Whitney Canada	Pratt & Whitney Canada	Pratt & Whitney Canada (2)
	model	PT6A-114	PT6A-114	PT6A-112
	shp	600	600	500 (each)
WEIGHTS lbs.	max takeoff	8,000	8,750	9,850
	max landing	7,800	8,500	9,360
	zero fuel	8,000	8,750	8,500
	empty	3,835	4,570 equipped	5,033
	useful load	3,885	4,215	4,525
SPEED kts.	max cruise	184	171	246
RANGE nm	cruise power	960	888	1,027
	range power	1,085	962	1,287
FUEL U.S. gal.	useable	332	332	475
TAKEOFF ft.	ground roll	1,205	1,575	2,121 (at 9,360 lbs)
	50 ft.obst.	2,210	2,840	2,485
LANDING ft.	ground run	745	915	1,327
	50 ft.obst.	1,655	1,740	2,485
SEATS	max	10	2	14
CARGO cu.ft.	Internal	254	340	233
	External pod	84	113	47

Cessna Out-of-Production Piston-Engine Aircraft

		152 AEROBAT	172 SKYHAWK	182 SKYLANE	210 CENTURION	310	GOLDEN EAGLE
ENGINE(S)	manufacturer	Lycoming	Lycoming	Continental	Continental	Continental	Continental
	model	O-235-L2C	O-320-H2AD	O-470-U	IO-520-L	IO-520-MB (2)	GTSIO-520M (2)
	TBO hrs.	2,000	2,000	1,500	1,500	1,500	1,200
PROPELLER	type	fixed pitch	fixed pitch	const.speed	const.speed	const.speed	const.speed
	blades	2	2	2	3	3	3
LANDING GEAR	type	fixed	fixed	fixed & RG	retractable	retractable	retractable
SEATS	number	2	4	4	6	6	10
TAKEOFF ft.	ground roll	725	805	705	1,250	1,335	1,788
	50 ft.obst.	1,340	1,440	1,350	2,030	1,700	2,367
CLIMB RATE	fpm	715	770	1,010	950	1,662 (400*)	1,575 (230*)
SPEEDS	max kts.	110	125	148	175	207	232
	75% power	107	122	144	171	195	217
	55% power	91	115	127	154	182	n/a
STALL	clean kts.	48	50	56	65	78	83
	dirty kts.	43	44	50	56	70	70
RANGE	75% nm	350	485	880	855	494	1,406
	55% nm	415	575	1,095	925	616	1,818
FUEL FLOW	75% pph	43.2	58.5	85.2	104.7	114.5 * 2	141.4 * 2
	55% pph	28.3	42.1	54.6	75.2	72.8 * 2	92.4 * 2
LANDING ft.	ground roll	475	520	590	765	640	1,100
	50 ft.obst.	1,200	1,250	1,350	1,500	1,700	2,130
FUEL	usable lbs.	147	240	528	534	600	2,064
WEIGHTS	ramp	1,675	2,307	2,960	3,812	5,535	8,450
	takeoff	1,670	2,300	2,950	3,800	5,500	8,400
	landing	1,670	2,300	2,950	3,800	5,400	8,100
	zero fuel					5,015	8,100
	empty	1,101	1,397	1,690	1,683	3,318	4,622
	useful load	574	910	1,260	2,117	2,182	3,778
FUSELAGE	length ft.	24.04	26.96	28	28.22	31.98	39.53
	height ft.	8.5	8.76	9.25	9.7	10.71	13.26
	span ft.	33.22	35.85	35.85	36.75	36.95	46.33
CABIN	length ft.	7.92	9	11.33	12.67	12.26	18.75
	height ft.	3.75	4	4.04	4.06	4.17	4.28
	width ft.	3.08	3.33	3.64	3.69	4.04	4.87

Cessna Aircraft Equipped with Edo Floats

		CESSNA 180 SKYWAGON	CESSNA 185 SKYWAGON	CESSNA 206	CESSNA 206 TURBO 206	CESSNA 185
ENGINE	manufacturer	Continental	Continental	Continental	Continental	Continental
	model	O-470-U	IO-520-D	IO-520-F	TSIO-520-M	IO-520-D
	rating hp	230	300	300	310	300
WEIGHTS	gross lb	2950	3265	3600	3600	3350
	empty lb	2213	2257	2254	2624	2420
	useful load lb	747	1020	1076	992	930
FUEL	capacity gal.	88	88	92	92	88
SPEEDS	maximum kts	129	135	138	150	135
	cruise kts	123	129	132	141	129
RATE OF CLIMB fpm		970	950	925	810	950
SERVICE CEILING ft.		15,300	16,100	13,900	25,100	16,100
RANGE	max, nm	815	715	770	530	715

Cessna Citation II.

Cessna Citation III.

Cessna Caravan II.

Cessna 152.

Cessna aircraft equipped with Edo floats.

CG range   The distance along the longitudinal axis of an airplane within which the CG must fall in order for the aircraft to be properly balanced. Aircraft loaded beyond the CG range might become uncontrollable.

chaff   Narrow strips of metallic reflectors, used to reflect radar energy. When dropped from an aircraft they tend to produce a large target on the radar screen.

Challenger   A family of wide-body executive jet aircraft produced by Canadair. The original design for the aircraft was created by Bill Lear. It was changed by Canadair and Lear, annoyed about not being consulted, then referred to the aircraft as "Fat Albert." (Page 114)

Challenger 600 wide-body corporate jet.

Canadair's CL-600 corporate jet.

Champion   A family of sport aircraft once produced by Bellanca Aircraft Corporation. It is no longer in production.

Champion Aviation Products Group   The aviation arm of Champion Spark Plug Company, probably the world's foremost manufacturer of aviation spark plugs, oil filters, turbine ignition leads, turbine igniters, and various accessories. (P.O. Box 910, Toledo, OH 43661. (419) 535-2463.)

Champion Decathlon   One of the Champion family of sport aircraft.

Chancellor   A pressurized twin-engine piston aircraft manufactured by Cessna Aircraft Company.

chandelle   An aerobatic maneuver to gain maximum altitude in a minimum distance and time, while reversing the direction of flight by 180 degrees. It starts with a dive to gain speed followed by a well-coordinated climbing turn ending in level flight, at minimum controllable airspeed, in the opposite direction.

changeover point   The point at which a pilot switches from one VOR, VORTAC, or DME station to the next, usually located approximately halfway between stations and assures reliable reception distance.

Chaparral   A high-performance single-engine aircraft once manufactured by Mooney Aircraft Corporation. It is no longer in production.

charlie   In aviation radio phraseology the term used for the letter C.

chart   An aeronautical or weather map.

chase aircraft   An aircraft flown close to a second aircraft, usually for the purpose of observing performance during testing.

chasing the needle   An expression used to imply sloppy flying.

checklist   Any list of items or procedures designed to guard against failures of the human memory. Using checklists is especially important during preflight, before takeoff and prior to landing.

checkout The training and flight test a pilot should undergo in order to become familiar with a particular aircraft.

Check pilot The pilot who checks out another pilot.

Checkpoint A geographical point or prominent landmark the location of which can be determined by reference to a chart and identified either visually or by radio.

Cheetah A single-engine fixed-gear piston aircraft manufactured by Gulfstream American Corporation. It was designed by Roy LoPresti and is no longer in production.

Cherokee A family of single-engine piston aircraft that was once produced by Piper Aircraft Corporation. No longer in production.

Piper Aircraft Corporation

Piper Cherokee Challenger.

Cheyenne   A family of high-performance pressurized turboprop aircraft manufactured by Piper Aircraft Corporation. The Cheyenne III and Cheyenne 400 are the two that are still in production. They are used by many airlines worldwide as training aircraft for jet aircraft pilots.

Piper Cheyenne IA.

CHG   Change.

Chieftain   A cabin-class piston twin once manufactured by Piper Aircraft Corporation. No longer in production.

Chichester Miles Ltd.   Manufacturer and consultant, has test-flown the Leopard, a light business jet powered by two Noel Penny jet engines developing 300 pounds of thrust each. Actual production is expected to commence in the early 1990s at an anticipated price of $650,000 in 1989 $s. (8 The Mews, Breadcroft Lane, Harpenden, Herts, England AL5 4TF. Phone: 0373 822037.)

chord   An imaginary line running from the leading edge to the trailing edge of the wing.

Christen Industries, Inc.   Manufacturer of the Christen Eagle, the Husky A-1 utility aircraft and the Pitts Special as well as kits and parts. (Office: P.O. Box 25033, Jackson, WY 83001. (307) 733-1789. Factory: South Washington Street, Afton, WY 83110. (307) 886-3151.) (Pages 117-118)

CHT   Cylinder head temperature gauge.

CIG   Ceiling.

Christen Industries Aircraft

		PITTS SPECIAL S-2S	PITTS SPECIAL S-2B	EAGLE	HUSKY A-1
ENGINE	manufacturer	Lycoming	Lycoming	Lycoming	Lycoming
	model	AEIO-540-D4A5	AEIO-540-D4A5	AEIO-540-D4B5	O-360-C1G
	rating hp	260	260	260	180
PROPELLER	manufacturer	Hartzell	Hartzell	Hartzell	Hartzell
	type	const.speed	const.speed	const.speed	const.speed
WEIGHTS lbs	gross, aerobatic	1500	1625	1478	1800
	gross, normal	1500	1700	1478	1800
	gross, competition			1262*	
	empty	1100	1150	997	1190
	useful load	400	475	481	610
FUEL U.S. gal	usable	34	28	25	50
	aux			20	
DIMENSIONS	span	20'	20'	19'11"	35'6"
	height	6'7.5"	6'7.5"	6'6"	6'7"
	length	17'4"	18'9"	18'6"	22'7"
SPEEDS knots	top speed	163	163	171	126
	cruise	152	152	149	122
	stall	50	52	52	37
	V_{ne}	177	183	183	n/a
RATE OF CLIMB	fpm	2800	2700	2640	1500
TAKEOFF	run ft	n/a	n/a	n/a	200
LANDING	roll ft	n/a	n/a	n/a	350
RANGE nm	standard fuel	352	277	304	696
	w. aux fuel			552	

* with 190-lb pilot

Christen Industries Incorporated

Christen Husky utility aircraft.

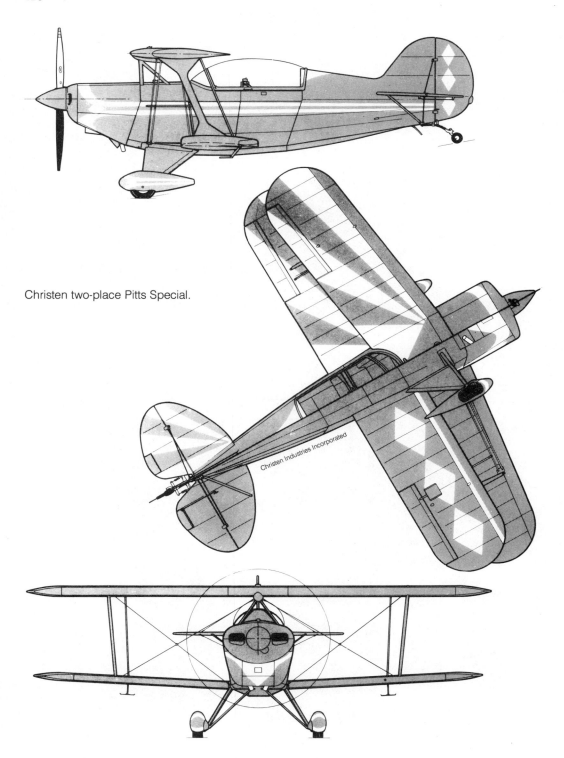

Christen two-place Pitts Special.

Christen Industries Incorporated

circle to land   A maneuver executed by the pilot to line up an aircraft on final approach to the active runway, when a straight-in landing from a given instrument approach is not possible. The maneuver requires prior ATC authorization and is permissable only after the pilot has established visual contact with the airport.

circle to runway (number)   A clearance expression used by ATC to inform the pilot that he must circle to land because the active runway is not aligned with the particular instrument landing procedure being flown.

circling approach   *See* CIRCLE TO LAND.

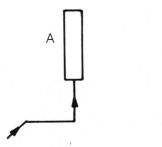

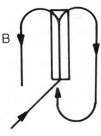

Use A when final approach course intersects runway centerline at less then 90°;

Use B if you see runway too late to fly pattern A.

Circling approaches.

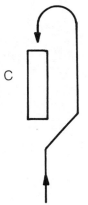

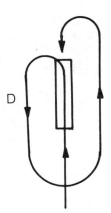

Use C to land in opposite direction from final approach course.

Use D if you see the runway too late to use pattern C.

circling minimums   Circling minimums are published on instrument approach charts and provide adequate obstruction clearance and pilots must not descend below the circling MDA until visual contact has been established with the airport and the aircraft is in a position to make the final descent for landing.

circuit breaker   A means of interrupting the flow of electrical current when an over-load occurs. The breaker can be reset by pushing a button. Its function is identical to that of a fuse.

cirrocumulus   A high cumuliform cloud occurring in bright puffs. When joined in a mass they have a rippling appearance, frequently referred to as "mackerel sky."

cirrostratus   Cirrus cloud in a solid or slightly broken layer, often topped by individ-ual cirrus clouds.

cirrus   A high stratiform cloud that occurs in bright filmy streaks or whisps through which the sun is easily visible. It consists of ice crystals.

Citabria   One of the Champion family of sport aircraft produced by Bellanca Air-craft Corporation. It is no longer in production.

Citabria on floats.

Citation   A family of executive jet aircraft manufactured by Cessna Aircraft Com-pany. (Page 121)

civil aviation   All non-military aviation.

CL   Control tower.

CLC   Course line computer; a component of RNAV systems.

CLD   Cloud.

David Clark Company, Inc.   Manufacturer of noise attenuating aviation headsets, voice-activated intercoms, voice-powered communication systems, and hearing protectors. (360 Franklin Street, P.O. Box 15054, Worcester, MA 01615-0054. (508) 756-6216.)

Cessna Citation V.

clean   Refers to aerodynamically clean, meaning with landing gear, flaps, and spoilers retracted.

clear   Sky conditions in which clouds cover less than 10 percent of the sky.

clear air turbulence (CAT)   Turbulence occurring in clear air and not associated with any cloud formation. Occurring most frequently in the vicinity of the jet stream.

clearance   An authorization by ATC for an aircraft to proceed under specified conditions within controlled airspace. Clearances are given based on known traffic in the affected area.

clearance delivery   At busy airports a separate ATC function with its own frequency, solely for the purpose of issuing clearances to departing IFR flights.

clearance limits   A point, determined either by time or navigation aids, at which the pilot must have further clearance from ATC in order to proceed.

clearance shorthand   Shorthand used by pilots when copying an ATC clearance. Use of this shorthand is recommended but not mandatory.

Clearance void if not off by (time)   A phrase used by ATC to inform the pilot that his departure clearance is automatically cancelled if he has not commenced his flight by the time given.

Cleared as filed   A phrase used by ATC to authorize a pilot to proceed on an IFR flight in accordance with the way in which he filed his IFR flight plan.

Cleared for approach   An authorization by ATC for the pilot to execute any type of published instrument approach of his choice.

Cleared for (type of) approach   An authorization by ATC for the pilot to commence the instrument approach specified in the clearance.

Cleared for takeoff   An ATC authorization for an aircraft to depart. It is frequently issued as "Cleared for immediate takeoff" when other traffic is on final approach.

Cleared for the option   An ATC authorization for an aircraft to execute a special maneuver such as a touch-and-go, stop-and-go, missed approach, etc.

Cleared through   An ATC authorization for an aircraft to make intermediate stops at specified airports without having to refile his flight plan.

Cleared to land   An ATC authorization for an aircraft to land.

clear ice   Ice that forms in smooth transparent layers from the gradual freezing of supercooled water. It is most prevalent on the smooth surfaces of an aircraft and tends to form most frequently when flying through freezing drizzle. Also called *glaze*.

clear of traffic   A phrase used by ATC to inform a pilot that previously issued traffic is of no further consequence.

climb   The portion of a flight during which the aircraft ascends from the ground to its cruising level; or any other time when the aircraft changes to a higher altitude or flight level.

climb-and-descent corridor   A narrow portion of airspace, usually established near military airports, where high-speed jet aircraft can climb or descend at speeds above 250 knots.

climbing turn   A turn, usually to a predetermined heading, made while climbing. It requires added power to maintain constant airspeed and rate of climb.

climb to VFR   An ATC authorization, usually issued in conjunction with a Special VFR clearance, for an aircraft to climb to VFR conditions within a control zone when the only weather factor is restricted visibility. It requires that the aircraft remain clear of clouds during the climb.

climbout   Flight between takeoff and cruising altitude.

clock   A clock with a sweep-second hand is a requirement for IFR flight. Recently, a wide variety of digital clocks and timers have appeared on the market, most designed to simplify the timing problems associated with nonprecision instrument approaches.

closed runway   A runway which, for one reason or another, is unusable for aircraft operation. Permanently closed runways must be marked by a large X.

closed traffic   Continuous activity involving takeoffs and landings during which the aircraft does not leave the traffic pattern.

cloud A visible mass of small water droplets condensed from the water vapor in the atmosphere, or, at higher altitudes, ice crystals. Cloud formation requires the presence of condensation nuclei and a drop in air temperature below the dew point at the altitude at which the formation takes place.

cloud bank A well-defined mass of clouds seen in the distance, covering a considerable portion of the horizon or sky.

cloud cover Sky cover.

CLR Clear.

CLRNC Clearance.

CLSD Closed.

clutter A term used to describe radar returns caused by precipitation, terrain, chaff, large numbers of aircraft or any other phenomenon producing an excessive number of targets in close proximity, and often making it difficult or impossible for ATC to provide effective radar service.

CNTR Center.

CNTRL Central.

cockpit The portion of an aircraft fuselage occupied by the flight crew.

cockpit voice recorder The instrument, often referred to in the press and on radio and TV as the *black box,* that records every sound heard in the cockpit, retaining the data for a given time period of the flight, constantly erasing old conversation as new data are added. *See also* FAIRCHILD-WESTON.

Cockpit voice recorder (CVR).

codes The number assigned by ATC to a transponder-equipped aircraft. VFR aircraft not in contact with ATC always squawk 1200. IFR aircraft and VFR aircraft under ATC control will be asked by ATC to squawk a given code number.

col A narrow neck between two highs or two lows, of the same pressure as the centers.

cold air mass   A mass of unstable air, colder than the surface over which it is moving. When warmed it results in convection currents and, in turn, clouds with vertical development. Visibility is usually good.

cold front   A front formed by a mass of cold high-pressure air moving under warm air and replacing it. It is usually associated with turbulent cumulonimbus clouds and line squalls. More often than not it doesn't last long because the front is shallow. It is indicated on a weather chart by a line with pointed triangular marks in the direction in which the front is moving.

Colemill Enterprises, Inc.   The company's slogan is "Making Great Planes Even Better." It has converted a large number of different aircraft by changing engines, propellers, and certain other items such as adding winglets, in order to improve the performance data of those aircraft. Among the aircraft so converted are the Beech Bonanza and Baron, the Piper Navajo and Chieftain, and the Cessna 310. (P.O. Box 60627, Cornelia Fort Airpark, Nashville, TN 37206. (615) 226-4256.)

collective   One of the primary flight controls on a helicopter.

Collins General Aviation and Avionics Divisions   Subsidiaries of Rockwell International. Manufacturers of avionics systems for general aviation, the airlines, and the military. With the introduction of the ProLine family of avionics for corporate aviation, the company greatly increased its use of microprocessor and digital technologies. In addition, the company has increased its efforts to have aircraft

Collins Pro Line II.

equipped with complete Collins instrument panels such as those designed for the Beech Starship and Beechjet, Learjet 55s, Falcon 20s, and others. (Cedar Rapids, IA 52498. (319) 396-1000.)

collision avoidance system   Cockpit instrumentation capable of warning the pilot of the proximity of other aircraft, especially those posing a threat if both aircraft continue on their present course. As of late 1991 TCAS II (*T*raffic alert and *Colli*sion *A*voidance *S*ystem) will be required on certain classes of civil aircraft. The systems require that all affected aircraft install a Mode S transponder to allow the exchange of traffic resolution information between aircraft. The systems that have been introduced or are in various stages of development are capable of detecting appropriately equipped aircraft and are capable of displaying suggested evasive action in terms of changes in altitude on cockpit displays.

com   Communications.

Comanche   A high-performance single- and twin-engine aircraft manufactured by Piper Aircraft Corporation. Comanches are no longer in production.

combined station/tower   A facility at which the functions of a control tower and a flight service station are combined.

combustion chamber   In a reciprocating engine the vacant area between the cylinder head and the highest point reached by the stroke of a piston. It is here that combustion of the fuel and air mixture occurs when ignited by the spark plug.

comm   Communications.

Commander   A family of single- and twin-engine aircraft once manufactured by the General Aviation Division of Rockwell International. It includes single-engine aircraft, twins, turboprops, and jets. The single-engine models were discontinued and the balance of the Commander family was purchased by Israel Aircraft Industries, which briefly manufactured the Jet Commander until replacing it by its original designs, the *Westwind I* and *Westwind II*.

Commander Aircraft Company   The company has acquired the rights to the single-engine Aero Commanders from Gulfstream Aerospace and is manufacturing an improved version of the Commander 114 as the 114B. (1155 21st Street N.W. #400, Washington, DC 20036. (202) 457-9060) (Page 126).

Commercial Computers, Inc.   Manufacturer of aviation management systems software for FBOs and corporate operators. (7875 N.W. 12th Street #120, Miami, FL 33165. (305) 593-2300.)

commercial license   A pilot certificate authorizing the pilot to carry passengers or freight for remuneration.

commercial pilot   *See* COMMERCIAL LICENSE.

common route   A segment of a route between an inland navigation aid and a coastal fix.

Commander Aircraft

		COMMANDER 114B
ENGINE	manufacturer	Lycoming
	model	IO-540-T4B5D
	cylinders	6
	rating h.p.	260
	TBO hrs	2,000
PROPELLER	manufacturer	McCauley
	model	B3D 34C 405/90DFA-13
	type	constant speed, hydraulic
	blades	3
	diameter	77"
DIMENSIONS	length	24'11"
	Wing span	32'9.1"
	height	8'5"
	cabin length	75"
	cabin width	47"
	cabin height	49"
FUEL	usable gal.	70
OIL	quarts	8
WING	area sq.ft.	152
	load lb/sq.ft.	21.4
SPEEDS	max kts	174
	75% kts	164
	65% kts	152
STALL	clean kts	61
	dirty kts	56
RANGE	max nm	734
TAKEOFF	ground run	1,040
	50 ft.obst.	2,000
LANDING	ground roll	720
	50 ft.obst.	1,200
RATE OF CLIMB	fpm	1,100
SERVICE CEILING	ft	17,500
PRICE 1989 $s	IFR equipped	$129,500

Commander 114B.

Communications Specialists, Inc.   Manufacturer of a hand-held 720-channel com transceiver that can also be panel mounted as a second com system in the cockpit. (426 West Taft Avenue, Orange, CA 92665-4296. (714) 998-3021 and (800) 854-0547.)

Communication transceiver, portable.

compass   A device for determining the direction of flight in the horizontal plane. The magnetic compass aligns itself automatically with the magnetic north. It tends to be unreliable during turns, climbs, and descents. A gyro compass must be intermittently set by the pilot to conform with the magnetic compass. (*See also* DIRECTIONAL GYRO.)

compass card   A circular scale in a magnetic compass or directional gyro, showing compass headings in degrees from 0 to 359. The readout might consist of a needle moving around the scale, or the card itself revolving with relation to a lubber line.

compass correction card   A card located in the cockpit and showing compass errors at various directions, caused by interference due to the airframe or instruments.

compass deviation   *See* COMPASS CARD.

compass error   Error in the reading of a magnetic compass induced by turns executed by the aircraft.

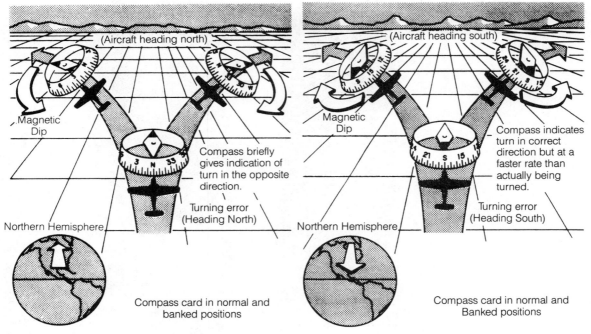

Magnetic compass card turn errors.

compass heading   The compass heading that must be flown in order to achieve a planned true course. It is arrived at by correcting the true course for magnetic variation, compass deviation and wind-drift angle.

compass locator   A low or medium frequency low-power radio beacon installed in conjunction with an ILS at the outer or middle marker. It is not usable for navigation at distances greater than 15 nm.

compass rose   *See* COMPASS CARD.

composite flight plan   A flight plan that combines VFR and IFR legs during one flight.

compression The degree of compression of the fuel and air mixture in reciprocating and turbine engines.

compressor The section of a turbine engine that compresses the air to the desired degree.

compressor blades Small metal blades attached to the compressor in a turbine engine.

compulsory reporting point Any position along an airway at which a pilot must report his position to ATC when not in radar contact. Compulsory reporting points are shown on radio-facility charts as solid black triangles.

computer Computers fall into two categories, analog computers and digital computers. Today virtually all computers are digital, using the binary method of information storage and manipulation. Computers are used extensively in modern avionics systems, providing varying degrees of automation. In addition, pilots use personal computers in the home and office to obtain weather information over telephone lines or to perform a variety of preflight tasks using different computer programs. Furthermore, there are self-contained laptop computers and programmable calculators that can be carried in the airplane in order to perform a multitude of in-flight calculations. And finally, the ATC system uses some of the most sophisticated mainframe computer banks for air traffic control and the maintenance of the national airspace system.

Computer Sciences Corporation Developer of time-sharing, facilities management, and communications systems software. (2100 East Grand Avenue, El Segundo, CA 90245. (213) 615-0311.)

Computer Training Systems, Inc. Developer of computer-based recurrent training programs for fixed- and rotary-wing aircraft. (P.O. Box 8500, Tenafly, NJ 07670. (201) 567-5639.)

Computing Technologies for Aviation Provides flight operations management systems. (P.O. Box 7624, Charlottesville, VA 22906. (804) 971-7624.)

COMSND Commissioned.

COMSNG Commissioning.

com transceiver A combination radio receiver and transmitter used for two-way radio communication. It might utilize VHF or HF frequencies. (Pages 130-131)

COND Condition.

condensation The process by which water vapor changes into liquid, usually because of a decrease in temperature. It is the opposite of evaporation.

condensation level The altitude at which a rising column of air reaches the condensation point and clouds begin to form.

condensation nuclei Impurities in the atmosphere, such as dust or sand, around which water vapor condenses to form precipitation or clouds.

Com Transceivers

MANU.	MODEL	PRICE	VOLT	#	FREQUENCIES range MHz	spc	stg	SQLCH A	M	MOUNT P	R	W	U	lbs	P	Remarks
Bendix/King	KY 92	2,160	13.75	720	116.000 to 135.975	25		¤		¤		7	1	2.8	*	Silver Crown *KX 99
Bendix/King	KA 93	3,070	14	720	116.000 to 135.975	25		¤			*	5	1	2.9		*base-station
	KA 94	2,435									#					#vehicle unit
Bendix/King	KY 96A	1,140	28	760	118.000 to	25	9	¤	¤	¤		5	1	2.9		Silver Crown
	KY 97A	1,140	14	760	136.975	25	9	¤	¤	¤		5	1	2.9		Silver Crown
Bendix/King	KY196A	3,060	28	760	118.000 to	25	9	¤		¤		16	1	2.8		Silver Crown
	KY197A	3,060	14	760	136.975	25	9	¤		¤		10	1	2.8		Silver Crown
Bendix/King	KTR908	8,310	27.5	720	118.000 to 135.975*	25	9	¤		¤	¤	20	2	4.3		Gold Crown -151.975 opt
Bendix/King	VCS 40	10,775	28	760	118.000 to 136.975	25		¤		¤	¤	20	2	6.1		Series III
Collins	VHF-21	n/a	28	760	118.000 to 136.975	25		¤			¤	16	1	4.2		ProLine II
Collins	VHF-422	n/a	28	760	118.000 to 136.975	25		¤			¤	16	1	4.7		ProLine II ARINC 429
Aire-Sciences	RT-551A	2,050	14	720	118.000 to 135.975	25			¤	¤			1	n/a		
Aire-Sciences	RT-661A	2,250	14	720	118.000 to 135.975	25			¤	¤			1	n/a		TSOd
Mentor	TR-12	730	14	1-10	select				¤	¤		8	1			add'l freq.$48
Mentor	TR-12	1,030	14	1-10	select				¤			8	1		¤	portable, „
Mentor	TR-12F	780	14	1-10	select				¤			8	1			Base unit
Mentor	TR-12F	970	115AC	1-10	select				¤			8	1			Base unit
Communicatn's Specialists	TR-720	195	12*	720	118.000 to 135.975	25			¤			3	3	1.2	¤	Portable **

** also receives 200 nav frequencies, 108.00 to 117.95.   Panel mount and power amplifier available.

PRICE:		uninstalled
VOLT:		input
FREQUENCIES	#:	number of frequencies
	range:	frequency range in MHz
	spc:	spacing kHz
	stg:	storage, number
SQLCH:	A:	automatic squelch
	M:	manual squelch
MOUNT:	P:	panel mounted
	R:	remote mounted
W:		transmitter output in watts
U:		number of units
P:		portable unit available

Collins Micro Line com transceiver.

condensation trail   A visible trail of condensed water vapor or ice crystals left behind an aircraft. Also called *contrail* or *vapor trail.*

conduction   The transfer of heat energy by contact of a cool region with a warm region.

cone of silence   The airspace above a LF/MF navaid in which no range signals can be heard because of the directional nature of the signals. It is usually co-located with a marker beacon.

cones   Cone shaped nerve ends in the center of the retina of the human eye. Cones are capable of distinguishing colors, but are ineffective under conditions of very low light levels. (*See* NIGHT VISION.)

Confederate Air Force   An organization, headquartered in Texas, that owns and maintains an impressive fleet of World War II military aircraft. The group maintains the Confederate Air Force Museum. (P.O. Box CAF, Harlingen, TX 78551. (512) 425-1057.)

CONFIG   Configuration.

conflict alert   An advisory by ATC with reference to conflicting traffic, usually in the form of: "Advise you turn right/left . . .climb/descend . . . etc."

connecting rod   A metal bar that converts back-and-forth motion of a piston into the rotating motion of the crankshaft in a reciprocating engine.

Conquest   An executive turboprop twin-engine aircraft manufactured by Cessna Aircraft Company.

Consolan   A low-frequency long-distance navaid useful in transoceanic navigation.

constant pressure chart   A chart showing the position of a line of constant pressure with changes in altitude in the upper air. It is plotted every 12 hours from measurements made by radiosondes.

constant speed propeller   A controllable-pitch propeller that maintains a constant rpm by automatically changing the blade angle in relation to engine output.

CONSTR   Construction.

CONSTRD   Constructed.

CONT   Continue, continuous.

Contact   A verbal warning shouted by the pilot, indicating that the engine is about to be started. An alternate term used is "Clear!" or "Clear prop!"

contact approach   A visual approach made by an aircraft on an IFR flight plan when operating with at least one mile visibility and when authorized by ATC. This approach must initially be requested by the pilot.

contact conditions   Weather conditions under which a pilot can navigate by reference to the ground.

contact flying   Flying by reference to the ground under visual flight rules (VFR).

conterminous U.S.   The 48 adjoining states and the District of Columbia.

contiguous U.S.   *See* CONTERMINOUS U.S.

continental control area   The airspace above 14,500 feet msl and at least 1,500 feet agl above the contiguous U.S. and most of Alaska. Prohibited and restricted areas are not included in the continental control area.

continental U.S.   The 49 states located on the North American continent plus the District of Columbia.

continuous transcribed weather broadcast   A continuous transmission of transcribed weather information and pertinent PIREPs by LF/MF stations and selected FSSs.

contour lines   Lines on aeronautical charts that link points of the same elevation and thus indicate ground relief.

contrail   Condensation trail.

control area   *See* CONTROLLED AIRSPACE.

controllable-pitch propeller   A propeller the blade angle of which may be changed by the pilot in flight in order to obtain the best or most economical performance.

controlled airport An airport at which all arriving and departing traffic and all traffic passing through the airport traffic area is governed by ATC.

controlled airspace All airspace in which all IFR traffic is subject to ATC. Also including all positive-control airspace in which all traffic is subject to ATC.

controller An employee of the FAA authorized to provide air traffic control service at en route and terminal ATC facilities. Not included is FSS personnel, known as flight service specialists.

controls Any and all devices used by the pilot in the process of operating an airplane.

control sector An area of airspace within horizontal and vertical limits over which a controller or group of controllers has jurisdiction. Usually a portion of the area controlled by a given ARTCC or approach/departure control facility.

control stick Control wheel or the yoke in an aircraft. The term is applicable whether it is a wheel or actually a stick, as in older and some current sport aircraft.

control surface Any movable airfoil such as aileron, rudder, elevator, trim-tab that can be operated by the pilot in order to achieve a desired reaction.

control tower Airport traffic control tower, the ATC facility at a controlled airport.

control wheel Control stick; yoke.

control zone A more or less circular area around a controlled airport, 10 miles in diameter including extensions necessary for instrument approaches, which is under ATC control. Control zones extend from the surface upward to the base of the continental control area or, where not underlying the continental control area, with no upper limit. They are shown on aeronautical charts by a broken blue line.

convection The transfer of heat through the atmosphere by the motion of vertical columns of air, usually resulting from uneven heating of the ground and producing turbulent conditions.

convection current A vertical current of air, commonly referred to as up or downdraft.

convection fog Fog, usually in the vicinity of large bodies of water, resulting from the air currents produced by the difference in heat absorption of land and water.

conventional gear Tail-wheel gear. Such airplanes are commonly known as taildraggers.

conversion charts Conversion tables.

conversion tables Tables or charts showing the comparative values of different means of identifying weights and measures:

Centigrade/Fahrenheit Conversion Table

To convert Fahrenheit (F.) to centigrade (Celsius) (C.) use: C. = F. − 32 / 9 * 5

To convert Celsius (C.) to Fahrenheit (F.) use: F. = C. * 9 / 5 + 32

C.	F./C.	F.	C.	F./C.	F.
−62	−80	−112	−4	25	77
−57	−70	−94	−2	30	86
−51	−60	−76	1	35	95
−46	−50	−58	4	40	104
−40	−40	−40	7	45	113
−34	−30	−22	10	50	122
−32	−25	−13	12	55	131
−29	−20	−4	15	60	140
−26	−15	+5	18	65	149
−23	−10	14	21	70	158
−21	−5	23	23	75	167
−18	0	32	27	80	176
−15	5	41	29	85	185
−12	10	50	32	90	194
−9	15	59	35	95	203
−7	20	68	37	100	212

Velocity Conversion Table

knots	mph/knots	mph	knots	mph/knots	mph
4	5	6	69	80	92
9	10	12	74	85	93
13	15	17	78	90	104
17	20	23	82	95	110
22	25	29	87	100	115
26	30	35	91	105	121
30	35	40	95	110	127
35	40	46	100	115	132
39	45	52	104	120	138
43	50	58	108	125	144
48	55	63	113	130	150
52	60	69	117	135	155
56	65	75	122	140	161
61	70	81	126	145	167
65	75	86	130	150	173

To convert mph into knots, divide by 1.15. To convert knots into mph, multiply by 1.15.

Converting Pressure Altitude to Density Altitude

The constant and the variables used in the algorithm are:

C = 288.15

PA = Pressure Altitude in feet (read at 29.92 in Hg)

DC = Degrees Centigrade

DA = Density Altitude in feet

DA = (145426.0*(1 − (((C − PA*.001981)/C)^5.2563/((273.15 + DC)/C))^0.235))

Calculating Range and Endurance

The variables used in the algorithm:

FB = Fuel on-board in gallons or pounds

FF = Fuel flow in gallons or pounds per hour

GS = Ground speed in knots

RG = Range with no reserves in nautical miles

HR = Hours and decimal fractions of hours

H1 = Hours

H2 = Minutes

The formula for no-reserve range:

RG = (FB / FF) * GS

The formula for endurance in hours and decimal fractions of hours:

HR = RG/GS

The formula that converts the decimal time format to hours and minutes:

H1 = int(HR)   [hours only]

H2 = (HR − H1) * 100   [fractions only]

H2 = H2 * 0.6   [converts decimal fractions to minutes]

Endurance = H1 hour(s) and H2 minutes(s)

Calculating the Effect of Wind on Ground Speed

The variables used in the algorithm:

TAS = True airspeed in knots

WD   = Wind direction

WV   = Wind velocity in knots

MC   = Magnetic course

MV   = Magnetic variation

WC   = Wind component
GS   = Ground speed in knots

WC = -1 * WV * COS((WD $-$ MC $-$ MV) / 57.2958)
GS = TAS + WC

Converting Altitude Change in Feet per Nautical Mile into Rate of Climb or Descent in Feet per Minute

The variables used in the algorithm:

GS   = Ground speed in knots
RG   = Rate of climb/descent
AC   = Altitude change in feet per nautical mile

RG   = (AC / 60) * GS

Figuring Time En Route by Distance Covered and Ground Speed

The variables used in the algorithm:

D   = Distance in nautical miles
GS   = Ground speed in knots
HM = Hours and decimal fractions of hours

HM = D / GS

Figuring Time En Route by Fuel Data

The variables used in the algorithm:

FB   = Fuel burned in gallons or pounds
FF   = Fuel flow in gallons or pounds per hour
HM = Hours and decimal fractions of hours

HM = FB / FF

Figuring Fuel Flow Data by Time and Fuel Burned

The variables used in the algorithm:

HM = Time en route in hours and minutes
FB   = Fuel burned in gallons or pounds
H   = Hours
M   = Minutes

H   = int(HM)   [hours only]
M   = HM $-$ H   [minutes only]

M   = M * 0.6   [converts minutes to decimal fractions]
HM = H + M   [combines hours and decimal fractions]
FF = FB / HM

Figuring Fuel Flow Data by
Distance Flown and Fuel Burned

The variables used in the algorithm:

FB = Fuel burned in gallons or pounds
D   = Distance covered in nautical miles
GS = Ground speed in knots
FF = Fuel flow in gallons or pounds per hour
FM = Fuel efficiency in gallons or pounds per nautical mile

FF = FB / (D / GS)
FM = D / FB

Determining the Point of Descent

The variables used in the algorithm:
F   = Current altitude in feet
E   = Destination airport elevation
AC = Altitude change in feet
GS = Ground speed
RC = Rate of descent in feet per minute
PD = Point of descent

AC = F − E
PD = AC / RC/60 * GS
      [nautical miles to destination]

Computing Time to Climb/Descent

The variables used in the algorithm:
CA = Current altitude in feet
NA = Next altitude in feet
RC = Rate of climb/descent in feet per minute
HM = Minutes
AC = Altitude change in feet

AC = ABS(CA − NA)
HM = AC /RC

Computing the Rate of Climb/Descent
in Feet per Minute

The variables used in the algorithm:

CA = Current altitude in feet
NA = Next altitude in feet
HD = Horizontal distance in nautical miles
FP = Rate of climb/descent in feet per minute

AC = ABS(CA − NA)
FP = HD / GS
FP = FP * 60
FP = AC / FP

Miscellaneous Conversion Factors

Multiply	By	To obtain
Acres	43,560	square feet
	4,047	square meters
	1.562×10^{-3}	square miles
Atmospheres	76	cm of mercury
	29.921	inches of mercury
	33.899	feet of water
	10,332	kilogram per sq. meter
	14,696	pounds per sq. inch
	2,116.2	pounds per sq. foot
	1.0133	bars
Bars	75.01	cm of mercury
	14.5	pounds per sq. inch
BTU	778.2	foot pounds
	$.3930 \times 10^{-3}$	horsepower hour
	$.2930 \times 10^{-3}$	kilowatt hour
	.2520	kilogram calorie
	107.6	kilogram meters
	1055	joules
Centimeters (cm)	.3937	inches
	.03281	feet

Miscellaneous Conversion Factors

Multiply	By	To obtain
cm of mercury	5.3524	inches of water
	.44603	feet of water
	.19337	pounds per sq. inch
	27.845	pounds per sq. foot
	135.95	kilogram per sq. meter
Cubic centimeters	10^{-3}	liters
	.06102	cubic inches
Cubic feet	28,317	cubic centimeters
	1,728	cubic inches
	.02831	cubic meters
	7.4805	gallons
	28.316	liters
Cubic feet per min.	.4717	liters per second
	.02832	cubic meters per min.
Cubic feet of water	62.428	pounds
Cubic inches	16.387	cubic centimeters
	.01639	liters
	4.329×10	gallons
	.01732	quarts
Cubic meters	61,023	cubic inches
	35,314	cubic feet
	264.17	gallons
Cubic yards	27	cubic feet
	.7646	cubic meters
	202	U.S. gallons
Degrees (arc), dynes	.01745	radians
	1.020×10^{-3}	grams
	2.248×10^{-6}	pounds
	7.233×10^{-5}	pounds

Miscellaneous Conversion Factors

Multiply	By	To obtain
Ergs	$.947 \times 10^{-10}$	BTU
	1	dyne centimeter
	7.376×10^{-8}	foot pounds
	1.02×10^{-3}	gram centimeters
	10^{-7}	joules
	2.388×10^{-4}	kilogram calories
Feet	.3048	meters
Feet of water	.0295	atmospheres
	.43353	pounds per sq. inch
	62.378	pounds per sq. foot
	304.8	kilogram per sq. meter
	.88367	inches of mercury
	.24199	centimeters of mercury
Feet per minute	.01136	miles per hour
	.01829	kilometers per hour
	.508	centimeters per second
	.009878	knots
Feet per second	.68182	miles per hour
	1.0973	kilometers per hour
	30.48	centimeters per second
	.3048	meters per second
	.59209	knots
Foot-pounds	.13826	meter-kilogram
Foot-pounds/min.	.00003	horsepower
Foot-pounds/sec.	.00182	horsepower
Gallons (imperial)	277.4	cubic inches
	1.201	U.S. gallons
	4.546	liters
Gallons, U.S., dry	268.8	cubic inches
	.1556	cubic feet

Miscellaneous Conversion Factors

Multiply	By	To obtain
	1.164	U.S. gallon, liquid
	4.405	liters
Gallons, U.S., liquid	231	cubic inches
	.13368	cubic feet
	3.7853	liters
	.83268	imperial gallons
	128	liquid ounces
Kilogram-meters	7.233	foot pounds
	9.8067×10^7	ergs
Kilogram per cu m	.06243	pounds per cubic foot
	.001	grams per cubic centimeter
Kilogram per meter	.67197	pounds per foot
Kilogram per sq. m	.00142	pounds per sq. inch
	.20482	pounds per sq. foot
	.0029	inches of mercury
	.00328	feet of water
	.1	grams per sq. centimeter
Kilometers	3,280.8	feet
	.62137	miles
	.53956	nautical miles
Kilometers per hr.	.91134	feet per second
	.53955	knots
	.62137	miles per hour
	.2777	meters per second
Kilowatts	.948	BTU per second
	737.7	foot-pounds per second
	1.341	horsepower
	.2389	kilogram calories per sec.

Miscellaneous Conversion Factors

Multiply	By	To obtain
Knots	1	nautical mile per hour
	1.6889	feet per second
	1,1516	miles per hour
	1.8532	kilometers per hour
	.51479	meters per second
Liters	1,000	cubic centimeters
	61.025	cubic inches
	.03532	cubic feet
	.26418	gallons
	.21998	imperial gallons
Meters (m)	39.37	inches
	3.2808	feet
	1.0936	yards
Meters per second	3.2808	feet per second
	2.2369	miles per hour
	3.6	kilometers per hour
	1.9451	knots
Miles (statute)	5,280	feet
	1.6093	kilometers
	.86839	nautical miles
Miles per hr. (mph)	1.4667	feet per second
	.44704	meters per second
	1.6093	kilometers per hour
	.86839	knots
Grams	15.432	grains
	.03527	ounces
	.0022	pounds
	1,000	milligrams
	.001	kilograms
	980.67	dynes

Miscellaneous Conversion Factors

Multiply	By	To obtain
Gram-calories	.00397	BTU
Grams per cm	.1	kilograms per meter
	.0672	pounds per foot
	.00559	pounds per inch
Grams per cu cm	1,000	kilograms per cu cm
	62.428	pounds per cu foot
Horsepower	33,000	foot-pounds per minute
	550	foot-pounds per second
	76.040	kilogram-meters per sec.
	1.0139	metric horsepower
Horsepower, metric	75	kilogram-meters per sec.
	.98632	horsepower
Horsepower-hours	2,545.1	BTU
	1,980,000	foot-pounds
	273,745	kilogram-meters
Inches	2.54	centimeters
Inches of mercury at 0°C.	.03342	atmospheres
	13.595	inches of water
	1.1329	feet of water
	.49116	pounds per sq. inch
	70.727	pounds per sq. foot
	345.32	kilograms per sq. meter
Inches of water	.07356	inches of mercury
	.18683	centimeters of mercury
	.03613	pounds per sq. inch
	5.1981	pounds per sq. foot
	25.4	kilograms per sq. meter

Miscellaneous Conversion Factors

Multiply	By	To obtain
Joules	$.9478 \times 10^{-3}$	BTU
	.7376	foot-pounds
	$.2388 \times 10^{-3}$	kilogram calories
	.10179	kilogram meters
	$.2777 \times 10^{-3}$	watt hours
	$.3725 \times 10^{-6}$	horsepower hours
	2.2046	pounds
Kilograms	32.274	ounces
	1,000	grams
	3.9685	BTU
Kilogram calories	3,087.4	foot-pounds
	426.85	kilogram-meters
Nautical miles	6080.2	feet
	.0625	pounds (avdp)
Ounces (avdp)	28.35	grams
	437.5	grains
Ounces, fluid	29.57	cubic centimeters
	1.805	cubic inches
Pounds	453.59	grams
	7,000	grains
	16	ounces
	32.174	poundals
Pounds per cu ft	16.018	kilograms per cu m
	.01602	grams per cu cm
Pounds per cu inch	1,728	pounds per cu ft
	27,680	grams per cu cm
Pounds per sq inch	2.0361	inches of mercury
	2.3066	feet of water
	.06805	atmospheres
	703.07	kilograms per sq meter

Miscellaneous Conversion Factors

Multiply	By	To obtain
	.07031	kilograms per sq cm
Radians	57.296	degrees (arc)
Radians per sec.	57.296	degrees per second
	.15916	revolutions per second
	9.8493	revolutions per minute
Revolutions	6.2832	radians
Revolutions per min.	.10472	radians per second
Square centimeters	.155	square inches
	.00108	square feet
Square feet	929.03	square centimeters
	144	square inches
	.0929	square meters
	.111	square yards
Square inches	645.16	square millimeters
	6.4516	square centimeters
Square kilometers	.3861	square miles
Square meters	10.764	square feet
	1.196	square yards
Square miles	2.59	square kilometers
	640	acres
Square yards	.83613	square meters
Yards	.9144	meters

For density altitude conversions, *see* DENSITY ALTITUDE.
For mach/knots conversions, *see* MACH.
For the effects of pressurization on cabin altitude, *see* PRESSURIZATION.

coordinated turn   A smooth turn accomplished by using the proper amount of aileron and rudder to prevent the airplane from either slipping or skidding. In a coordinated turn the ball in the turn-and-bank indicator remains centered.

coordinates   Latitudes and longitudes determining a given geographical point on the surface of the earth.

coordination fix   A fix where ATC facilities will turn the control of an IFR aircraft over from one to another.

copilot   The second in command, occupying the right seat in the cockpit.

copy   A term that refers to having received and understood a radio message, such as: "Did you copy?" It has nothing to do with writing it down.

coriolis force   A force caused by the rotation of the earth that, in the northern hemisphere, deflects moving bodies to the right of their course and has the opposite effect in the southern hemisphere. It does not have an effect on their velocity and it tends to make winds move parallel to the isobars.

corporate aviation   Aviation activity conducted by major corporations for the purpose of improving productivity. With the trend of locating factories and facilities away from major metropolitan areas, corporate aviation has become increasingly important. More than half of *Fortune* magazines's list of the 1,000 largest corporations operate their own aviation departments with fleets of aircraft.

correction   In aviation radio communication a phrase which means that an error has been made in the transmission.

Cougar   A light piston twin once manufactured by Gulfstream American Corporation. No longer in production.

coupler   A means of coupling an autopilot to any number and variety of nav instruments, such as a VOR, localizer, flight director, etc.

course   The planned direction of flight in the horizontal plane.

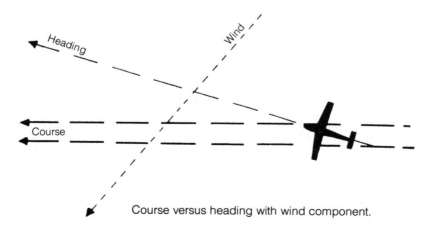

Course versus heading with wind component.

course   Any leg of an LF/MF range.

course deviation indicator (CDI)   The vertical needle of an omni-bearing indicator (OBI) that shows where the aircraft is in relation to the VOR radial selected on the omni-bearing selector (OBS). On course, the needle is centered. Off course, the radial is located in the direction that the needle has moved away from center.

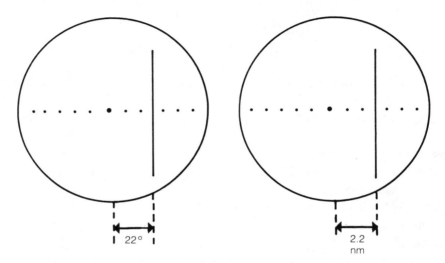

En route the CDI needle indicates *degrees* of deviation while in the approach phase it indicates *nautical miles* of deviation.

course line computer (CLC)   An integral part of area navigation systems, effecting the electronic relocation of VORTAC stations.

course selector   Omni-bearing selector (OBS).

cowl flap   A movable door or shutter in an engine cowling designed to regulate the flow of cooling air around the engine. It may be adjusted on the ground or in the air to achieve the desired cylinder head temperatures.

cowling   A removable cover or housing containing the engine or any other aircraft component.

crab   To turn partly into the wind to the right or left of course in order to compensate for wind drift.

crab angle   Wind correction angle.

crankshaft   A rotating shaft that, by means of the connecting rod, gives movement to the pistons in a reciprocating engine, as well as transferring piston motion to the propeller.

critical altitude   The highest altitude at which, due to decreasing atmospheric density, an airplane can maintain its maximum allowable continuous power setting. Above this altitude, even with full throttle, the power will begin to fall off. Turbocharging a reciprocating engine greatly increases the critical altitude.

critical angle-of-attack   *See* BURBLE POINT.

critical engine   The engine in a twin-engine aircraft that, if it fails, would most adversely affect the performance and handling characteristics of the aircraft.

cross-country   Any flight other than a local flight that requires some degree of navigation, usually to an airport 25 or more miles distant from the takeoff point. A cross-country flight returning to the point of departure without intermediate landing is referred to as a round-robin.

cross (fix) at (altitude)   An ATC clearance requiring the pilot to cross a certain fix at a given altitude.

cross (fix) at or above (altitude)   An ATC clearance requiring the pilot to cross a certain fix at or above a given altitude.

crossing altitude   The minimum altitude that must be maintained when crossing a given fix or area.

cross pointer instrument   An instrument such as the combination localizer/glide scope indicator or certain flight director pictorial displays that require coordinating separate vertical and horizontal readings on one instrument.

crosswind   Wind blowing at any angle across the line of flight and causing the aircraft to drift.

crosswind component   The wind component in knots, at 90 degrees to the direction of the runway or course. It can be figured out using the wind-correction portion of the average E6b, or similar, flight computer. If a calculator or computer is handy, the algorithm is:

Wind Component = − 1 * Wind Velocity * COS((Wind Direction − Magnetic Course − Magnetic Variation) /57.2958)

and the ground speed will be:

Ground Speed = True Airspeed + Wind Component

crosswind leg   A flight plan at right angles to the landing runway off its upwind side.

CRS   Course.

CRT   Cathode ray tube.

cruise   To fly at a speed a given percentage below maximum power at a constant altitude, which results in good range and economy.

cruise   A phrase used by ATC in a clearance to indicate that the pilot may climb to the assigned altitude and may leave it at his own discretion.

cruise climb   Climbing at an angle less than that required for the best rate of climb. Though it takes longer to arrive at the desired altitude, it is more comfortable for pilot and passenger, tends to keep the engine cooler, and covers a greater distance during climb.

cruise performance chart A chart in aircraft flight manuals showing the various cruise speeds that can be maintained at various altitudes with varying rpm and manifold pressure settings. It also shows fuel consumption and maximum range for each combination.

cruising altitude Altitudes at which aircraft should cruise under various conditions, according to the hemispherical rules.

cruising speed Any speed in level flight, usually resulting from a power setting recommended in the appropriate cruise performance chart.

CSDRBL Considerable.

CST Coast.

CS/T Combined station and tower facility.

CTC Contact.

CTL Control.

CTLD Controlled.

Cuban eight A maneuver in which the airplane completes about three fourths of a normal loop, rolls over and repeats the loop portion in the other direction, resulting in a vertical figure eight pattern.

Cubic Corporation Manufacturer of training systems, data links, simulators, radars, antennas. (9333 Balboa Avenue, San Diego, CA 92138. (619) 277-6780.)

cumuliform Clouds having rounded or dome-shaped upper surfaces with some protuberances. They usually have flat bases and are formed by rising convection currents in unstable air, and occur separated from each other by downward currents, leading to turbulence in the vicinity of the clouds.

cumulonimbus A cumuliform cloud with a dark base and extensive vertical development, usually producing thunderstorms. Also called thunderheads.

Cumulonimbus cloud in the formation stage.

cumulus   Cumuliform cloud that develops vertically from a low flat bottom to a billowing top. It is not as high as a cumulonimbus.

customs facilities   Facilities available at international airports, airports of entry and, upon prior notification, at certain other airports, to check international flights into and out of the country. When returning to the U.S. from another country, it is advisable to time the arrival to coincide with the hours during which customs facilities are staffed by on-duty personnel, as overtime charges can be rather steep.

Cutlass   A retractable-gear single-engine piston aircraft manufactured by Cessna Aircraft Company. No longer in production.

Cessna Cutlass RG.

CVR   *See* COCKPIT VOICE RECORDER.

CVR   Cover.

Cyclic pitch control   The control stick of a helicopter used to induce pitch or roll.

cyclone   A low pressure area.

cyclone   A storm occurring in a low pressure area.

cylinder   The hollow tube-like structure in a reciprocating engine in which the piston moves back and forth. It forms the circular wall of the combustion chamber.

cylinder head temperature   The temperature generated by the combustion chamber.

cylinder head temperature gauge (CHT)   An engine instrument that indicates the heat being produced by the combustion chamber in reciprocating engines. Usually calibrated in degrees F. A green arc indicates the normal operating temperature range and a red line or arc indicates that the engine is overheating. Overheating of a reciprocating engine is usually the result of pre-ignition or detonation and can produce catastrophic engine failure within a very short period of time. (Pages 151-152)

Cylinder-head temperature gauge (CHT) for a four-cylinder single-engine aircraft.

ALCOR Incorporated

Cylinder head temperature gauge (CHT) for a twin-engine aircraft. It reads only the hottest cylinder in each engine.

ALCOR Incorporated

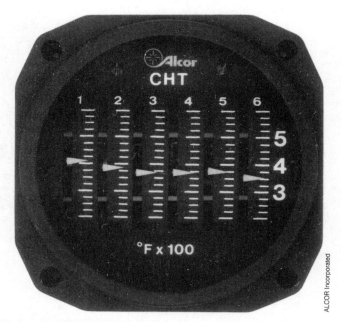

Cylinder head temperature gauge (CHT) vertical readout for a six-cylinder single-engine air-craft.

D Day (instrument approach charts.)

D Delta (in the phonetic alphabet.)

D Dust (in sequence reports.)

DABRK Daybreak.

DABS Discrete-address beacon system.

Dakota A single-engine aircraft manufactured by Piper Aircraft Corporation.

Piper Aircraft Corporation

Piper Dakota.

DALGT Daylight.

Daniel Systems, Inc. Aviation software programs/systems: maintenance, spares inventory, flight logs, trip and crew planning, passenger reservations, preparation of FAA in special programs for FAR 91 and 125 aircraft. (4391 N.W. 150th Street #A, Opa Locka Airport, FL 33054-2360. (305) 685-6286.)

Dash 7 A four-engine turboprop aircraft with STOL capabilities, manufactured by Boeing of Canada, deHavilland Division. (Page 154)

de Havilland Dash 7 four-engine turboprop.

Dash 8/400   A stretched twin-engine turboprop aircraft with STOL capabilities, manufactured by Boeing of Canada, deHavilland Division.

de Havilland Dash-8 twin-turboprop.

Dassault   *See* FALCON JET.

Data link   A phrase used to describe technology in which computers communicate with one another, issuing and accepting commands.

Dauphin   A family of turbine helicopters manufactured by Aerospatiale in France.

Davtron, Inc.   Manufacturer of digital clocks, VORs, ADFs, digital readout for encoding altimeters, and aircraft instruments. (427 Hillcrest Way, Redwood City, CA 94062. (415) 369-1188.)

dB   Decibel.

DBA   Doing business as . . ..

DC   Direct current (electric).

DCE   Distance calculating equipment.

DCR Decrease.

dead reckoning A method of navigation by which the course and time of an aircraft between two given points is estimated by taking course, speed and wind components calculated with a wind triangle into consideration. Applicable only in VFR conditions. The phrase "dead" has nothing to do with death, but is a bastardization of the terms deduced reckoning.

dead-stick landing A landing made without engine power, usually only in an emergency.

Decathlon One of the Champion family of sport aircraft that were manufactured by Bellanca Aircraft Corporation. No longer in production.

deceleration A decrease in velocity and the rate at which such decrease takes place.

decibel A unit for expressing the relative intensity of sound on a scale from zero for the average least perceptible sound to about 130 for the average sound intensity producing physical pain.

decision height (DH) The altitude at which a pilot making a precision instrument approach (ILS or PAR) must have the airport in sight in order to legally continue the approach. If the airport is not in sight, he must make a missed approach.

decoder A device used in ATC radar operations to differentiate among signals received from transponders, resulting in their display as selected codes on the radar scope.

ded reckoning Dead reckoning.

deepening Increasingly low air pressure in a moving low, usually in its center.

defense visual flight rules (DVFR) Rules applicable to operations within an air defense indentification zone (ADIZ) under visual flight rules.

Defiant A kit-built push-pull twin-engine four-seat aircraft designed and built by Burt Rutan, distinguished by the typical Rutan canard wings. The kits are no longer being produced. *See* RUTAN AIRPLANE FACTORY.

deflation port The opening in a hot-air or gas balloon that can be operated by the pilot and, when opened, permits hot air or gas to escape, thus either stopping ascent or producing descent. (Page 156)

DEG Degree.

de-icing equipment *See* ANTI-ICING EQUIPMENT.

deHavilland Division *See* BOEING OF CANADA, LTD.

Delay indefinite because (reason), expect approach/further clearance at (time) Phrase used by ATC to inform the pilot of a delay for which an accurate time estimate is not available.

Delco Electronics Corporation Manufacturer of avionics and computer guidance navigation systems. (700 East Firmin Street, MS A211, Kokomo, IN 46902. (317) 451-2353.)

delta In aviation radio phraseology the term for the letter D.

Hot-air balloon with the deflation port partly open.

DEMOL Demolition.

DEMSND Decommissioned.

denalt computer A small computer used to determine density altitude.

density altitude Pressure altitude corrected for prevailing temperature conditions. Awareness of density altitude is important in calculating takeoff distance and climb performance, especially when operating to or from an airport at a high elevation. The following table shows the density altitude at various elevations under given temperature conditions. (Page 157)

departure control An ATC service that monitors and directs IFR, and in some instances VFR, traffic at a controlled airport.

Density Altitude Conversion Table

ELEVATION	Temperature in degrees F./C.										
	97/36	90/32	82/28	75/24	68/20	61/16	54/12	47/8	39/4	32/0	25/-4
Sea level	2500	2100	1600	1100	600	100	-400	-900	-1400	-1900	-2300
500	3100	2700	2200	1800	1300	800	300	-200	-700	-1200	-1600
1000	3700	3200	2800	2400	1900	1400	900	500	-100	-600	-1100
1500	4300	3900	3400	3000	2500	2000	1500	1100	600	100	-500
2000	4900	4500	4000	3600	3100	2600	2200	1700	1200	700	200
2500	5500	5100	4600	4200	3700	3200	2800	2300	1800	1300	800
3000	6300	5700	5200	4800	4300	3800	3400	2900	2500	2000	1500
3500	6800	6300	5900	5400	4900	4400	4000	3500	3100	2600	2100
4000	7500	7000	6600	5900	5500	5000	4600	4100	3700	3200	2700
4500	8000	7500	7100	6500	6000	5500	5100	4600	4200	3600	3200
5000	8500	8000	7600	7100	6500	6100	5600	5200	4700	4200	3700
5500	9100	8600	8200	7700	7100	6700	6200	5800	5300	4700	4300
6000	9700	9200	8800	8300	7800	7300	6900	6400	5900	5300	4900
6500	10300	9800	9400	8800	8400	7800	7400	7000	6400	6000	5600
7000	10800	10400	10000	9500	9000	8500	8100	7600	7100	6700	6200
7500	11400	11000	10600	10200	9700	9200	8700	8300	7800	7300	6800
8000	12100	11600	11200	10800	10300	9800	9200	8800	8400	7900	7500

These figures have been rounded off, but are sufficiently accurate for everyday use. To determine the actual density altitude, the mathematical formula which can be entered into a computer or calculator program is as follows:

The constant used in the formula is

C = 288.15

and the variables used in the algorithm are:

PA = Pressure Altitude in feet (read at 29.92 in Hg)
DC = Degrees Centigrade
DA = Density Altitude in feet

$$DA = (145426.0*(1-(((C-PA*.001981)/C)^{5.2563}/((273.15+DC)/C))^{0.235}))$$

where the variable DA represents the exact density altitude.

departure leg   The airborne path of an aircraft immediately after takeoff.

departure time   The time at which an aircraft becomes airborne.

DEP CON   Departure control.

depression   A low pressure air mass.

depth perception   The ability to judge distances with reasonable accuracy.

DER   Designated engineering representative of the FAA.

descending turn   A turn made during a descent, usually to a predetermined heading, using power appropriate to maintain constant airspeed and rate of descent.

designated engineering representative   A person designated by the FAA and authorized to issue supplementary type certificates.

detonation   The burning of a fuel-and-air mixture by explosion rather than steady burning. It tends to occur when the wrong grade of fuel is used and results in rapidly rising cylinder head temperatures. Prolonged detonation will bring about catastrophic engine failure.

DEV   Deviation.

deviation   The error in the reading of a magnetic compass induced by installation or by magnetic disturbances in the aircraft. It is the difference between the magnetic heading and the compass reading. Such errors are recorded on the compass-deviation card that must be displayed in the cockpit.

deviation card   Compass correction card.

DeVore Aviation Corporation   Manufacturer of aircraft tail floodlighting, bleed air systems, vented fuel-recovery systems, PLASIs (approach lights), and seaplane and amphibious floats. (6104-B Kircher Blvd. N.E., Albuquerque, NM 87109. (505) 345-8713.)

DEW   Distant early warning.

DEWIZ   Distant early warning identification zone.

dew point   The temperature to which air must cool in order for condensation to take place without change in pressure or vapor content.

DF   Direction finder.

DF approach procedure   This procedure is used under emergency conditions when an alternate instrument procedure is unavailable or cannot be executed. Such DF guidance is given by ATC facilities with DF capability.

DF fix   The geographical location of an airplane in flight, obtained by using one or more direction finders.

DF guidance   DF steer.

DF steer   When giving a DF steer to an aircraft, a facility equipped with DF capability gives the aircraft specific headings to fly which, when followed, will guide the aircraft to an airport, back on its course, or to any other predetermined point. DF steers are given aircraft in distress and other aircraft upon request by the pilot. Pilots are encouraged to request practice DF steers as controllers and/or flight service specialists are supposed to give a certain number of DF steers over a fixed period of time in order to stay proficient. Practice DF steers are given on a workload-permitting basis.

DFUS   Diffuse.

DG   Directional gyro compass.

DH   Decision height.

digital computer   A type of electronic computer that translates all information input into combinations of two digits (zero and one, or plus and minus, or positive and negative), performs the necessary calculations and then translates its two-digit language into whatever comprehendible type of readout is desired. Today, virtually all computers used in aviation are the digital type.

digital timers Timers and clocks with no moving parts that display time or elapsed time in digital form.

Digital Timers

MANUFACTURER	MODEL	PRICE	POWER A	B	HOURS	TIME	COUNT U	D	#	X	ALARM V	A	lbs	REMARKS
Astrotech	LC-2	129.50		¤	12/24	24-hr			1				4oz	Lights 14/28 VDC
Astrotech	LC-6	349.00		¤	12/24	24-hr		¤	6*			¤	4oz	* selectable.
Astrotech	LC-2P	169.00		¤	12/24	24-hr			1				4oz	for Piper control wheels
Astrotech	LC-6P	349.00		¤	12/24	24-hr		¤	6*			¤	4oz	* selectable.

PRICE:		uninstalled
POWER	A:	aircraft electrical system
	B:	separate battery
HOURS:		time of day, 12 or 24 hours
TIME:		displays elapsed time to minutes
COUNT	U:	count up to minutes
	D:	count down to minutes
#:		number of displays
X:		automatically activated by external signal
ALARM	V:	visual alarm
	A:	audio alarm

Digital timer.

digitizer   The instrument that reads the altitude off the altimeter and transmits that information to the transponder.

dihedral   The angle at which the wing is attached upward from the horizontal axis of the airframe. Also applies to the horizontal tail and other airfoils.

direct   Flight in a straight line between two points or fixes. When IFR pilots fly off airways direct, any point used to define the direct route segments becomes a compulsory reporting point unless the aircraft is in radar contact.

direct entry   One of the three recommended (but not compulsory) means of entering a holding pattern. In a direct entry the pilot flies along one leg of the holding pattern directly toward the fix and, when passing the fix, turns right and flies the pattern.

directional gyro   A gyroscopic flight instrument that, when set to conform with the magnetic compass, will continue to indicate the aircraft heading for some time. It tends to gradually develop heading errors (preset) and must be adjusted intermittently by the pilot.

direction finder (DF)   A direction finder is a radio receiver that is equipped with a directional sensing antenna capable of taking bearings on a radio transmitter when that transmitter is being activated. When using DF to guide a pilot, the controller or flight service specialist will ask the pilot to depress the transmit button on his mike for a given number of seconds, which then enables the controller to determine the position of the aircraft. DF services are provided by control towers and FSSs listed in Part 2 of AIM.

dirigible   A lighter-than-air craft equipped with a power source and a means of directional control.

DISCNTD   Discontinued.

discrete address beacon system (DABS)   The DABS surveillance system is similar to ATCRBS in that there are ground interrogators and airborne transponders. DABS, however, provides garble-free replies, better quality data, and a means of implementing a digital data link. Each DABS interrogation is addressed to one specific aircraft, which then replies only after it has recognized its own address rather than replying to all interrogators within line of sight.

discrete code   Any one of the 4,096 codes that can be selected in a Mode 3-A transponder except those ending in two zeroes. (0020; 2301; 4356 etc.) Non-discrete codes are used by radar facilities that are incapable of discrete decoding and some are reserved for special use: 1200/VFR; 7600/two-way communication radio failure; 7700/emergency; 3500/being hijacked.

discrete frequency   A separate frequency being used by a controller in dealing with one or a limited number of aircraft, thus reducing frequency congestion.

displaced threshold   The touchdown point located on a runway at a point other than the beginning of that runway.

dissymmetry of lift   The difference in lift produced by the advancing and retreating motion of a helicopter blade during each rotation cycle.

DIST   District.

distance calculating equipment   A cockpit instrument developed by Collins Avionics Division that is capable of calculating distance to station, time to station and ground speed, as long as the aircraft is within reception distance of two VORs. Unlike DME, it can operate with standard VORs and does not require that the navaids be VORTACs. It uses input from standard on-board VOR receivers to effect its computation and the digital readout shows distance or time to the station, ground speed, or the bearing to either station. While capable of performing most functions normally obtained from a DME, it cannot be legally used during instrument approaches that require a DME.

distance from VOR   By flying at a distance past a VOR the distance from the VOR can be calculated by noting the time it takes to pass a given number of radials, assuming the ground speed is known. Or ground speed can similarly be calculated if the distance from the VOR is known. The formula for this computation looks like this:

Time between radials in seconds divided by degrees of radial change equals minutes to the station. Or, ground speed (if not known, use TAS) times the time in minutes between radials divided by the number of degrees of radial change equals miles to the station. (Statute miles if speed is figured in mph, nautical miles if speed is figured in knots.)

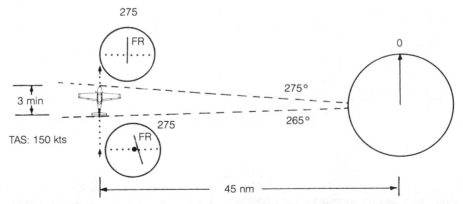

If it takes an aircraft flying at 150 knots three minutes to cross 10 degrees of radials, the distance to the station is 150 times 3 divided by 10 = 45 nautical miles.

distance measuring equipment (DME)   A combination of airborne and ground equipment that gives a distance reading from the airplane to the ground station by measuring the time lapse of a signal generated in the airplane and bounced off the ground station. The recorded distance is the slant range in nm from the airplane to the station. The difference between the slant range and the actual horizontal distance is of no practical consequence at altitudes below 18,000 feet when approximately 10 or more miles from the station. When closer to the station, both distance and ground-speed readings become unreliable. Some very sophisticated and expensive DMEs, designed primarily for use in airliners and corporate jets, automatically compute the slant range and produce reliable readouts regardless of altitude and distance from the station. (Page 163)

Distance Measuring Equipment (DME)

MANUFACTURER	MODEL	PRICE	VOLT	RANGE	+/-	MINS	KTS	CHNL	DISPLAY D	E	M	G	HOLD	LBS	REMARKS
Bendix/King	KN 62A	4,515	14/28	389	.1	99	999	200	¤		¤	¤		2.6	Silver Crown
Bendix/King	KN 63	6,850	14/28	389	.1	99	999	200	¤		¤	¤		3.6	Silver Crown
Bendix/King	KN 64	2,085	14/28	389	.1	99	999	200	¤		¤	¤		2.6	Silver Crown
Bendix/King	KDM 706	9,590 11,295	28	389	.1	99	999	252	¤		¤	¤		4.7	Gold Crown, w/o ind. 5.5 with indicator
Bendix/King	DMS 44	15,690	28	300	.1	1199	999	200	¤		¤	¤		9.32	Series III
Collins	DME-42	n/a	28	300		120	999	252	¤		¤	¤		3.3	ProLine II
Collins	DME-442	n/a	28	300		120	999	252	¤		¤	¤		3.3	Same. ARINC 429 int.
Foster AirData	DME670	n/a	28	400	.1	yes		200	¤	¤		¤		5.8	Displays data from 2 nav receivers

PRICE: uninstalled
VOLT: input
RANGE: display range in nm
+/-:   accuracy in nm
MINS: time to station in minutes (0 to x)
KTS: ground speed in knots (0 to x)
CHNL: number channels
DISPLAY:
          D: digital;
          E: electric;
          M: mechanical;
          G: gas discharge
HOLD: hold feature
RNAV: RNAV compatible
lbs.:   weight in pounds

DME single system digital display.

DME master and slave units.

ditching   Making an emergency off-airport landing.

dive   A steep descent with or without power at a speed greater than normal.

dive brakes   Spoiler-type systems in the wings of some jet aircraft and all gliders that, when extended, produce drag and, in turn, reduce airspeed.

DL   Direct line (interphone).

DLA   Delay.

DME   Distance measuring equipment.

DME fix   A geographical point determined by reference to DME instrument readings. Shown on instrument approach charts in terms of distance in nm and radial degrees from the appropriate navaid.

DME separation   Separation of aircraft in terms of nm determined by using DME.

DMSH   Diminish.

DN   Day and night (on instrument approach charts.)

DNS   Dense.

DNSLP   Downslope.

DO   Ditto.

DOD   Department of Defense.

DOD FLIP   Department of Defense Flight Information Publications.

doldrums   The general circulation pattern of a calm or light and variable wind around the equator between the two regions of tradewinds.

dope   A glue-like varnish used to fill the weave and weatherproof fabric surfaces of aircraft.

Doppler effect   A change in the frequency with which sound, light or radio waves from a given source reach an observer when the source and the observer are in rapid motion with respect to one another, so that the frequency increases or decreases according to the speed with which the distance is increasing or decreasing. (Named after Christian J. Doppler.)

Doppler radar   A radar system that uses the Doppler effect for measuring velocity.

Dorne & Margolin, Inc.   Designer and manufacturer of airborne, mobile and portable antennas for communications, satellite communication, navigation, data link, interrogation and EW purposes operating in the 30 MHz to 16 GHz and Omega frequencies; antenna couplers, ELTs, portable ELT homing systems. (2950 Veterans Memorial Highway, Bohemia, NY 11716. (516) 585-4000.)

Dornier GmbH   Manufacturer of the Dornier 228 corporate or regional airline twin turboprop aircraft, powered by two Garrett TPE 331-5 fixed-shaft engines. The aircraft features a rectangular fuselage that results in exceptional cabin headroom and legroom. In the regional airline configuration it can accommodate up to 20 seats. In the corporate configuration interior designers can add toilets, galleys, or any other convenience. The aircraft is designed to be operated on wheels or skis in corporate, passenger, cargo, or emergency medical service. In addition, the company is developing the Model 328 pressurized 30-passenger commuter aircraft, with first flight expected in 1990 and customer deliveries slated to begin in late 1991 or early 1992. Unlike the 228, the $5 million 328 will have a T-tail and a somewhat wider cabin to allow for three-abreast seating. (P.O. Box 2160, 8000 Munich, West Germany. Phone: 0 89-84 1080. U.S. sales office: Dornier Aviation, 1213 Jefferson Davis Highway, Suite 1001, Arlington, VA 22202. (703) 769-7228.)

Dornier Aviation Incorporated

Dornier 238.

DOS   Disk operating system. The operating system used by microcomputers to operate the data storage media such as floppy or hard disks.

DOT   Department of Transportation.

Downdraft   A convection current that moves downward. Popularly and falsely called *air pocket*.

Downwind Moving in the direction in which the wind is blowing; or being located on the lee side of a mountain or other geographic point.

Downwind landing A landing made with the wind rather than into it and used only in emergencies or occasionally under light wind conditions in order to expedite traffic. It results in a longer landing roll and, under adverse conditions, can cause the aircraft to run off the end of the runway.

Downwind leg The flight path parallel to the landing runway in the direction opposite to landing. It is part of the standard traffic pattern.

DP Deep.

DPNG Deepening.

DPTG Departing.

DPTR Departure.

Drag The force created by the friction of the air on objects in motion. It must be overcome by thrust in order to achieve flight parallel to the relative wind. There are two types of drag, induced drag and parasite drag. Induced drag is drag created through the process of producing lift. Parasite drag is all drag from surfaces that do not contribute to lift. It increases with an increase in airspeed.

Drag chute A type of parachute that can be deployed from the rear of an aircraft in order to reduce the landing roll.

Dragging The lead or lag capability of each helicopter rotor blade in relation to each other rotor blade.

DRFT Drift.

Drift The gradual displacement of an airplane from its course as the result of a steady crosswind component.

Drift angle The off-course angle that is corrected by the wind-correction angle.

Drizzle Precipitation of tiny droplets, usually from stratus clouds. Shown in sequence reports as L.

Droop stops Means of preventing articulated helicopter rotor blades from drooping too close to the ground during start-up and shutdown.

Drop line A rope, usually approximately 150 feet long, carried in balloons and dropped to the ground to slow lateral movement or to facilitate assistance in landing by the ground crew.

DRZL Drizzle.

DSB Double sideband.

DSIPT Dissipate.

dsnt distant.

Dual control Having a double set of controls in the cockpit, permitting either pilot or copilot (or instructor or student) to control the aircraft.

duty priorities The order in which services must be provided by ATC controllers and FSS specialists.

ATC controller priorities:

1) Separation of aircraft and issuing radar safety advisories.
2) Other required services not involving separation of aircraft.
3) Additional services to the extent possible.
4) Priorities with reference to emergencies must be left at the controller's discretion because of the great variety of possible emergency situations.

FSS specialist priorities:

1) Action involving emergencies in which life or property might be in immediate danger.
2) Action required because of navaid malfunctions.
3) Service to airborne aircraft.
4) Weather observations and PIREPs.
5) Preflight pilot briefings.
6) Unscheduled broadcasts.
7) Teletype operations.
8) Transcribed weather broadcasts and pilot automatic telephone weather answering service.
9) Scheduled broadcasts.

DVFR Defense visual flight rules.

DVLP Develop.

DX Duplex.

Duchess A light piston twin once manufactured by Beech Aircraft Corporation. No longer in production.

Beechcraft Duchess.

Duke A heavy, pressurized piston twin, once manufactured by Beech Aircraft Corporation. No longer in production.

Beech Aircraft Corporation

Beechcraft Duke.

duplex Simultaneously using two frequencies, one for transmitting, the other for receiving.

DURG During.

E East.

E Eastern Standard Time.

E Echo (in the phonetic alphabet).

E Equatorial air mass.

E Estimated (in sequence reports).

E Sleet (in sequence reports).

E6b A circular slide rule type of flight computer. The name is a leftover from some obscure military origin and has absolutely no meaning. *See also* FLIGHT COMPUTER.

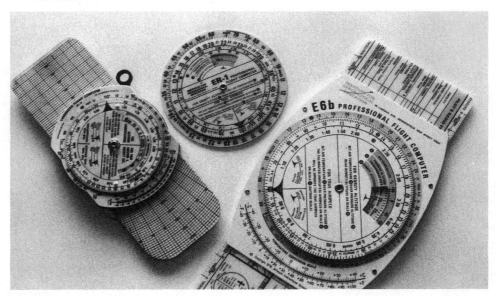

E6b flight computer.

EAA Experimental Aircraft Association.

EAS Equivalent airspeed.

echo The term used in aviation-radio phraseology for the letter E.

eddy   A local whirling current of air different from the general flow, usually given in feet msl.

Edo Corporation   Manufacturer of floats for different general aviation aircraft. (14-04 111 Street, College Point, NY 11356. (718) 445-6000.) (Page 171)

Aircraft Approved to be Used with Edo Floats

FLOAT MODEL	AIRCRAFT MFR.	MODELS
1650A	Cessna	150, G, H, J, K
	Piper	PA-18, S125, S135, S150
	Champion	7ECA, 7GCAA, 7KCAB, 7GCBC
2000, 2000A	Arctic	Tern S1B2
	Cessna	170, A, B; 172A through N
	Piper	PA-12, -20 S135, -22 S135, S150, S160, -28 S160, S180, -18 S150, AS150
	Champion	7GCBC, 8GCBC
	Aeronca	S15AC
2440B	Cessna	172 Plus II, D, E, F, G, H, I, K; 172 XP, R172K
	Maule	M4 210T, 220 C, S, T, M5 210C, 220C, 235C, M6, M7
3430	Cessna	206, P206, A, U206, A thru G, TP206, Turbo 206, TU206 A thru G, 185, A185E, A185F
	Piper	PA-32 S300
	Helio	H250, H295/800
2790	Cessna	180, G, H, J, K, 185 A thru F, A185E, A185F
2960	Cessna	180 G, H, J, K, 185 A thru F, A185E, A185F
4930	DeHavilland	Piston Beaver DHC2
	Pilatus	Porter
	Piper	Aztec E Nomad
	Sea	Thrush
2130	Cessna	172, L, M, N, P, Cutlass II
	Bellanca	Scout 8GCBC
3500	Cessna	U206, TU 206, 1285
	Helio	H295/800
2500	Maule	M5 235, M6 235, M7 235

Cessna equipped with Edo amphibious floats.

EDO Corporation

Cessna equipped with Edo seaplane floats.

EDT Eastern Daylight Time.

EFCTV Effective.

EFIS *See* ELECTRONIC FLIGHT INSTRUMENTATION SYSTEM.

EGT Exhaust gas temperature gauge.

EHF Extremely high frequency (30,000 to 300,000 MHz).

Elastomeric bearings. Bearing consisting of bonded elastomers and metal in sandwich layers, said to be exceptionally maintenance free.

electronic flight instrumentation system A family of flight instruments that include as displays cathode ray tubes on which computer-generated images replace the analog images used in conventional instruments. Cockpits equipped with EFIS instruments are referred to as "glass cockpits." (Page 172)

Electronic Flight Instrument Systems (EFIS)

| MANUFACTURER | MODEL | PRICE | VOLT | TUBES | ADI | HSI | DISPLAYS RADAR degress with | | | | ALTITUDE | REMARKS |
							NO DATA	NAV	VOR/CDI	HSI		
Bendix/King	EFS-10	118,885	28VDC	3 5x5	¤	¤	120	360	120	360	55,000	2/strke/rstr
		134,400	28VDC	4 5x5	¤	¤	120	360	120	360	55,000	2/strke/rstr
		186,085	28VDC	5 5x5	¤	¤	120	360	120	360	55,000	2/strke/rstr
Collins	EFIS-85A	n/a	28VDC	5 5x5	¤	¤	120	360	120	360	n/a	5x6" avail.
Collins	EFIS-86A	n/a	28VDC	5 5x5	¤	¤	120	360	120	360	n/a	5x6" avail.
Collins	EFIS-85B	n/a	28VDC	5 5x5	¤	¤	120	360	120	360	n/a	5x6" avail.
Collins	EFIS-86B	n/a	28VDC	5 5x5	¤	¤	120	360	120	360	n/a	5x6" avail.

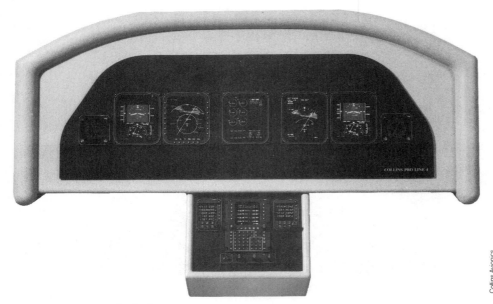

Collins Avionics

Different types of EFIS displays.

Bendix/King Avionics

EFIS display showing weather radar display superimposed over nav display and the way-points for the route around the heavy weather.

Electronique Aerospatiale   Manufacturer of a variety of avionics equipment (B.P. No. 4, 93350 Aeroport le Bourget, France.)

ELEV   Elevation.

elevation The height of airports, terrain features, or man-made objects on the ground, generally given in feet msl.

elevator A primary control surface attached to the horizontal stabilizer that can be moved up or down to control the pitch of the aircraft with reference to its lateral axis.

ELSW Elsewhere.

ELT Emergency locator transmitter.

Embraer Aircraft Corporation A Brazilian manufacturer of a family of turboprop aircraft used in commuter and corporate service. The two models that are original Embraer designs and are in production are the EMB 120 Brasilia and the EMB-110 Banderante. (The company also manufactures other types of aircraft under contracts with Piper and other manufacturers.) (U.S. address: Ft. Lauderdale International Airport, 276 SW 34th Street, Ft. Lauderdale, FL 33315.)

Embraer Aircraft

	EMB-110 P1 Bandeirante	EMB-110 P2 Bandeirante	EMB-120 Brasilia
ENGINES	Pratt & Whitney	Pratt & Whitney	Pratt & Whitney
MODEL	PT6A-34	PT6A-34	PW118
RATING shp	750	750	1,800
PROPELLER	Hartzell	Hartzell	Hamilton Standard
blades	3	3	4
RAMP WEIGHT pounds	12,662	12,566	25,529
TAKEOFF WEIGHT pounds	12,500	12,500	25,353
LANDING WEIGHT pounds	12,500	12,500	24,802
ZERO FUEL WEIGHT pounds	12,015	12,015	23,148
EMPTY WEIGHT pounds	7,751	7,751	15,082
BASIC OPERATING WEIGHT pounds	8,415	8,309	15,869
WING SPAN	50.26 ft.	50.26 ft.	64.90 ft.
LENGTH	49.54 ft.	49.54 ft.	65.62 ft.
HEIGHT	16.54 ft.	16.54 ft.	20.87 ft.
CABIN LENGTH	31.2 ft.	31.2 ft.	30.77 ft.
WIDTH	5.24 ft.	5.24 ft.	6.9 ft.
HEIGHT	5.24 ft.	5.24 ft.	5.77 ft.
FUEL usable, pounds	2,884	2,884	5,732
SPEED, maximum, knots	221	221	300
long range, knots	181	181	246
RANGE, with full load	800	800	780
TAKEOFF FIELD LENGTH	4,000 ft	4,000 ft.	4,659 ft.
LANDING FIELD LENGTH	4,400 ft.	4,400 ft.	4,495 ft.
RATE OF CLIMB, 2 engines	1,650 fpm	1,650 fpm	2,120 fpm
1 engine	340 fpm	340 fpm	675 fpm
SERVICE CEILING, 2 engines	21,500 ft.	21,500 ft.	29,800 ft.
1 engine	9,500 ft.	9,500 ft.	17,200 ft.

The EMB-120 Brasilia is being certificated for Garrett TPE331-16 twin turboprops driving twin pusher propellers for increased performance and reduced noise.

Emergency Beacon Corporation   Manufacturer of a family of emergency locator transmitters, direction finders and airborne monitors that respond with audio and visual indications to ELT signals. (P.O. Box 1291, 15 River Street, New Rochelle, NY 10801. (914) 576-2700.)

emergency, declaring an emergency   A pilot declaring an emergency for whatever reason, automatically has the right of way over all other aircraft (except balloons). Once the emergency is over, he is expected to make a detailed report about it to the FAA.

emergency frequency   Civil: 121.5 MHz; military: 243.0 MHz. Both frequencies are continually guarded by most but not all FAA facilities. Also called guard frequencies.

emergency locator transmitter   A transmitter carried aboard the aircraft that is automatically activated by the impact during a crash or by immersion in water. It can also be activated by the pilot. When activated it transmits a wailing tone on the two emergency frequencies, permitting DF-equipped aircraft to determine the location of the transmitter and, in turn, of the aircraft in trouble.

emergency radar flight patterns   Triangular flight patterns flown by a pilot to indicate to an ATC controller that an emergency exists. If both transmitter and receiver are inoperative, the pattern is flown to the left. If the transmitter is inoperative but the receiver is working, the pattern is flown to the right. In each instance each leg of the triangular pattern is flown for two minutes with all turns made at one half standard rate. The pattern is to be flown twice and repeated at 20-minute intervals. Tests flown by pilots to determine the effectiveness of this procedure have proved that it is seldom spotted and that it hardly ever works in a radar environment with a great deal of traffic activity.

EMGCY   Emergency. (Pages 175-176)

empennage   The tail section of an aircraft, including horizontal and vertical stabilizers, rudder, and elevators.

empty operating weight   The weight of an aircraft including all necessary equipment but excluding fuel.

empty weight   The weight of the aircraft itself including all undrainable fluids. The figure is always given in the aircraft flight manual. Any optional equipment installed must be added to the empty weight in weight-and-balance calculations.

encoding altimeter   Altitude encoder.

ENDG   Ending.

endurance   The time an aircraft can stay aloft at the current rate of fuel consumption, based on the amount of fuel on board and the fuel-burn rate. To figure the endurance divide the IFR range or the no-reserve range by the ground speed. For the formula to figure the range data, see range or conversion tables.

ENG   Engine.

Visual emergency signals

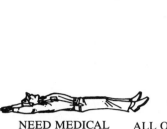

NEED MEDICAL
ASSISTANCE—URGENT
Used only when life

ALL OK—DO NOT WAIT
Wave one arm
overhead

CAN PROCEED SHORTLY—
WAIT IF PRATICABLE
One arm horizontal

NEED MECHANICAL HELP
OR PARTS—LONG DELAY
Both arms horizontal

USE DROP MESSAGE
Make throwing motion

OUR RECEIVER IS
OPERATING
Cup hands over ears

DO NOT ATTEMPT
TO LAND HERE
Both arms waved
across face

LAND HERE
Both arms forward
horizontally, squatting and
point in direction of
landing-Repeat

NEGATIVE (NO)
White cloth
waved horizontally

AFFIRMATIVE (YES)
White cloth
waved vertically

PICK US UP—
PLANE ABANDONED
Both arms vertical

AFFIRMATIVE (YES)
Dip nose of plane
several times

NEGATIVE (NO)
Fishtail plane

HOW TO USE THEM

If you are forced down and are able to attract the attention of the pilot of a rescue airplane, the body signals illustrated on this page can be used to transmit messages to him as he circles over your location, as seen from the air. Go through the motions slowly and repeat each signal until you are positive that the pilot understands you.

GROUND-AIR VISUAL CODE FOR USE BY SURVIVORS

NO.	MESSAGE	CODE SYMBOL
1	Require assistance	V
2	Require medical assistance	X
3	No or Negative	N
4	Yes or Affirmative	Y
5	Proceeding in this direction	C

IF IN DOUBT, USE INTERNATIONAL SYMBOL   SOS

INSTRUCTIONS

1. Lay out symbols by using strips of fabric or parachutes, pieces of wood, stones, or any available material.
2. Provide as much color contrast as possible between material used for symbols and background against which symbols are exposed.
3. Symbols should be at least 10 feet high or larger. Card whould be taken to lay out symbols exactly as shown.
4. In addition to using symbols, every effort is to be made to attract attention by means of radio, flares, smoke, or other available means.
5. On snow covered ground, signals can be made by dragging, shoveling or tramping. Depressed areas forming symbols will appear black from the air.
6. Pilot should acknolwedge message by rocking wings from side to side.

	GROUND-AIR VISUAL CODE FOR USE BY GROUND SEARCH PARTIES	
NO.	MESSAGE	CODE SYMBOL
1	Operation completed.	LLL
2	We have found all personnel	LL
3	We have found only some personnel.	+ +
4	We are not able to continue. Returning to base.	XX
5	Have divided into two groups. Each proceeding in direction indicated.	⤲
6	Information received that aircraft is in this direction.	→
7	Nothing found. Will continue search.	NN

"Note: These visual signals have been accepted for international use and appear in Annex 12 to the Convention on International Civil Aviation."

engine analyzer An exhaust gas temperature gauge with probes and readouts for each cylinder of each engine.

engine instruments All instruments that indicate condition or performance of the engine, including rpm and manifold pressure. They are usually grouped on the right side of the instrument panel.

engine, piston Reciprocating engine, usually with four or more cylinders, burning a mixture of aviation gasoline and air. The average piston engine used in aviation today is air-cooled, horizontally opposed, and generates anywhere from under 100 to approximately 400 horsepower. Most piston engines powering singles and twins are in the 200- to 300-hp range. Normally aspirated (non-turbocharged) piston engines are capable of producing full power only up to about 6,000 feet, above which altitude the power output drops off because of the reduction in the density of the atmosphere. When equipped with turbochargers, full power is available up to two or three times that critical altitude. All pressurized piston-engine aircraft are turbocharged as the turbocharger provides the pressurization capability.

engine, turbine All jet engines, pure jets, fan-jets, and turboprops. For details *see* JET ENGINES.

engine, turbocharged *See* ENGINE, PISTON.

en route air traffic control service The positive control given aircraft operating on an IFR flight plan, generally by ARTCCs, when such aircraft are in flight between departure and destination airport areas. It functions in the low altitude as well as the jet route system.

en route descent To determine the point along the route of flight at which descent should be started in order to arrive at the pattern altitude of the destination airport without wasting either time or fuel:
Divide the difference in altitude between cruise and the pattern altitude at the destination airport by the rate of descent in feet per minute. Divide the result by 60 and multiply that result by the ground speed in nautical miles. The result is the distance in nautical miles from the destination at which descent should be initiated.

en route flight advisory service A service that is designed to provide the pilot with weather and other information pertinent to his particular type of flight, route of flight, and altitude. It is available at the pilot's request only. Also referred to as *flight watch service.*

en route frequency The frequency used for air-ground communication, usually with center sectors, on or off airways between departure and approach control zones.

en route low altitude chart Aeronautical charts showing radio and navigation facilities but no topographical features. Scales vary from 10 to 30 nm per inch. These

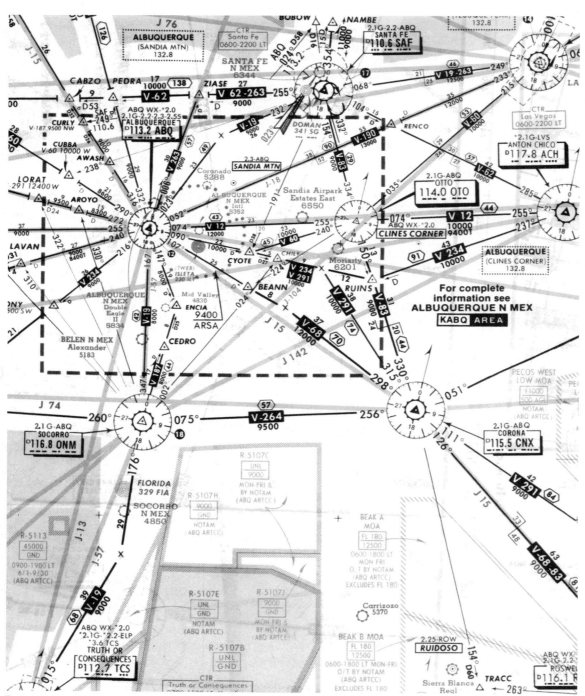

En route low altitude chart.

charts are available from the government or from Jeppesen Sanderson, Inc. It takes 28 of the government charts to cover the contiguous U.S. and 32 of the Jeppesen charts. The charts can also be obtained from the AOPA.

Enstrom Helicopter Corporation   Manufacturer of the three-place F-28F Falcon, and 280FX Shark piston-engine helicopters. (P.O. Box 277, Twin County Airport, Menominee, MI 49858. (906) 863-9971.)

Enstrom Helicopters

	F28F FALCON	280FX SHARK
ENGINE, manufacturer	Lycoming	Lycoming
model	HIO-360-F1AD turbocharged	HIO-360-F1AD turbocharged
hp	225	225
WEIGHT, gross, pounds	2,600	2,600
empty, pounds	1,570	1,585
useful load, pounds	1,030	1,015
WIDTH, tip to tip	28 ft.	28 ft.
HEIGHT	9 ft.	9 ft.
LENGTH	28.1 ft.	28.7 ft.
FUEL, standard, gallons	40	40
w. aux tank, gallons	53	53
SPEED, maximum, knots	97.4	101.7
economy, knots	88.7	93
RANGE, max, no reserve, nm	229	261
RATE OF CLIMB at gross weight	1,150 fpm	1,179 fpm
HOVER IGE	13,200 ft.	13,200 ft.
OGE	8,700 ft.	8,700 ft.

envelope   The hot-air or gas balloon itself, minus gondola and other attachments and systems.

envelope bag   The bag containing the envelope (balloon) when it is being transported on the ground.

ENTR   Entire.

EOW   Empty operating weight.

EPNdB   Estimated perceived noise in terms of decibels.

EQPMT   Equipment.

equator   The horizontal line around a balloon at a point where the diameter is greatest.

equatorial air mass   A warm air mass that originates in the doldrums around the equator.

equilibrium   When flying a balloon, the condition when the lifting capacity of the hot air or gas equals the force of gravity, resulting in constant altitude.

equivalent airspeed   Calibrated airspeed corrected for compression of air in the pitot system at various altitudes and generally important only at speeds approaching Mach 1. It is equal to the calibrated airspeed at sea level.

ETA   Estimated time of arrival.

ETD   Estimated time of departure.

ETE   Estimated time of en route.

European Helicopter Corporation   Manufacturer of the EH101 heavy triple-turbine helicopter.

European Helicopter Corporation Aircraft

		EH101
ENGINES	manufacturer	General Electric (3)
	model	CT7-2A or CT7
	installed hp	4311 or 6000
	takeoff hp	n/a
	max continuous hp	n/a
WEIGHTS lbs	gross	31,500
	external	31,500
	empty	18,876
	useful load	12,624
DIMENSIONS ft	total length	75.3
	fuselage length	52
	height	21.3
	width	n/a
MAIN ROTOR	diameter ft	61
	number of blades	5
FUEL gal	usable, standard	1134
	aux.	n/a
SPEEDS knots	V_{ne}	167
	max cruise	160
	economy cruise	150
SERVICE CEILING	ft	n/a
HOVER	IGE	9000
	OGE	5500

eustachian tube   A passage between the pharynx and the inner ear, providing humans with a sense of balance. This sense is reliable only when continuously monitored and corrected by visual cues. When no visual cues are available, the sense of balance is disturbed and might cause a pilot, flying in clouds, to believe he is flying straight and level when, in fact, he is in a steep bank.

evaporation   The process by which water is transformed into vapor, usually by heating the water. The opposite of condensation.

EVE   Evening.

EW   Sleet showers (in sequence reports.)

EWAS   En route weather advisory service.

EXCP   Except.

execute missed approach   ATC phraseology meant to have the pilot take the following action: Continue inbound to the MAP, then execute the missed approach procedure as described in the instrument approach chart. The missed approach
procedure and/or any turns associated with it should not be started prior to reaching MAP. In the event that the approach being conducted is a radar approach
(ASR or PAR), the missed approach procedure is to be started immediately after
receiving the instruction.

executing missed approach   Phrase used by the pilot to inform ATC of his intention
to execute a missed approach. Alternate phrase: commencing missed approach.

Executive   A high-performance single-engine aircraft once manufactured by Mooney
Aircraft Corporation.

exhaust gas temperature gauge   A means of measuring the exhaust gas temperature
from one or several cylinders and displaying the reading in the cockpit. It is
accomplished by installing a probe in the exhaust manifold(s) and transmitting the
information thus obtained to a gauge located on the instrument panel. Units measuring single cylinders are referred to as EGTs and are always installed in the
exhaust manifold of the hottest running cylinder. Units with probes in all cylinder
exhaust manifolds are often called engine analyzers. EGTs and engine analyzers
are the only reliable means of scientifically leaning the mixture of fuel and air to
the exact proportion suggested in the engine owner's manual, or as desired by the
pilot. By operating the aircraft with the leanest mixture permitted by the engine
manufacturer at any given altitude, great fuel savings can be realized. When gradually leaning the mixture the EGT needle will climb up to a maximum position. If
leaning is continued, it will begin to drop again. The maximum position is
referred to as *peak* and represents the mixture at which close to 100 percent of the
fuel-air mixture is being burned (but it is not the setting producing best power).
Both manufacturers of piston engines (Continental and Lycoming) suggest that the
engine be run full rich while operating at 75 or more percent of power. As soon as
power is reduced below 75 percent, leaning should commence, regardless of the
altitude of the aircraft. Virtually all piston engines can be operated safely at 25
degrees below peak and some may be operated at peak or even at 25 degrees the
other side of peak (assuming a power setting less than 75 percent). Operating
manuals and pilot experience should be the guide. (Pages 182-183)

EXPC   Expect.

expect (altitude) at (time or fix)   ATC phrase that informs the pilot when to expect
clearance to another altitude.

expect approach clearance at (time)   ATC phrase to inform the pilot, possibly
while holding, when to expect clearance for the approach. In instances of an
anticipated delay, ATC should advise the pilot at least five minutes prior to reaching the clearance limit of the expected approach clearance time.

Exhaust Gas Temperature Gauges, Cylinder Head Temperature Gauges, and Related Equipment

MANUFACTURER	MODEL	TYPE OF EQUIPMENT	PRICE	REMARKS
KS Avionics	EGT-1	Single channel analog	148	Exhaust gas temperature gauge
KS Avionics	CHT-1	Single channel analog	127	Cylinder head temp. gauge
KS Avionics	EGT/CHT1T	Single channel analog	278	Combined EGT/CHT
KS Avionics	EGT/CHT 2	Single channel analog	270	Combined EGT/CHT 2.25" add $50
KS Avionics	EGT-2	Single channel analog	311	2.25' mount add $50
KS Avionics	CHT-2	Single channel analog	269	2.25" mount add $50
KS Avionics	EGT-1D	Digital engine monitor	203	Toggle switch for twins
KS Avionics	CHR-1D	Digital engine monitor	183	Toggle switch for twins
KS Avionics	EGT.CHT1D	Digital engine monitor	260	Toggle switch for twins
KS Avionics	TSA-1	Thermal stress alert	210	Available for twins
KS Avionics	TSA-1D	Thermal stress alert	265	Digital. Available for twins
KS Avionics	TETRA	Multi-channel analog	702	Toggle switch for twins
KS Avionics	TETRA C	Multi-channel analog	835	Toggle switch for twins
KS Avionics	TETRA II	Multi-channel analog	1,174	Toggle switch for twins
KS Avionics	TETRA ST	Multi-channel analog	1,062	Toggle switch for twins
KS Avionics	TETRA CST	Multi-channel analog	1,286	Toggle switch for twins
KS Avionics	TETRAIIST	Multi-channel analog	1,674	Toggle switch for twins
KS Avionics	HEXAD	Multi-channel analog	1,017	Toggle switch for twins
KS Avionics	HEXAD C	Multi-channel analog	1,147	Toggle switch for twins
KS Avionics	HEXAD II	Multi-channel analog	1,621	Toggle switch for twins
KS Avionics	HEXAD ST	Multi-channel analog	1,605	Toggle switch for twins
KS Avionics	HEXAD CST	Multi-channel analog	1,689	Toggle switch for twins
KS Avionics	HEXADIIST	Multi-channel analog	2,343	Toggle switch for twins
KS Avionics	E4 4 CYL	4-cylinder upgrade	182/430	Specify aircraft voltage
KS Avionics	E6 6 CYL	6-cylinder upgrade	290/690	Specify aircraft voltage
KS Avionics	C4 4 CYL	4-cylinder upgrade	116/313	Specify aircraft voltage
KS Avionics	C6 6 CYL	6-cylinder upgrade	187/470	Specify aircraft voltage
	monitors 1 cylinder only:			
Alcor	211-110-0	single-engine EGT	233.95	For Cherokee Six add $7.10
Alcor	213-101-0	single-engine CHT	248.50	For Cherokee Six add $4.05
Alcor	221-310-0	twin-engine EGT/EGT	589.95	Except Aerostars, Aero Commanders
Alcor	222-111-0	single-engine EGT/CHT	572.50	For Cherokee Six add $11.15
Alcor	223-301-0	twin-engine CHT/CHT	612.85	Except Aerostars, Aero Commanders
	monitors all cylinders:			
Alcor	211-140-0	single-engine EGT	635.90	2.25" ($803.90 for 6 cyl)
Alcor	213-104-0	single-engine CHT	664.10	2.25" ($841.20 for 6 cyl)
Alcor	221-340-0	twin-engine EGT	1414.90	2.25" ($1844.90 for 6 cyl)
Alcor	222-144-0	single-engine EGT/CHT	1270.10	2.25" ($1615.20 for 6 cyl)
Alcor	223-304-0	twin-engine CHT	1446.50	2.25" ($1882.30 for 6 cyl)
Alcor	321-340-0	twin-engine EGT	1609.95	3.125" ($2039.95 for 6 cyl)
Alcor	322-144-0	Single-engine EGT/CHT	1450.15	3.125" ($1795.25 for 6 cyl)
Alcor	323-304-0	twin-engine CHT	1651.55	3.125" ($2087.35 for 6 cyl)

(All prices 1989 $s)

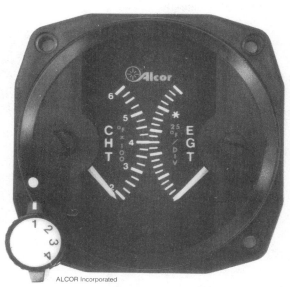

Cylinder head temperature gauge (CHT) and exhaust gas temperature gauge (EGT) combination for a four-cylinder single-engine aircraft.

Exhaust gas temperature gauge (EGT) for a four-cylinder single-engine aircraft.

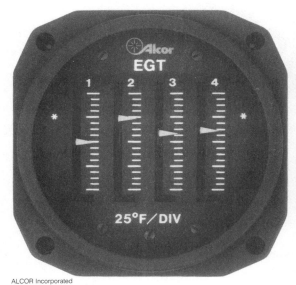

Exhaust gas temperature gauge (EGT) for a twin with six-cylinder engines.

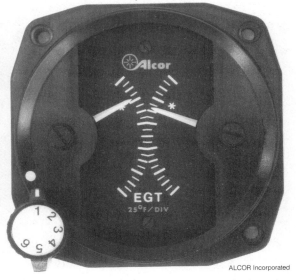

Exhaust gas temperature gauge (EGT) vertical readout for a four-cylinder single-engine aircraft.

expect departure clearance at (time)   Used primarily to avoid having aircraft hold on the ground prior to departure and burning fuel while doing so. It refers to the expected time at which the aircraft will be released from the loading gate to commence taxi and takeoff without additional delays.

expect further clearance at (time)   ATC phrase indicating the time at which the pilot can expect further clearance. If a delay is anticipated, ATC should inform the pilot for the anticipated duration of such a delay at least five minutes prior to his reaching the clearance limit.

experimental   Any homebuilt aircraft. A placard reading EXPERIMENTAL must be displayed on homebuilt aircraft and on aircraft that, for one reason or another, are not currently certificated.

Aircraft placarded as EXPERIMENTAL.

Experimental Aircraft Association (EAA)   The second largest organization of pilots and aircraft owners, comprised primarily of home builders and antiquers.

external loads   Loads carried by a helicopter outside the fuselage. Also referred to as sling loads.

EXTRM   Extreme.

EXTSV   Extensive.

extrusion   A means of forming metal or plastic into any variety of complicated shapes by squeezing it through a form.

F. Fahrenheit.

F Fog (in sequence reports).

F Foxtrot (in the phonetic alphabet).

FA Area forecast.

F/A Fuel-air ratio.

FAA Federal Aviation Administration.

FAA General Aviation District Offices Offices concerned with general aviation matters (GADOs). The offices are within the flight standards district office (FSDO).

Alaskan Region:
> 1714 East 5th Avenue, Anchorage, AK 99501
>
> 5640 Airport Way, Fairbanks, AK 99701
>
> Star Route 1, Box 592, Juneau, AK 99801

Central Region:
> 228 Administration Bldg., Municipal Airport, Des Moines, IA 50321
>
> Fairfax Municipal Airport, Kansas City, KS 66115
>
> Municipal Airport, Wichita, KS 67209
>
> 9275 Glenaire Drive, Berkeley, MO 63134
>
> Municipal Airport, Lincoln, NE 68524

Eastern Region:
> National Airport, Washington, D.C. 20001
>
> Friendship International Airport, Baltimore, MD 21240
>
> 510 Industrial Way, Teterboro, NJ 07608
>
> Country Airport, Albany, NY 12211
>
> Republic Airport, Farmingdale, NY 11735
>
> Monroe County Airport, Rochester, NY 14517
>
> Allentown-Bethlehem-Easton Airport, Allentown, PA 18103
>
> Harrisburg-York State Airport, New Cumberland, PA 17070
>
> North Philadelphia Airport, Philadelphia, PA 19114

Allegheny County Airport, West Mifflin, PA 15122
Aero Industries, 2nd Floor, Sandston, VA 23150
Kanawha County Airport, Charleston, WV 25311

Great Lakes Region:

P.O. Box H, Dupage County Airport, West Chicago, IL 60185
R.R.2, Box 3, Springfield, IL 62705
St. Joseph County Airport, South Bend, IN 46628
5500 44th Street SE, Grand Rapids, MI 49508
6201 34th Avenue South, Minneapolis, MN 55450
4242 Airport Road, Cincinnati, OH 45226
4393 East 175th Avenue, Columbus, OH 43219
General Mitchell Field, Milwaukee, WI 53207

New England Region:

1001 Westbrook Street, Portland, ME 14102
Municipal Airport, Box 280, Norwood, MA 02062
P.O. Box 544, Westfield, MA 01085

Northwest Region:

3113 Airport Way, Boise, ID 83705
5401 NE Marine Drive, Portland, OR 97218
FAA Building, Boeing Field, Seattle, WA 98108
P.O. Box 247, Parkwater Station, Spokane, WA 99211

Pacific Region:

Room 715, Terminal Building, International Airport, Honolulu, HI 96819

Rocky Mountain Region:

Jefferson County Airport, Broomsfield, CO 80020
Logan Field, Billings, MT 59101
P.O. Box 1167, Helena, MT 59601
P.O. Box 2128, Fargo, ND 58102
R.R.2, Box 633B, Rapid City, SD 57701
116 North 23rd West Street, Salt Lake City, UT 84116
Air Terminal, Casper, WY 82601
P.O. Box 2166, Cheyenne, WY 82001

Southern Region:

6500 43rd Avenue North, Birmingham, AL 35206
P.O. Box 38665, Jacksonville, FL 38665
P.O. Box 365, Opa Locka, FL 33054
Clearwater International Airport, St. Petersburg, FL 33732

Fulton County Airport, Atlanta, GA 30336
Bowman Field, Louisville, KY 40205
P.O. Box 5855, Jackson, MS 39208
Municipal Airport, Charlotte, NC 28208
P.O. Box 1858, Raleigh, NC 27602
Box 200, Metropolitan Airport, West Columbia, SC 29169
P.O. Box 30050, Memphis, TE 38103
Metropolitan Airport, Nashville, TE 37217

Southwest Region:
Adams Field, Little Rock, AR 72202
Lakefront Airport, New Orleans, LA 70126
Downtown Airport, Shreveport, LA 71107
P.O. Box 9045, Sunport Station, Albuquerque, NM 87119
Wiley Post Airport, Bethany, OH 72008
International Airport, Tulsa, OK 74115
Redbird Airport, Dallas, TX 75232
6795 Convair Road, El Paso, TX 79925
P.O. Box 1689, Meacham Field, Fort Worth, TX 76016
8345 Telephone Road, Houston, TX 77017
P.O. Box 5247, Lubbock, TX 79417
1115 Paul Wilkins Road, San Antonio, TX 78216

Western Region:
2800 Sky Harbor Boulevard, Phoenix, AZ 85034
Air Terminal, Fresno, CA 93727
2815 East Spring Street, Long Beach, CA 90806
P.O. Box 2397, Oakland, CA 94614
International Airport, Ontario, CA 91761
Municipal Airport, Sacramento, CA 95822
3750 John J. Montgomery Drive, San Diego, CA 92123
1887 Airport Boulevard, San Jose, CA 95110
3200 Airport Avenue, Santa Monica, CA 90405
7120 Hayvenhurst Avenue, Van Nuys, CA 91406
5700-C South Haven, Las Vegas, NV 89109
2601 East Plum Lane, Reno, NV 89502

FAA Headquarters: 800 Independence Avenue, Washington, D.C.

FAAP   Federal Aid Airport Program

FAA Standard   Any rule, regulation, standard of comparison, or procedure issued by the FAA, adherence to which is necessary in the interest of the safety of efficiency of the National Airspace System.

FAC Facility. Also FACIL.

FAD Fuel advisory departure.

FAF Final approach fix.

Fahrenheit (F.) A temperature scale with 32 degrees as the melting point of ice (freezing point of water) and 212 degrees as the boiling point of water, assuming standard atmospheric conditions at sea level. F. equals $^9/_5$ of the C. reading plus 32 degrees. Currently the predominantly used temperature scale in the U.S., it is gradually being replaced by C. (Celsius, centigrade) as part of the trend toward adopting the metric system.

FAI Federation Aeronautique Internationale. The international agency supervising record attempts and concerned generally with a variety of standards of international importance.

Fairchild Weston Systems, Inc. Manufacturer of cockpit voice recorders and flight systems recorders for corporate aircraft operated under Part 91 and 135 and for the airlines. The models A100/A100A are cockpit voice recorders that have been in production since 1963 and are installed on just about every type of airline aircraft in the free world. The Model 800 was introduced as a flight recorder that can display real time data while the unit is still on the aircraft as an aid to maintenance personnel. The model GA100 is the latest cockpit voice recorder model, designed for use on corporate aircraft. (P.O. Box 3041, Sarasota, FL 34230-3041. (813) 371-0811.)

fairing A covering or structure installed on an aircraft to help produce smooth airflow.

Falcon A family of corporate jet aircraft produced in France by Avions Marcel Dassault-Breguet.

Falcon Jet Corporation U.S. distributors of the Falcon family of corporate jet aircraft manufactured in France as Mystère by Avions Marcel Dassault Breguet. (Teterboro Airport, Teterboro, NJ 07608. (201) 288-5300.) (Pages 189-191)

fan Popular jargon for propeller.

fan Blower (in hot-air ballooning.)

fan-jet A high-bypass turbine engine in which a fan, for all practical purposes a multi-bladed shrouded propeller, produces a portion of the thrust. Fan-jets are quieter than pure jets, but lose a degree of their thrust capability at very high altitudes. (Page 192)

fan marker Marker beacon.

FAP Final approach point.

FAR Federal Aviation Regulation.

FAS Flight Assistance Service.

Fasteners So-called Dzus fasteners used primarily to secure those portions of the cowling that must repeatedly be opened for engine inspection.

Falcon Jet Aircraft

		FALCON 100	FALCON 20F	FALCON 200	FALCON 50	FALCON 300
ENGINES	manufacturer	Garrett	Gen'l Electric	Garrett	Garrett (3)	Garrett (3)
	model TFE 731-2-1C	CF 700-2D2	ATF 3-6A-4C	TFE 731-3-1C	TFE 731-5A-1C	
	thrust, sea level lbs	3,230	4,500	5,200	3,700	4,500
WEIGHTS	ramp lbs	18,740	28,660	32,000	38,800	45,500
	takeoff lbs	18,740	28,660	32,000	38,800	45,500
	landing lbs	17,640	27,320	28,880	35,715	42,000
FUEL	usable lbs	5,912	9,098	10,684	15,520	19,065
WING	area sq.ft.	259.4	440	440	504	527.4
	span ft.in	42.11	53.6	53.6	61.10	63.5
AIRFRAME	length ft.in	45.6	56.3	56.3	60.9	66.4
	height ft.in	15.2	17.6	17.6	22.11	24.8
CABIN	length inches	155	294	286	282	468
	width inches	60	73	73	73	92
	height inches	58	68	68	71	74
	passenger seats	9	9	9	10	19
SPEEDS	max thrust KTAS	490	457	473	480	502
	long range KTAS	417	n/a	n/a	410	428
	V_{ref} KIAS	103	103	103	104	106
	M_{mo} above 25,000 ft.	Mach 0.87	Mach 0.88	Mach 0.865	Mach 0.86	Mach 0.87
RANGE nm	long range, full fuel	1,948	1,630	2,611	3,529	4,200
TAKEOFF ft.	balanced field length 4,500	4,900	5,200	4,700	4,900	
LANDING ft.	distance 2,750	2,450	2,660	2,900	3,500	

In early 1989 the Falcon 20 was certificated with a Garrett TFE731-5AR engine, resulting in a range increase to 1,900 nm for the C model and 2,200 for the F model, based on a projected cruise speed of Mach .72 with eight passengers.

Falcon Jet Corporation

Falcon 20.

Falcon 50.

Falcon 100.

Falcon Jet Corporation

Falcon 200.

Falcon Jet Corporation

Falcon 900.

Garrett TFE731 fan-jet engine.

fast file   A system by which the pilot files a flight plan by phone. It is automatically tape recorded and transmitted to the appropriate ATC facility.

fatigue   Pilot tiredness caused by lack of sleep, overwork, excessive noise, or other factors.

fatigue   With reference to metal or aircraft structures the process of wear that might eventually lead to failure.

FAX   Facsimile.

FBO   Fixed base operator; fixed base operation.

FCC   Federal Communications Commission.

FCS   Flight control system.

FCST   Forecast.

FD   Flight director.

FD   Winds aloft forecast.

FDR   Flight data recorder.

FE   Flight engineer.

feather   To change the blade angle of a controllable-pitch propeller so that the blades are turned with the edge facing into the line of flight. It prevents the windmilling of the propeller of an inoperative engine. On helicopters, aligning the rotor blade with the relative wind.

feathered propeller   *See* FEATHER.

Federal Aviation Administration (FAA)   The branch of the Department of Transportation (DOT) responsible for the safety, regulation, and promotion of civil aviation, and the safe and orderly use of the National Airspace System. Originally an independent agency, called the Federal Aviation Agency, established by the Federal Aviation Act of 1958 during the Eisenhower administration as a means of upgrading the inefficient Civil Aviation Administration (CAA). (800 Independence Avenue, Washington, D.C. 20591; Alaskan Regional Office, 701 C Street, Anchorage, AK 99513; Central Regional Office, 601 East 12th Street, Kansas City, MO 64106; Eastern Regional Office, JFK Int'l. Airport, Jamaica, NY 11430; Great Lakes Regional Office, 2300 East Devon Avenue, Des Plaines, IL 60018; New England Regional Office, 12 New England Exec. Park, Burlington, MA 01803; Northwest Mountain Regional Office, 17900 Pacific Highway South, Seattle, WA 98168; Southern Regional Office, Box 20636, Atlanta, GA 30320; Southwest Regional Office, Box 1689, Ft. Worth, TX 76101; Western Pacific Regional Office, Box 92007 Worldway Postal Center, Los Angeles, CA 90009.)

Federal Air Regulations (FARs)   The basic rules covering the safe and orderly conduct of civil aviation.

Federal Aviation Act of 1958   The federal law that, during the Eisenhower administration, established the Federal Aviation Agency (FAA).

Federal Communications Commission (FCC)   The independent agency of the U.S. government charged with the efficient use of radio frequencies. It issues radio-station licenses and operator permits to the aviation community and allots frequencies to the FAA for use in navigation and communication.
Address: Federal Communications Commission,
1919 M Street, NW, Washington, D.C. 20554.
Phone: 202-655-4000.

feeder airline   A commuter airline serving a limited region and connecting with major airlines.

feeder route   A flight path shown on instrument approach charts which designates routes to be flown from the en route structure to the initial approach fix (IAF).

ferry flight   A flight conducted in order to return an aircraft to its base, delivering an aircraft to another location or moving an aircraft to or from a maintenance facility. Special flight permits can be obtained to ferry a partially disabled but flyable aircraft to another location for repair. No passengers may be carried on such a flight.

FHP   Friction horsepower.

FIDO   Flight Inspection District Office.

field elevation   Height in feet msl of the highest usable portion of a landing area. When known, may be used to set the altimeter before commencing a flight or to check its accuracy.

FIFO Flight inspection field office.

fifteen-meter class A class of sailplanes with a wingspan of 15 meters or less.

filed Used primarily in conjunction with filing an IFR flight plan with ATC. Having filed means operating IFR.

FILG Filling.

filling Changing to a higher air pressure in the center of a moving low.

fin A fixed vertical airfoil attached to the fuselage for the purpose of providing stabilization.

final Commonly used phrase meaning that an aircraft is on final approach or is aligned with the direction of the active runway.

final approach The flight path of an airplane from a specific fix or from its turn after completing the base leg toward the active runway. The third leg of the standard traffic pattern.

final approach course A straight line extending from the localizer or runway centerline, without regard to distance from the runway.

final approach fix (FAF) The designated fix from which the final approach may be initiated by an aircraft operating IFR. It identifies the starting point of the final approach segment of an instrument approach.

final approach point The point within the published limits of an approach procedure where the aircraft is established on the final approach course and from which the final descent may be started. It is applicable only in nonprecision approaches where an FAF has not been established.

final approach segment Segment of an instrument approach procedure.

FINFO Flight Inspection National Field Office.

Fire Fighting Amphibian A twin-engine high-wing aircraft designed and manufactured by Canadair for the specific purpose of fighting forest and brush fires. The aircraft can scoop up huge amounts of water to be used in water drops. Two versions are built, one powered by two piston engines, the other by turboshaft engines. (Page 195)

fix A geographical location determined either by visual reference or by electronic navaids, such as the intersection of two VOR radials or bearings or the DME distance from a navaid on a given radial or bearing.

fixed base operation (FBO) A commercial operation, on an airport, that provides such services as fueling, tiedown, maintenance, flight instruction, aircraft sales, restaurant services, etc. or any part thereof.

fixed base operator (FBO) The owner or operator of a fixed base operation.

fixed-pitch propeller A propeller, the blade angle of which was set during construction and cannot be changed.

fixed-wing aircraft Any heavier-than-air craft, other than a helicopter or gyrocopter.

Canadair Incorporated

Fire Fighting Amphibian.

fixed-wing special IFR   Flight operations, usually conducted by agricultural or industrial aircraft, under a waiver agreement with the FAA. They must be flown by instrument rated pilots in IFR equipped aircraft.

fixed-wing special VFR   *See* SPECIAL VFR (S/VFR).

FL   Flight level.

flag   A usually red tag incorporated into electronic navigation instruments in the cockpit to alert the pilot to the fact that the instrument is either inoperative or beyond reception distance from the navaid to which it is tuned.

flag alarm   *See* FLAG.

flameout   Unintentional loss of combustion in a turbine (jet) engine, resulting in loss of power.

flap   An auxiliary control surface usually located on the trailing edge of the inner wing panels, between the fuselage and the ailerons. It can be extended and/or turned down to increase the wing camber and/or surface, creating additional lift and drag. It is commonly used to increase control during slow flight and to increase the glide angle prior to landing. (*See also* FOWLER FLAP; FULL-SPAN FLAP.) Certain high-performance jets and STOL aircraft have leading-edge flaps which can be deployed by the pilot or which deploy automatically at very low speeds.

flap operating range   The range of airspeeds at which flaps may safely be extended. It is shown on the airspeed indicator by a white arc.

flapping   The up and down motion of helicopter rotor blades resulting from aerodynamic loads and changes in control input.

flare   A smooth leveling of the aircraft between glide to a landing and touchdown.

flare out   Bringing the airplane to its touchdown attitude inches above the runway.

flares   Emergency lights that can either be dropped from an aircraft prior to a night emergency landing in order to light up the terrain below, or can be fired from a flare gun or tube by a pilot after an off airport emergency landing in order to draw attention of passing aircraft or vehicles.

FLASHG   Flashing.

flashing beacon   Anti-collision light.

FLD   Field.

FLG   Falling.

flight   Being airborne.

flight check   In-flight check of navigational aids to determine whether they operate reliably.

flight computer   Originally the flight computer used by virtually all pilots was circular slide rule (known as E6b for some obscure reason) that could be used to calculate the problems that tend to arise with reference to flight planning, navigation, time en route, fuel consumption, etc. Today it has frequently been replaced by pocket-sized computers like the AvStar and ProStar from Jeppesen-Sanderson, programmable calculators like Hewlett-Packard's HP-41C or Texas Instruments' TI59, or any one of a variety of personal computers. (Page 197)

flight control system   A combination of flight director, autopilot, and other systems, all interlocked to result in near automatic flight. (Page 198)

flight data recorder   The instrument, often referred to as one of the black boxes, that records all the control settings and actions as they occur during the flight. *See also* FAIRCHILD-WESTON. (Page 199)

flight deck   Cockpit.

flight director   A computer equipped flight instrument that collects information from all nav instruments and displays the findings in one pictorial display. It relieves the pilot of the need of scanning all instruments and tells him at a glance what action to take in order to achieve the desired result. When coupled to an autopilot, it becomes a flight control system. (Pages 199-200)

flight indicator   Gyro horizon.

flight information region   Airspace of specific dimensions in which flight information and flight alerting services are provided. Information services refer to giving advice and information aimed toward the safe and efficient conduct of flight. Alerting services refer to contacting the NTSB (National Transportation Safety Board) and/or other appropriate organizations with reference to an aircraft requiring search and rescue operations.

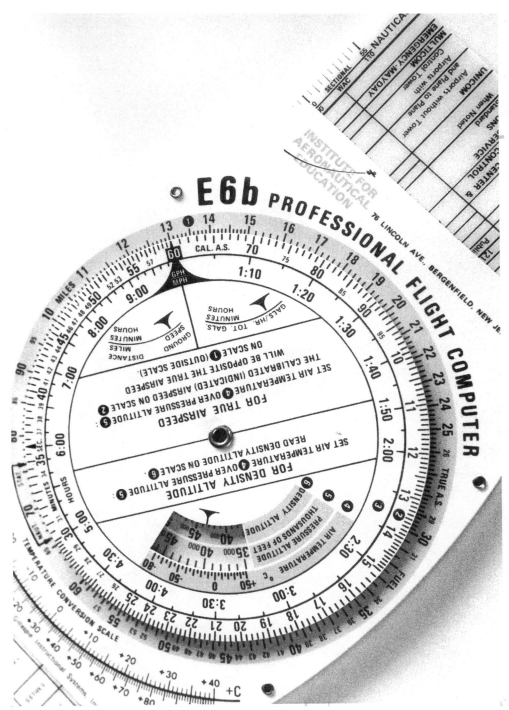

Circular flight computer (E6b).

Flight Control Systems

MANUFACTURER	MODEL	PRICE	VOLTS DC	AC	INTER	TRQ M	E	SENSR D	R	V	COMP D	C	A	X	F	G	H	I	FUNC N	T	B	G	P	S	R	W	K	ADI	HSI	lbs	REMARKS
Bendix/King	KFC150	21,510	14 ¤					¤	¤		¤	¤	¤	¤	¤		¤		¤	¤		¤							¤	25.25	
	KAP150	13,835	/28					¤		¤		¤	¤	¤		¤	¤		¤	¤					¤	AH	DG	18.05	
	KAP100	8,320	¤					¤					¤		¤		¤		¤			¤				AH	DG	10.93	
Bendix/King	KFC200	23,085	14 ¤			¤ ¤		¤			¤ ¤	¤	¤	¤	¤				¤ ¤			¤ ¤		¤			¤	28.30	2-axis systm
		26,980	/28 ¤			¤ ¤ ¤		¤			¤ ¤ ¤	¤	¤	¤	¤				¤ ¤			¤ ¤ ¤		¤			¤	32.76	3-axis systm
		39,900	¤			¤ ¤ ¤ ¤		¤		¤	¤ ¤ ¤ ¤	¤	¤	¤	¤			¤ ¤ ¤ ¤	¤		¤ ¤ ¤ ¤		¤			¤	36.86	w.alt.preslct
Bendix/King	KFC250	70,630	28 26	¤		¤ ¤ ¤ ¤ ¤				¤ ¤ ¤ ¤ ¤ ¤ ¤ ¤				¤ ¤ ¤ ¤ ¤ ¤ ¤ ¤		¤	49.76	4-inch displ.
		44,505																										40.26	3-inch displ.
Bendix/King	KFC400	194,815	28 26	¤		¤ ¤ ¤ ¤ ¤ ¤ ¤ ¤ ¤ ¤ ¤ ¤ ¤				¤ ¤ ¤ ¤ ¤ ¤ ¤ ¤		¤	117.4	3 EFIS displ.
		210,330																										127.3	4 EFIS displ.
		262,015																										153.6	5 EFIS displ.

PRICE:		uninstalled	
VOLTS	DC:	DC input voltage	
	AC:	AC 400 Hz input voltage	
INTER:		flight director interface	
TRQ	M:	mechanical torque limiter	
	E:	electrical torque limiter	
SENSR	D:	directional sensor	
	R:	rate sensor	
	V:	vertical sensor	
COMPUTER	D:	air data	
	C:	air speed compensation	
	A:	altitude	
	X:	expanded localizer	
	F:	fault monitor	

G:	glide slope gain
H:	heading
I:	intercept
N:	navigation
T:	turbulence
B:	back course
G:	glide slope
P:	altitude preset
S:	heading preset
R:	go around
W:	control wheel steering
K:	air speed hold

FUNCT'S listing (right column): G: glide slope gain, H: heading, I: intercept, N: navigation, T: turbulence, B: back course, G: glide slope, P: altitude preset, S: heading preset, R: go around, W: control wheel steering, K: air speed hold
ADI: ADI display
HSI: HSI display

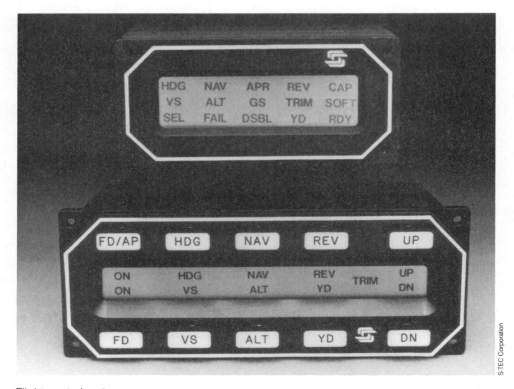

Flight control system.

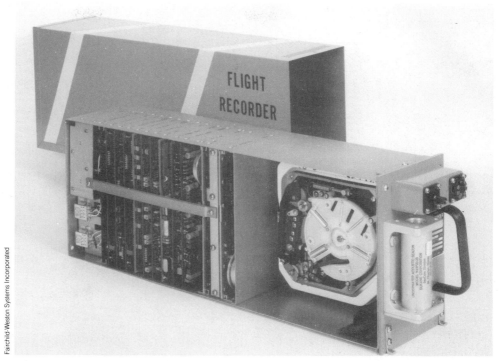

Fairchild-Weston Systems Incorporated

Flight data recorder.

Flight Directors

MANUFACTURER	MODEL	PRICE	VOLTS DC	AC	DISPLAY V	C	H	FUNCTIONS A	W	I	M	V	READOUTS C	D	W	T	INTER	SEN A	H	lbs	REMARKS
S-Tec	65	11,995	14 28		3			□	□			□	□		□	□	□		□	□	15.8	Yaw damper option
Bendix/King	KFC150	21,510	14 28		3			3 □	□			□			□	□	KAP100 KAP150	□	□	18.42 26.47	
Bendix/King	KFC200	23,085	14 28		3			3 □	□			□		□	□	□	KAP200	□	□	28.3 32.9	2-axis system 3-axis system
Bendix/King	KFC250	44,505 62,520	28	26	4 3			4 □ 3	□			□		□	□	□	□	□	□	49.75 40,26	4-inch system 3-inch system
Collins	FDS-84	n/a	28	26	4			4 □	□	□	□	□ □	□	□	□		□	□	□	11.4	ProLine
Collins	FDS-85	n/a	28	26	5			5 □	□	□	□	□ □	□	□	□		□	□	□	15.6	ProLine
Collins	FD-108	n/a	28	26	5			5 □	□	□	□	□ □	□	□	□		□	□	□	n/a	ProLine
Collins	FD-109	n/a	28	26	5			5 □	□	□	□	□ □	□	□	□		□	□	□	n/a	ProLine
Century	2000	n/a	14 28		3			3 □	□								□		□	□	18.3	The system consists of 5 modules incl. yaw damper
Astronautics	ADIs	n/a	14 28		3-6			□	□		□□		□	□						4-7.7	ADIs for use with flight directors
Astronautics	2-CUE	n/a	14 28			3		3 □	□			□	□	□	□	□		□	□	n/a	
Astronautics	3-CUE	n/a	14 28			3		3 □	□			□	□	□	□	□		□	□	n/a	

PRICE:		uninstalled		FUNCTIONS	A: altitude			D:	DME
VOLTS:	DC:	DC input voltage		W:	control wheel steering			W:	MDA.DH warning
	AC:	AC 400 Hz input voltage		I:	indicated airspeed			T:	turn rate
DISPLAY	V:	V-bar ADI, diameter in inches		M:	Mach		INTER:		autopilot interface
	C:	cross pointer ADI, diameter in inches		V:	vertical speed		SEN:	A:	altitude sensor
	H:	slaved HSI		READOUTS	C: digital course			H:	heading sensor

Flight director ADI (attitude director indicator).

Attitude director indicator (ADI) display.

flight inspection *See* FLIGHT CHECK.

flight instruments All instruments displaying information about the aircraft's course, speed, altitude, and attitude.

flight level (FL) An altitude based on a reference atmospheric pressure of 29.92, stated in digits representing hundreds of feet. It is usually used only for altitudes above 18,000 feet msl. FL 230 means 23,000 feet.

flight log A record of a specific flight or of all flight activity by a pilot.

flight manual Part 1 of AIM.

flight path The actual line, altitude, and course along which an aircraft is flying.

flight path deviation indicator Course deviation indicator (CDI).

flight plan An outline of a proposed cross-country flight, filed with an FSS before departure and closed at the end of the flight. For instrument flight in controlled airspace, flight-plan filing is mandatory. For IFR flights in uncontrolled airspace and for VFR flights, filing a flight plan is voluntary. The only purpose of a VFR flight plan is to activate search and rescue activities in the event that the aircraft fails to arrive at its destination.

Flight plan form.

flight plan sequence The sequence in which flight plan information should be provided:

1. Type of flight plan (VFR; IFR; DVFR)
2. Aircraft identification number
3. Aircraft type and equipment

4. Estimated TAS
5. Departure point
6. Departure time (Zulu time)
7. Cruising altitude
8. Route of flight
9. Destination
10. Estimated time en route
11. Remarks
12. Fuel on board in hours and minutes
13. Alternate airport (IFR only)
14. Pilot's name, address, telephone number, and aircraft homebase.
15. Number of persons on board
16. Color of aircraft
17. Destination contact, telephone optional

Flight Safety International   A major pilot training operation, operating simulators for most major corporate aircraft. (Marine Air Terminal, LaGuardia Airport, Flushing, NY 11371. (718) 565-4100.)

flight service station (FSS)   A facility operated by the FAA with the prime responsibility for preflight briefing, communication with VFR flights, assisting lost VFR aircraft, originating and disseminating NOTAMs, broadcasting aviation weather, and operating the national weather teletype system, plus other functions as they arise. (*See also* DUTY PRIORITIES.)

Flight service station (FSS) interior.

flight service specialist An employee of the FAA performing his duties in an FSS.

Flight Simulator II and III A computer game that realistically copies the behavior of an actual aircraft. It is available for a wide variety of personal computers.

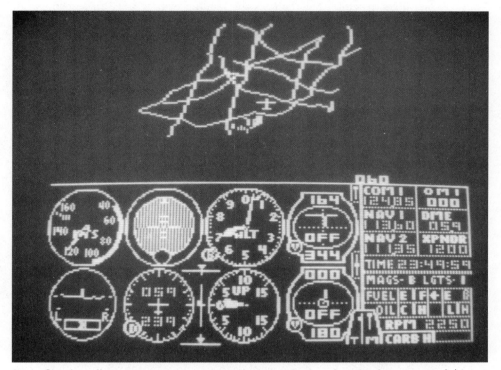

Flight Simulator II computer program, here depicting the Los Angeles freeways at night.

Flight Standards District Office (FSDO) A field office of the FAA, serving a given geographical area and primarily serving the aviation industry in that area in matters relating the flight standards, such as the certification of aircraft or systems. Other duties involve certification of airmen, accident prevention, investigation, enforcement of rules and regulations and matters related thereto.

flight test The in-flight evaluation of an applicant for a pilot certificate or rating by an authorized examiner.

flight test The in-flight investigation of the flight characteristics of an aircraft, an aircraft component, or system.

flight time The total time from the moment an aircraft first moves under its own power for the purpose of subsequent flight until it comes to rest at the next point of landing. Also known as block time.

flight visibility The distance it is possible to see while in flight. The visibility from one point in the air to another point in the air.

flight watch En route flight advisory service.

FLIP Flight information publications.

Flite Liner A light single-engine piston training aircraft once manufactured by Piper Aircraft Corporation. No longer in production.

float A boat-like structure that replaces the landing gear wheels on a seaplane or amphibian, used to take off and land on water.

Float-equipped aircraft.

float The action of a airplane that continues to remain airborne after the flare prior to landing.

float A part of the carburetor that measures the amount of fuel required for the correct mixture of fuel and air.

floater An aircraft that tends to float after the flare prior to landing.

floater A sailplane with an exceptional L/D ratio.

float plane Seaplane; usually the type that floats on its hull.

flow control Routines designed to regulate the flow of traffic along an airway or other route or en route to an airport or a given portion of airspace.

FLRY Flurry.

FLT Flight.

flutter Self-excited oscillations of one or several components of an aircraft, deriving its energy from the airstream. Flutter is dependent upon the elastic and inertia characteristics of the affected component.

FLW Follow.

FLWG Following.

fly (heading/degrees)   An ATC phrase to tell the pilot which heading to fly. If compliance involves a turn, the pilot is expected to turn in the shorter direction to the new heading.

fly-by-wire   Aircraft in which the flight controls are largely computerized.

Flying   A monthly aviation magazine with worldwide circulation approaching 500,000. (Editorial address: 1515 Broadway, New York, NY 10036. (212) 503-4200.)

flying tail   An empennage structure in which the entire tail assembly is moved as part of the elevator movement.

FM   Frequency modulation.

FM   Fan marker.

FN   Regional forecast.

FOB   Fuel on board.

foehn gap   In a mountain-wave system marked by clouds, the foehn gap is an area of blue sky between the mountain's cap clouds and the lenticular clouds over the first lee wave.

foehn wind   A warm, dry wind blowing down the slopes of a mountain range (such as the chinook in the Rocky Mountains).

fog   A cloud formed at or near the surface of the earth, giving a visibility of less than one kilometer ($^5/_8$ mile). Fog results from the condensation of tiny water droplets when low altitude air is cooled to or below the dew point. Sequence report symbol: F.

fogged in   Forced to stay on the ground by fog or low visibility caused by any source.

Fokker Aircraft   A manufacturer of airline turboprops and jets, some of which are used by corporations as corporate aircraft. The F27 twin turboprop and F28 twin fan-jet were replaced in 1986 by the Fokker 50 twin turboprop and the much larger Fokker 100 fan-jet. (U.S. Address: 1199 North Fairfax Street, Alexandria, VA 22314. (703) 838-0100.) (Page 206)

Fokker Aircraft

Fokker F-27 twin turboprop.

Fokker F-28 twin fan-jet.

Fokker F-50 twin-turboprop.

Fokker F-100 twin fan-jet.

FONE Telephone.

forced landing A landing made necessary by mechanical malfunction, weather, or getting lost at some point other than the intended destination. It may be at an airport or at a location other than an airport. Such forced landings frequently involve short-field technique or the ability to successfully land without the use of power.

formation flight Several aircraft that, by prior agreement among the pilots, operate as one with reference to navigation, position reporting, etc. Among aircraft participating in a formation flight separation between aircraft is the responsibilty of the participating pilots.

FORNN Forenoon.

forward slip A maneuver in which the aircraft is deliberately cross controlled by using opposite aileron and rudder. It can be used during the final approach in order to achieve rapid loss of altitude, or for the purpose of correcting for wind drift by slipping into the wind.

Foster Airdata Systems, Inc. Manufacturer of Loran-C, Loran/TACAN/VOR-DME, GPS navigation equipment, databases and DME systems, and airborne TACAN. (7020 Huntley Road, Columbus, OH 43229. (614) 888-9502.)

four forces The four primary dynamic forces that make flight possible: lift, weight, thrust, drag.

four stroke cycle The basic operating method of the reciprocating engine; the four movements of each piston: 1) Intake stroke; the movement toward the crankshaft that draws fuel and air into the cylinder. 2) The compression stroke; movement toward the top of the cylinder that compresses the fuel-air mixture for ignition by the spark plug. 3) The power stroke; when pressure of the burning mixture forces the piston back toward the crankshaft that, in turn, is moved by the correcting rod. 4) The exhaust stroke; the piston moves back toward the top of the cylinder, which forces what remains of the burned mixture out through the exhaust valve.

Fowler flap A flap consisting of several individual flaps, capable of initially extending the wing surface without appreciably adding drag, then, when extended further, moving downward, increasing both camber and drag.

foxtrot In aviation-radio phraseology the term used for the letter F.

FP Flight plan.

fpm Feet per minute.

FPR Flight planned route.

FQT Frequent.

FRACTO Prefix used with cloud types to indicate that they are broken.

Frasca International, Inc. A leading manufacturer of fixed base flight simulators for fixed- and rotary-wing aircraft. The types of simulators produced include some for general use and others designed to represent specific aircraft. The company also offers a remanufactured version of the venerable GAT-1 two-axis motion simulator. In March 1989 Frasca built and delivered to the Piper Personal Aviation Training Center a Malibu Mirage simulator. (606 South Neil Street, Champaign, IL 61820-5279. (217) 359-3951.) (Pages 208-210)

free balloon A free-flying balloon, not tethered to the earth. (Page 211)

freezing rain Precipitation starting as rain turning into ice when striking a colder object such as an aircraft or the ground.

FREQ Frequency.

Frasca Simulators

	Model 141	Model 142	Model 146	Model 242	Model 242T
Type of aircraft Single engine	Twin engine	Single engine	Twin Engine	Twin Turboprop	Two pilot
			Twin engine	Two Pilot	
Standard equipment	Fuselage	Fuselage	Fuselage	Fuselage	Fuselage
plotter	variable scale	variable scale	variable scale	variable scale	variable scale
controls	engine	engine	engine	engine	engine
instruments	flight, nav	flight, nav	flight, nav	flight, nav	flight, nav
sound	engine	engines	engine(s)	engines	engines
	aerodynamic	aerodynamic	aerodynamic	aerodynamic	aerodynamic
operator statn	console	console	console	console	console
	computer	computer	computer	computer	computer
motion system			2-axis		
avionics					
Bendix/King	audio panel	audio panel	audio panel	audio panel	audio panel
	marker beacon	marker beacon	marker beacon	marker beacon	marker beacon
	nav receivers	nav receivers	nav receivers	nav receivers	nav receivers
dual	digital RMI	digital RMI	digital RMI	digital RMI	digital RMI
dual	com radios	com radios	com radios	com radios	com radios
dual	ADF, DME	ADF, DME	ADF, DME	ADF, DME	ADF, DME
	transponder	transponder	transponder	transponder	transponder
Options				instrument grp	instrument grp
copilot	yes	yes	yes	yes	yes
Silver Crown	yes	yes	yes	yes	yes
HSI	yes	yes	yes	yes	yes
flt.director	yes	yes	yes	yes	yes
visual system					
Base price 1989 $s	55,050	71,045	70,100*	145,050	365,100
			85,100**		

* Single-engine version
** Twin-engine version
The Model 146 is a modified and upgraded version of the GAT-1 simulator. In either case, the price
assumes that the basic GAT-1 simulator is provided by the customer.

In addition to the above, Frasca manufactures type-specific custom simulators for

    MBB Bo 105 helicopter
    Bell 205 helicopter
    Bell 212 helicopter
    Hughes 300 helicopter
    Cessna Citation II
    Pilatus PC-7
    Piper Seneca III
    Piper Navajo
    Cessna T-303
    Beech Bonanza A36
    Cessna 310
    Cessna 310R

plus a variety of custom-built simulators to represent specific corporate and airline aircraft.

Frasca model 142 twin-engine simulator, with color visual system.

Frasca simulator McFadden three-axis motion base.

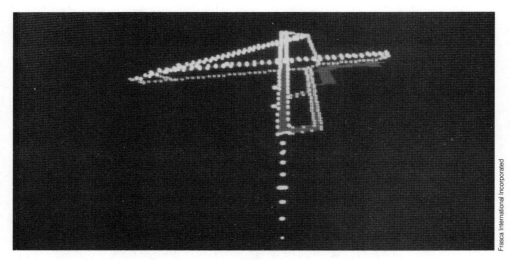

Frasca simulator color visual system for night approach.

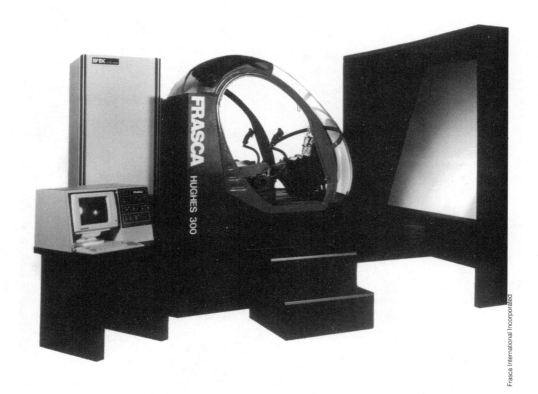

Frasca Hughes 300 helicopter simulator.

Free hot-air balloon.

frequency   A figure expressing cycles (Hertz) per second of a wave of electro-magnetic energy. Radio receivers are designed to select a specific frequency while cutting out all others.

frequency bands   The radio frequencies utilized in aviation navigation and communication lie in a relatively narrow range of the electromagnetic spectrum between 3,000 cycles (Hertz) and 300,000,000,000 cycles (Hertz). (The total range of the known electro-magnetic spectrum ranges from approximately 85 cycles per second to 100,000,000,000,000,000,000 cycles per second.)

The range applicable to aviation is divided into frequency bands, more or less in accordance with their propagation characteristics:

Below 30 kHz	VLF (Very low frequency)
30 kHz to 300 kHz	LF (Low frequency)
300 kHz to 3MHz	MF (Medium frequency)
3 MHz to 30 MHz	HF (High frequency)
30 MHz to 200 MHz	VHF (Very high frequency)
200 MHz to 3 kMHz	UHF (Ultra high frequency)
3 kMHz to 30 kMHz	SHF (Super high frequency)
30 kMHz to 300 kMHz	EHF (Extremely high frequency)

The propagation characteristics (reception distance) of these bands breaks down as follows:

VLF   worldwide

(continued)

LF, MF   3,000 to 5,000 miles

Others   Line of sight

frequency drift   The tendency of certain radio receivers to drift from the frequency to which they have been tuned.

frequency management system   Sophisticated avionics systems that permit the pilot to tune any number of navigation and communication radios through one central input unit, usually a keyboard.

friction horsepower   The amount of the total horsepower absorbed by engine friction and not available to produce thrust.

front   The boundary or zone of transition between two air masses with different properties or pressures. Fronts are identified as cold, warm, occluded, or stationary. (Pages 213-214

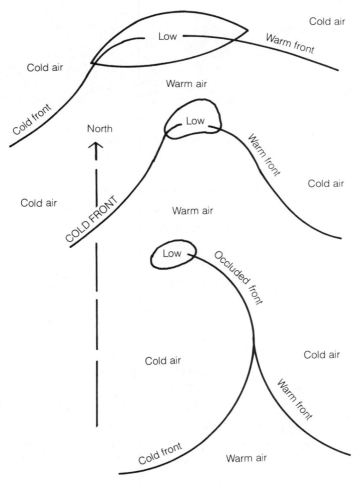

Low pressure areas are associated with cold and warm fronts.

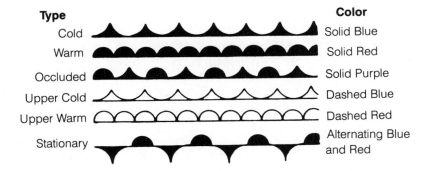

Type		Color
Cold		Solid Blue
Warm		Solid Red
Occluded		Solid Purple
Upper Cold		Dashed Blue
Upper Warm		Dashed Red
Stationary		Alternating Blue and Red

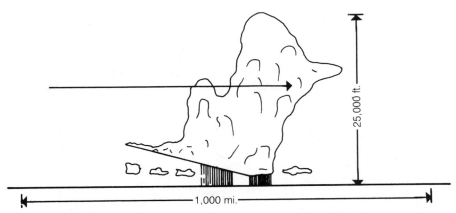

Cold fronts are usually smaller in area than warm fronts, but more violent.

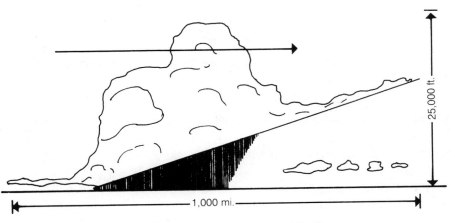

Warm fronts and their effects might extend as far as 1,000 miles.

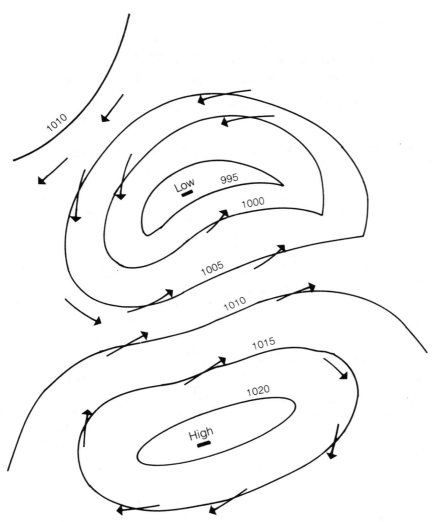

The air circulation is always clockwise around a high pressure system and counterclockwise around a low pressure system.

frontogenesis   The development of a front, or an increase in intensity of an existing front.

frontolysis   The dissipation of a front, usually caused by horizontal mixing within the frontal area.

FROPA   Frontal passage.

FROSFC   Frontal surface.

frost   A layer of crystals of ice formed like dew when the temperature is below 32 degrees F. or when a freezing surface comes in contact with warmer moist air.

FRST   Frost.

FRZ   Freeze.

FRZLVL   Freezing level.

FRZN   Frozen.

FSDO   Flight Standards District Office.

FSL   Full-stop landing.

FSS   Flight Service Station.

FT   Foot, feet.

FT   Fort.

FT   Terminal forecast.

FTHR   Further; farther.

fuel   A hydrocarbon compound that burns when compressed and mixed with air and then ignited. In doing so it heats and expands, providing the energy necessary to drive the engine.

fuel advisory departure   Procedures devised to reduce fuel consumption when delays are expected at an airport.

fuel and air mixture   The mixture of fuel and air channelled into the combustion chamber. A burnable mixture can be classified as lean (excessive percentage of air) or rich (excessive percentage of fuel). The perfect mixture for combustion in the case of aviation gasoline is 15 parts of air to one part of fuel.

fuel and air ratio   The ratio of fuel to air drawn into the combustion chamber and controlled by the mixture-control knob on the instrument panel.

fuel consumption   The amount of fuel used by an aircraft per unit of time, usually expressed in gallons or pounds per hour.

fuel dumping   The release of usable fuel while airborne, usually for the purpose of reducing aircraft weight prior to landing.

fuel efficiency   The fuel required to travel one nautical mile. It can be determined by: Dividing the total distance covered in nautical miles by the amount of fuel burned. *See also* CONVERSION TABLES.

fuel flow   The rate at which fuel is burned by the engine(s). Usually expressed in gallons or pounds per hour (gph or pph). To determine the fuel flow two methods are available: Fuel burned divided by time en route in hours and decimal fractions of hours, or, fuel burned divided by the result of dividing distance covered by ground speed. *See also* CONVERSION TABLES.

fuel gauge   The cockpit instrument that displays the amount of fuel left in the tank(s). Fuel gauges are historically inaccurate and should never be solely relied on during the last quarter of fuel quantity shown.

fuel injection   A process, doing away with the carburetor, by which fuel is forced under pressure directly into the combustion chamber.

fuel monitoring systems Systems containing a computer and a computer memory. Once told the amount of fuel on board, they keep careful track of the amount of fuel being burned, the amount remaining etc. One of the most popular and reliable fuel monitoring systems is produced by Silver Instruments (16100 S.W. 72nd Avenue, Portland, OR 97224. (503) 684-1600.)

fuel quantity indicator Fuel gauge.

fuel rate Gallons or pounds per hour.

fuel siphoning Unintentional loss of fuel because of a loose fuel cap, leaking tank, or such.

fuel strainer A filter that removes impurities from the fuel before it reaches the carburetor or injectors. It should be checked during preflight and cleared after refueling.

fuel venting Fuel dumping.

full flaps The position of the flaps when they are extended as far as possible, providing a maximum amount of additional lift and drag. On some light aircraft it can be dangerous to use full flaps during a crosswind landing.

full lean The leanest mixture at which a reciprocating engine will barely continue to operate. Not recommended for prolonged operation.

full rich The setting of the mixture control that results in the highest possible proportion of fuel to air that can be supplied to an engine. To be used during takeoff and when operating at 75 or more percent of power.

full-span flaps Flaps that either extend the entire length of the wing (such as on the Mitsubishi MU-2, which used spoilers instead of ailerons) or that continue underneath the fuselage.

full throttle Maximum available power at any given altitude.

fuselage The main body of the airplane, housing crew, passengers, and baggage/cargo space.

FWD Forward.

FXD Fixed.

FYI For your information.

G   Golf (phonetic alphabet)

G   Gusts (in sequence reports)

G   Gravity; the force equal to the gravitational pull of the earth. For instance, in a steep bank an aircraft might produce a three-G pull on the pilot and on the structure of the aircraft itself; a force equal to three times the pull of gravity of the earth.

G-I, G-II, G-III, G-IV   Gulfstream I, II, III, and IV.

G forces   The gravity forces caused by unusual maneuvers or by rapid acceleration have the following effects on the human body.

- 3.5 to 4 g: loss of peripheral vision; possibly dimming of all vision; greyout.
- 4 to 4.5 g: complete loss of vision; blackout.
- Above 4.5 g: loss of consciousness.
- In order to operate under conditions of greater G forces, the pilot must be wearing a pressure suit.

G forces created by banking the aircraft:

Angle of bank	G load	Increase in stall speed
0	1	0
20	1.065	3
40	1.31	14.4
60	2	41.4
80	5.76	140
90	infinite	infinite

G suit   Pressure suit.

GA   Glide angle.

Gables Engineering, Inc.   Manufacturer of avionics controls, displays, and audio systems. (P.O. Box 140880, Coral Gables, FL 33114. (305) 442-2578.)

GADO   General Aviation District Office (FAA).

gage   Gauge.

GAL   Gallon.

galley   On-board equipment for food and beverage storage and service.

Garrett Turbine Engine Division   Manufacturer of a wide variety of turboshaft and turbofan engines for fixed-wing and rotary-wing aircraft. (Page 219)

- The TFE 731 family of turbofan engines is used on a wide variety of business jets.
- The TPE 331 family of turboshaft engines is used in a large number of business turboprop aircraft.
- The ATF3-6A high-bypass turbofan engine incorporates the latest in business aircraft jet-engine sophistication.
- The T800 1,300 shp engine which in 1988 was selected by the U.S. Army to power the LHX (light experimental helicopter), was developed jointly by Garrett and Allison.

(111 South 34th Street, P.O. Box 5217, Phoenix, AZ 85010. (602) 231-2589.)

Garrett TPE331-14 turboshaft engine.

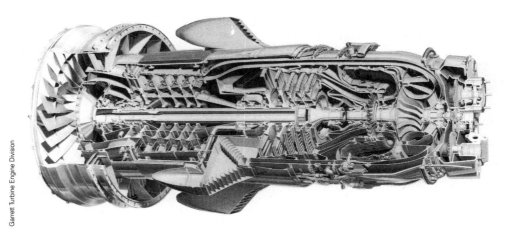

Garrett ATF3 high-bypass turbofan engine.

GAS Gasoline.

gas The lifting agent used in gas balloons: helium, hydrogen, or kitchen gas.

gas balloon A balloon deriving its buoyancy from gas rather than hot air.

gascolator Fuel strainer.

gasoline Fuel used in reciprocating engines. Jet engines, though able to function with gasoline in an emergency, normally burn kerosene.

gate The passenger loading and unloading position at an air terminal.

gate hold procedures Procedures at certain busy airports designed to hold aircraft at the gate or other designated positions when anticipated departure delays exceed five minutes.

Gauge An instrument displaying fuel quantities or other measurements. Also spelled *gage*.

Gazelle A single-engine turbine helicopter with a shrouded tail rotor, manufactured by Aerospatiale in France.

GCA Ground controlled approach.

gear-up landing A landing during which the gear is either accidentally or purposely kept in the retracted position. Also *belly landing*.

Genave, Inc. Manufacturer of a variety of avionics equipment. (802 East Lord Street, Indianapolis, IN 46202. (317) 262-2000.)

general aviation All aviation other than military and the airlines.

General Aviation District Office (GADO) FAA offices concerned with serving general aviation. For addresses, *see* FAA.

General Electric Aircraft Engine Business Group Designer and manufacturer of turbine engine for commercial and military turbine aircraft. (1 Neumann Way, Cincinnati, OH 45215-6301. (513) 243-2000. General Electric Company headquarters: 3135 Easton Turnpike, Fairfield, CT 06431. (203) 373-2211.)

General Services Administration   The agency of the U.S. government concerned with general housekeeping chores.

general warning signal   An alternating red and green light signal that warns the pilot of a no-radio aircraft to exercise extreme caution.

generator   A device, identical in construction to an electric motor, that generates electricity and continuously recharges the battery.

GF   Ground fog (in sequence reports.)

GICG   Glaze icing.

Giovanni Agusta S.p.A   *See* AGUSTA AEROSPACE CORPORATION.

Glasflugel   Manufacturers of high-performance sailplanes. (7311 Schlettstall Krs., Nurtingen, West Germany. U.S. representative: Graham Thompson Ltd., 3200 Airport Avenue, Santa Monica, CA 90405.)

glaze   Clear ice.

GLDR   Glider.

glide   A sustained forward flight in which speed is maintained by sacrificing altitude, power on or power off. Every airplane has a glide airspeed depending on load and altitude that, in the event of engine failure, will enable it to achieve the maximum distance over the ground. For details, see the flight manual of the particular aircraft.

glide path   The downward flight path of a gliding aircraft.

glider   Sailplane. An aircraft without an engine. It is supported in flight by the dynamic action of the air on the lifting surfaces. By taking advantage of rising air currents a high-performance sailplane can stay aloft for many hours and cover distances of a thousand miles or more. The world altitude record for a sailplane is over 46,000 feet.

glide ratio   Usually expressed in terms of L/D (lift over drag) it is the ratio of forward distance traveled to altitude lost assuming still air. An L/D number of 45 (highest achieved by a sailplane to date) means that it will travel 45 miles while losing one mile in altitude, assuming still air.

glide slope   A single direction VHF radio beam, part of an ILS system that establishes a glide path at a vertical angle of about 2.5 to 3 degrees relative to the runway. It activates a cockpit display that, when kept centered, shows the pilot that he has achieved the correct rate of descent.

glide slope   Any proper glide path toward a landing, such as might be shown by a visual approach slope indicator (VASI).

glide slope intercept altitude   The minimum altitude at which the glide slope must be intercepted on a precision approach in order to assure safe obstacle clearance. It is shown on instrument approach charts.

gliding distance   The maximum distance a heavier-than-air craft can glide, without power, from any given altitude.

glitch Jargon for any trouble problem, usually of a mechanical nature.

global positioning system (GPS) A long-range navigation system that takes navigational input from transmissions generated by a series of satellites in synchronous orbit. At this writing, while the system is technically feasible, it is not yet fully operational, though it is expected to be one of the most important and reliable worldwide navigation systems in years to come.

Canadian Marconi Company

Global positioning system.

Canadian Marconi Company

Global positioning system (GPS) interior.

Global-Wulfsberg Systems

Global-Wulfsberg GNS-X flight management system.

Global – Wulfsberg Systems   Manufacturer of VLF/Omega long-range navigation systems, flight management, and information systems, in-flight telephone, and communication systems. (2144 Michelson Drive, Irvine, CA 92715. (714) 851-0119.)

GMT Greenwich mean time.

GND Ground.

GNDFG Ground fog.

go ahead Proceed with your message. In aviation radio practice it may not be used for any other purpose.

go around ATC instruction to the pilot to abandon the approach and landing, usually followed by additional instructions.

going by the book An expression used by the air traffic controllers to justify slowdowns in intermittent labor disputes with the FAA. Controllers are by law prohibited from calling a strike, therefore they use the slowdown technique instead. The "book" being referred to is the controller's handbook that specifies spacing between aircraft during IFR conditions. When these spacings are extended into VFR conditions, massive delays tend to result at major airports. In 1981 the controllers did go on strike in defiance of the law, as a result of which then President Ronald Reagan fired all of the members of PATCO, the controllers union, causing a fairly severe controller shortage that lasted for a considerable number of years.

Golden Eagle A pressurized piston twin once manufactured by Cessna Aircraft Company. No longer in production.

golf In aviation radio phraseology the term used for the letter G.

gondola The basket of a hot-air or gas balloon.

B.F. Goodrich Aerospace and Defense Division Manufacturer of wheels and brakes for general aviation, the airlines, and the military, aircraft tires, aircraft instruments, and avionics through its Castleberry and Jet Electronics and Technology subsidiaries, de-icing systems, and aircraft evacuation systems. (250 North Cleveland-Massilon Road, Akron, OH 44313-0501. (216) 374-2000.)

Goodyear Aerospace Manufacturer of aircraft tires and brake systems. (1210 Massilon Road, Akron, OH 44315.)

Gould, Inc. Manufacturer of a variety of aircraft instrumentation. (10 Gould Center, Rolling Meadows, IL 60008. (312) 640-4000.)

GP Glide path.

gph Gallons per hour.

GPS Global Positioning System.

GPWS Ground proximity warning system.

gradient Change in value per unit of distance, such as the pressure gradient in meteorology. IFR approach charts frequently include gradient instructions consisting of changes in altitude of so many feet per nautical mile. To convert such instructions to a more meaningful feet per minute: Divide the altitude change in feet per nautical mile by 60 and multiply the result by the ground speed in knots. The result is the rate of climb or descent in feet per minute.

gravity   The force exerted by the mass of the earth or any object at or near its surface, pulling the object toward the center of the earth. Roughly equivalent to weight.

gravity feed   A type of fuel system that depends on gravity to move the fuel from the tanks to the carburetor or injectors.

GRDL   Gradual.

greasing it on   Making a perfect landing.

grease job   Perfect landing.

great circle   A circle on the surface of the earth, an arc of which connecting two terrestial points constitutes the shortest distance between those two points.

great circle route   A route flown along the great circle or a portion thereof. Flying the great circle route from New York to Paris, for instance, saves 145 miles over the straight (rhumb) line.

Great Lakes   An aerobatic biplane, no longer in production.

Greenwich mean time   Zulu time. The time at the Prime Meridian in England, used in aviation the world over in order to avoid confusion with reference to time zones. Officially referred to as Coordinated Universal Time and abbreviated, oddly, UTC.

grayout   Blurred vision caused by excessive G forces.

gross weight   The full weight of the aircraft prior to takeoff, consisting of empty weight plus useful load. It must not exceed the maximum allowable gross weight for the particular aircraft. While gross weight usually is identical to the maximum takeoff weight, in some aircraft the so-called ramp weight is greater than the maximum takeoff weight, allowing for fuel burn while waiting for takeoff clearance. Also many aircraft include a maximum landing weight that may not be exceeded and that, under certain conditions, would require dumping or burning off fuel before landing. Finally, there is the zero fuel weight that is the maximum allowable weight of the aircraft with empty fuel tanks.

ground clutter   Patterns produced by ground returns on radar scopes. Such returns tend to degrade other radar returns. Ground clutter can be minimized by using a moving target indicator (MTI), the effect of which is that the radar will pick up only targets that are in motion.

ground control   An ATC service at controlled airports, responsible for the safe and efficient movement of aircraft and airport vehicles on the ground.

ground controlled approach (GCA)   A nonprecision approach using surveillance radar. It makes instrument landings possible for pilots flying aircraft equipped only with a com transceiver and attitude flight instruments by transmitting precise heading and rate-of-descent instructions by voice. When precision approach radar (PAR) is used in a GCA, it becomes a precision instrument approach.

ground crew   In ballooning, the crew that follows the balloon on the ground and eventually assists in the landing procedure.

Ground crew following hot-air balloon.

ground effect   A certain amount of additional lift that takes effect when the aircraft is close to the ground. Low-wing aircraft are more susceptible to ground effect than are high-wing aircraft.

ground handling   The ease or lack of ease with which an aircraft can be maneuvered on the ground.

ground handling ropes   The ropes attached to a hot-air or gas balloon, used to control its movements during inflation and prior to liftoff.

ground loop   An uncontrollable abrupt turn of an aircraft while taxiing or during the ground roll of a takeoff or landing. Tailwheel aircraft are specially prone to ground loop during crosswind conditions.

ground proximity warning systems   Sophisticated avionics systems capable of warning the pilot when he gets too close to the ground. Usually employing radar technology.

ground roll   Landing roll.

ground run   The distance an airplane taking off or landing travels down the runway. The ground run is affected by density altitude, wind, runway surface conditions and other variables.

ground speed (GS)   The speed with which an aircraft travels across the ground. Its relation to TAS is affected by the prevailing winds.

ground visibility   The horizontal visibility near the earth's surface as reported by an authorized observer. Always given in statute miles, or, in the case of runway visual range (RVR), in feet.

ground wire   A wire attached to the aircraft from a grounding point during refueling to avoid the possibility of static electricity buildup.

Grumman Corporation   Originally the developer and manufacturer of the Gulfstream I (G-I) and subsequently of a line of single-engine general aviation aircraft under the Grumman American company name. The entire civil aircraft operation was purchased by Allen Paulson who dropped the single-engine aircraft and proceeded to develop the family of Gulfstream corporate jets under his Gulfstream Aerospace operation. Grumman produces only military aircraft: The A-6F, A-6E, F-14, OV-1D, E-2C, and the EF-111A. (Bethpage, NY 11714. (516) 575-5287)

Grumman EF-111A.

Grumman F14A4.

GRVL Gravel.

GS Glide slope.

GS Ground speed.

GSA General Services Administration.

GTCL Great circle.

guard To listen to. An ATC instruction to guard a given frequency.

guard frequency Emergency frequency.

Gulfstream I, II, III, IV A family of high-performance corporate aircraft manufactured originally by Grumman and subsequently by Gulfstream American Corporation. The G-I was a twin turboprop and the G-II, G-III, and G-IV are twin turbofan aircraft, with only the G-IV being manufactured. (Page 228)

Gulfstream Aerospace GIV.

Gulfstream Aerospace Aircraft

		II	III	IV
ENGINE	manufacturer	Rolls-Royce	Rolls-Royce	Rolls-Royce
	model	Spey Mk 511-8	Spey Mk 511-8	Tay Mk 611-8
	rated at lb thrust	11,400	11,400	13,850
WEIGHTS lbs	ramp	66,000	66,000	73,600
	takeoff	65,500	65,500	73,200
	landing	58,500	58,500	58,500
	zero fuel	42,000	42,000	45,500
	basic operating			42,500
	useful load	28,814	28,280	31,100
FUEL	capacity lbs	26,800	26,680	29,500
DIMENSIONS	span			77'10"
	length			88'4"
	height			24'5"
WING AREA	lb/ft_2			950.39
CABIN	length			45'1"
	height			6'1"
	width			7'4"
PASSENGERS	max	19	19	19
PRESSURE	psi	9.45	9.45	9.45
SPEEDS	M_{mo}	.85 Mach	.85 Mach	.88 Mach
	high speed cruise	501 knots	501 knots	.85 Mach
	long range cruise	430 knots	430 knots	.8 Mach
TAKEOFF	balance field length			5,280 ft
LANDING	distance			3,386 ft
RANGE	max	3,180 nm	3,600 nm	4,220 nm
	w. eight passengers	2,680 nm	3,080 nm	4,220 nm
CEILINGS	max operating	43,000 ft	45,000 ft	45,000 ft
	single engine	24,300 ft	25,000 ft	27,000 ft
PRICE $1988 $s	without interior	n/a	n/a	16,500,000
	including completions			18,500,000

Gulfstream Aerospace Corporation, a Chrysler Company   Manufacturers of the Gulfstream family of corporate twin-turbofan aircraft. The aircraft are the Gulf-stream I turboprop, and the II, III and IV turbofans, of which only the IV is currently in regular production. Also being manufactured are a specially modified Gulfstream IV, known as the Gulfstream SRA-4, that is used by various military and government agencies as a platform for specialized support missions. The U.S. Air Force uses Gulfstream IIIs for special air missions.

Finally, Gulfstream Aerospace has embarked on a 21st Century Gulfstream-SST business jet concept development program, designed to study the needs of business in the year 2000 and beyond, an aircraft with a speed of 1.5 to 2.0 Mach and a 3,500 to 4,000 range, carrying 10 to 12 passengers, to cruise at an altitude of 50,000 to 60,000 feet. The company states at this time (February 1989) that it has determined that there is a market for such an aircraft priced in the $30 to $50 million range. (P.O. Box 2206, Savannah, GA 31402. (912) 964-3000.)

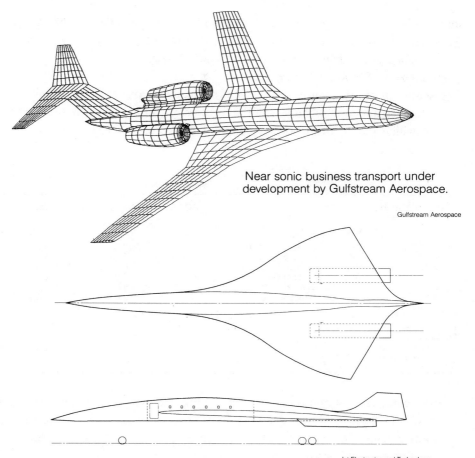

Near sonic business transport under development by Gulfstream Aerospace.

Gulfstream Aerospace

Jet Electronics and Technology

Supersonic business transport under development by Gulfstream Aerospace.

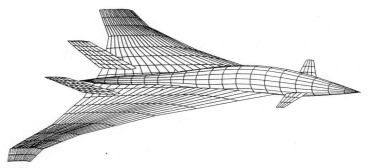

Supersonic business transport under development by Gulfstream Aerospace.

gust   An abrupt but brief increase in the velocity of the wind, generally caused by friction between the air and ground features or by uneven heating of the earth's surface.

gust loads   The load factor caused by gusts and acting upon the aircraft structure.

gust lock   Devices to hold control surfaces in place while the aircraft is tied down, designed to avoid structural damage caused by gusts of wind.

gyro horizon   *See* ARTIFICIAL HORIZON.

gyroscope   A rotating wheel that tends to maintain its position in space relative to a reference direction regardless of the forces exerted on it. It is the basic principle on which the artificial horizon, direction gyro, and inertial guidance systems work.

Gyroscopes

MANUFACTURER	MODEL	TYPE	POWER	WEIGHT	PRICE	REMARKS
J.E.T.	AI-804	2" Gyro Horizon	115VAC 3∅	2.5	$ 7,780	Standby system
J.E.T.	AI-804	2" Gyro Horizon	28 VDC	2.5	$ 8,272	Standby system
J.E.T.	AI-904	3" Gyro Horizon	115VAC 3∅	4.25	$12,811	Self contained system
J.E.T.	AI-904	3" Gyro Horizon	28 VDC	4.25	$14,260	Self contained system
J.E.T.	VG-208	Vertical Gyro	115VAC	4.8	$ 9,435	Remote mounted
J.E.T.	VG-401D	Vertical Gyro	28 VDC	4.0	n/a	Misc. mount options
J.E.T.	DG-710	Directional Gyro	18-32.2 VDC	7.4	n/a	Remote mounted

Prices in 1989 $s
Weights in pounds
AC current requires 400 Hz

gyrosyn compass   A compass system combining a remote mounted magnetic compass (usually located near the wing tip or other magnetic-interference-free location) a remote compass transmitter, a directional gyro, an amplifier, and the heading indicator. Also referred to as a slaved gyro.

H Haze (in sequence reports).

H Hotel (phonetic alphabet).

HAA Height above airport.

HAA Helicopter Association of America. The name was subsequently changed to Helicopter Association International (HAI).

HADIZ Hawaiian Air Defense Identification Zone.

HAI Helicopter Association International.

hail Precipitation of irregular balls of ice, often of such size as to be capable of causing considerable damage to aircraft in flight and on the ground, built up by continuously rising and falling in the atmosphere, usually in thunderstorms, until heavy enough to fall to the ground. The sequence report symbol for hail is A.

HAL Height above landing.

hammerhead stall An aerobatic maneuver in which the aircraft climbs almost vertically to the point of stalling and then is tipped right or left in a wingover, ending in a 180-degree change in direction.

hand off The action of passing control of, and communication with, an aircraft from one controller to another within the same facility or between facilities without interrupting radar contact.

hand signals Signals used by line personnel in directing aircraft on the ground. (Page 232)

hangar An enclosed structure for the purpose of parking aircraft or performing maintenance and repair work. Too often misspelled hanger.

hangar flying An expression used for rehashing a flight or talking about real or imagined flight experiences.

hangar session A meeting of a pilot group, regardless of whether it takes place in a hangar or elsewhere.

hang glider A winged contraption with or without operable flight controls, having neither engine nor fuselage. The pilot usually hangs under a pair of fabric wings and controls the flight by shifting the weight of his body.

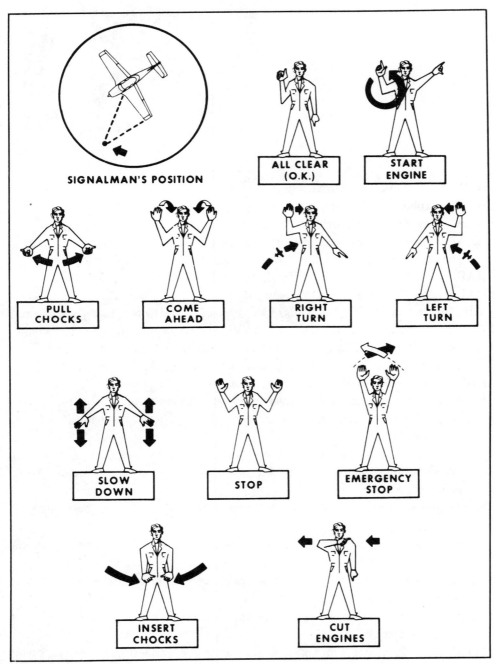

SIGNALMAN'S POSITION

ALL CLEAR (O.K.)

START ENGINE

PULL CHOCKS

COME AHEAD

RIGHT TURN

LEFT TURN

SLOW DOWN

STOP

EMERGENCY STOP

INSERT CHOCKS

CUT ENGINES

Hand signals used by ramp personnel.

hang gliding   The action of flying a hang glider. It is the only aviation activity so far not under the jurisdiction or control of the FAA.

Hartzell Propeller, Inc.   Manufacturer of propellers, governors, and spinners. (One Propeller Place, Piqua, OH 45356-2634. (513) 778-4200.)

HAT   Height above touchdown.

have the numbers   Expression used by pilots when approaching an airport or getting ready to depart, to inform the tower or ground controller that they have received the current information with regard to weather, wind, active runway, and so on.

Hawk XP   A single-engine four-place high-wing piston-powered aircraft once manufactured by Cessna Aircraft Company. No longer in production.

Hawker Siddeley Aviation Ltd.   Manufacturers of a variety of aircraft. (Richmond Road, Kingston upon Thames, KT2 5Qs, Surrey England. U.S. representative: British Aerospace, Inc., P.O. Box 17414, Washington, D. C. 20041).

haze   Restriction to visibility caused by dust, industrial pollution, salt particles in the air, or other causes. The sequence report symbol for haze is H.

Hazeltine Corporation   Manufacturer of expandable modular microwave landing system (MLS) hardware. Its MLSs are installed, among other locations, at New York's Wall Street heliport; Cadillac, Michigan; Houston, Texas; Alberta and Nanaimo, Canada. (500 Commack Road, Commack, NY 11725. (516) 266 5623.) *See also* MICROWAVE LANDING SYSTEMS.

Hazeltine Model 2500-22N MLS AZ-EL stations co-located at Wall Street Heliport, New York City.

HDI   Horizontal deviation indicator. *See* ARTIFICIAL HORIZON.

heading   A direction expressed in numbers of degrees from a given reference point, counting clockwise. Headings can be true (based on true north), magnetic (based on magnetic north) or compass headings.

heading indicator   Directional gyro.

headset   A combination earphone(s) and microphone that is worn on the head in order to be able to communicate while keeping one's hand free. (Pages 235-236)

Headsets

MANUFACTURER	MODEL	SENS	FREQU Hz	IMPED	MIKE	RESP	OUTPUT	IMPED	CORD	oz	TYPE
Telex	PEV 77	117dB	200-3000	150-600					5' C	2	Head
Telex	PEM 77	117dB	200-3000	150-600					5' C	2	Head
Telex	PEM 78	117dB	200-3000	150-600					5' S	2	Head
Telex	HTW-2A	120dB	100-3000	150-600					5' S	4	Head
Telex	A-610	100dB	100-5000	150-600					5.5' S	8	Head
Telex	Airm.760	90dB	100-3000	150-600					5.5' S	3	Head
Telex	H-960	103dB	100-10000	150-600					5.5' S	15.2	Head
Telex	H-630	105dB	100-4000	150-600					5' S	8	Head
Telex	ProAir*	103dB	100-5000	150-600					6' S	18	Head
Telex	66C(RA)				C	200-4500	-48 dB	50-150	5' C	8	Mike
Telex	66T(RA)				D	100-5000	-48 dB	50-600	5' C	9	Mike
Telex	100TRA				D	100-5000	-48 dB	50-600	5' C	9	Mike
Telex	500T				E	100-8000	-48 dB	50-600	5' C	6.5	Mike
Telex	38T				E	300-3000	-48 dB	50-600	6' C	8	Mike
Telex	HS500	109dB	20-4000	600	E	100-10000	-51 dB	50-600	5' C	12	Mike
Telex	ProAir**	103dB	100-5000	150-600	E	100-5000	-51 dB	50-600	5.75'S	19	Boom
Telex	ProAir***	103dB	100-5000	150-600	E	100-5000	-51 dB	50-600	6' C	19	Boom
Telex	D-950	103dB	100-10000	150-600	D	100-6000	-48 dB	50-600	5.5' S	16.7	Boom
Telex	E-951	103dB	100-10000	150-600	E	100-8000	-48 dB	50-600	5.5' S	16.7	Boom
Telex	MRB600	100dB	100-5000	150-600	C	200-4500	-48 dB	50-150	5' S	12	Boom
Telex	Airm.750	90dB	100-3000	150-600	E	300-5000	-50 dB	50-600	6' S	4	Boom
Telex	Mark IIE	111dB	100-3000	150-600	E	100-4000	-48 dB	50-600	6' S	6	Boom
Telex	PRO 1R	120dB	100-3000	150-600	E	100-10000	-48 dB	50-600	6' S	8	Boom
Telex	PRO III	125dB	100-3000	150-600	E	100-10000	-48 dB	50-600	6' S	6	Boom
David Clark	H10-80		100-1000		E				5' S		Boom
David Clark	H10-86		100-1000		E				6' C		Boom
David Clark	H10-30				D				5' S		Boom
David Clark	H10-36+				D				5' C		Boom
David Clark	H10-40				E				5' S		Boom
David Clark	H10-46+				E				5' C		Boom
David Clark	H10-00								5' C		Head
David Clark	M-1A				D			220-1000			Mike
David Clark	M-7				E			150-1000			Mike

*	ProAir 1500	
**	ProAir 2000E	
***	ProAir 2000HE	
+	For use in helicopters	

RESP:	Microphone frequency response in Hz
OUTPUT:	Microphone output
IMPED:	Microphone impedance in ohms
CORD:	Length
S:	Straight
C:	Coiled
oz.:	Weight in ounces
TYPE: Head:	Headphones
Mike:	Microphones
Boom:	Boom microphone headsets

SENS:	Headphone sensitivity
FREQU:	Headphone usable frequency response
IMPED:	Headphone impedence in ohms
MIKE:	Microphone type
C:	Carbon
D:	Dynamic
E:	Electret

David Clark Company

Headset with helmet.

head-up display (HUD)   A means of presenting nav information in a manner that permits the pilot to see both this information and outside through his windscreen.

headwind   Wind blowing directly against the line of flight of the aircraft.

headwind component   The amount of reduction in ground speed resulting from wind blowing toward the aircraft at an angle more or less coinciding with the direction of travel. Even a 90° crosswind produces a headwind component. To

Telex Communications Incorporated

ProAir 2000E Aviation Headset.

determine the ground speed under headwind conditions, use the following formula: The wind component is −1 times the wind velocity in knots times the cosine of (wind direction minus magnetic course minus magnetic variation) divided by 57.2958). The ground speed is: true airspeed plus the wind component. For the exact mathematical formula *see* CONVERSION TABLES.

heavy aircraft Aircraft capable of takeoff weights of 300,000 pounds or more, regardless of the weight at which they are operating at any given time.

heavy iron Vernacular for heavy corporate jets like the Gulfstream II, III and IV and for airline jets.

height above airport (HAA) The height of the MDA above the surface of the airport, as used in connection with the published IFR circling approach minimums.

height above landing (HAL) The height above a designated helicopter landing area. Used only in helicopter IFR approach procedures.

height above touchdown (HAT) The height of the MDA or DH above the highest elevation of the touchdown zone. It is published on instrument approach charts in connection with straight-in approach minimums.

helicopter A rotary-wing aircraft in which both lift and speed are produced by an engine or two engines driving a rotor, the blades of which tilt in a manner that results in both lift and thrust. While helicopters usually fly in a forward direction, they can be flown sideways and even backwards. Helicopters are powered by piston or turboshaft engines.

Helicopter Association International Formerly Helicopter Association of America. *See* AVIATION ORGANIZATIONS.

Helio A family of high-performance STOL aircraft equipped with automatic leading edge slats for extra lift at low speeds. No longer in production.

Helio Courier STOL aircraft in steep climbout at Reading Air Show.

helipad   The actual touchdown portion of a heliport. Any temporary or permanent installation designed to permit helicopter landings.

heliport   An area designed to be used for landing, takeoff, and loading of helicopters. It might be on land, on water, or atop a building.

helium   A non-flammable gas used as a lifting agent in gas balloons and dirigibles.

hemispheric rules   FARs governing the altitudes at which an aircraft should fly, depending on which half circle of the compass (hemisphere) its magnetic heading falls, in order to achieve a reasonable degree of vertical separation. *See* CARDINAL ALTITUDES.

Hertz (Hz)   A measurement of the frequency of radio waves equal to one cycle per second. It is named after Heinrich R. Hertz who proved the existence of electromagnetic waves.

HF   High frequency.

HF transceivers   High frequency com equipment.

Hg   Mercury (hydrargyrum.) Used primarily in expressing manifold pressure in inches of mercury (in. Hg).

HGT   Height.

HI   High.

HIALS   High intensity approach light system.

HIGE   Hovering in ground effect. Used with reference to helicopters to give the service ceiling for hovering in ground effect. Given in feet msl.

high   A region of atmospheric pressure surrounded by lower pressure and, in the northern hemisphere, by clockwise winds. Also called anticyclone.

high clouds   Clouds with bases above 20,000 feet.

high frequency (HF)   Radio frequencies from three to 30MHz (3,000 to 30,000 cycles per second).

high frequency communications   Com radios using the HF band for long-range communications.

high lift devices   Any device, generally attached to the wing of an aircraft, used to increase lift, primarily during slow flight, takeoff or landing. Trailing edge flaps and leading edge slats are the most frequently used high lift devised.

high pressure system   *See* HIGH.

high-speed exit   A taxiway angled to the runway in such a way as to permit aircraft to exit the active runway without the need for excessive speed reduction.

high-speed stall   A stall occurring at high airspeeds. An airfoil of a given shape always stalls at a specific angle-of-attack. An airplane can be made to stall at high speed by a rapid change of the angle-of-attack, such as might occur in a snaproll. The stall speed of an airplane increases with an increase in wing loading caused by the amount of weight carried in the aircraft or by the increase in wing loading effected by steep turns.

High Frequency (HF) Transceivers

MANUFACTURER	MODEL	PRICE	VOLTS DC AC	CHANNELS #		A	S	C	AC	PC	MNT P R	PEP	A	S	V	U	lbs	REMARKS
Bendix/King	KHF950	16,860	28	280,000	¤ ¤		¤		¤		¤ ¤	150	¤			5	22	
Bendix/King	KHF990	19,270	28	280,000	¤ ¤		¤		¤		¤ ¤	150	¤	¤		4	22	Helicopter system, Gold Crown
Collins	HF-230	n/a	28	280,000	¤ ¤ ¤ ¤		¤			¤	¤ ¤	100	¤	¤		3	15	ProLine II
Collins	HF-9000	n/a	28	280,000	¤ ¤ ¤ ¤		¤			¤	¤ ¤	175	¤	¤		3	39	ProLine II
Sunair	ASB500	n/a	28	32,000	¤ ¤		¤		¤		¤ ¤	100	¤	¤		3	23	
Sunair	ASB850A	n/a	28	280,000	¤ ¤		¤		¤		¤ ¤	100	¤	¤		3	36	

PRICE: uninstalled
VOLTS: DC: DC input voltage
          AC: AC 400 Hz input voltage
CHANNELS #:   number of channels
          A: AM
          S: single sideband
          C: CW
AC: automatic antenna coupler

PC: Pretuned antenna coupler
MNT   P: panel mounted
      R: remote mounted
PEP: power output, watts, PEP
A: power amplifier
S: shock mounts
V: Portable unit available
U: number of units

high-speed taxiway *See* HIGH-SPEED EXIT.

high-speed turnoff *See* HIGH-SPEED EXIT.

high tow In soaring, the method of towing a glider behind a powered aircraft during which the glider flies above the flight path of the tow plane.

High tow, where the sailplane rides above the altitude of the tow plane.

high wing   The position of the wing at or near the top of the fuselage on a mono-plane.

Hiller Aviation Division   *See* ROGERSON HILLER CORPORATION.

Rogerson-Hiller Helicopters

		UH-12E HAULER	RH-1100M
ENGINE	manufacturer	Lycoming	Allison
	model	VO-540-C2A	250-C20B
	rating	305 hp	n/a shp
WEIGHTS	maximum lbs	3,100	3,200
	empty	1,759	1,515
	useful load	1,341	1,335
SPEEDS	max knots	83.5	110
	cruise knots	78.3	110
RANGE	max nm	150	340
RATE OF CLIMB	max fpm	1,290	1,600
	vertical fpm	740	800
SERVICE CEILING ft.		15,000	17,300
HOVER	IGE feet	10,400	17,000
	OGE feet	6,800	12,000
FUSELAGE	length feet	28.5/40.7	28.4/41.3
	width feet	7.5	7.23
	height feet	9.3	9.2
ROTOR DIAMETER	main feet	35.4	35.4
	tail feet	5.5	6.0
PRICE	1988 $s	n/a	$405,000

HIRL   High intensity runway light system.

HLF   Half.

HLSTO   Hailstones.

HND   Hundred.

HOGE   Hovering out of ground effect. Used with reference to helicopters to give the service ceiling when hovering out of ground effect. Given in feet msl.

holding   Flying a race-track shaped pattern while waiting for further clearance.

holding fix   A specified location that can be recognized by the pilot either by reference to a ground feature or by using one or several navaids, and used to establish and maintain a given position of an aircraft while holding.

holding pattern   A precise pattern, usually elliptical, based on one or several navaids that an airplane is supposed to fly at an altitude given by ATC while waiting for further clearance. Frequently assigned holding patterns are shown on the low altitude en route charts.

holding pattern entries   Procedures recommended by the FAA (but not mandatory) that are designed to make it relatively easy for a pilot to establish himself in a holding pattern. There are three basic types: direct entry, parallel entry, and tear-drop entry. (Page 241)

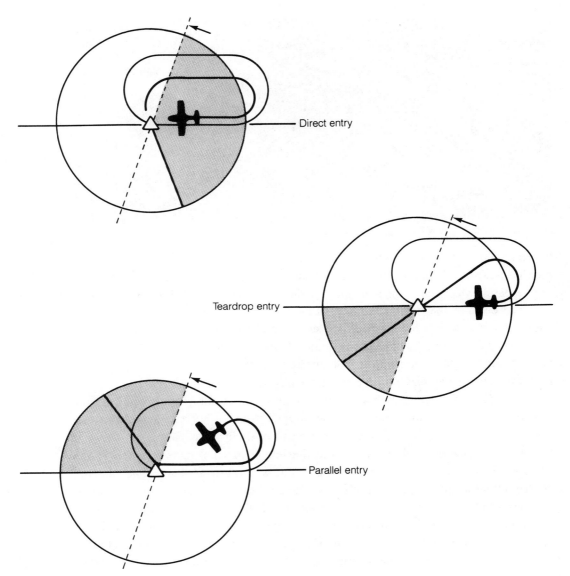

Direct entry

Teardrop entry

Parallel entry

Holding pattern entry.

holding procedure   A standard maneuver used in the air or on the ground to keep an aircraft within a given geographical area while awaiting further clearance.

homebuilt   An aircraft on which at least 51 percent of the construction was performed by an amateur builder. (Page 242)

Homebuilt aircraft at the EAA get-together at Oshkosh, Wisconsin.

homing   Flying toward a navaid.

homing beacon   A nondirectional radio beacon (NDB) that broadcasts a constantly repeating Morse code signal identifying the station. It uses M/LF frequencies and is received by the ADF in the aircraft.

hood   A contraption worn by flight students during instrument flight instruction to prevent them from being able to see outside the aircraft.

hop   A short flight from one airport to another nearby.

horizon   The line at which the earth and the sky appear to be meeting.

horizon   The reference line on an artificial horizon representing the actual horizon with reference to the attitude of the aircraft. Similar horizon indications are included in the pictorial displays that are part of flight-director systems.

horizontally opposed engine   A reciprocating engine in which pairs of cylinders are opposite to one another on a horizontal plane with the crankshaft between them.

horizontal situation indicator (HSI)   A cockpit display activated by nav receivers and usually including a slaved compass card that, by means of various moving indicators, shows the pilot his position relative to certain given navaids. Most HSIs include a VOR and ADF readout as well as a heading information and glide scope indication, all in one instrument. HSIs are a standard component of flight director systems, but can be installed and used without a flight director. (Page 243)

horizontal stabilizer   The fixed horizontal section of the empennage to which the elevators are attached. Some aircraft are equipped with so-called stabilators, in which case the entire horizontal stabilizer can be moved by the pilot, acting as an elevator in its entirety.

horsepower   A unit of energy equal to the power needed to raise 550 pounds one foot in one second. Generally used in measuring engine output.

hotel   In aviation radio phraseology the term used for the letter H.

Horizontal Situation indicators (HSI)

MANUFACTURER	MODEL	PRICE	VOLTS DC AC	V	MOUNT P R	OUTPT AP RM	S	U	lbs	REMARKS
Bendix/King	KCS 55A	7,750	14 28	¤	¤ ¤	¤ ¤*	¤	5	2	* optional Silver Crown
Collins	EHSI74	n/a	28	¤	¤ ¤	¤ ¤	¤	3	9.5	ProLine II
Astronautics		n/a	14 28	¤		¤	¤	1	6-8	5-, 4- and 3-inch systems

PRICE: uninstalled
VOLTS   DC: DC input voltage
              AC: AC 400 Hz input voltage
V: vacuum required
MOUNT   P: panel mounted
              R: remote mounted
OUTPT   AP: output to autopilot
              RM: output to RMI
S: slaved
U: number of units

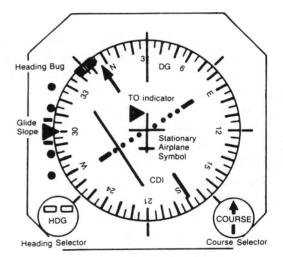

The components of a typical horizontal situation indicator (HSI).

Horizontal situation indicator (HSI).

Combined HSI and DME.

hovering   The ability of a helicopter to retain a given altitude without forward, rearward, or lateral movement.

Dee Howard Company   A company specializing in aircraft modification. The most recent project involves re-engining the BAC 111 with a pair of Rolls-Royce Tay engines producing 12,800 pounds of thrust. (9610 John Saunders Road, P.O. Box 17300, International Airport, San Antonio, TX 78216. (512) 828-1341.)

How do you hear me?   Radio phraseology for, "Did you understand what I said?"

How do you read (me)?   Same as "how do you hear me?" Often abbreviated: Do you read?

hp   Horsepower.

HR   Hear.

HR   Here.

hr   hour.

HS-125   A family of corporate jet aircraft originally manufactured by Hawker Siddeley Aviation in England. Subsequently built by deHavilland as the DH 125 and by Beech Aircraft as the BH 125. Today the rights belong to British Aerospace, which manufactures a new version as the BAe 800.

HSI   Horizontal situation indicator.

HST   Hawaiian Standard time.

hub   A major airport.

HUD   Head-up display.

Hughes Helicopters   Manufacturer of a variety of piston- and turbine-powered helicopters. The company was acquired by McDonnell Douglas, which continues to manufacture the 500-series helicopters under its own name while the Hughes 300 is being manufactured by Schweizer Aircraft Corporation. *See* McDONNELL DOUGLAS HELICOPTERS and SCHWEIZER AIRCRAFT CORPORATION.

Hughes 300 helicopter now manufactured by Schweizer Aircraft Corporation.

Hughes Training Systems, Inc. A combination of four companies that specialize in flight training for corporate and airline crews: Hughes Aircraft Company; Rediffusion Simulation, Inc.; Hughes Support Systems; and Hughes Technical Service Company. The organization provides training for a variety of fixed- and rotary-wing aircraft for corporate aviation, the airlines, and especially the military. A variety of visual systems are employed using a database design for quick access. (2200 Arlington Downs Road, Arlington, TX 76011. (817) 640-5000.)

humidity The amount of water vapor in the air, expressed either in terms of absolute or relative humidity.

hunting and dragging *See* DRAGGING.

HURCN Hurricane.

hurricane A tropical cyclone with wind speeds of 64 knots or more, usually originating in the vicinity of the West Indies.

HVY Heavy.

HWY Highway.

HWVR However.

hydraulics A branch of science that deals with practical applications of liquids in motion, such as the transmission of energy by compressing liquids.

hydraulic system An aircraft system of valves, lines, and pipes that uses the pressure of fluids, usually some type of oil, to move a structure or structures. It is based on the scientific fact that pressure applied to a fluid will pass through it and be concentrated in a small area of least resistance. Thus small pressures on the controls will turn into large pressures capable of moving the control surfaces, landing gear, or other systems. Hydraulic systems must always maintain a given amount of fluid under given pressure.

hydrogen A highly flammable gas used as a lifting agent in gas balloons and dirigibles. Being vastly less expensive than the safer (non-flammable) helium, it continues to be used. The inability of Germany to obtain and pay for helium in the operation of its Zeppelins, resulted in the use of hydrogen and, in the final analysis, the Hindenburg disaster.

hygrometer An instrument that measures humidity.

hypoxia A deficiency of oxygen reaching the tissues of the body. It occurs when flying at high altitudes without supplemental oxygen, initally producing a misleading feeling of euphoria, then inhibiting the pilot from being able to function efficiently and eventually resulting in unconsciousness. Initial onset of hypoxia can be detected by the color of the fingernails, which tend to turn blueish purple.

Hz Hertz.

I

I   India (phonetic alphabet).

IAF   Initial approach fix.

IAP   Instrument approach procedure.

IAS   Indicated airspeed.

IATA   International Air Transport Association.

IC   Ice crystals (in sequence reports).

ICAO   International Civil Aviation Organization.

ice   One of the two most dangerous phenomena in aviation. The other: thunderstorms.

ice fog   Ice fog consists of tiny ice crystals, in fact, frozen water vapor. It tends to be most prevalent in the vicinity of populated areas (and airports) where man-made pollutants are the nuclei around which the ice crystals form.

ice protection systems   A variety of systems is employed in aviation to protect aircraft from the effects of ice accumulation: pulsating de-icing boots on the leading edges of airfoils; a means of spraying alcohol onto the propeller blades in flight; heated windshields and heating system in the leading edges of wings or other airfoils. And, to counteract carburetor ice, the carburetor heat system.

ICG   Icing.

ICGIC   Icing in clouds.

ICGICIP   Icing in clouds and precipitation.

ICGIP   Icing in precipitation.

icing conditions   Weather conditions conducive to depositing ice on an aircraft while in flight. Usually characterized by visible moisture in the air and temperatures around the freezing level. Pilots encountering icing conditions are urged to issue PIREPs immediately. When ice buildup occurs, the best evasive action is to climb or descend to either colder or warmer air.

IDC   Intercontinental Dynamics Corporation.

ident   Phrase used by ATC to ask the pilot to push the ident button on the transponder for positive identification on the radar scope.

IDENT   Identification.

ident feature   One of the features of the ATC radar systems (ATCRBS) used to instantly distinguish one radar return from another.

idle   To run the engine(s) at low speed, preferably at an rpm setting recommended by the manufacturer.

IDO   International District Office (FAA).

IF   Ice fog (in sequence reports).

IFF   Identification, friend or foe.

If feasible reduce (increase) speed to (speed)   An ATC phrase used to ask the pilot to make an adjustment in his speed, usually for the purpose of maintaining safe separation between aircraft.

IFIM   International Flight Information Manual.

If no transmission received for (minutes) or by (time)   An ATC phrase used during or prior to instrument approaches to tell the pilot what action to take in the event of communication failure.

IFR   Instrument flight rules.

IFR   Instrument Flight Research Corporation.

IFR aircraft   An aircraft operating under ATC control, or an aircraft appropriately equipped to operate in IFR conditions.

IFR conditions   Weather conditions below the minimums required for VFR flight.

IFR flight   Flight in below VFR conditions, under ATC control when in controlled airspace.

IFR minimums   Minimums in terms of ceiling and (or) visibility under which IFR departures and (or) approaches are permissible. They are listed on the instrument approach charts. There are no IFR departure minimums for flights carrying neither passengers nor freight for revenue.

IFR over the top   The operation of an aircraft when cleared by ATC to operate in and maintain VFR conditions on top (above clouds).

IFR reserves   A 45-minute reserve in terms of fuel that must be aboard the aircraft when reaching its destination on an IFR flight.

IFR Systems, Inc.   Manufacturer of avionics test equipment. (10200 West York Street, Wichita, KS 67215. (316) 522-4981.)

IFSS   International Flight Service Station.

ignition check   Part of the preflight procedure during which the pilot of a piston-engine aircraft checks the action of the spark plugs by alternately switching from one set to the other.

ignition switch   The switch that activates the ignition system of an aircraft.

ignition system   A system of dual spark plugs, generally powered by magnetos, that provides the spark for igniting the fuel-air mixture in the combustion chamber. It is not part of the electrical system of an aircraft.

IHP   Indicated horsepower.

ILS Instrument landing system.

ILS categories There are five categories of ILS approaches; all except one require special certification of the pilot and special instrumentation in the aircraft over and above that required for a standard ILS approach.

> Category I (CAT I)—The basic ILS approach, calling for an HAT of not less than 200 feet and an RVR of not less than 1,800 feet.

> Category II (CAT II)—Calls for an HAT of not less than 100 feet and an RVR of not less than 1,200 feet.

> Category III is divided into three sub-categories:

> CAT IIIA—Calls for no decision height minimum but an RVR of not less than 700 feet.

> CAT IIIB—No DH and an RVR of not less than 150 feet.

> CAT IIIC—No DH and no RVR minimum. In other words, zero-zero conditions.

IM Inner marker.

IMC Instrument meteorological conditions.

IMD Immediate.

IMDTLY Immediately.

IMEP Indicated mean effective pressure.

immediate Used by ATC in the context of "Cleared for immediate takeoff," usually because another aircraft is on final.

immediately Used by ATC to inform the pilot that he must comply with an instruction without delay in order to avoid a possibly critical situation.

Immelmann The Immelmann is an aerobatic maneuver consisting of the first half of a loop followed by a half roll to level flight. It derived its name from the German WW I ace who is said to have first perfected the maneuver for the purpose of rapidly gaining altitude while, at the same time, reversing his direction of flight.

impeller A vital part of a centrifugal turbine engine. Air enters the impeller through inlet guide vanes. The impeller rotates at high speed, compressing the air by centrifugal action.

IMPT Important.

in Inch; inches.

inbound Flying toward an airport or navaid.

inches of mercury—(in Hg) A unit of measurement of atmospheric pressure, indicating the height in inches to which a column of mercury (Hg) will rise in a glass tube in response to the weight of the atmosphere exerting pressure on a bowl of mercury at the base of the tube.

incident A minor accident or failure or malfunction of an aircraft component or system. Certain incidents require notification of the National Transportation Safety Board (NTSB).

INCR Increase.

Increase speed to (speed)   An ATC instruction to the pilot to increase the speed of his aircraft, usually in order to maintain safe separation between aircraft.

INDC   Indicate.

INDEF   Indefinite; indefinitely.

India   In aviation radio phraseology the term used for the letter I.

indicated airspeed   The airspeed of an aircraft as displayed on its airspeed indicator (IAS).

indicated altitude   Height above sea level as shown on the altimeter when it has been set to the appropriate barometric pressure corrected to msl.

indicated horsepower   The actual power produced in the engine combustion chamber.

indicated mean effective pressure   The average of combustion pressures exerted on the combustion chamber.

induced drag   Drag created through the process of producing lift.

induction system   The air scoop and related plumbing.

induction system icing   Under certain atmospheric conditions ice might form and eventually block the induction system. For this reason most aircraft are equipped with an alternate air source that, when used, takes air from the cabin or other area permanently protected from ice. Using alternate air usually results in a reduction of power.

inertia   The property of matter by which it remains at rest or in uniform motion in the same straight line unless acted upon by some external force.

inertial navigation   Navigating by using the principle of inertia. A gyroscopic instrument on the aircraft senses acceleration, deceleration and changes in direction and, feeding this information into a computer, tells the pilot his position at any given time, assuming the computer has been told the departure point in terms of latitude and longitude.

inertial navigation system   The hardware required for inertial navigation. Prices for these systems are extremely high and as a result such systems are only found on airliners and corporate jets used for intercontinental flights.

inflation   The act of feeding hot air or gas into a balloon or blimp.

inflation sleeve   The sleeve attached to a gas balloon through which gas is fed into it.

INFO   Information.

information request (INREQ)   A request for information originated by an FSS in an effort to locate an overdue or missing aircraft.

in Hg   Inches of mercury.

initial approach fix (IAF)   A fix shown on instrument approach charts and representing the start of the first segment of the instrument approach procedure.

initial approach segment   The first segment of an instrument approach, starting at the IAF.

injection Fuel injection.

inner ear The portion of the ear providing a sense of balance. *See also* EUSTACHIAN TUBES.

Our motion sensing system is located in each inner ear in the approximate position shown.

Semicircular tubes

sac

Enlarged, this system is shaped about as shown. It contains fluid and the sensory organs for detecting angular acceleration, and gravity and linear acceleration.

ANGULAR ACCELERATION

The semicircular tubes are arranged at approximately right angles to each other, in the roll, pitch and yaw axes.

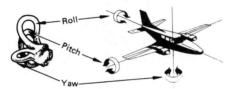

Roll

Pitch

Yaw

A sensory organ, which consists of small sensory hairs that project into a gelantinous substance, is located in each tube. When the head starts to turn (angular acceleration), or speeds up, slows down, or stops its turning, the sensory hairs in the tube in the axis of turning are temporarily deflected due to the motion of the fluid lagging behind the motion of the tube wall. This causes the sensation of turning.

Sensory hairs

tube

A

NO TURNING

No sensation

C

CONSTANT RATE TURN

No sensation after fluid accelerates to same speed as tube wall

B

START OF TURN

Sensation of turning as moving fluid deflects hairs.

D

TURN STOPPED

Sensation of turning in opposite direction as moving fluid deflects hairs in opposite direction.

GRAVITY AND LINEAR ACCELERATION

A sensory organ for detecting gravity and linear acceleration is located in the bottom and side of the sac. It consists of small sensory hairs that project upward into a gelatinous substance containing chalk-like crystals. The weight borne by these sensory hairs changes with every head movement with respect to gravity and with every linear acceleration (up, down, left, right, forward, backward), so causing the sensation of tilting the head or body.

MOVEMENT

Functions of the inner ear.

inner marker A marker beacon used primarily in CAT II approaches. It is located more or less halfway between the middle marker (MM) and the runway threshold.

INOP Inoperative.

INREQ Information request.

INS Inertial navigation system.

inspection of aircraft The FARs require periodic inspection of aircraft by an inspector authorized by the FAA. Such inspections must be logged in the aircraft logbook and initialed by the inspector.

INST Instrument.

installation error Error in the reading of an airspeed indicator caused by the difference between the actual and theoretical comparison between pitot and static pressure. Calibrated airspeed accounts for this error and makes the appropriate correction.

instrument approach Any approach made by reference to instruments and ground-based navigation aids or communication systems.

instrument approach procedures chart A chart of a specific airport area, showing the airport and facility diagrams in detail, plus giving all directions needed for making an instrument approach and landing at that particular airport. Such charts are issued by the government and by Jeppesen-Sanderson. (Pages 253-258)

instrument error Error in the reading of an instrument, such as a magnetic compass, that is inherent in that particular instrument, and the degree of which is known.

Instrument & Flight Research Corporation Manufacturer of encoding altimeters and other aircraft instrumentation. (2716 George Washington Blvd., Wichita, KS 67210. (316) 684-5177.)

Instrument Flight Research, Inc. Manufacturers of on-board in-flight weather simulator for pilot training and testing. (3002 Aviation Way, West Columbia, SC 29169. (803) 796-7400.)

instrument flight rules (IFR) Rules governing the procedures for flight under IFR conditions and (or) under the direction of ATC. (FAR Part 61 and 91).

instrument flying Flying by reference to instruments, ground-based navaids, or communication with ATC.

instrument landing system (ILS) An electronic system of landing aids that provide precise directional and altitude information to the pilot through instrument display(s) in the cockpit. Directional information is supplied by the localizer, altitude information by the glide slope. ILS minimums generally are a 200-foot ceiling and a half mile visibility. An ILS is a precision approach. (Page 259)

instrument meteorological conditions Weather conditions in terms of ceiling, visibility, and cloud types below those which constitute VFR minimums.

instrument panel The panel housing the instrument displays (though not necessarily the complete instruments) in front of the pilot and copilot. (Page 260)

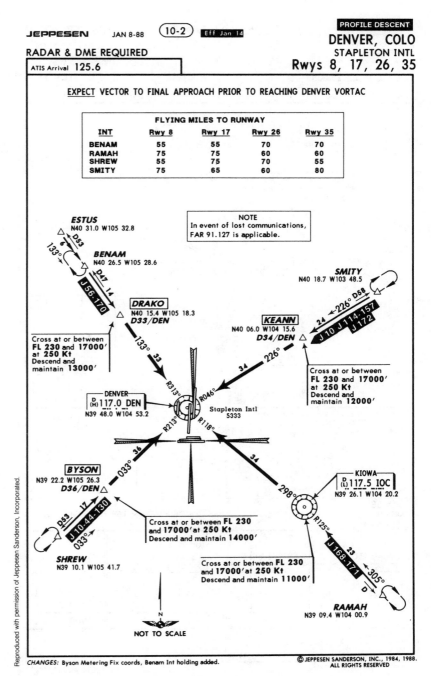

JEPPESEN   JAN 8-88   (10-2) Eff Jan 14

PROFILE DESCENT
DENVER, COLO
STAPLETON INTL
Rwys 8, 17, 26, 35

RADAR & DME REQUIRED

ATIS Arrival 125.6

EXPECT VECTOR TO FINAL APPROACH PRIOR TO REACHING DENVER VORTAC

FLYING MILES TO RUNWAY

INT	Rwy 8	Rwy 17	Rwy 26	Rwy 35
BENAM	55	55	70	70
RAMAH	75	75	60	60
SHREW	55	75	70	55
SMITY	75	65	60	80

NOTE
In event of lost communications,
FAR 91.127 is applicable.

ESTUS
N40 31.0 W105 32.8

BENAM
N40 26.5 W105 28.6

DRAKO
N40 15.4 W105 18.3
D33/DEN

SMITY
N40 18.7 W103 48.5

KEANN
N40 06.0 W104 15.6
D34/DEN

133° 33

Cross at or between
FL 230 and 17000'
at 250 Kt
Descend and
maintain 13000'

Cross at or between
FL 230 and 17000'
at 250 Kt
Descend and
maintain 12000'

DENVER
D
(H) 117.0 DEN
N39 48.0 W104 53.2

Stapleton Intl
5333

BYSON
N39 22.2 W105 26.3
D36/DEN

KIOWA
D
(L) 117.5 IOC
N39 26.1 W104 20.2

Cross at or between FL 230
and 17000' at 250 Kt
Descend and maintain 14000'

SHREW
N39 10.1 W105 41.7

Cross at or between FL 230
and 17000' at 250 Kt
Descend and maintain 11000'

RAMAH
N39 09.4 W104 00.9

N
NOT TO SCALE

Instrument approach chart.

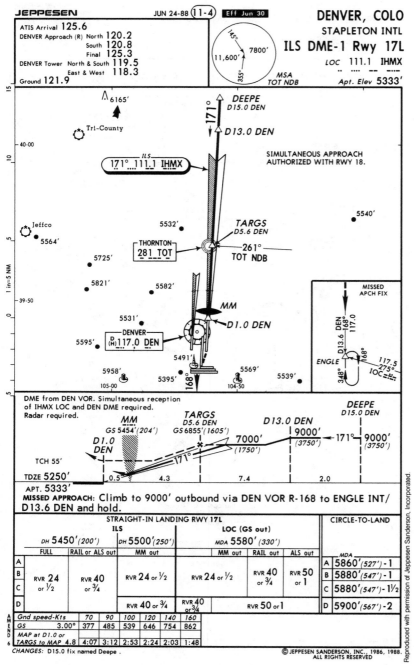

ILS DME instrument approach chart.

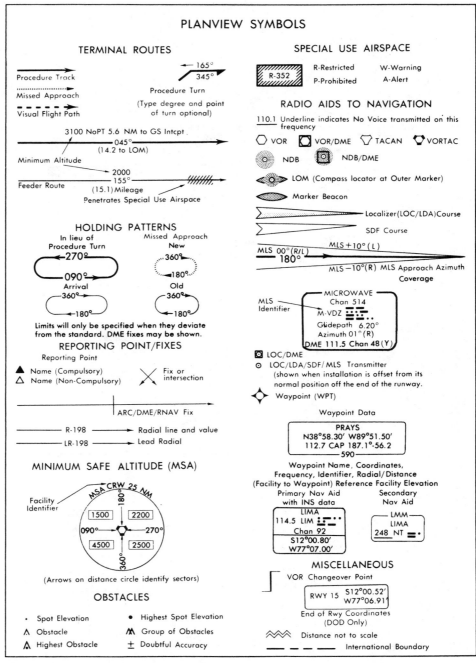

PLANVIEW SYMBOLS

TERMINAL ROUTES

Procedure Track

Missed Approach

Visual Flight Path

Procedure Turn

165°
345°

(Type degree and point of turn optional)

3100 NoPT 5.6 NM to GS Intcpt
045°
(14.2 to LOM)

Minimum Altitude

2000
155°
(15.1) Mileage
Penetrates Special Use Airspace

Feeder Route

HOLDING PATTERNS

In lieu of
Procedure Turn

Missed Approach
New

270°
090°

360°
180°

Arrival

360°
180°

Old

360°
180°

Limits will only be specified when they deviate from the standard. DME fixes may be shown.

REPORTING POINT/FIXES

Reporting Point

▲ Name (Compulsory)
△ Name (Non-Compulsory)

Fix or
intersection

ARC/DME/RNAV Fix

R-198 → Radial line and value

LR-198 → Lead Radial

MINIMUM SAFE ALTITUDE (MSA)

Facility
Identifier

MSA CRW 25 NM
180°

1500 | 2200
090° 270°
4500 | 2500

360°

(Arrows on distance circle identify sectors)

OBSTACLES

· Spot Elevation
⋀ Obstacle
⋀ Highest Obstacle

● Highest Spot Elevation
⋀⋀ Group of Obstacles
± Doubtful Accuracy

SPECIAL USE AIRSPACE

R-352

R-Restricted
P-Prohibited

W-Warning
A-Alert

RADIO AIDS TO NAVIGATION

110.1 Underline indicates No Voice transmitted on this frequency

○ VOR ◇ VOR/DME ▽ TACAN ⬡ VORTAC

⬤ NDB ⬤ NDB/DME

LOM (Compass locator at Outer Marker)

Marker Beacon

Localizer(LOC/LDA)Course

SDF Course

MLS 00°(R/L)
180°

MLS +10°(L)

MLS -10°(R) MLS Approach Azimuth
Coverage

MLS
Identifier

MICROWAVE
Chan 514
M-VDZ ▬▬·
Glidepath 6.20°
Azimuth 01°(R)
DME 111.5 Chan 48(Y)

▣ LOC/DME
⊙ LOC/LDA/SDF/MLS Transmitter
(shown when installation is offset from its normal position off the end of the runway.

◆ Waypoint (WPT)

Waypoint Data

PRAYS
N38°58.30' W89°51.50'
112.7 CAP 187.1°-56.2
590

Waypoint Name, Coordinates,
Frequency, Identifier, Radial/Distance
(Facility to Waypoint) Reference Facility Elevation

Primary Nav Aid
with INS data

LIMA
114.5 LIM ▬·
Chan 92
S12°00.80'
W77°07.00'

Secondary
Nav Aid

LMM
LIMA
248 NT ▬·

MISCELLANEOUS

VOR Changeover Point

RWY 15 S12°00.52'
W77°06.91'

End of Rwy Coordinates
(DOD Only)

〜〜 Distance not to scale

▬ ▬ ▬ International Boundary

Instrument approach procedures chart legend.

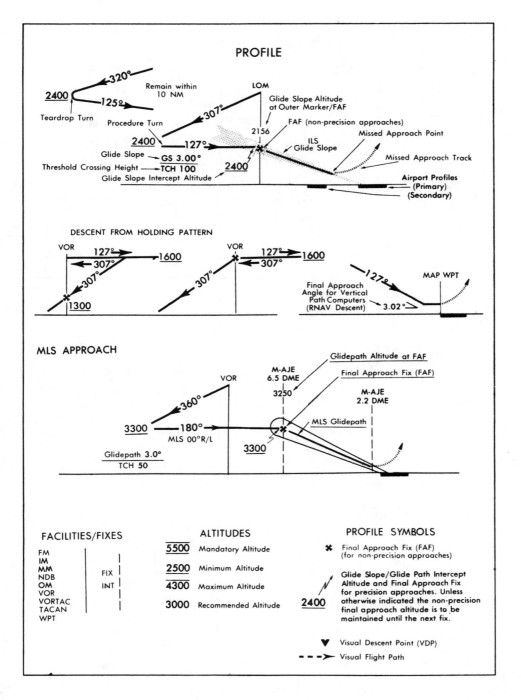

AIRPORT DIAGRAM/AIRPORT SKETCH

Runways

Hard Surface	Other Than Hard Surface	Overruns, Taxiways, Parking Areas	Displaced Threshold

Closed Runways	Closed Taxiways	Under Construction	Metal Surface	Runway Centerline Lighting

Arresting Gear

uni-directional   bi-directional   Jet Barrier

REFERENCE FEATURES

Buildings . . . . ■

Tanks . . . . ●

Obstruction . . . . ∧

Airport Beacon # . . . . ☆

Runway Radar Reflectors . . . . ✕

Control Tower # . . . . ▪

Runway length depicted is the physical length of the runway (end-to-end, including displaced thresholds if any) but excluding areas designated as overruns. Where a displaced threshold is shown, an annotation is added to indicate the landing length of the runway; e.g., Rwy 13 ldg 5000'.

Helicopter Alighting Areas   Ⓗ ✳ Ⓗ ⚠ ⊞

Negative Symbols used to identify Copter Procedure landing point . . . . Ⓗ ⊞ Ⓗ ⚠ ⊞

Runway TDZ elevation . . . . TDZE 123

Total Runway Gradient . . . . 0.8%→UP

     (shown when runway gradient exceeds 0.3%)

▣ U.S. Navy Optical Landing System (OLS) "OLS" location is shown because of its height of approximately 7 feet and proximity to edge of runway may create on obstruction for some types of aircraft.

Approach light symbols are shown on a separate legend.

Airport diagram scales are variable.

True/magnetic North orientation may vary from diagram to diagram.

Coordinate values are shown in 1 or ½ minute increments. They are further broken down into 6 second ticks, within each 1 minute increment.

Positional accuracy within ±600 feet unless otherwise noted on the chart.

When Control Tower and Rotating Beacon are co-located, Beacon symbol will be used and further identified as TWR.

NOTE:
Airport diagrams that are referenced to the World Geodetic System (WGS) (noted on appropriate diagram), may not be compatible with local coordinates published in FLIP.

Runway Gradient

FIELD ELEV 174   Rwy 2 ldg 8000'

0.7% UP→

20

9000 X 200   ←023.2°   1000 X 200

Runway End Elevation — ELEV 164

Runway Dimensions (in feet)

Runway Heading (Magnetic)

Overrun Dimensions (in feet)

Runway Identification

GENERAL INFORMATION (NOS)
SCOPE

Airport diagrams are specifically designed to assist in the movement of ground traffic at locations with complex runway/taxiway configurations and provide information for updating Inertial Navigation Systems (INS) aboard aircraft. Airport diagrams are not intended to be used for approach and landing or departure operations. Requisition for the creation of airport diagrams must meet the above criteria and will be approved by the FAA or DOD on a case-by-case basis.

MINIMA DATA

△ Alternate Minimums not standard. Civil users refer to tabulation. USA/USN/USAF pilots refer to appropriate regulations.

△ NA Alternate minimums are Not Authorized due to unmonitored facility or absence of weather reporting service.

▽ Take-off Minimums not standard and/or Departure Procedures are published. Refer to tabulation.

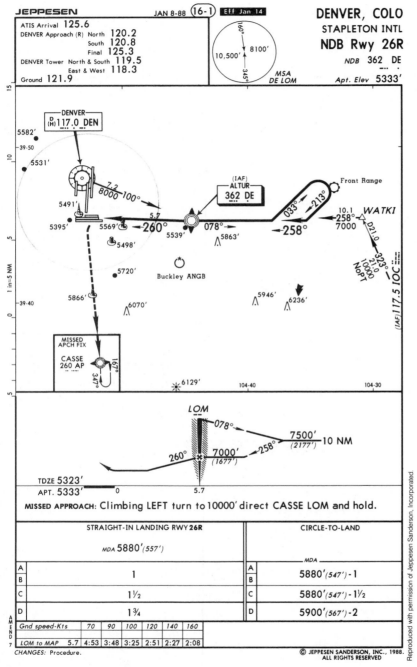

NDB instrument approach chart.

ILS

[FAA INSTRUMENT LANDING SYSTEM]

STANDARD CHARACTERISTICS AND TERMINOLOGY

ILS approach charts should be consulted to obtain variations of individuals systems.

VHF LOCALIZER

Provides Horizontal Guidance.

108.10 to 111.95 MHz. Radiates about 100 watts. Horizontal polarization. Modulation frequencies 90 and 150 Hz. Modulation depth on course 20% for each frequency. Code identification (1020 Hz, 5%) and voice communication (modulated 50%) provided on same channel.

1000 ft typical. Localizer transmitter building is offset 250 ft minimum from center of antenna array and within 90° ±30° from approach end. Antenna is on centerline and normally is under 50/1 clearance plane.

Point of intersection, runway and glide slope extended

3000' to 6000' from threshold

Runway length 7000 ft (typical)

250 to 600 ft from centerline of runway

Sited to provide 55 ft (± 5 ft) runway threshold crossing height

UHF GLIDE SLOPE TRANSMITTER

Provides Vertical Guidance.

329.3 to 335.0 MHz. Radiates about 5 watts. Horizontal polarization, modulation on path 40% for 90 Hz and 150 Hz. The standard glide slope angle is 3.0 degrees. It may be higher depending on local terrain.

∠200'

MIDDLE MARKER

Indicates Approximate Decision Height Point. Modulation 1300 Hz, 95% Keying: 95 Alternate Dot & Dash Combinations/Minute

Amber Light

Flag indicates if facility not on the air or receiver malfunctioning

OUTER MARKER

Provides Final Approach Fix For Non-Precision Approach

Modulation 400 Hz, 95%

Keying: Two dashes/second

Blue light

Localizer modulation frequency
90 Hz   150 Hz

90 Hz   150 Hz
Glide slope modulation frequency

Outer marker located 4 to 7 miles from end of runway, where glide slope intersects the procedure turn (minimum holding) altitude, ±50 ft vertically.

All marker transmitters approximately 2 watts of 75 MHz modulated about 95%

Approximately 1.4° width (full scale limits.)

0.7° (approx.)

3° above horizontal (optimum)

Course width varies; between 3°-6° tailored to provide 700 ft at threshold (full scale limits)

* Figures marked with asterisk are typical. Actual figures vary with deviations in distances to markers, glide angles and localizer widths.

NOTE:

Compass locators, rated at 25 watts output 190 to 535 KHz, are installed at many outer and some middle markers. A 400 Hz or a 1020 Hz tone, modulating the carrier about 95%, is keyed with the first two letters of the ILS identification on the outer locator and the last two letters on the middle locator. At some locators, simultaneous voice transmissions from the control tower are provided, with appropriate reduction in identification percentage.

RATE OF DESCENT CHART
(feet per minute)

Speed (Knots)	Angle			
	2 1/2°	2 3/4°	3°	
90	400	440	475	
110	485	535	585	
130	575	630	690	
150	665	730	795	
160	707	778	849	

Instrument panel in a corporate jet.

instrument rating The rating that a pilot must have in order to fly approved IFR flights. Obtaining an instrument rating requires a minimum of 125 hours as pilot in command, considerable flight training, and a written as well as a flight test.

instrument runway A runway equipped with the appropriate electronic and visual aids for which an instrument approach, either precision or nonprecision, has been approved and published.

instrument ticket Instrument rating.

insurance Aviation related insurance (liability, hull, etc.) is a very specialized field and should be discussed with, and purchased from, a person or company specializing in aviation insurance.

INT Intersection.

integrated autopilot/flight director systems Flight control systems in which the autopilot is coupled to the flight director and takes its commands from the flight director. These systems can be manually overridden at the pilot's discretion.

intercept The action of flying toward and then aligning the aircraft with a VOR radial or bearing.

Interception Intercept.

Intercontinental Dynamics Corporation   Manufacturer of a wide variety of aircraft instruments. (220 Daniel Webster Highway, Merrimack, NH 03054. (603) 889-2500.)

interiors   While most general-aviation aircrafts are manufactured and delivered with standard interiors, many of the higher priced corporate aircraft are ordered with custom interiors, and there are a number of expert companies in various parts of the country which specialize in the design, manufacture and installation of custom interiors.

intermediate approach segment   The segment of an instrument approach between the initial approach segment and the final approach.

internal combustion engine   Reciprocating engine.

international airport   An airport of entry offering customs service; a landing rights airport where permission to land must be obtained in advance from customs authorities; airports designated under the convention on international civil aviation as an airport to be used by international air transport and general aviation flights.

International Aviation Organizations   While internationally there are literally hundreds of aviation organizations, the ones that are included here are the ones that are most likely of interest to pilots traveling in the countries in question. (For a list of the international member organization of the AOPA, contact the AOPA, 421 Aviation Way, Frederick, MD 21701. Phone: (301) 695-2220.)

Abbotsford International Airshow Society, P.O. Box 361, Abbotsford, BC, Canada V2S 4N9. (604) 859-9211.

Aero Club of Brazil, Ave. Alvorado 2541 Via 11, Rio de Janeiro, RJ, Brazil. Phone: 21 224-5621.

Aero Club of Czechoslovakia, Opletalova 29, C-11631 Prague 1, Czechoslovakia. Phone: 223544. Publication: *Letectvi & Kosmonautika.*

Aero Club of France, 6 Rue Galilee, F-75016 Paris, France. Phone: 1 472-37252. Monthly publication: *Aero France.*

Aero Club of India, United India Life Bldg. 3rd Floor, F Block, Connaught Pl., New Delhi, India 110001. Phone: 40721 662361.

Aero Club of Indonesia, Tebet Utara Dalam No. 21, Jakarta, Indonesia. Phone: 21 881331.

Aero Club of Italy, Viale Marescialto Pilsudski 124, I-00197, Rome, Italy. Phone: 6 879641.

Aero Club of Luxembourg, C.P. 131, 2011, Luxembourg. Phone: 433269.

Aero Club of Monaco, 14 Ave. de Fontvieille, Monaco.

Aero Club of Portugal, Ave. de Liberdade 226, 1200 Lisbon, Portugal. Phone: 1 572146.

Aero Club of South Africa, P.O. Box 1993, Halfway House, 1685 Johannesburg, South Africa. Phone 011 805-3106. Publication (10 issues a year): *Aeronews.*

Aero Club of Switzerland, Lidostr. 5, CH-6006 Lucerne, Switzerland. Phone: 41 312121. Monthly publications: *Aero-Revue, Cockpit.*

Aero Club of Zimbabwe, P.O. Box 3371, Harere, Zimbabwe. Phone: 761181.

Aero Federation of Chile, P.O. Box 1074, Ave. J. Arrieta No. 7698-B, Santiago. Chile. Phone: 2 260067.

Aeronautical Chamber of Commerce, Missouri 1465, Montevideo, Uruguay. Phone: 2 591619.

Aeronautical Federation of Bulgaria, 48 Blvd. Christo Botev, 1000 Sofia, Bulgaria. Phone 2 880261.

Aeronautical Federation of Hungary, Szamuely U 44, H-1093 Budapest, Hungary. Phone: 311500.

Aeronautical Sports Association of the Peoples Republic of China, 9 Tiyuguan Rd., Beijing, China. Phone: 751313. Quarterly Publication: *Model Airplane.*

Aeronautical Union of Yugoslavia, P.O. Box 872, Uzun Mirkova 4/1, YU-11001 Belgrade, Yugoslavia. Phone: 011 627290.

Air League of New Zealand, Inc., 68 Evelyn Rd., Howick, Auckland, New Zealand. Phone 768870.

Algerian Federation of Sport Aviation, 20 Blvd. Zighoud Youcef, Alger, Algeria. Phone: 641573.

Argentinian Confederation of Sport Aviation, Anchorena 275, 1170 Buenos Aires, Argentina. Phone: 1 872320. Monthly publication: *Aerodeportes.*

Association of Sport Aviation of the U.S.S.R., Box 395, D-362 Moscow, U.S.S.R. Phone: 491-8661.

Australian Federation of Air Pilots, 132 Albert Road, South Melbourne, Vic., Australia 3205. Phone: 03 699-4200. Publication: *Australian Air Pilot.*

Australian Women Pilots Association, 35 St. Leonards Ave., West Leedersville, WA, Australia 6007. Phone: 09 381-3034. Quarterly publication: *Airnews.*

Austrian Aviation Association, Box 12, Schwechat Airport, A-1300 Vienna, Austria. Phone: 0222 777-02730. Quarterly publication: *Flug-Magazin.*

Aviation Society of Antwerp, Morckhovenlei 22, B-2200 Borgerhout, Belgium. Phone: 3 322 1513. Bimonthly publication: *Aeronews of Belgium.*

British Balloon and Airship Club, British Gliding Association, Kimberly House, Vaughan Way, Leicester, England LE1 4SG. Phone: 0533 531051.

Canadian Business Aircraft Association, Suite 1317, 50 O'Connor Street, Ottawa, ON, Canada K1P 6L2. Phone: (613) 236 5611. Quarterly publication: *CBAA Newsletter.*

Canadian Owners and Pilots Association, Box 734, Station B, Ottawa, ON, Canada K1P 5S4. Phone: (613) 236-4901. Monthly publication: *Canadian General Aviation News.*

Central Aeronautical Association of North Korea, Munsingdon 2, Dondalwon District, Pyongyang, North Korea. Phone: 32798.

Danish Pilots Association, Gammel Kongevej 3, DK-1610 Copenhagen V, Denmark. Phone: 01 310643.

East German Aero Club, Langenveckstrasse 36-39, DDR-1272 Neuenhagen, East Germany. Phone: 37 38890.

Finnish Aeronautical Association, Malmin Lantoasema, SF 00700 Helsinki 70, Finland. Phone: 0 378055. Publication: *Ilmailu.*

German Aero Club, Postfach 710243, Lyoner Str. 16, D 6000 Frankfurt am Main, West Germany. Phone 069 666-6731.

Iceland Aero Club, P.O. Box 1378, Reykjavik Airport, Reykjavik IS-121, Iceland. Phone 91 29330. Quarterly publication: *Flug.*

Iraqui Aero Federation, P.O. Box 441, Baghdad, Iraq. Phone: 98874.

Irish Aviation Council, Bodeen Ratoath, County Meath, Ireland. Phone 372503.

Israeli Aero Club, P.O. Box 26261, 67 Hayarkon St. Tel Aviv, Israel. Phone: 03 655038.

Japan Aircraft Pilot Association, Kokukaikan-Bunken, 18-2 Shinbashi 1-chome, Minato-ku, Tokyo, Japan 105. Phone: 03 501-0433. Bimonthly publication: *Pilot.*

Korea Aeronautic Association, 132-5 1-Ka, Bongnae Dong, Choong-Ku, I.P.O.Box 3855, Seoul, South Korea. Phone: 2 285341.

Mexican Federation of Sport Aviation, Cubiculo No. 6 del 3er Piso del Edif. de la C.D.M., Ave. Rio de Churubusco, Puerta 9, Magdalena Mixhuca 8, DF, Mexico. Phone: 519-2040.

Polish Aero Club, Krakowskie Przedmiescie 55, PL-00-071 Warsaw, Poland. Phone: 22 262021. Weekly publication: *Skrzydlata Polska.*

Romanian Aeronautical Association, 165 Str. Vasile Conta, Bucharest 1, Romania. Phone: 120469.

Royal Aero Club of Belgium, 1 Rue Montoyer, B-1040 Brussels, Belgium. Phone: 2 511-7947. Monthly publication: *Carnets de Vol/La Conquete de L'Air.*

Royal Aero Club of Spain, Carrera San Jeronomo 15, Madrid E-28014, Spain. Phone: 1 429-5034. Monthly publication: *Avion.*

Royal Swedish Aero Club, Box 20081, S-161 20 Bromma, Sweden. Phone: 08 764-6092. Bimonthly publication: *Flygrevyn.*

Turkish Aero Club, Ataturk Bulvari 33, Ankara, Turkey. Phone: 41 111294.

International Aviation Theft Bureau   A clearing house for information leading to the recovery of stolen aircraft and aircraft instruments.

International Civil Aviation Organization   An agency of the United Nations concerned with matters related to international civil air transport.

International Data Systems, Inc.   Software for maintenance, record keeping, systems training, and developers of custom software. (4640 East Elwood, Phoenix, AZ 85040. (602) 968-2244.)

International Flying Farmers   *See* AVIATION ORGANIZATIONS.

interrogator   The signal sent by a radar beacon to be re-transmitted by a transponder.

intersecting runways   Two or more runways that cross or meet one another.

intersection   A point at which the signal from two or more navaids cross, usually given a name related to some nearby geographic location or landmark. Shown on charts by open triangles or crossed arrows.

Intersection departure   A takeoff initiated at a point where the runway intersects a taxiway or another runway. Intersection departures may be suggested by tower controllers in order to expedite traffic, but may be refused by the pilot if he prefers to have the entire length of the runway available for takeoff.

intersection takeoff   Intersection departure.

INTL   International.

INTMT   Intermittent.

INTR   Interior.

INTS   Intense.

INTSFY   Intensify.

INTSV   Intensive.

INTXN   Intersection.

inversion   A fairly shallow layer of the atmosphere in which the lapse rate is reversed and temperature increases instead of decreasing with altitude. It is usually caused by cooling of the air at the surface without extensive vertical mixing. In an inversion the air is usually smooth, but it tends to hold restrictions to visibility, such as smog, close to the ground.

inverted attitude recovery   The process of transition from inverted to normal flight, accomplished by rolling toward the bank index pointer on the artificial horizon.

inverted flight   Flying upside down; an aerobatic maneuver.

inverted outside loop   It begins from normal level flight, followed by a push-over as for a steep dive. This stick position is maintained until the loop is completed and level flight regained.

inverted spin   A relatively unpleasant maneuver resulting in considerable negative G forces. It is accomplished by holding the yoke full forward as the aircraft stalls in an inverted or extreme nose high position. To maintain the spin the yoke must continue to be held forward. Releasing the yoke will usually convert the maneuver into a normal spin.

inverter An electrical instrument that transforms DC current of a given voltage into AC current, usually of a different voltage.

ionosphere A region of strongly ionized particles in the atmosphere, about 35 to 300 miles above the surface of the earth. It reflects radio waves around the curvature of the earth.

IOVC In the overcast.

IPV Improve.

IR Ice on the runway.

ISA Standard atmospheric conditions. The abbreviation stands for ICAO Standard Atmosphere.

I say again I am about to repeat what I said.

isobar An imaginary line or a line on a chart connecting places on the surface of the earth where barometric pressure, reduced to sea level, is the same at a given time or for a given period.

isogonic lines Lines of identical easterly or westerly magnetic variation, shown on aviation charts with the number of degrees of the variation.

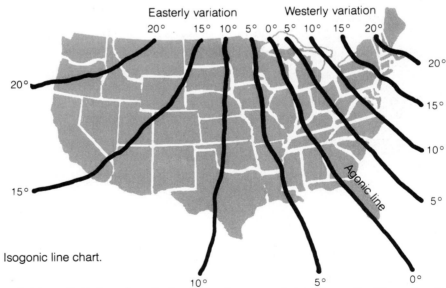

Isogonic line chart.

Israel Aircraft Industries, Ltd. Manufacturer of a variety of military hardware plus the Astra and Westwind I and II business jets. (Ben Gourion International Airport, 70100 Tel Aviv, Israel. Phone: 03 971-3111. U.S. Office: 1700 North Moore Street, Room 1923, Arlington, VA 22209. (703) 243 2227) (Page 266)

ITT Intake turbine temperature.

Israel Aircraft Industries' Westwind

		WESTWIND I
ENGINES	manufacturer	Garrett (2)
	model	TFE 731-3-1G
	thrust lb each	3,700
WEIGHT lbs	ramp	23,000
	takeoff	22,850
	landing	19,000
	zero fuel	16,000
	max payload	2,400
	payload w. full fuel	1,104
DIMENSIONS ft	length	52.3
	height	15.8
	span	44.8
CABIN ft	length	15.3
	height	4.9
	width	4.8
WINGS	area ft^2	308.3
	loading lb/ft^2	74.1
PRESSURIZATION	psi	8.8/9
FUEL lbs	usable	8,710
	w. max payload	7,404
FUEL FLOW pph	per engine, hi speed	2,156
	economy	1,896
SPEEDS knots	V_r	134
	V_2	141
	V_{mo}	360
	M_{mo}	.765
	cruise, hi speed	424
	economy	401
SERVICE CEILING ft	2 engines	45,000
RANGE nm	hi speed, max fuel	2,210
	economy	2,440

J Jet route structure.

J Juliett (phonetic alphabet).

jamming Interference, either electronic or mechanical, that disrupts radio transmissions or the ability of radar to display the desired targets.

jato Jet assisted takeoff. Small rocket engines attached to aircraft and used to effect extremely steep short-field takeoffs. Used primarily by the military and jettisoned after use.

Jeppesen charts Radio facility and instrument approach charts produced and marketed by Jeppesen Sanderson.

Jeppesen Sanderson, Inc. Producer of aviation charts and audio-visual flight training materials. (8025 East 40th Avenue, Denver, CO 80207.)

Jet advisory area Certain areas along some jet routes designated primarily to provide air carrier jets and certain other aircraft with flight following, traffic information, and vectoring service.

jet blast Jet engine exhaust. Jet blast can be dangerous to light aircraft positioned behind a jet on the ground. It should not be confused with wake turbulence.

Jet Cruzer A six- to eight-place canard-equipped all-composite turboprop pusher aircraft is being test flown by Aerodynamics and Structures, the Olympia, WA, company that will be manufacturing and marketing the aircraft, priced at under $1 million in 1989 dollars. Powered by a single Allison 250-C20S gas turbine engine, installed by Soloy Conversions, the aircraft is expected to cruise at 220 knots.

Jet Electronics and Technology, Inc. A subsidiary of Goodrich Aerospace and Defense Division. Manufacturer of gyros and flight instruments, avionics systems, power conversion systems, monitoring systems, head-up displays, and related products. (5353 52nd Street S.E., P.O. Box 8239, Grand Rapids, MI 49508-0239. (616) 949-6600.) (Page 268)

jet engines Turbine engines.

Jet Ranger A family of single-engine turbine helicopters manufactured by Bell Helicopter Textron. (Page 269)

Jet Electronics' standby heading indicator.

Jet Electronics' remote attitude indicator.

JetRanger III.

jet route   Airways to be used by aircraft flying at altitudes above FL 180 (18,000 feet) and up to and including FL 450 (45,000 feet msl), designated by the letter J plus a number, such as J-107.

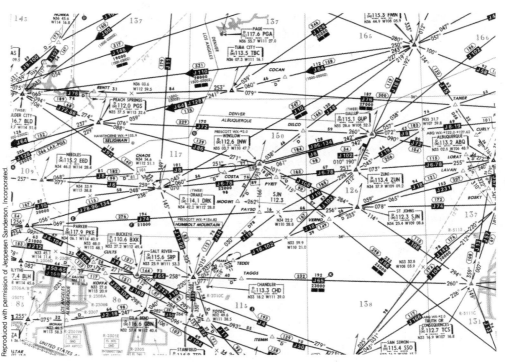

Jet route chart.

jet route structure   The network of jet routes.

JetStar   The first jet aircraft designed specifically for corporate aviation. It was manufactured by Lockheed as a four-engine jet and was later modified by Garrett who replaced the rather noisy jet engines with four powerful fan-jets. The modified version is known as the 731 JetStar because of the TFE 731 engines. Subsequently, Lockheed manufactured a limited number of fan-jet-powered aircraft known as the JetStar II.

Lockheed JetStar II

		JetStar II
ENGINE	manufacturer	Garrett (4)
	type	TPE 731-3
	lb thrust each	3,700
	TBO hours	progressive, modular
WEIGHTS lbs	ramp	44,500
	zero fuel	27,500
	useful load	20,150
	max payload	2,750
	payload with full fuel	2,004
FUEL lbs	with max payload	17,250
DIMENSIONS ft	length	60.4
	height	20.4
	span	54.4
WINGS	area ft^2	542.5
	loading lb/ft^2	82
CABIN ft	length	28.1
	height	6.1
	width	6.2
PRESSURIZATION	psi	8.9
SEATS	crew + passengers	2 + 10
TAKEOFF	balanced field length	6,525
	ISA + 20°	8,425
RATE OF CLIMB	4 engines	4,100
	3 engines	2,250
SERVICE CEILING	4 engines	43,000
	3 engines	28,000
SPEEDS kts	V_r	136
	V_2	151
	V_{mo}	350
	M_{mo}	.82
	cruise, high speed	475 @ 38,000 lbs
	cruise, long range	422 @ 38,000 lbs
RANGE nm	hi speed, max fuel	2,292
	with max payload	2,175
	long range w. max fuel	2,603
FUEL FLOW pph	per engine, hi speed	830
	economy	598
NOISE, EXTERIOR	EPNdB	87.7 - 97.4

Aircraft is no longer in production.

jet stream A narrow migrating stream of winds with velocities ranging from 50 knots up to 250 knots and occasionally more. It is usually located somewhere between 20 degrees and 70 degrees north latitude at altitudes between 20,000 and 40,000 feet, though it has been known to occasionally dip down to 15,000 feet and below. Flow is west to east.

jettisoning external stores The release of tiptanks, jato engines, or other hardware attached to the outside of the aircraft while in flight.

joints Any juncture of two or more pieces of metal or other materials used in the construction of the airframe.

joint use restricted area Restricted areas within which flight may be authorized by the FAA when the area is not being used by the controlling agency.

joy stick Jargon for control stick, control wheel, yoke.

JTSTR Jet stream.

jug Slang meaning cylinder of a reciprocating engine.

juliett In aviation radio phraseology the term used for the letter J.

jumbo jet Very large aircraft, such as the Boeing 747, the McDonnell Douglas DC-10, the Lockheed L-1011, or the military C-5A.

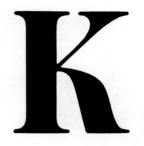

k Cold (as a designation of an air mass).

K Kilo (phonetic alphabet).

k Kilo (1,000 of any measure).

k kiloHertz

K In computer usage stands for one kilobyte or 1,024 bytes.

K Kilometer.

K Smoke (in sequence reports).

katabatic wind The downslope or drainage wind caused by radiation cooling of a shaded slope.

Kawasaki Heavy Industries, Ltd. Manufacturer of the BK 117 twin-turbine helicopter in partnership with MBB/Messerschmitt-Bölkow-Blohm GmbH. (Aircraft Group, World Trade Center Building, 4-1 Hamamatsu-Cho 2-Chome, Minato-ku, Tokyo, 105, JAPAN. Phone: 03 435-2971.)

kg Kilogram (1,000 grams).

kHz KiloHertz (1,000 Hertz; electromagnetic waves propagating at 1,000 cycles per second).

Kilo In aviation radio phraseology the term used for the letter K.

Kilogram (kg) 1,000 grams.

KiloHertz (kHz) 1,000 Hertz; radio magnetic waves propagating at 1,000 cycles per second.

Kilometer (km) 3,281 feet; $5/8$ of a statute mile. *See* CONVERSION CHARTS.

Kilowatt (kw) 1,000 watts.

kinesthetic sense The sense of position and balance that detects and estimates motion without reference to vision or hearing. It tends to become unreliable during maneuvers in IFR conditions.

King Air A family of corporate twin turboprop aircraft manufactured by Beech Aircraft Corporation. (Pages 274-275)

King Radio Corporation *See* BENDIX/KING GENERAL AVIATION AVIONICS DIVISION.

kitchen gas Ordinary natural gas used occasionally as lifting agent in gas balloons. It is highly flammable and less effective than helium, but also less expensive.

Beechcraft King Air C90A.

Beechcraft King Air C99.

Beechcraft King Air A100.

Beechcraft King Air B100.

Beechcraft Super King Air B200.

Instrument panel of the Beechcraft Super King Air 300.

km   Kilometer; 1,000 meters.

kmh   Kilometers per hour.

knot   Nautical miles per hour. One knot equals one nautical mile or 1.15 statute miles per hour.

known traffic   Aircraft, whether IFR or VFR, whose position, altitude, and intentions are known to ATC.

Koch chart   A chart showing the percentage increase in the required takeoff distance and the reduction in climb capability caused by an increase in density altitude (airport elevation and temperature).

Kollsman Avionics Division   Manufacturer of a wide variety of avionics and flight instruments. (220 Daniel Webster Highway South, Merrimack, NH 03054. (603) 889-2500.)

Kollsman window   The window on an altimeter displaying the barometric pressure to which the altimeter is set.

KS Avionics, Inc.   Manufacturer of EGTs and other avionics and flight instruments. (25216 Cypress Avenue, Hayward, CA 94544. (415) 785-9407.)

kt   Knot.

kw   Kilowatt; 1,000 watts.

kwh   Kilowatt hour.

L   Drizzle (sequence reports).

L   Lights.

L   Lima (pronounced leemah) (phonetic alphabet).

Lake Aircraft, Inc.   Manufacturer of amphibian aircraft and seaplanes. (Laconia Airport, Laconia, NH 03246. (603) 524-5868.)

Lake Aircraft

		RENEGADE	TURBO RENEGADE
ENGINE	manufacturer	Lycoming	Lycoming
	model	IO-540	TIO-540
	rating hp	250	270
DIMENSIONS	wing span ft	38	38
	length	28 ft 2 in	28 ft 2 in
	height ft	10	10
FUEL	usable gal	90	90
WEIGHTS	useful load lbs	1200	1120
SPEEDS	knots	132	155
	stall	49	49
RANGE	nm	870	783
RATE OF CLIMB	3140 lbs, fpm	850	1030
	2600 lbs, fpm	1200	1250
TAKEOFF RUN	3140 lbs, land, ft	980	880
	2600 lbs, land, ft	600	600
	3140 lbs, water, ft	1350	1250
	2600 lbs, water, ft	800	800

Alodined and chromated inside and out for salt-water operation.

lake, island, and mountain reporting service   A special service provided by FSSs in certain areas.

Lama   A high-performance utility turbine helicopter manufactured by Aerospatiale in France.

Lambert conformal conic projection   A relatively accurate means of representing the curved surface of the globe on the flat surface of a chart or map.

laminar airfoil   An airfoil shaped in a way to maintain laminar flow over much of its upper surface.

laminar flow   Air flowing smoothly over and adhering to the surface of an airfoil.

laminated   Bonded by means of adhesive agents rather than rivets.

Lance   A high-performance single-engine piston aircraft, a member of the Cherokee family, manufactured by Piper Aircraft Corporation. No longer in production.

Piper Lance II and Turbo Lance II.

land breeze   The movement of air from land to sea at night. It reverses to a sea breeze in the daytime.

landing   The act of bringing the airplane down to the surface of the earth (or water). Technically, it starts at DH or MDA and includes flare out, touchdown and roll-out.

landing area   Any area of land or water intended to be used for the landing of aircraft, regardless of whether such an area includes actual runways, service facilities, and the like.

landing direction indicator   Tetrahedron.

landing distance   The horizontal distance required to bring an aircraft to a complete stop. It might be measured from the point of touchdown or from an altitude of 50 feet prior to touchdown. It depends on many variables including aircraft weight, wind, runway surface conditions, touchdown speed, use of flaps, etc. Aircraft flight manuals contain landing distance charts for standard conditions.

landing gear   The entire mechanism including hinges, supports, wheels, tires (or floats) necessary in order to support the aircraft on the ground (or water). Landing gear might be fixed or retractable.

landing gear doors   Doors that cover the gear wells when landing gear is retracted.

landing-gear-extended speed   The maximum speed at which a retractable-gear aircraft may safely be flown with the gear in the extended position.

landing-gear-operating speed   The maximum speed at which a retractable-gear aircraft may be flown while the gear is in the process of being extended (or retracted). On some aircraft it is lower than the landing-gear-extended speed because gear doors and related apparatus may be susceptible to damage from high-speed airflow when in the process of opening or closing.

landing weight   The maximum gross weight condition under which an aircraft may be landed. Under certain conditions it may be necessary to dump or burn off fuel before landing in order to comply with the landing weight restrictions.

landing minimums   The minimums in terms of ceiling and visibility applicable to the published instrument approaches for any given airport.

landing pattern   The standard pattern, consisting of downwind leg, base leg and final approach, which should be flown prior to and during the landing unless clearance for a straight-in or other approach has been given by the control tower.

landing roll   The distance from touchdown to where the aircraft has been brought to a complete stop. Also called ground run or landing run.

landing run   Landing roll.

landing sequence   The order in which aircraft are positioned and follow one another for landing.

landing site   In ballooning, any area free of obstructions that lends itself to the landing of a balloon.

landing speed   The minimum speed at which an aircraft can touch down while under control by the pilot.

lapse rate   The rate at which atmospheric temperature decreases with altitude. Under standard conditions this is 5.5 degrees per 1,000 feet. *See* ADIABATIC RATE.

large aircraft   An aircraft of more than 12,500 pounds maximum certificated takeoff weight, regardless of its actual operating weight at any given time.

Laser 300   *See* OMAC, INC.

OMAC Laser 300 Single-Turbine Aircraft

		LASER 300
ENGINE	manufacturer	Pratt & Whitney
	type	PT6A-135A
	rating shp	904, flat rated to 750
PROPELLER	diameter inches	106
	blades	3
	type	constant speed, full feathering, reversing
WEIGHTS lbs	max takeoff	7800 (8350[*])
	basic empty	5100
	useful load	2700 (3250[*])
FUEL U.S. gallons	usable	297
DIMENSIONS	length	29'7"
	height	9'5"
	rear wing span	41'6"
	front wing span	23'6"
CABIN	length	14'7"
	height	5'
	wodth	5'6"
PRESSURIZATION	psi	5.5
WINGS	rear wing area ft^2	260
	front wing area ft^2	66
	rear wing load. lb/ft^2	19
	front wing ld. lb/ft^2	32
SPEEDS kts	max cruise	253
RANGE nm	max cruise speed	1500
	economy cruise	2097
RATE OF CLIMB	fpm	2010
CEILING	certified ft.	25,000
	service ft.	34,000
TAKEOFF ft.	50 ft.obstacle	2000
LANDING ft.	50 ft.obstacle	2300

[*] anticipated

last assigned altitude   The last altitude or flight level assigned by ATC and acknowl-
edged by the pilot.

LAT   Latitude.

lateral axis   The imaginary line running from wingtip to wingtip through the center
of gravity of the aircraft. Also known as pitch axis.

lateral separation   The lateral spacing of aircraft flying at the same altitude, regardless of the direction of flight.

latitude   Any line circling the earth parallel to the equator, measured in degrees,
minutes, and seconds north and south of the equator.

latitude   Permissible deviation from the norm, such as, a pilot has a certain amount
of latitude in selecting an rpm setting relative to the manifold pressure setting
being used.

Latitude/longitude chart.

launch site   In ballooning, a large fairly flat area suitable for inflating the balloon
and free of downwind obstructions. (Page 282)

Hot-air balloon instrument panel.

Lawyer Pilots Bar Association *See* AVIATION ORGANIZATIONS.

lazy eight A coordination maneuver in which the nose of the aircraft is made to describe a pattern resembling a figure eight lying on its side on the horizon.

lb Pound.

lbs Pounds.

LC Local telephone number of an FSS.

LCL Local.

LCLZR Localizer.

LCTD Located.

LCTN Location.

L/D Lift-drag ratio; or lift over drag.

LDA Localizer type directional aid.

leading edge The forward edge of any airfoil.

lead/lag *See* DRAGGING.

lead sled In sailplane parlance, a heavy glider with a poor glide ratio.

lean To adjust the fuel mixture so that it contains less fuel and more air.

LearAvia Company formed by William P. Lear on Reno Stead Airport for the purpose of manufacturing his revolutionary LearFan pusher turboprop. After his death, his wife attempted to continue development and eventual manufacture of the aircraft, but in the final analysis the obstacles were too great.

LearFan   A revolutionary design by William P. Lear for a turboprop in which two turboshaft engines would drive a single pusher propeller. *See* LEARAVIA.

Lear Jet   The original spelling of the corporate jet aircraft designed and built by William P. Lear.

Lear Jet 23, first flight.

Lear Jet 23 prototype.

Learjet   A family of corporate jet aircraft.

Learjet Corporation   Manufacturer of the Learjet family of corporate jet aircraft. (P.O. Box 7707, Wichita, KS 67277-7707. (316) 946-2000.) (Page 284)

Learjets

		MODEL 31	MODEL 31ER	MODEL 35A	MODEL 36A	MODEL 55C	MODEL 55C/ER	MODEL 55C/LR
ENGINE	mfr.	Garrett	Garrett	Garrett	Garrett	Garrett	Garrett	Garrett
	model	TFE 731-2	TFE 731-2	TFE 731-2	TFE 731-2	TFE 731-3A	TFE 731-3A	TFE 731-3A
	thrust lb.	3500	3500	3500	3500	3700	3700	3700
WEIGHTS	takeoff	15,500	15,500	18,300	18,300	21,000	21,500	21,500
	landing	15,300	15,300	15,300	15,300	18,000	18,000	18,000
	empty	9,857	9,896	9,838	9,838	12,622	12,686	12,816
FUEL	usable lbs	4,107	4,596	6,198	7,397	6.693	7,048	7,705
FUSELAGE	length ft	48.58	48.58	48.58	48.58	55.10	55.10	55.10
	height ft	12.25	12.25	12.25	12.25	14.70	14.70	14.70
WING	span ft	43.79	43.79	39.50	39.50	43.79	43.79	43.79
	area sq.ft	264.5	264.5	253.3	253.3	264.5	264.5	264.5
PASSENGERS max		10	10	10	10	10	10	10
CABIN	length in	205	191	205	160	200	188	184
	width in	59	59	59	59	70.8	70.8	70.8
	height in	52	52	52	52	68.5	68.5	68.5
BALANCED FIELD LNGTH		2,970	3,370	4,972	4,972	5,039	5,299	5,299
LANDING	distance ft	2,950	3,010	3,075	3,075	3,250	3,250	3,250
SERVICE CEILING		51,000	51,000	45,000	45,000	51,000	51,000	51,000
SPEED	cruise,kts	447	447	462	462	461	461	461
RANGE	nm	1,630	1,850	2,236	2,664	2,221	2,337	2,510

Learjet 31.

Learjet 35A.

left-right indicator On-course indicator.

left seat Flying the left seat is frequently used jargon for being pilot in command, regardless whether the crew consists of one or more persons.

leg A segment of a flight as in San Diego-Los Angeles leg.

leg Any of the four courses of an L/MF radio range.

leg Part of the traffic pattern; downwind leg, base leg.

lenticular cloud A high cloud in the approximate shape of a double-convex lens, usually indicating severe turbulence below. Generally associated with mountain waves.

letter of agreement A written agreement between the FAA and the operator of an aircraft, permitting him to operate in a manner inconsistent with the regulations covering a given area of airspace.

level action valve In ballooning, a blast valve.

level flight Flight in which level altitude is maintained for a prolonged period of time.

level turn A turn without losing or gaining altitude, usually while maintaining a constant rate of turn and airspeed until the desired heading has been reached.

LF Low frequency.

LF/MF radio range A (largely antiquated) navigation facility that radiates four overlapping signal patterns. The overlapping areas are called legs, and the area between them, quadrants, identified by Morse code signals A (. –) or N(– .).

LFR LF/MF radio range.

LGT Light.

LGTD Lighted.

LGTG Lightning.

lift The generally upward force created by the difference in pressure between the upper and lower surfaces of an airfoil in motion. In level flight it is balanced by the force of gravity. The force always acts at right angles to the flight path.

lift component The portion of lift that acts on the wing perpendicular to the direction of its motion through the air.

lift drag ratio (L/D) The ratio of lift to drag of any structure. It is an indication of the efficiency of an airfoil at any given angle-of-attack.

liftoff The moment when the wheels break contact with the ground during takeoff.

light aircraft An aircraft with a maximum certificated gross weight of 12,500 pounds or less, regardless of the operating weight at any given moment.

lighted airways Airways, usually in remote parts of the country, marked by lights flashing course identification in Morse code. Remnants of the original airways system and, for all practical purposes, extinct.

lighted airport An airport where runway and obstruction lighting are available. There need not be a rotating beacon. At small airports such lighting might be available only on demand, either by contacting the nearest FSS (or unicom, if in operation), or in some cases by repeatedly depressing the mike button using a given transmitting frequency.

lighter-than-air craft Balloons, dirigibles, blimps.

Lighter-Than-Air Society, Inc. (LTA) *See* AVIATION ORGANIZATIONS.

light gun Located in control towers, it is a hand-held directional light-signaling device that emits a narrow bright signal of light (white, green, red). It can be operated by the tower controller in communicating with no-radio aircraft or aircraft experiencing radio failure. The color of the light and the frequency of flashes tells the pilot what action he is supposed to take. The pilot should acknowledge having received the message by rocking his wings or, when able, flashing his landing lights.

light-light twin   An unofficial designation for twin aircraft with a maximum certificated takeoff weight of 4,000 pounds or less.

lightning   Immensely powerful electrical discharges occurring in and near thunderstorms. Lightning can strike from cloud to ground or from cloud to cloud. Lightning strikes on aircraft are relatively rare but, when occurring, can cause damage to the aircraft skin and have been known to knock out electrical systems due to a momentary overload. Lightning usually occurs in areas of maximum turbulence and should be given a wide berth.

light signals   The signals used by a tower controller using the light gun. Steady green means cleared for takeoff (aircraft on the ground) or landing (aircraft in the air); flashing green means cleared for taxi (aircraft on the ground) or return and land (aircraft in the air); steady red means stop (on the ground) or yield to other aircraft (in the air); flashing red means taxi clear of runway (on the ground) or do not land (in the air); flashing white means return to starting point (used only for aircraft on the ground).

light twin   An unofficial designation for aircraft with certificated takeoff weights of between 4,000 and 6,000 pounds.

lima   In aviation radio phraseology the term used for the letter L. Pronounced leemah.

limited remote communications outlet   An unmanned ground facility capable of forwarding transmissions and receptions to the associated VOR or VORTAC.

limit-load factor   The maximum theoretical load factor that an airplane is expected to encounter. It is generally 3.8 G in a normal category light plane and is well below the ultimate load factor, thus offering a substantial safety margin.

line inspection   Preflight.

line-of-sight   Literally the straight line from a person's eye to the horizon and from there out into space. Frequencies propagating according to the line-of-sight principle do not follow the curvature of the earth and are thus limited in reception distance. All VHF radio signals, both nav and com, fall into this category.

line squall   A chain of cumulonimbus clouds along or ahead of a cold front, with violent winds, rain, lightning (and thunder) and the possibility of heavy hail. Such line squalls (lines of thunderstorms) might extend for hundreds of miles and tend to reach up very high. They cannot safely be overflown or circumvented except by certain turbine aircraft equipped with airborne weather radar. More often than not they don't last more than a few hours.

liquid oxygen system   In these systems liquid oxygen is stored in supercooled (vacuum insulated) containers and can be turned into breathing oxygen (gas) when needed. The volumetric proportion between liquid and gaseous oxygen is 1 to 800.

LIRL   Low intensity runway edge lights.

liter   A liquid or volumetric measure used in countries operating on the metric system. *See* CONVERSION TABLES.

Litton Aero Products   Manufacturer of inertial, Omega, and GPS nav systems. (6101 Condor Drive, Moorpark, CA 93021-2601. (805) 378-2000.)

LKLY   Likely.

L/MF   LF/MF radio range.

LMM   Compass locator middle marker; part of an ILS.

LMT   Limit.

LND   Land.

LNDG   Landing.

load   The total force acting on a structure, especially the wings and control surfaces of an airplane. It consists of static loads caused by gravity, dynamic loads resulting from certain maneuvers, or a combination thereof. *See also* PAYLOAD, USEFUL LOAD, EMPTY WEIGHT, GROSS WEIGHT, AND GUST LOADS.

load factor   The ratio of the total of loads exerted on an airplane to its original weight. A load factor of one G is in effect during level flight.

load tapes   The horizontal and vertical tapes incorporated into the structure of a hot-air or gas balloon, which carry most of the load.

LOC   Localizer; part of an ILS.

local aeronautical chart   A chart of a large terminal area at a scale of 1:250,000.

local control frequency   Tower frequency.

localizer   The portion of an ILS system which sends out directional VHF signals which show the pilot on his OBI and the action of the CDI whether he is aligned with the centerline of the runway, or off course to either left or right.

localizer type directional aid   Similar to a localizer, it is not associated with an ILS system, may not be used for precision approaches, and is frequently not aligned with the centerline of the runway.

localizer usable distance   The maximum distance from which the localizer signal can be reliably received by an aircraft flying at a given altitude.

local traffic   Aircraft operating in the traffic pattern or within sight of the tower, usually consisting of training flights and practice VFR or IFR approaches.

locator beacon   ELT.

Lockheed Dataplan, Inc.   Provides computerized flight planning, text/graphic weather services, worldwide ATC route structure, and aircraft performance loads. (121 Albright Way, Los Gatos, CA 95030. (408) 866-7611.)

Lockheed Georgia Company Manufacturer of the JetStar, the L-1011 wide-body airliner, and the military C-130 Hercules family of aircraft, the KC-130T tanker aircraft designed for aerial refueling, the C-141 Starlifter, and the C-5A and C-5B, which, with its 261,000-pound payload capacity, is doubtlessly one of the largest transport aircraft. (86 South Cobb Drive, Marietta, GA 30063. (404) 424-4411.)

Lockheed KC-130T refueling a pair of Sikorsky CH53-E Super Stallions.

log A flight-by-flight record of all operations involving a specific aircraft, engine, or pilot, listing flight times, areas of operation, maintenance, repairs, etc. There are generally three types of logs: The pilot logbook that must list all mandatory flight experience and flight tests, though logging other types of flying is voluntary. The airframe logbook that records the hours flown and all inspections, maintenance, and repair work. And the engine log, which does the same for the engine.

logbook Log.

LOM Compass locator outer marker; part of an ILS.

Lomcevak A violent aerobatic maneuver in which the aircraft is made to tumble tail-over-prop through one-and-a-half revolutions. Only a handful of pilots have performed the true lomcevak, and not all aerobatic aircraft have the capability.

LONG Longitude.

longitude Any line from the north to the south pole, measured in degrees, minutes, and seconds of a circle, east or west of the Prime Meridian, which runs roughly through Greenwich, England.

longitudinal axis An imaginary line running length-wise through the airplane from the nose to the tail through the center of gravity. It is the axis about which the aircraft banks or rolls. Also called roll axis.

longitudinal separation   The separation between aircraft flying at the same altitude and in (more or less) the same direction.

long-range navigation   Navigation beyond the limits of the North American VOR/VORTAC system.

long-range navigation systems   Avionics systems capable of precision navigation independent of the VOR/DME/VORTAC navigation network. They generally fall into three distinctly different types.

One, known as INS (inertial navigation system) is either controlled by a gyroscopic device or by a series of lasers. In each case it is entirely independent of any ground-based navaids, producing navigational guidance by remembering the lat/long coordinates at takeoff and computing all motion in terms of speed, direction, and so on, in order to produce exact current location information at all times.

Another is referred to as VLF/Omega. It uses the signals obtained continuously from a worldwide network of low-frequency transmitters to produce precise navigational guidance anywhere in the world. (Pages 290-291)

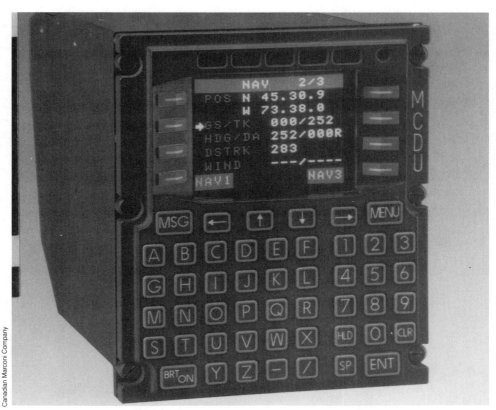

Canadian Marconi Company

Long-range navigation management system.

The third is Loran-C, which uses the signals produced by a network of Loran transmitters to produce accurate navigational guidance. It is usable primarily in North America and has some geographical limitations because of areas of unsatisfactory reception.

Loran-C Systems

MANUFACTURER	MODEL	VOLT	U	WEIGHT	G.CIRCLE	RHUMB	CROSS	RESOL	PLAN	WAY	DBASE	REMARKS
Foster Airdata	F4 Phoenix	10-32 12 w.	3 2	4.97 1.55	0 - 9999	0 - 299.9	+/-99	0.1nm* 1 nm**	20/9	200	62UDC	$2,191
Foster Airdata	500	10-32 8 w.	3 2	4.15 1.55	0 - 9999	0 - 299.9	+/-99	0.1nm* 1 nm**	26/9	200	62UDC	$1,295
Terra	TLC 120	11-35	1	2.5			+/-20		4/9	120		
II Morrow	Apollo II 612	6.5-48 15 w.	1	3.75			0.1 nm	0.01 nm		100	Fly-brary	
II Morrow	Apollo II 612B	6.5-48 15 w.	1	3.75			0.1 nm	0.01 nm		100	Fly-brary	
II Morrow	Apollo II 618	6.5-48 15 w.	1	3.75			0.1 nm	0.01 nm		500		
II Morrow	Apollo 614R	6.5-48 16.5 w.	3	4.97			0.1 nm	0.01 nm		100	Fly-brary	IFR appr.
II Morrow	Apollo 618R	6.5-48 15.6 w.	3	4.97			0.1 nm	0.01 nm		500	Fly-brary	VFR only
II Morrow	Apollo 604FB	6.5-48 9 w.	1	3.187			0.1 nm	0.01 nm		100	Fly-brary	Dead Reckoning comp
II Morrow	Voyager 612C	6.5-48 15 w.	1	3.5			0.1 nm	0.01 nm		100	Fly-brary	Circular display
ARNAV	R25/50									100	Jeppsn	TCA Alert $3,795
ARNAV	R40									100	Jeppsn	IFR appr. $3,915
Advanced Navigation	ANI-7000	28+-4 30 w.	2	18.1			0.1 nm	0.01 nm	99	200		IFR appr.
Terra	TLC 120	11-35 10 w.	1	2.5			1 nm		4	120		

VOLT	1st line: input voltage, DC. 2nd line: watts
U	number of units
WEIGHT	pounds
G.CIRCLE	Great circle computation range in nautical miles
RHUMB	Rhumb line computation range in nautical miles
CROSS	either +/- to/from left or right in nautical miles or resolution increments in nautical miles
RESOL	distance resolution in nautical miles * at distances from 0 to 99.9 nm ** at distances of 100 nm and greater
PLAN	number of flight plans stored/maximum waypoints per each
WAY	maximum number of user-defined waypoints
DBASE	data base available for use

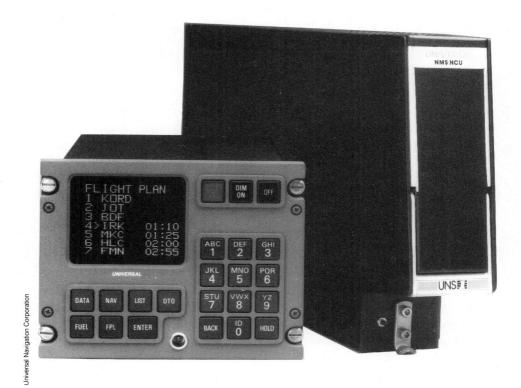

Universal Navigation UNS-1 long-range navigation management system.

LongRanger   A single-engine turbine helicopter of the JetRanger family, manufactured by Bell Helicopter Textron.

LongRanger III.

loop　An aerobatic maneuver in which the airplane, without banking, describes a complete vertical circle in the sky. In an inside loop the head of the pilot points to the center of the circle. In an outside loop it points away from it.

loop　A type of directional antenna used to receive low and medium frequency transmissions by the ADF.

loop/sense antenna　A recent invention in the design of ADF antennas, eliminating the actual loop and reducing size and thus drag of the antenna installation.

loran　Long range aid to navigation. In the past a rather complicated low-frequency system involving fixes by triangulation between so-called master and slave stations. With these calculations being rather difficult to perform in flight, Loran was becoming obsolete until computer science produced a more practical solution to its use. *See* LORAN-C.

Loran-C　Loran-C (Loran is an acronym for *LO*ng *RA*nge *N*avigation) uses the same signals as the old Loran system, but it includes computers that perform all the necessary computations, giving the pilot up-to-the-minute navigational guidance at all times. In addition, if, for instance, the lat/long coordinates of the destination are keyed into the system, Loran-C will display the correct heading, the distance and, depending on the specific equipment, a large amount of related information. Loran stations are located near both coasts in the United States and Canada, in Iceland, several European countries, in Saudi Arabia, Japan, South Korea and on several Pacific islands. One is located in Tunisia but there are none in the rest of Africa and none in Australia and Central and South America. The reason for their coastal locations is that they were originally intended as aids for maritime navigation.

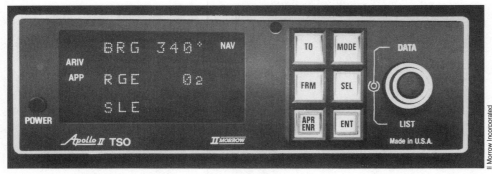

II Morrow Apollo II model 612 Loran-C system.

lost communications　*See* TWO-WAY RADIO FAILURE.

L over D　L/D.

low　A region of low atmospheric pressure surrounded by higher pressure. The winds around a low flow counterclockwise (in the northern hemisphere). Also called cyclone or depression.

low altitude airway structure   The complete network of airways serving traffic up to, but not including, 18,000 feet msl.

low altitude chart   Radio facility chart for operations below 18,000 feet msl.

low altitude en route chart   Low altitude chart.

low approach   An approach followed by a low flight over the runway, but without landing. Usually used after a practice instrument approach. Low approaches must have tower clearance at controlled airports.

low clouds   Any clouds with bases below 6,000 feet agl.

low frequency   Radio-magnetic waves with frequencies from 30 to 300 kHz (30,000 to 300,000 cycles per second).

low-frequency radio range   *See* LF/MF RADIO RANGE.

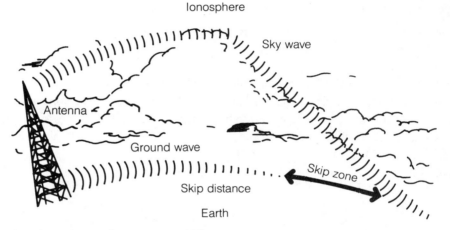

Low frequency radio wave propagation.

low pressure system   A low.

low tow   In sailplaning an airplane tow in which the sailplane flies below the flight-path of the tow plane (not recommended).

low wing   Having the wing of a monoplane attached at or near the bottom of the fuselage.

LPG   Liquefied petroleum gas (propane).

LRCO   Limited remote communication outlet.

LRS   Lake reporting service. A special flight watch service offered over the Great Lakes, the Long Island Sound, and other areas where an emergency landing would be difficult or not impossible.

LSR   Light snow on the runway.

LTA   Lighter than air (craft).

LTA   Lighter-than-Air Society, Inc.

LTL Little.

LTLCG Little change.

LTR Later.

lubber line The reference line on a magnetic compass or other instrument indicating heading. It is aligned with the longitudinal axis of the aircraft.

Lucas Aerospace Ltd. Designer, developer, and manufacturer of engine control systems, digital controls, composite materials structures, nacelles, thrust reversers, small gas turbine, electrical power generating systems, engine starting systems, pneumatic, electric and mechanical actuation systems, de-icing systems, and related equipment. (Bryeton House, New Road, Solihull, West Midlands, England B91 3TX. Phone: 021 704-5171. U.S. address: Lucas Aerospace, Inc., 11150 Sunrise Valley Drive, Reston, VA 22091-4399. (703) 264-1704.)

Lunar Rocket A single-engine fixed-gear tailwheel STOL aircraft once manufactured by Maule Aircraft. No longer in production.

LVL Level.

LWR Lower.

Lycoming Manufacturer of piston and turbine engines for fixed-wing and rotary-wing aircraft. The piston engines fall into five major groups. The company's turboshaft engines are used, among others, in the Bell 222 helicopters. (Textron Lycoming/Subsidiary of Textron, Inc., 652 Oliver Street, Williamsport, PA 17701. (717) 323-6181.) (Page 295)

LYR Layer.

Lycoming IO-720 piston engine.

Lycoming Piston Engines

Cubic In	Horsepower	Cylinders	TBO hours	Drive	Rotation	Comments
235	100 to 118	4	2,400	direct		Carbureted
320	140 to 160	4	2,000	direct	L & R	Carbureted or fuel injected *
360	180 to 210	4	2,000	direct **	L & R	Carbureted or fuel injected ***
540	235 to 450	6	2,000		L & R	Carbureted or fuel injected ***
720	375 to 400	8	1,800	direct		Fuel injected

* Turbocharged model available
** Direct drive and geared drive
*** Turbocharge model available. Intercooling available

M   Mach number.

m   Maritime air mass.

M   Measured (in sequence reports).

M   Megahertz (MHz)

M   In computer usage, MB, one megabyte or 1024 kilobytes or 1,048,576 bytes.

m   Meter(s).

M   Mike (phonetic alphabet).

M   Missing (in sequence reports).

MAA   Maximum authorized altitude.

Mach number   The ratio of TAS or IAS to the speed of sound. Mach 1 is the speed of sound under standard atmospheric conditions. Named after Ernst Mach. In the accompanying table are some typical examples of the indicated and true airspeeds in nautical miles as converted to subsonic Mach numbers at different altitudes under standard atmospheric conditions.

Subsonic Airspeeds as Mach Numbers

ALTITUDE	Mach 0.76	Mach 0.80	Mach 0.84	Mach 0.88	Mach 0.92	Mach 0.96
10,000 ft.	425 IAS 485 TAS	450 IAS 511 TAS	472 IAS 537 TAS	495 IAS 562 TAS	518 IAS 585 TAS	541 IAS 610 TAS
20,000 ft.	353 IAS 467 TAS	373 IAS 492 TAS	393 IAS 516 TAS	412 IAS 541 TAS	434 IAS 565 TAS	452 IAS 589 TAS
31,000 ft.	280 IAS 445 TAS	297 IAS 469 TAS	314 IAS 493 TAS	330 IAS 516 TAS	346 IAS 540 TAS	365 IAS 564 TAS
43,000 ft.	209 IAS 438 TAS	223 IAS 462 TAS	235 IAS 485 TAS	250 IAS 507 TAS	265 IAS 530 TAS	278 IAS 553 TAS

mackerel sky   Cirrocumulus clouds in a large, rippling layer.

MacCready speed ring   A rotable bezel around a variometer, used in sailplanes to show the best speed to fly between thermals for the fastest speed in terms of lateral distance covered.

mag   Magneto.

MAG   Magnetic.

magnetic compass   A compass that is always aligned with the magnetic north except during periods of turns, acceleration, deceleration, steep climbs.

magnetic course (MC)   True course corrected for magnetic variations.

magnetic deviation   Error in the reading of the magnetic compass due to installation error or magnetic interference caused by cockpit instruments. It should be displayed in the cockpit on the compass correction chart.

magnetic heading   True heading corrected for magnetic variations.

magnetic north   The region, some distance from the geographic north pole, where the earth's magnetic lines concentrate. A magnetic compass points to the magnetic north.

magnetic variation   The angle between the magnetic and true north. It differs at various points on the earth due to local magnetic disturbances. It is shown on charts as isogonic lines marked with degrees of variation, either east or west, degrees that must be subtracted from or added to the true course to get the magnetic course. Easterly variations are deducted, westerly variations added (east is least, west is best).

magneto   A self-contained generator that supplies electrical current to the spark plugs in the ignition system.

Magneto.

main gear   The principal portion of the landing gear, usually two wheels located on either side of the fuselage, in tricycle-gear aircraft behind the center of gravity, and in tailwheel aircraft ahead of the center of gravity.

MAINT   Maintain.

MAINT   Maintenance.

maintain   Concerning altitude, it is usually used by ATC in phrases like "Climb to and maintain . . ." or "Descend to and maintain . . ." At other times it might be used in such phrases as: "Maintain VFR."

maintenance   Inspection, overhaul, repair, preservation, and replacement of parts. Different classes of aircraft and aircraft used either commercially or non-commercially are subject to different maintenance rules: but all aircraft must have one annual inspection and commercially used light aircraft must be inspected every 100 hours.

main wheels   *See* MAIN GEAR.

make short approach   An ATC instruction, asking the pilot to enter final approach and land as quickly as possible, usually because of other traffic approaching to land. It is not a command. If the pilot feels that a short approach would be less than safe for him, he can refuse, in which case he might be asked to extend his downwind leg in order to permit the other traffic to land ahead of him.

Makila   A turbine engine manufactured by Turbomeca in France and used to power the Aerospatiale Super Puma helicopter, among other aircraft.

Malibu Mirage   A pressurized high-performance single-engine piston aircraft, manufactured by Piper Aircraft Corporation.

Piper Malibu Mirage.

MALS Medium intensity approach light system.

MALSF Medium intensity approach light system with sequenced flashers.

MALSR Medium intensity lighting of simplified short approach light system with RAIL.

maneuver Any intentional change in the attitude or movement of an aircraft.

maneuvering speed The maximum speed at which abrupt control changes may be made without exceeding the load limits of the aircraft design.

maneuvering vent The vent near the apex of a hot-air or gas balloon, which can be opened and closed by the pilot, in flight, in order to increase or decrease lift.

manifold pressure The pressure of the fuel-air mixture in the intake manifold.

manifold pressure gauge The cockpit instrument showing the manifold pressure. It works on the principle of an aneroid barometer and reads in terms of inches of mercury (in Hg).

manufacturers Major manufacturers of aircraft, components, instruments, and avionics are listed alphabetically along with their addresses. A complete listing of all companies in any way involved with any phase of aviation may be found in the *World Aviation Directory*. (McGraw-Hill, Inc. 1221 Avenue of the Americas, New York, NY 10020. (212) 512-2528. Editorial offices: 1156 15th Street N.W., Washington, D.C. 20005. (202) 822-4600. Published semi-annually in March and September.)

MAP Missed approach point.

Marathon Battery Company and Marathon Power Technologies Manufacturers of nicad, magnesium, and carbon-zinc aircraft batteries, chargers and analyzers, DC-to-AC and DC-to-DC static inverters, and temperature monitors. (P.O. Box 8233, Waco, TX 76714-8233. (817) 776-0650.)

Marconi Elliott Avionics Systems Manufacturers of a sophisticated line of avionics. (Christopher Martin Road, Basildon, Essex SS14 3EL, England.)

maritime air mass An air mass that originated over a large body of water and has a high moisture content concentrated in the lower layers. It may be polar or tropical.

marker beacon A 75 MHz transmitter which sends an elliptical signal pattern straight up with the size of the pattern expanding with altitude. It provides precise fixes at low altitudes.

marker beacon receiver A cockpit instrument which is designed to receive signals from marker beacons and to trigger visual and/or audio signals. (Page 301)

Marquise One of the family of MU-2 corporate turboprop aircraft manufactured in part by Mitsubishi Heavy Industries in Japan and assembled and completed by Mitsubishi Aircraft International. No longer in production.

master switch A switch on the instrument panel of most aircraft, designed to turn the entire electrical system either on or off.

Terra Radio

Marker beacon receiver in audio panel.

MAX   Maximum.

max   Frequently used expression in combinations such as max fuel, max payload, etc.

maximum allowable gross weight   The gross weight to which a particular aircraft may be loaded in accordance with its certification.

maximum continuous horsepower   Maximum cruise power.

maximum flap extended speed   The maximum allowable structural speed at which an aircraft may be operated with flaps extended. It is shown as the upper limit of the white arc on the airspeed indicator.

maximum fuel with a given payload   The maximum amount of fuel that may be carried in the tanks relative to the weight of passengers or freight being carried. Many aircraft are not designed to carry max fuel and max payload at the same time without exceeding maximum allowable gross weight.

maximum payload   A greatest load in terms of weight, not counting the fuel and, in aircraft flown by a professional crew, the crew, which the aircraft can legally carry.

maximum power   The greatest power available in an aircraft for use in emergencies.

maximum structural cruise speed   The highest airspeed at which a given aircraft may be flown in rough air. Designated on the airspeed indicator by the upper limit of the green arc.

mayday   An emergency voice message indicating to anyone receiving it anywhere in the world that the pilot is in trouble. Derived from the French phrase *m'aider,* meaning "help me!"

MB   Marker beacon (receiver).

MB   Millibars.

MBB Helicopter Corporation   Marketing, technical support, and customer service for MBB BO 105 CB, BO 105 CBS and BK 117 helicopters in the U.S., Mexico, Latin America and the Caribbean. (P.O. Box 2349, 900 Airport Road, West Chester, PA 19380. (215) 431-4150.)

mc   Megacycles. Now called MHz, megaHertz.

MC   Magnetic course.

MCA   Minimum controllable airspeed.

MCA   Minimum crossing altitude.

McDonnell Douglas Helicopter Company   Formerly Hughes Helicopters, manufacturer of the McDonnell Douglas 500D, E, F helicopters, and the no-tail-rotor MDX. (5000 East McDowell Road, Bldg. 510/A290, Mesa, AZ 85205. (602) 891-3000.) (Page 303)

McDonnell Douglas 500E helicopter operated by Los Angeles County Sheriff's Department.

McDonnell Douglas Helicopters

		MD 500E	MD 530F
ENGINE	manufacturer	Allison	Allison
	model	250-C20R	250-C30
	rating shp	450	650
	takeoff shp	375	425
	continuous shp	350	350
WEIGHTS pounds	gross, normal	3,000	3,100
	gross, external load	3,550	3,750
	empty, standard	1,496	1,591
	empty, industrial	1,396	1,491
	useful load, standard	1,504	1,509
	useful load, industrial	1,604	1,609
	external, standard	2,054	2,159
	external, industrial	2,154	2,259
MAIN ROTOR	diameter ft.	26.4	27.4
	blades	5	5
TAIL ROTOR	diameter ft.	4.6	4.8
	blades	2	2
AIRCRAFT	height ft.	8.6	8.5
	length ft.	24.6	24.6
SPEEDS kts.	sea level	137 @ 2,000 lbs.	136 @ 2,150 lbs.
	sea level	135 @ 3,000 lbs.	134 @ 3,100 lbs.
	5,000 ft.	143 @ 2,000 lbs.	142 @ 2,150 lbs.
	5,000 ft.	137 @ 3,000 lbs.	136 @ 3,100 lbs.
RANGE nm	sea level	247 @ 2,000 lbs.	211 @ 2,150 lbs.
	sea level	233 @ 3,000 lbs.	206 @ 3,100 lbs.
	5,000 ft.	285 @ 2,000 lbs.	247 @ 2,150 lbs.
	5,000 ft.	258 @ 3,000 lbs.	232 @ 3,100 lbs.
ENDURANCE hours	sea level	2.3	2.0
SERVICE CEILING	certification limit	16,000	16,000
RATE OF CLIMB	sea level fpm	3,260 @ 2,000 lbs.	3,573 @ 2,150 lbs.
	sea level fpm	1,770 @ 3,000 lbs.	2,069 @ 3,100 lbs.
	ISA + 20°C day	3,304 @ 2,000 lbs.	3,610 @ 2,150 lbs.
	ISA + 20°C day	1,776 @ 3,000 lbs.	2,061 @ 3,100 lbs.
HOVER	IGE std. day	16,000 @ 2,000 lbs.	16,000 @ 2,150 lbs.
	IGE std. day	11,300 @ 3,000 lbs.	14,300 @ 3,100 lbs.
	IGE ISA + 20°C day	16,000 @ 2,000 lbs.	16,000 @ 2,150 lbs.
	IGE ISA + 20°C day	6,900 @ 3,000 lbs.	12.000 @ 3,100 lbs.
	OGE std. day	16,000 @ 2,000 lbs.	16,000 @ 2,150 lbs.
	OGE std. day	9,346 @ 3,000 lbs.	12,300 @ 3,100 lbs.
	OGE ISA + 20°C day	15,700 @ 2,000 lbs.	16,000 @ 2,150 lbs.
	OGE ISA + 20°C day	5,160 @ 3,000 lbs.	9,750 @ 3,100 lbs.
FUEL U.S. gallons	usable	64	64
PRICE	1988 $s	$450,000	$625,000

MCHP   Maximum continuous horsepower.

MDA   Minimum descent altitude.

MEA   Minimum en route altitude.

mean sea level   The sea level midway between the mean high and the mean low water, used as the standard reference point from which to measure altitude or elevation.

measurements   *See* CONVERSION CHARTS.

mechanically aspirated engine   Turbocharged or supercharged engine.

medical certificate   The official proof or evidence that a pilot meets the medical standards required by the FARs. Examinations must be conducted by an approved aviation medical examiner. There are three classes of such certificates: A private pilot needs a third class certificate, which must be renewed every 24 months. A commercial pilot needs a second class certificate, renewable every 12 months. Air transport pilots need a first class certificate, renewable every six months.

medical examiner   A medical doctor authorized by the FAA to conduct medical examinations of pilots. Names and addresses can be obtained from the nearest FAA GADO office.

medium frequency   The band of radio magnetic waves propagating at frequencies of from 300 to 3,000 kHz (300,000 to 3,000,000 cycles per second.)

MEL(S)   Multiengine land (sea); a pilot rating.

Melmoth   An all-metal high-performance single-engine two-seat aircraft designed and built by Peter Garrison. It became famous when he flew it first across the Atlantic to Europe and then across the Pacific to Japan and back. Subsequently it was turbocharged. The aircraft was destroyed on John Wayne Airport in Orange County, California, when, while waiting off the active runway for takeoff clearance, a Cessna Centurion landed on top of it. Garrison, miraculously, walked away unharmed. Since then he has been working on a "new and improved" version, but no completion date is envisioned at the time of this writing. [**Editor's note:** Peter Garrison is the son of author Paul Garrison.] (Page 305)

Melmoth at the EAA fly-in Oshkosh, Wisconsin.

Melmoth

		MELMOTH (homebuilt)
ENGINE	manufacturer	Continental
	model	TSIO-360
	rating hp	210
	TBO hrs	1400
PROPELLER	number of blades	2
	type	constant speed
LANDING GEAR	tricycle	retractable
WEIGHTS	takeoff	2950 lbs
	landing	2950 lbs
	useful load	1450 lbs
	max payload	525
FUEL U.S. gal	usable	154
WINGS	area ft^2	93
	loading lb/ft^2	31.7
DIMENSIONS ft	span	23.3
	length	21.5
	height	8.3
TURBOCHARGER	manufacturer	Rajay
	type	manual waste gate
EQUIPMENT	installed	VHF nav, com, marker
		glide slope
		audio panel
		transponder
		encoding altimeter
		EGT, CHT
		ADF, DME
		HF transceiver
		angle of attack indicator
		autopilot
		fuel totalizer

Mentor Radio Company Manufacturer of VHF transceivers, amplifiers, intercoms, cockpit audio systems, avionics, marker receivers. (1561 Lost Nation Road, Willoughby, OH 44094. (216) 942-2025.)

Mercator chart A chart using the Mercator projection.

Mercator projection A chart or map on which the meridians are drawn parallel to each other and the parallels of latitudes are straight lines whose distance from one another increases with the distance from the equator. Named after Gerhardus Mercator.

meridian Any line of longitude.

Merlin A family of corporate turboprop aircraft once manufactured by Swearingen Aviation Corporation.

MES Multiengine sea; a pilot rating.

Messerschmitt-Bölkow-Blohm GmbH The West German parent company of MBB Helicopter Corporation.

MBB Helicopters

		BO 105 CB/CBS	BO 105 LS A-3	BK 117
ENGINE	manufacturer	Allison (2)	Allison (2)	Lycoming (2)
	model	250-C20-B	250-C28C	LTS 101-750 B-1
RATING shp	max takeoff	420	410	592
	continuous	400	373	550
MAIN ROTOR	blade each in	387.4	387.4	441
	number	4	4	4
TAIL ROTOR	diameter in	74.8	74.8	77
	number	2	2	2
WEIGHTS	gross, max lb	5511	5732	7055
	empty lb	2868	3153	3807
	useful load	2643	1170	3248
FUEL lbs	standard	1005	1005	1230
	w. aux tanks	1711		1583
SPEEDS	V_{ne} kts	131	145	150
	cruise kts	131	131	134
RATE OF CLIMB	fpm	1375	2080	1910
HOVER	IGE ft.	5000	14,000	9600
	OGE ft.	1500	11,100	4900
OPERATING ALT.	max ft.	10,000 *	20,000	10,000 *
RANGE nm	standard fuel	308	282	308
PRICE	1988 $s	$1,160,000	$1,375,000	$1,855

* Certification limit

MBB Bo 105LS helicopter.

meteorology Science dealing with the atmosphere and its phenomena; specifically with weather and weather forecasting.

meter Metric means of measuring distance. *See* CONVERSION CHARTS.

meter valve In ballooning, part of the plumbing that meters the propane gas to the burner, which heats the air in a hot-air balloon.

Metro A turboprop commuter airliner once manufactured by Swearingen Aviation Corporation.

MF Medium frequency.

MFOB Minimum fuel on board.

MH Magnetic heading.

MH Nondirectional homing beacon operating on less than 50 watts.

MHA Minimum holding altitude.

mHz MicroHertz.

MHz MegaHertz (1,000,000 cycles per second).

mi Mile.

Microcomputer A personal computer that uses microprocessors for its operation.

Micro Line A family of high-quality avionics designed especially for high-performance singles and light twins by Collins Radio.

Micrologic Avionics Manufacturer of Loran-C navigation systems. (20801 Dearborn Street, Chatsworth, CA 91311. (818) 998-1216.)

microphones The portion of a transmitting system that accepts the human voice (and other sound) and, via a diaphram or similar device, transforms it into transmittable electrical energy.

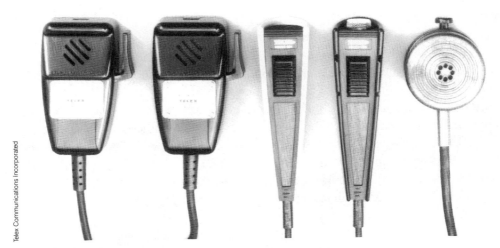

Telex Communications Incorporated

Aircraft microphones.

microwave landing system MLS is an approach and guidance system with an extremely accurate approach azimuth and glide path coupled with DME or Precision DME (PDME). The system uses the MLS C-band and DME/PDME L-band frequencies, providing superior stability. The final approach and glide path can be selected by the pilot in the cockpit and can be offset at an angle left or right of the runway centerline in order for aircraft to be able to fly offset approaches to avoid obstacles. MLS can provide precision instrument approaches to airports on which previous precision guidance systems could not be installed.

middle clouds   Clouds with bases between 6,000 and 20,000 feet; usually lower in the winter and higher in the summer.

middle marker beacon   A marker beacon located approximately 3,500 feet from the threshold of the runway in an ILS, triggering aural and (or) visual signals in the cockpit.

midfield RVR   The runway visual range numbers obtained by equipment located at or near the half-way point of the runway.

MIDIZ   Mid-Canada identification zone.

mike .   In aviation radio phraseology, the term used for the letter M.

mike   Microphone.

mile-high club   A humorous name for a fictitious organization of pilots that claim to have made love while at least one mile agl.

millibar   A unit of pressure equal to a force of 1,000 dynes per square centimeter or $1/1000$ of a bar. It is also equal to about .03 in Hg.

military operations area   A portion of airspace designed to separate military operations from IFR traffic. Non-participating IFR traffic may traverse such areas only if ATC can assure safe IFR separation.

min   minute.

minimum control speed   The lowest speed at which a twin-engine aircraft is controllable with the critical engine inoperative and the other at takeoff power.

minimum cross altitude   The minimum altitude at which an aircraft may cross a fix under IFR conditions, usually based on obstructions.

minimum crossing altitude   Minimum cross altitude.

minimum descent altitude (MDA)   The lowest altitude measured in feet msl, to which an aircraft may descend under IFR conditions when executing a nonprecision instrument approach. If no visual contact has been established with the airport or clearly airport related terrain when MDA is reached, the pilot must maintain that altitude until reaching the missed approach point and then must execute a missed approach.

minimum en route altitude (MEA)   The altitude between radio fixes which assures acceptable navigational radio signal reception and meets the necessary obstruction clearance requirements.

minimum fuel   Means that the aircraft has sufficient fuel on board to reach its destination, assuming little or no undue landing delays. It is not a declaration of an emergency.

minimum holding altitude   The lowest altitude prescribed for a holding pattern, meeting obstruction clearance requirements and acceptable radio signal reception.

minimum IFR altitudes   Unless otherwise indicated on the appropriate aviation charts, the minimum IFR altitude in non-mountain areas is 1,000 feet above the highest obstacle within a horizontal distance of five statute miles from the intended course. In mountainous areas it is 2,000 feet instead.

minimum obstacle clearance altitude (MOCA)   The lowest possible altitude between fixes on or off airways that meets obstacle clearance requirements for that route segment. At this altitude radio signal reception is guaranteed for only 22 nm from a VOR.

minimum reception altitude (MRA)   The lowest altitude required to receive reliable signals from navaids needed for navigation in the particular route segment.

minimum safe altitude   The minimum altitudes specified for various operations in heavily populated, lightly populated and unpopulated areas in the FARs Part 91. Instrument approach charts show minimum safe altitudes and emergency safe altitudes that provide for 1,000 foot obstacle clearance within a given distance of a navaid. They are for emergency use only and do not guarantee reliable reception of radio signals.

minimums   Plural of minimum; also and technically more correctly expressed as minima.

minimum sink speed   The indicated airspeed at which a sailplane loses altitude most slowly, usually a little above stalling speed and below the best glide speed.

minimum vectoring altitude   The lowest altitude in terms of feet msl at which an aircraft will be radar vectored by a controller except as authorized in conjunction with radar approaches, departures or missed-approach procedures. Minimum vectoring altitudes, sometimes lower than the published MEAs, are depicted on charts available to controllers but not normally to pilots.

minute (') $1/60$ degree of a circle.

MISG   Missing.

missed approach   A mandatory maneuver that must be initiated whenever an aircraft on an instrument approach has reached the missed approach point at MDA or DH without making visual contact with the airport. The missed approach procedures to be followed at individual airports are depicted and described on instrument approach charts.

missed approach point (MAP)   The point shown on each published instrument approach chart at which a missed approach must be initiated if visual contact with the airport has not been established.

missed approach segment   The portion of the published instrument approach procedure that must be flown in accordance with those published directions after the decision has been made to miss the approach.

mission   Term used to describe a flight from takeoff to landing. Most often used in conjunction with business and corporate aviation activities.

mission profile   The various numbers (fuel consumption, rate of climb, speed, rate of descent, etc.) associated with a specific mission.

mist   Thin fog giving a visibility in excess of one kilometer ($^5/_8$ mile).

mist   Commonly used term for drizzle.

Mitsubishi Aircraft International, Inc.   Manufacturers of the MU-2 family of twin-turboprop aircraft and the Diamond corporate jet. The Diamond was sold to Beech Aircraft Corporation and is now being manufactured as the Beechjet, while manufacture of the MU-2s (Solitaire and Marquise) has ceased altogether.

Mitsubishi MU-2 Aircraft

		SOLITAIRE	MARQUISE
ENGINE	manufacturer	Garrett (2)	Garrett (2)
	model	TPE 331-10-501M	TPE 331-10-501M
	flat rated shp	778	727
	TBO hrs	3,000	3,000
WEIGHTS lbs	ramp	11,625	10,520
	takeoff	11,575	10,470
	landing	11,025	9,955
	zero fuel	9,950	9,700
	useful load	3,975	3,510
FUEL lbs	usable	2,700	2,700
	with max payload	1,675	820
PAYLOAD lbs	max	2,300	2,945
	with full fuel	1,275	810
DIMENSIONS ft	span	39.22	39.22
	length	39.4	33.25
	height	13.7	12.95
CABIN ft	length	21.5	13.4
	height	4.26	4.26
	width	4.95	4.95
PRESSURE	psi	6	6

mixture   The mixture of fuel and air necessary for combustion in reciprocating engines.

mixture control   A control knob in the cockpit permitting the pilot to adjust the mixture of fuel and air.

MKR   Marker beacon.

MLS   Microwave landing system.

mm   Millimeter; $^1/_{1000}$ meter.

MM   Middle marker.

MOA   Military operations area.

MOCA   Minimum obstruction clearance altitude.

mod   Term used for an alteration or modification of a standard aircraft.

mode   A letter (or number in the military) assigned to particular pulse spacing of radar signals. Mode A is the standard mode used in the air traffic control radar beacon system (ATCRBS). Mode C implies altitude reporting capability (in conjunction with an encoding altimeter or altimeter digitizer combination).

modified Lambert conformal conic projection   The standard Lambert conformal conic projection cannot be used in depicting the polar regions. It is therefore not used above the 80-degree parallel. The modified version allows for this and produces a chart representation usable for navigation.

moment   A figure representing the rotating force times its perpendicular distance from the axis of rotation. It is used in calculating the cg range of an aircraft.

momentarm   The distance from the axis of rotation, affecting the moment.

Mooney Aircraft Corporation   Manufacturer of exceptionally fast high-performance single-engine aircraft, with the basic designs of the models currently in production credited to Roy LoPresti. In the summer of 1987 the company announced the formation of a joint venture between itself and Aerospatiale of France to develop a six-to-eight-place single-engine pressurized 300-knot turboprop aircraft to sell in the area of $1 million. Initial deliveries were expected to commence in late 1989. (P.O. Box 72, Kerrville, TX 78029. (512) 896-6000.) (Pages 312-313)

Mooney Aircraft

		201SE	252TSE	PFM	TLS
ENGINE	manufacturer	Lycoming	Continental	Porsche	Lycoming
	model	IO-360-A3B6D	TSIO-360-MB1	PFM 3200 NO3	TIO-540-AF1A
	rating hp	200	210	217	270
	TBO hrs	1800	1800	2000	2000
PROPELLER	manufacturer	McCauley	McCauley	Hartzell	McCauley
	blades	2	2	2	3
	diameter inches	74	74		75
	type	const.speed	const.speed		const.speed
WEIGHTS lbs	gross	2740	2900	2900	3200
	empty	1671	1800	n/a	2012
	takeoff		2900		3200
	landing		2900		3200
	useful load		1100		1188
FUEL U.S. gal	usable	64	75.6	60.5	90
DIMENSIONS ft	span	36.1	36.1	36.1	36.1
	length	n/a	25.45	26.92	24.92
	height	8.3	8.3	8.3	8.3
WING LOADING	lb/ft^2	15.7	16.6	16.6	18.3
SPEEDS kts	max	175	219	161	223
	economy	152	202		200
RANGE nm	@ % of power	951 @ 75%	1172 @ 78.6%	921 (max)	1070
RATE OF CLIMB	fpm	1030	1080	640	1230
STALL	clean kts		61	64	65
	dirty	53	59	57	60
SERVICE CEILING	ft	18,600	28,000	19,300	25,000

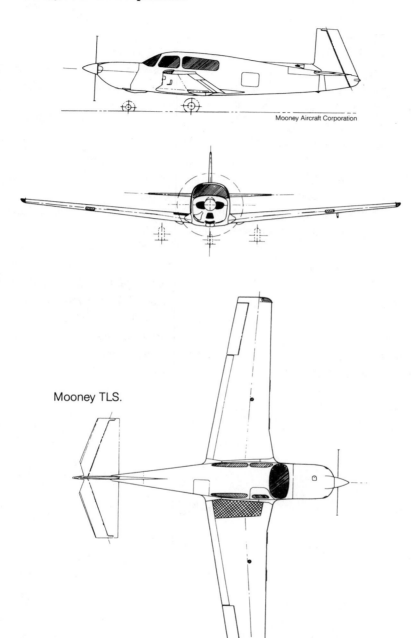

Mooney Aircraft Corporation

Mooney TLS.

Mooney/Aerospatiale TB 700 single-engine turboprop.

Morse code   The internationally accepted code of audible or visual dots and dashes representing all letters of the alphabet and digits from zero to nine:

A • –	M – –	Y –• – –
B –• • •	N –•	Z – –• •
C –• –•	O – – –	0 – – – – –
D –• •	P • – –•	1 • – – – –
E •	Q – –• –	2 • • – – –
F • • –•	R • –•	3 • • • – –
G – –•	S • • •	4 • • • • –
H • • • •	T –	5 • • • • •
I • •	U • • –	6 –• • • •
J • – – –	V • • • –	7 – –• • •
K –• –	W • – –	8 – – –• •
L • –• •	X –• • –	9 – – – –•

motorglider   A glider or sailplane with either a detachable or permanently built-in engine that can be shut off in flight whenever the pilot wants to soar. (Page 314)

mountain flying   Flying in mountainous areas that requires specialized knowledge of the effects of density altitude, air currents, and weather phenomena indigenous to the mountains.

mountain wave   Turbulent movement of strong air currents on the lee side of mountain ranges. Mountain waves are often associated with updrafts some distance from the mountain range and have been responsible for various altitude records set by sailplanes. Often associated with lenticular clouds capping so-called rotor currents, they tend to result in extremely rough rides for light aircraft.

Motorglider.

movement area   Runways, taxiways, and other portions of the airport used for moving aircraft rather than parking or tiedown.

moving target indicator   An electronic means of emphasizing returns from moving targets on a radar display, capable of minimizing the confusing effect of ground clutter.

mph   Statute miles per hour.

mps   Meters per second.

MRA   Minimum reception altitude.

MRKD   Marked.

MRKG   Marking.

MRTM   Maritime.

MSA   Minimum safe altitude.

msl   Mean sea level.

MST   Mountain standard time.

MTBF   Mean time between failures.

MTCA   Minimum terrain clearance altitude.

MTI   Moving target indicator.

multi engine aircraft   Any aircraft with more than one engine.

multi engine rating   The primary purpose of the training associated with obtaining a multi engine rating is to know how to continue to safely control the aircraft in the event of a failure of one engine (or several engines in the case of three-, four-, or more-engine aircraft.)

MU-2   A family of corporate twin-turboprop aircraft manufactured jointly by Mitsubishi Heavy Industries in Japan and by Mitsubishi Aircraft International. The entire operation was sold to Beech Aircraft Corporation as a result of which the Mu-2s are no longer being produced. *See* DIAMOND.

Multi Service Corp. Integrated multi-user systems software for flight planning with integrated real-time weather. (8650 West College Blvd. #205, Overland Park, KS 66210. (913) 451-2400.)

MUN Municipal.

Murphy's Law If anything can go wrong, eventually it will.

mush To sink in a nose-high attitude in which the aircraft is not able to effectively respond to normal control inputs.

mushing Flying along in a nose-high attitude at low speed, always just at the edge of a stall.

MVA Minimum vectoring altitude.

N Night (instrument approach charts).

N November (phonetic alphabet).

NA Not available (used frequently in aviation publications to indicate data not furnished by the manufacturer of a product). Also, not applicable.

n/a *See* NA.

NAA National Aeronautical Association.

NAAA National Agricultural Aircraft Association.

NAAS Naval Auxiliary Air Station.

nacelle A streamlined housing or compartment on an airplane, especially engine enclosures not attached to the fuselage.

NAFEC National Aviation Facilities Experimental Center; an activity of the FAA, located in Atlantic City, NJ.

NAFI National Association of Flight Instructors.

Narco Avionics, Inc. Manufacturer of electronic navcom equipment for general aviation. (270 Commerce Drive, Ft. Washington, PA 19034. (215) 643-2900.)

NAS National Airspace System.

NAS Stage A Refers to the entire complex of hardware and software comprising the ATC en route system, such as radars, computers, computer programs, communication apparatus, etc.

NAS Stage A alert function A computer controlled function capable of alerting controllers to potential traffic conflicts before they become critical.

NASA National Aeronautics and Space Administration.

NASAO National Association of State Aviation Officials.

NASP National Aerospace Plane, the Mach-25 X-30 being developed by Rockwell International Corporation. For more details, *see* ROCKWELL INTERNATIONAL.

NATA National Air Transportation Association.

National Aeronautical Association (NAA) *See* AVIATION ORGANIZATIONS.

National Agricultural Aviation Association (NAAA) *See* AVIATION ORGANIZATIONS.

National Airspace System (NAS)   The national aviation complex of the U.S., consisting of all elements, aircraft, airmen, airports, airspace, navaids, communication facilities, traffic control facilities and personnel, aeronautical charts and information, weather information, rules, regulations, procedures, technical information, and the FAA as a whole.

National Air Transportation Association (NATA)   *See* AVIATION ORGANIZATIONS.

National Association of Flight Instructors (NAFI)   *See* AVIATION ORGANIZATIONS.

National Association of Priest Pilots   *See* AVIATION ORGANIZATIONS.

National Association of State Aviation Officials (NASAO)   *See* AVIATION ORGANIZATIONS.

National Aeronautics and Space Administration (NASA)   A government agency concerned with space exploration and sophisticated research and development in the areas of aviation, space, and many related subjects.

National Business Aircraft Association (NBAA)   *See* AVIATION ORGANIZATIONS.

National Flight Data Center (NFDC)   A Washington-based FAA facility operating a central aeronautical information collection and dissemination service for government, industry, and the aviation community. It publishes the Flight Data Digest.

National Flight Data Digest (NFDD)   A daily publication of the flight data collected by the Flight Data Center.

Nationality mark   The letter or letters or combinations of letters and digits used to identify the nationality or country or registry of an aircraft:

AN	Nicaragua	3C	Equatorial Guinea
AP	Pakistan	D	Germany
3A	Monaco	EC	Spain
5A	Lybia	EI	Ireland
B	China	EJ	Ireland
5B	Cyprus	EL	Liberia
CC	Chile	EP	Iran
CF	Canada	ET	Ethiopia
CN	Morocco	F	France
CP	Bolivia	G	United Kingdom
CR	Portugal	9G	Ghana
CS	Portugal	HA	Hungary
CU	Cuba	HB	Liechtenstein
CX	Uruguay	HB	Switzerland
HC	Ecuador	00	Belgium
HH	Haiti	0Y	Denmark

HI	Dominican Republic	6OS	Somali
HK	Colombia	PH	Netherlands
HL	Republic of Korea	PI	Philippines
HP	Panama	PJ	Netherlands Antilles
HR	Honduras	PK	Indonesia
HS	Thailand	PP	Brazil
HZ	Saudi Arabia	PT	Brazil
5H	Tanzania	7P	Lesotho
9H	Malta	8P	Barbados
I	Italy	7QY	Malawi
JA	Japan	4R	Ceylon
9J	Zambia	5R	Madagascar
JY	Jordan	9Q	Leopoldville
9K	Kuwait	8R	Guyana
LN	Norway	SE	Sweden
LQ	Argentina	SP	Poland
LV	Argentina	ST	Sudan
LX	Luxembourg	SU	United Arab Republic
LZ	Bulgaria	SX	Greece
9L	Sierra Leone	TC	Turkey
9M	Malaysia	TF	Iceland
N	United States	TG	Guatemala
5N	Nigeria	TI	Costa Rica
9N	Nepal	TJ	Cameron
OB	Peru	TL	Central African Republic
OD	Lebanon	TN	Brazzaville
OE	Austria	TO	South Yemen
OH	Finland	TR	Gabon
OK	Czechoslovakia	TS	Tunisia
TT	Chad	XW	Laos
TU	Ivory Coast	XY	Burma
TY	Dahomey	XZ	Burma
TZ	Mali	3X	Guinea
5T	Mauretania	4X	Israel
7T	Algeria	5X	Uganda
5U	Burundi	YA	Afghanistan
VH	Australia	YI	Iraq
VT	India	YK	Syria
5V	Togo	YR	Romania
6V	Senegal	YS	El Salvador (Continued)

9V	Singapore	YV	Venezuela
4W	Yemen	5Y	Kenya
5W	Western Samoa	6Y	Jamaica
6W	Senegal	9Y	Trinidad and Tobago
XA	Mexico	ZK	New Zealand
XB	Mexico	ZL	New Zealand
XC	Mexico	ZM	New Zealand
9XR	Rwanda	ZP	Paraguay
XT	Upper Volta	ZS	Union ofSouth Africa
XU	Cambodia	ZT	Union of South Africa
XV	Vietnam	ZU	Union of South Africa
YU	Yugoslavia		

National Oceanic and Atmospheric Administration (NOAA) The government agency concerned with weather reporting and forecasting. Also publishers of aeronautical charts.

National Pilots Association (NPA) The organization has been merged with AOPA.

National search and rescue plan An agreement among various agencies to coordinate search and rescue efforts of all types.

National Transportation Safety Board (NTSB) The agency of the government that investigates all transportation related accidents, and makes recommendations, based on its findings, to minimize the chance of a repetition of such accidents.

National Weather Service A service of the National Oceanic and Atmospheric Administration. (8060 13th Street, Silver Spring, MD 20910. (301) 427-7675.)

NATL National.

nautical mile (nm) 6,076 feet or 1.15 statute mile. It is equal to one minute of latitude.

nav Navigation.

nav aid or navaid Navigation aid such as VOR, NDB, etc.

Navajo A family of piston-powered cabin-class twin-engine aircraft manufactured by Piper Aircraft Corporation. No longer in production.

navcom Radio systems combining the functions of navigation and communication. Some navcoms use the receiver portions for both functions (often referred to as one-and-a-half systems) while others combine two entirely separate units in one box (referred to as one-plus-one or two-systems). (Page 321)

navigable airspace All airspace at or above the minimum altitudes prescribed in the FARs, plus the lower airspace required for takeoff and landing.

navigation Any one of several methods of getting an aircraft from one predetermined point to another and means of establishing present position.

VHF Navcom Systems

MANUFACTURER	MODEL	PRICE	VOLT	FREQUENCIES COM	kHz	NAV	kHz	E	M	S	C	A	P	R	G	U	lbs	REMARKS
Bendix/King	KX 99	595	+	118.000 - 136.975	25	108.00 - 117.95	50	¤		10						1	1.75	Portable navcom system. Many opts
Bendix/King	KX165	5,930	27.5	118.000 -	25	108.00 -	50	¤		4		¤			*	1	5.65	optional
	KX155	4,010	13.75	135.975		117.95				¤		4			¤	*	5.30	Silver Crown
Aire-Sciences	RT-553A	2,175	14	118.000 - 135.975	25 50*	108.00 - 117.95	50		¤	1						1	n/a	2 com selectors *
Aire-Sciences	RT-563A	2,995	14	118.000 - 135.975	25 50*	108.00 - 117.95	50		¤	1	¤					1	n/a	2 com selectors *
Terra	TXN920	n/a	14	118.000 - 135.975	25	108.00 - 117.95	50		¤			¤			*	1	2.15	optional *
Terra	TXN960	n/a	14	118.000 - 135.975	25	108.00 - 117.95	50	¤	¤						*	1	3.75	optional *

+ Rechargable nicad battery

PRICE:		uninstalled	M:	mechanical readout
VOLT:		input voltage	S:	storage for number of frequency channels
FREQUENCIES	COM:	com range	C:	automatic radial centering
	kHz:	spacing in kHz	A:	automatic squelch
	NAV:	nav range	P:	marker beacon plug-in
	kHz:	spacing in kHz	R:	RMI output
E:		electric readout	G:	glide slope
			U:	number of units

Navcom system with OBI.

navigational aid Navaid.

navigation lights The lights at the wing tips and tail of the aircraft. A red light is located at the left wing tip, a green light at the right wing tip and a white light at the tail. Also known as position lights. Navigation lights are mandatory for night flight.

navigator   In multi-person crews, the third crew member who handles navigation-related chores.

nav instruments   The various cockpit instruments designed to receive and display signals from ground-based navaids. (Page 323)

Navigation Management Systems

MANUFACTURER	MODEL	VOLT DC	AC	SYSTEM R V O I G L	OUTPUTS P T E W G	INPUTS H H T D V A	WP	NV	lbs	REMARKS
Foster AirData	LNS616B	18-32		¤	¤ ¤ ¤ ¤ ¤	¤ ¤ ¤ ¤	234	¤	19.75	26 flight plans, 9 WP each $9,000 to 34,200 1989 $s
Global-Wulfsberg	GNS500A	28		¤ ¤ ¤ ¤	¤ ¤ ¤ ¤ ¤	¤ ¤ ¤ ¤ ¤	250	¤	48.4	Includes data pages for nav, data, flight plans, weather, fuel, messages etc.
Global-Wulfsberg	GNS X	28	26	¤ ¤ ¤	¤ ¤ ¤ ¤ ¤ ¤	¤ ¤ ¤ ¤ ¤ ¤	1470	¤	44.95	A regional system expandable to worldwide
Canadian Marconi	CMA900	28	115	¤ ¤ ¤ ¤ ¤	¤ ¤ ¤ ¤ ¤	¤ ¤ ¤ ¤ ¤ ¤	4000	¤	28 +	Modular system using user-selectable options
Universal Navigation	UNS-1	28	26	¤ ¤ ¤ ¤ ¤ ¤ ¤ ¤ ¤ ¤ ¤	¤ ¤ ¤ ¤ ¤ ¤		22000	¤	n/a	Database options: 1) Worldwide; 2)Canada, US & Latin America; 3)US, Latin & South America; 4)Europe, Middle East, Africa; 5)Eastern Europe, Pacific; 6)Helicopter for Eastern US.
Universal Navigation	UNS-1A	28	26	¤ ¤ ¤ ¤ ¤ ¤ ¤ ¤ ¤ ¤ ¤	¤ ¤ ¤ ¤ ¤ ¤		3000	¤	22 +	Includes a large selection of data pages.
Universal Navigation	Compact	28	26	¤ ¤ ¤ ¤ ¤ ¤ ¤ ¤ ¤ ¤ ¤	¤ ¤ ¤ ¤ ¤ ¤		3000	¤	18.9	Includes a large selection of data pages.
Bendix/King	KNS660	28	26	¤ ¤ ¤ ¤ *	¤ ¤ ¤ ¤ ¤	¤ ¤ ¤ ¤ ¤ ¤	800	¤	39.26	* GPS optional

VOLT	DC: DC input voltage		W: Time to waypoint
	AC: AC 400 Hz input voltage		G: Ground speed
SYSTEM	R: RNAV		H: HSI
	V: VLF	INPUTS	H: Heading
	O: Omega		T: True airspeed (TAS)
	I: Inertial guidance systems (INS)		D: DME
	G: Global positioning systems (GNS)		V: VOR
	L: Loran-C		A: Altitude
OUTPUTS	P: Position	WP:	Number of waypoints
	T: Track	NV:	Non-volatile memory
	E: Error	lbs:	Weight in pounds

Navion   A high-performance single-engine aircraft. No longer in production.

nav receiver   A radio receiver designed to receive signals from VORs.

NBAA   National Business Aircraft Association.

NDB   Nondirectional beacon.

negative   Expression used in aviation radio phraseology in place of *no* or *not available*. For instance, *negative transponder* means that the aircraft is not equipped with a working transponder.

VHF Navigation Receivers

MANUFACTURER	MODEL	PRICE	VOLTS DC	AC	MNT P	R	FREQUENCY range MHz	kHz	S	CHANNELS VOR	GS	D	R	E	M	B	I	U	lbs	REMARKS
Bendix/King	KN 53	3,355 / 2,680	14 / 28		¤		108.00-117.95	50	2	200	40	¤	¤			*		1	3	* 3 types of displays / low price w/o glide slp
Bendix/King	KNS 80	8,205	14 / 28		¤		108.00-117.95	50	2	200	40	¤	¤	¤		¤		2	6	Silver Crown
Bendix/King	KNS 81	6,290	14 / 28		¤		108.00-117.95	50	10	200	40	¤	¤	¤		¤	¤	3	5	Silver Crown
Bendix/King	KNR634	13,310	28		¤	¤	108.00-117.95	50	9	200	40	¤	¤	¤		¤	¤	4	4.7	Gold Crown III
Bendix/King	VNS 41	12,695	28		¤	¤	108.00-117.95	50		200	40		¤			¤	¤	2	6.24	Series III
Collins	VIR-351	n/a	14		¤		108.00-117.95	50		200				¤	¤		¤	1	2.7	Micro Line
Collins	VIR-32	n/a	28			¤	108.00-117.95	50		200	40	¤						1	4.5	ProLine II
Collins	VIR432	n/a	28			¤	108.00-117.95	50		200	40	¤						1	4.5	ProLine II / ARINC 429 tuning
Collins	VIR-31	n/a	28	26		¤	108.00-117.95	50		200	40	¤				¤	¤	2	6.6	ProLine
Terra	Tri-NAV	n/a	14		¤		108.00-117.95	50		200		¤				¤	¤	1	1.25	CDI only
Terra	Tri-NAV C	n/a	14		¤		108.00-117.95	50		200		¤				¤	¤	1	1.25	CDI only. Includes Loran-C readout

PRICE: uninstalled

VOLTS
DC: DC input voltage
AC: AC 400 Hz input voltage

MNT
P: panel mounted
R: remote mounted

FREQUENCY range:
MHz: frequency range MHz
kHz: spacing in kHz
S: storage for number of frequencies

CHANNELS
VOR: number of VOR channels
GS: number of glide slope channels
D: DME
R: RNAV output
FRO
E: electric frequency readout
M: mechanical frequency readout
B: radial/bearing readout
I: RMI output
U: number of units

Collins Avionics

Collins Micro Line nav receiver.

negative contact Phrase used by pilots to inform ATC that announced traffic is not in sight; or that the pilot has been unable to get a response on a given frequency.

negative dihedral The dihedral of the wing is downward from the lateral axis.

negative lift The force that will cause an airfoil to want to move downward rather than up. Many horizontal stabilizers are designed to produce a degree of negative lift.

never-exceed speed The highest speed at which an airplane may be flown in smooth air according to its certification parameters. Shown on the airspeed indicator by a red line. Also called red-line speed.

NFDC National Flight Data Center.

NFDD National Flight Data Digest.

NGT Night.

nicad battery Nickel-cadmium battery.

nickel-cadmium battery A type of battery using the interaction of nickel and cadmium to generate electricity. It usually consists of a large number of individual cells, each producing between one and 1.5 volts. They are connected in sequence to produce the needed voltage. Nicad batteries are found primarily in turbine-powered aircraft. Charging procedures and maintenance are extremely critical. *See* THERMAL RUNAWAY.

night The time between the end of official evening twilight and the beginning of official morning twilight.

night effect The tendency of an ADF to fluctuate during dusk, night, and dawn, when tuned to an appropriate navaid or standard broadcast station.

night error Night effect.

night flying There is little difference between flying at night or during the day, assuming that the pilot is able to control the aircraft by means of instruments alone, and that he can navigate with a minimum or total lack of outside visual cues. Night flight in single-engine aircraft adds the complication that in the event of an engine malfunction, an emergency landing cannot successfully be made in total darkness.

night vision The ability to use the rods rather than the cones of the eye by moving the direction of the eye from side to side to take advantage of the peripheral vision capability of the rods and to minimize the effect of the blind spot straight ahead, caused by the inability of the centrally located cones to see under minimum light conditions. (Page 325)

nimbostratus Middle stratiform cloud of a uniform dark grey color; usually associated with snow or steady rain.

nimbus A suffix or prefix (usually nimbo-) used with cloud types that are associated with rain.

niner In aviation radio phraseology the term used for the number nine.

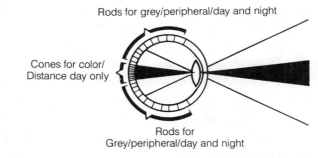

Rods for grey/peripheral/day and night

Cones for color/
Distance day only

Rods for
Grey/peripheral/day and night

To see the target most clearly at night,
Don't look directly at it

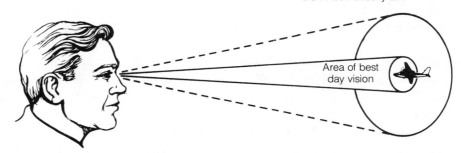

Area of best
day vision

Area
of
Best
Night

Blind spot

Vision

Night vision restrictions.

Ninety-Nines An organization of women pilots originally founded by Amelia Earhart and 98 other female pilots. *See* AVIATION ORGANIZATIONS.

nm Nautical mile.

N-number The identification number of an aircraft of U.S. registry. *See also* NATIONALITY MARK.

NO Number.

NOAA National Oceanic and Atmospheric Administration.

no contact Negative contact.

no-gyro approach A radar approach provided pilots with inoperative or malfunctioning gyro instruments (DG, AH). In a no-gyro approach the controller will instruct the pilot: "Turn right (left) . . . stop turn."

no-gyro vector   A vector accomplished in the same manner as a no-gyro approach.

noise   Sound at a level unpleasant to the human ear. The interior noise level of aircraft can eventually cause a degree of hearing loss. This can be avoided by wearing effective earplugs.

noise   Visual clutter on a radar display, often caused by atmospheric disturbances.

noise   The exterior noise created by certain aircraft during takeoff or landing is resulting in an increasing number of airports attempting to institute some kind of curfew or to ban certain aircraft altogether from the airport.

noise regulation   FAR Part 36 spells out current and future regulations with reference to permissable exterior noise levels.

noncontrolled airport   Uncontrolled airport.

nondirectional   Omni-directional; sending or receiving equally to or from all directions.

nondirectional beacon (NDB)   A LF/MF navaid sending nondirectional signals which can be received by an ADF in the aircraft and used for navigation. Though not intended as such, standard broadcast stations can be used in the same way as NDBs for VFR flight.

nonprecision approach   Any instrument approach with no ground-based vertical guidance system such as a glide slope or precision approach radar. Nonprecision approaches include localizer approaches (front and back course), VOR and ADF approaches, all circling approaches and a number of variations of the above.

nonradar   Used as a prefix in connection with other terms such as: nonradar approach, route, separation, etc., indicating that no radar coverage is available or being used.

nonradar approach control   An approach control facility without radar capability.

NoPT   No procedure turn (on instrument approach charts).

NORAD   North American Air Defense Command.

Nordam   Manufacturer of honeycomb structures, wing panels and assemblies, helicopter components, radomes, and miscellaneous plastic, plexiglas, fiberglass, and composite structures. (P.O. Box 3365, Tulsa, OK 74101-3365. (918)587-4105.)

Norden Systems   Manufacturer of long-range navigation systems, exclusively for the military. (P.O. Box 5300, Norden Place, Norwalk, CT 06856. (203)852-5000.)

NORDO   No-radio aircraft.

normal climb   A climb at airspeed and power setting that produces the most efficient combination or gain in altitude and forward progress for the time and amount of fuel used.

normal glide   A glide at an airspeed and angle that results in the greatest forward distance covered for a given loss of altitude. Also called maximum glide.

normally aspirated   A non-turbocharged piston engine.

normal operating range   The range of airspeeds within which a particular aircraft is supposed to be operated under normal conditions. It corresponds with the green arc on the airspeed indicator.

normal operating range   With reference to instruments other than those associated with airspeed (tachometer, oil pressure, oil temperature, cylinder head temperature, exhaust gas temperature, etc.) the range within which it is safe to operate. Most such instruments also have a green marking of some kind to show the limits of the normal operating range.

normal operating speed   Cruising speed.

normal spin   A spin deliberately entered into by stalling the aircraft and from which recovery is made at the discretion of the pilot.

normal stall   A deliberately created stall condition by slowly increasing the angle-of-attack, either with or without power.

North Atlantic Route   A coded route designed to utilize specific coastal fixes for transatlantic flight.

northerly turning error   The error in the reading of a magnetic compass when an aircraft in the northern hemisphere banks on a north-south heading. The vertical pull of the earth's magnetic field turns the compass card as the aircraft banks. An opposite effect takes place in the southern hemisphere.

Norton Performance Plastics   Manufacturer of radomes, radome kits, Doppler radomes, and fiberglass assemblies. (P.O. Box 3660, Akron, OH 44309. (216)296-9948.)

nose-heavy   Tendency of the aircraft to pitch forward when elevator control is released. Caused by faulty trimming or by forward-center of gravity loading.

nose-high   Flying with the nose of the aircraft higher than normal in relation to the level of flight. Usually caused by flying at a slow speed that requires a greater-than-normal angle-of-attack.

nose-low   The exact opposite of nose-high; usually achieved at very high speeds, though barely noticeable.

nosewheel   The (usually steerable) wheel under the nose of the fuselage in a tricycle gear aircraft.

NOTAM   Notice to airmen.

notice to airmen   An advisory distributed by the FAA giving current information about conditions or changes in any part or component of the National Airspace System.

november   In aviation radio phraseology the term used for the letter N.

no voice   An indication on an aeronautical chart that a navigation facility has no capability for voice communication.

nozzle   A narrow orifice through which fuel is fed to the carburetor or, in fuel injection systems, into the combustion chamber.

NPA   *See* NATIONAL PILOTS ASSOCIATION.

NSSFC   National Severe Storm Forecast Center in Kansas City.

NTSB   National Transportation Safety Board.

null   The condition of a radio receiver when minimum reception is achieved.

null position   The position of a loop antenna that produces minimum reception. In that position the sides of the loop antenna point to and from the station.

numerous targets vicinity (fix)   An ATC traffic advisory to pilots, indicating a large number of radar returns and, in turn, a large number of aircraft at a given location.

NWS   National Weather Service.

O Oscar (phonetic alphabet).

OAT Outside air temperature.

OB Olive branch routes.

OBI Omni bearing indicator.

OBNR Oil burner route.

OBS Omni bearing selector.

obscuration A sky cover report indicating that the sky cannot be seen at all because it is obscured by surface phenomena such as fog, smog, smoke, rain, snow, or dust extending upward from the ground. The sequence report symbol is X.

obstacle Buildings, chimneys, trees, powerlines, broadcast towers, or other natural or man-made objects reaching to the height where they interfere with aviation.

obstacle clearance altitude Sufficient altitude to safely clear any obstacle in the vicinity.

OBSTN Obstruction.

obstruction Obstacle.

obstruction light A light or group of lights, usually red, mounted on the surface of a structure or terrain feature to warn pilots of the presence of a flight hazard. In recent years many obstruction lights on broadcast towers and other high obstacles have been replaced with strobe lights that are easier to see under limited visibility conditions.

OCAC Oceanic air traffic control.

occluded front The front remaining on the surface after a cold front has overtaken a warm front. It may be cold or warm depending on which front displaces the other to the upper altitudes by the low pressure motion at their point of intersection. It is indicated on weather charts by a line with alternating points and rounded marks. Also called occlusion, it can occasionally present a situation hazardous to light aircraft.

occlusion Occluded front.

OCT Octane.

octane rating   A measurement of the ability of fuel to burn smoothly and without detonation, compared to a pure test fuel called octane. Most aircraft require fuel with an octane rating in excess of 80. But because many companies have stopped producing 80 octane av gas, newer aircraft engines are designed to use low lead 100 octane fuel.

OFAS   Overseas flight assistance service.

off-route vector   An ATC radar vector that takes the aircraft along a route other than that previously assigned.

offset parallel runways   Runways with parallel centerlines but with thresholds that are not aligned with one another.

Offshore Navigation, Inc.   Manufacturer of Loran-C navigation systems, data link, and flight following systems. (P.O. Box 23504, New Orleans, LA 70183. (504) 733-6790.)

oil burner route   Areas with low altitude high speed military flight training activity. The routes and hours of use are published in the special operations section of the Airman's Information Manual.

oil canning   The rattling sound caused by the bulging in and out of fuselage skin during flight because of inadequate stiffeners. It is unpleasant but not necessarily dangerous.

oil pressure gauge   An engine instrument that shows the pressure with which the lubricating oil is circulating through the moving parts of the engine. The readout is usually calibrated in psi, with the normal operating pressure indicated by a green bar or line.

oil temperature gauge   An engine instrument that shows the temperature of the lubricating oil, indicating the normal operating range (usually by a green bar or line) and the point beyond which the temperature should not be permitted to rise. It can be used to judge engine temperatures in aircraft without a cylinder head temperature gauge, though, when available, the latter is more accurate and to be preferred for that purpose.

oleo strut   An assembly that dissipates shock by hydraulic action. Used primarily in landing gears to absorb the landing shock.

olive branch routes (OB)   Flight paths used by the Air Force and Navy in jet aircraft training in VFR and IFR conditions, at altitudes from the surface to a published flight level. Information about the operational status of any particular route can be obtained by contacting the nearest FSS.

OM   Outer marker beacon.

OMAC, Inc.   (Old Man Aircraft Company) Manufacturer of the Laser 300 single-engine turboprop pusher aircraft. (P.O. Box 3530, 1 Rockwell Avenue, Albany, GA 31708. (912) 436-2425.)

Omega   A long-range navigation system in which the on-board navigation receiver uses the signals from a limited number of low-frequency transmitters to determine present position.

omni   VOR.

omni bearing indicator (OBI)   The cockpit display used in VOR navigation, consisting of three components: 1) The omni bearing selector (OBS) with which the pilot selects the radial from or bearing to a particular VOR. 2) The course-deviation indicator (CDI) consisting of a swinging needle or horizontally moving vertical bar which shows whether the aircraft is on the selected radial or bearing, or to either side of it. (Recently some manufacturers have begun to market CDIs with electronic displays. Typical of these is the Bendix 2000.) 3) The ambiguity or TO-FROM indicator which shows the pilot whether the selected radial is, in fact, a radial FROM the station or the bearing TO the station.

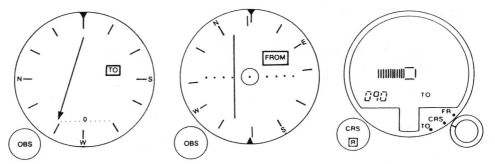

Three faces of an OBI, one with a swinging needle, one with a vertical needle moving horizontally, and one with electronic bars that determine the off course distance of the aircraft.

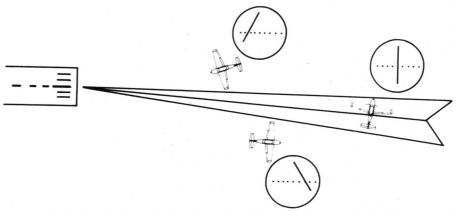

Indications of the OBI when crossing or flying in the reception area of a localizer.

omni bearing selector (OBS)   The element of the OBI used to select the bearing to or radial from the VOR.

omni course indicator   Omni bearing indicator.

omni range   The system of VORs and VORTACs on which the Victor airway system is based.

on course   Phrase used to indicate that the aircraft is established on the centerline of its route.

on course   Phrase used by ATC to inform a pilot making an instrument radar approach that he is correctly lined up with the final approach course.

on-course indicator   Any airborne instrument which shows the pilot that he is flying the desired course or what action he must take in order to intercept the desired course.

on instruments   Flying IFR.

on the gauges   Flying IFR.

OPERG   Operating.

OPERN   Operation.

Optica Scout   A slow-speed low-level observation aircraft with eight-hour loitering capability. *See* BROOKLANDS AIRCRAFT COMPANY.

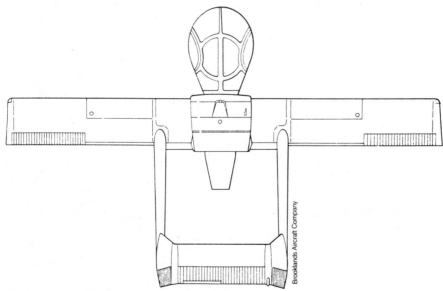

The Optica Scout observation platform.

optimum range   The longest distance a particular aircraft can travel, usually using higher altitudes and lower rpm settings than would be employed in normal cruise.

option approach An instrument approach, usually used for training purposes, that terminates either in a low approach, touch-and-go, missed approach, or full-stop landing. *See* CLEARED FOR THE OPTION.

Organized Flying Adjusters *See* AVIATION ORGANIZATIONS.

organized track system A system of oceanic routes between Europe and North America that is adjusted twice daily to take advantage of the prevailing winds aloft.

orientation flight A flight made to permit a pilot to familiarize himself with a particular aircraft or a geographic area. Usually conducted in the company of a pilot familiar with either the aircraft or the area.

ORL Overrun lights.

oscar In aviation radio phraseology the term is used for the letter O.

oscillation A continuous movement of the aircraft around its pitch or lateral axis.

OSHA Occupational Safety and Health Administration.

OSV Ocean station vessel.

OTS Out of service.

out In aviation radio phraseology the term used to indicate that the conversation is ended and no further reply is expected.

OUTBND Outbound.

outbound Flying away from the station or fix.

outer compass locator Compass locator co-located with the outer marker in an ILS system.

outer fix A general ATC term used with reference to terminal area fixes other than those associated with the final approach.

outer marker Outer marker beacon.

outer marker beacon (OM) A beacon, part of the ILS, located between four and seven miles from the threshold of the runway. It radiates a fan shaped vertical signal and is identified in the cockpit by visual or aural signals of the marker beacon receiver. It constitutes usually the beginning of the ILS final approach and aircraft should intercept it at an altitude that permits immediate interception of the glide slope.

outside air temperature gauge A thermometer mounted in such a way that it senses the temperature outside the fuselage and presents a readout inside the cockpit.

outside loop An aerobatic maneuver in which the aircraft executes a loop during which the pilot's head points away from the center of the loop. It may be entered from normal flight by a push over as for a steep dive, or from inverted flight with forward stick pressure throughout the maneuver.

over In aviation radio phraseology the term used to imply that the transmission is ended but that a reply is expected.

overcast A sky cover report indicating that the clouds cover more than 90 percent of the sky.

overcontrol To make large and usually erratic control movements that cause the aircraft to overreact. Also referred to as chasing the needle.

overdevelopment A term used primarily in soaring, indicating a rapid increase in the extent of cumulus cloud cover, reducing the sun's ability to heat the surface of the earth and thus slowing thermal activity.

overhead approach A series of maneuvers used by military pilots under VFR conditions as an entry into the traffic pattern.

overload To exceed the maximum allowable gross weight of a particular aircraft.

overshoot To fly beyond a designated or selected spot on the runway, frequently resulting in having the aircraft run off the end of the runway before it can be brought to a stop.

overtaking A faster aircraft approaching and then passing a slower aircraft from the rear. In this situation the aircraft being overtaken has the right of way and the overtaking aircraft should pass well to the right of the slower aircraft.

over the top VFR on top.

owner-flown aircraft In business and corporate aviation referring to aircraft that are usually flown by the owner or persons other than a professional crew.

owner's handbook Aircraft flight manual.

owner's manual Aircraft flight manual.

OXY Oxygen.

oxygen A colorless, tasteless, odorless gas that forms about 21 percent of the atmosphere at sea level. The percentage of oxygen in the atmosphere decreases with altitude and supplemental oxygen is required when flying at higher altitudes. According to the FARs, supplemental oxygen must be used by the pilot (crew) when flying above 12,500 feet msl up to and including 14,000 feet msl for periods exceeding 30 minutes. When operating above 14,000 feet msl the pilot (crew) must use supplemental oxygen continuously; and when flying above 15,000 feet msl each occupant of the aircraft must be provided with supplemental oxygen.

oz Ounce.

ozone A triatomic form of oxygen that is a bluish, irritating gas of pungent odor. It is formed naturally in the upper atmosphere by the photochemical reaction with solar ultraviolet radiation.

ozone layer The atmospheric layer at an altitude between 20 and 30 miles msl, distinguished by a heavy concentration of ozone.

ozonosphere Ozone layer.

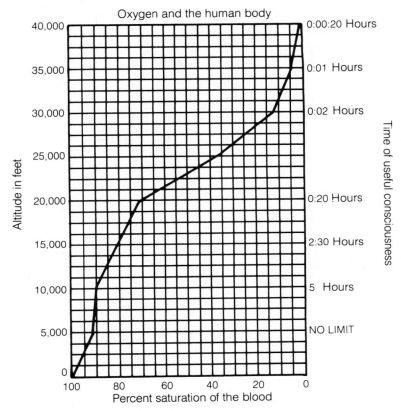

Oxygen requirements at altitude.

P

P Papa (phonetic alphabet).

P Polar air mass.

P Precipitation ceiling (in sequence reports).

PA Pressure altitude.

Pacer Systems, Inc. Manufacturer of cockpit procedures and instrument flight trainers, customized simulators, either fixed or including a three-degree of freedom motion base, and either with or without visual systems. In addition the company manufactures and markets a tabletop instrument procedures trainer. (4 Horsham Business Center, 300 Welsh Road, Horsham, PA 19044. (215) 657-7800.)

Tabletop instrument procedures trainer.

pan   An emergency message indicating that the pilot needs help, but that the emergency is not as serious as it would be if he radioed Mayday.

pancake landing   A landing in which the aircraft, usually unintentionally, is stalled somewhat too high above the landing surface and literally falls to the ground in a nose high attitude. It can be used intentionally to reduce the landing roll on a short field, or in the case of an emergency off airport landing, it will help to shorten the after landing skid or roll on rough terrain.

panel   Instrument panel.

panel mounted   When used in relation to instruments or avionics, the term implies that the entire piece of equipment or most of its components are mounted behind the instrument panel. *See also* REMOTE MOUNTED.

pants   Streamlined fairings enclosing the wheels of many fixed-gear aircraft, designed to reduce drag. Also called spats.

papa   In aviation radio phraseology the term used for the letter P.

PAR   Precision approach radar.

PAR approach   A precision instrument approach in which the controller, using PAR, gives instructions to the pilot with reference to the final approach course, the glide slope and the distance to the touchdown points. Today, few civil airports have PAR capability and it is used primarily by the military and in civil aviation emergencies.

parachute   Originally, an umbrella shaped fabric contraption of sufficient size to convey a person or freight safely to earth. In recent years parachutes have been designed in a variety of shapes, most intended to reduce the speed of descent and to increase the parachutist's ability to steer his chute to a predetermined landing spot.

parallel   Latitude line.

parallel entry   A suggested (but not mandatory) means of entering a holding pattern. The pilot approaches the holding fix from a direction more or less opposite of the direction in which the pattern is to be flown. He flies the first leg parallel to the holding pattern, makes a left procedure turn, and then re-enters the holding pattern in the right direction.

parallel offset course   A track that runs parallel to an established airway, either to the left or right, usually by appropriately RNAV-equipped aircraft.

parallel runways   Two or more runways at one airport, the centerlines of which are parallel. At such airports the runways, in addition to the usual numbers, are identified with one of three letters: L for left, C for center, R for right. In some instances, such as Los Angeles International Airport, where there are three or more parallel runways, one or two quite a distance from the other pair, the additional runways might be given a number that is one or two digits removed from the others, in order to avoid confusion. (At LAX the runways are 25L and 25R and 24L and 24R despite the fact that they are actually parallel.)

parasite drag   All drag produced by aircraft surfaces that do not contribute to creating lift. It increases with an increase in airspeed.

parking brake   A brake, usually a handbrake, that locks the wheels when the aircraft is parked or tied down.

parrot   A slang term used for transponder.

partial panel   A panel on which one or several of the basic flight instruments are either inoperative or covered up by the flight instructor. Executing certain maneuvers with a partial panel is part of instrument flight instruction.

Pathfinder 235   One of the Cherokee family of single-engine piston aircraft manufactured by Piper Aircraft Corporation. No longer in production.

PATN   Pattern.

pattern   Landing pattern, holding pattern, or any pre-determined or generally accepted manner in which to fly in order to achieve a given result.

PATWAS   Pilot's automatic telephone weather answering service.

Pawnee   Agricultural aircraft manufactured by Piper Aircraft Corporation. No longer in production.

payload   Useful load minus the weight of fuel and oil and, in the case of professionally flown aircraft, the crew and its baggage.

PC   A term used by Mooney Aircraft Corporation to identify the permanently-on wing leveler installation in its aircraft. PC stands for positive control.

PC   Personal computer.

PCA   Position control area.

PCPN   Precipitation.

PD   Period.

peak envelope power   The maximum power in terms of watts, produced by a com transmitter.

PEP   Peak envelope power.

performance chart   Charts, usually part of the aircraft flight manual, showing speeds, fuel consumption, rates of climb, minimum field lengths, etc., under a variety of engine settings and other conditions.

performance numbers   Octane ratings in excess of 100 in fuel designed for high compression engines.

performance parameters   The ranges in terms of speed, distance, service ceiling, and so on, within which an aircraft is capable of performing safely.

periodic inspection   The inspections of the airframe and engines and certain instruments that must be performed by authorized inspectors at intervals spelled out in the FARs.

peripheral vision   The ability to see and recognize objects located to either side or above or below the direction in which we are looking. Especially important in night flight when the eye develops a blind spot straight ahead.

permanent echo   A radar return, usually caused by fixed objects on the ground, representing a known location and sometimes used in directing aircraft to a desired position.

PERMLY   Permanently.

personal computer   Microcomputer. Any electronic computer, using microprocessors, other than a minicomputer or a mainframe computer.

P-factor   An unevenness in thrust produced by the propeller during changes in aircraft attitude. It combines with torque to cause the aircraft to want to yaw in one direction or another during periods of maximum or minimum power. In typical U.S. aircraft in which the propeller turns to the right (as seen from the position of the pilot), the aircraft will try to yaw to the left (requiring right rudder) during full power takeoff roll and climbout, and to the right (requiring left rudder) during a power off glide to a landing.

phonetic alphabet   The words used internationally for letters and digits:

A	—	Alpha	M	—	Mike	Y	—	Yankee
B	—	Bravo	N	—	November	Z	—	Zulu
C	—	Charlie	O	—	Oscar	0	—	Zero
D	—	Delta	P	—	Papa	1	—	Wun
E	—	Echo	Q	—	Quebec (Kebek)	2	—	Too
F	—	Foxtrot	R	—	Romeo	3	—	Tree
G	—	Golf	S	—	Sierra	4	—	Fow-er
H	—	Hotel	T	—	Tango	5	—	Fife
I	—	India	U	—	Uniform	6	—	Six
J	—	Juliett	V	—	Victor	7	—	Sev-en
K	—	Kilo	W	—	Whiskey	8	—	Ait
L	—	Lima (Leemah)	X	—	Exray	9	—	Nin-er

phugoid   The tendency of an aircraft to intermittently dive and climb, gaining speed during the dive portion until the added speed causes it to start to climb, losing speed until the cycle is repeated.

Piaggio   Rinaldo Piaggio, the Italian manufacturer of the Avanti canard equipped twin turboprop pusher corporate aircraft and the P.166-DL3-SEM twin turboprop utility aircraft distinguished by its gull-wing design. (Rinaldo Piaggio S.p.A., 4 Via Cibrario, I-16154 Genova-Sestri, ITALY. (010) 6004-325) (Pages 341-342)

PIC   Pilot in command.

Rinaldo Piaggio

Piaggio Avanti twin-turboprop pusher aircraft.

Rinaldo Piaggio

Piaggio P.166-DL3-SEM twin-turboprop utility aircraft.

Piaggio Turboprop Aircraft

		AVANTI P180	P.166-DL3-SEM[*]
ENGINES	manufacturer	Pratt & Whitney (2)	n/a
	type	PT6A-66	n/a
DIMENSIONS ft	length	47.25	n/a
	height	13.04	n/a
	span	45.66	n/a
	wing area ft^2	172.22	n/a
CABIN ft	width	6.07	n/a
	height	5.74	n/a
WEIGHTS lbs	ramp	10,900	n/a
	max takeoff	10,810	9,480
	max landing	10,270	n/a
	basic operating	7,370	n/a
	empty, equipped	7,200	n/a
	max payload	1,630	n/a
	fuel	2,846	n/a
	payload with full fuel	684	n/a
SPEEDS	max kts	400	224
	M_{mo} Mach	0.67	
	V_{mo} kts	300	162
	stall (dirty) kts	90	69
RANGE nm	IFR reserves	1,500	
	VFR reserves	1,820	1,110
SERVICE CEILING ft	2 engines	41,000	30,500
	1 engine	n/a	16,000
PRESSURIZATION	psi	9.0	n/a
TAKEOFF ft	50 ft.obstacle	2,770	2,000
LANDING ft	50 ft.obstacle	2,330	1,360
RATE OF CLIMB fpm	2 engines	3,100	2,570
	1 engine	950	740

[*] Gull wing design powered by two turboprop engines driving pusher propellers

pictorial display   Any navigation instrument display that attempts to pictorially represent the attitude of the aircraft with reference to the horizon or other fixed parameters. In contrast to displays using digits or needles to convey that information.

Pilatus Britten-Norman Ltd.   Manufacturer of the Islander ten-seat twin piston-engine high-wing aircraft and the Turbine Islander. (Bembridge Airport, Bembridge, Isle of Wight, England P035 5PR. Phone: 0983 872511.)

Pilatus Fugzeugwerke A.G.   Manufacturer of the Turbo Porter single-engine multi-purpose utility aircraft; the Turbo Trainer single-engine fully aerobatic training aircraft and the PC-9 high-performance turboprop trainer. (CH-6370 Stans, Switzerland. Phone: 041 636111.)

Pilatus Porter   A family of Swiss-built STOL aircraft.

pilot   Airman. Anyone who flies a powered fixed-wing or rotary-wing aircraft, a glider, balloon, blimp, or dirigible. (One who flies only hang gliders or uses high-performance, or other types, of parachutes is not a pilot.)

pilotage   Navigation by reference to visible landmarks. Used usually in conjunction with aviation charts on which all meaningful landmarks are shown.

pilot briefing   A service provided by flight service specialists at FSSs to help the pilot determine the weather and other conditions that might affect a planned flight.

pilot in command   The pilot responsible for the safe conduct of a flight. Regardless of the circumstances or of any ATC clearances or instructions, the pilot in command is responsible for the aircraft, passengers, crew, and conduct of the flight.

pilot light   On a hot-air-balloon heater the flame needed to activate the heater and replenish the supply of hot air and, in turn, lift.

pilot-light valve   In a hot-air balloon, the valve that controls the pilot light.

pilot report (PIREP)   An observation of weather or other phenomena, their intensity, location and time made by a pilot in flight and reported to the nearest FSS which, at its discretion, may then transmit the report on the nationwide teletype system.

pilot's automatic weather answering service (PATWAS)   Prerecorded and periodically updated weather information, available at locations and during hours when on-site personnel is not available to brief pilots on flight conditions.

pilot's discretion   An ATC phrase used with reference to altitude assignments. It means that the pilot may start his climb (or descent) whenever he wishes and that he may climb (or descend) at any rate of his choice. He might, if he so desires, temporarily level off at an intermediate altitude, but once having vacated a given altitude, he cannot return to it.

pilot self-briefing terminal (PSBT)   A facility that gives pilots direct access to a computer for preflight briefing, obtaining information, and filing flight plans. The pilot uses a keyboard telephone to convey his requests to the computer, and the computer replies either through alphanumeric displays on a TV screen or through computer-generated voice messages.

pilot weather report   Pilot report.

Piper Aircraft Corporation   Manufacturer of a full line of aircraft. (2626 Piper Drive, Vero Beach, FL 32960. (407) 567-4361.) (Pages 344-348)

piston   Any structure that moves back and forth within a tube. More specifically, the circular ram that moves within the cylinder of reciprocating engines and represents the moving base of the combustion chamber. Also the moving inner part of an oleo strut.

piston engine   Reciprocating engine.

Piper Single-Engine Fixed-Gear Aircraft

	SUPER CUB	CADET	WARRIOR II	ARCHER II	DAKOTA	SARATOGA
ENGINE						
MODEL	Lycoming	Lycoming	Lycoming	Lycoming	Lycoming	Lycoming
	O-320-A2B	O-320-D3G	O-320-D3G	O-360-A4M	O-540-J3A5D	IO-540-K1G5
RATING hp	150 @ 2700 rpm	160 @ 2700 rpm	160 @ 2700 rpm	180 @ 2700 rpm	235 @ 2400 rpm	300 @ 2700 rpm
				178 @ 2650 rpm		294 @ 2600 rpm
TBO hours	2000	2000	2000	2000	2000	2000
PROPELLER	Sensenich 2/74	Sensenich 2/74	Sensenich 2/74	Sensenich 2/76	Hartzell 2/80	Hartzell 2/80
	fixed pitch	fixed pitch	fixed pitch	fixed pith	const.speed	const.speed
RAMP WEIGHT	1750	2332	2447	2558	3011	3615
TAKEOFF WT.	1750	2332	2440	2550	3000	3600
LANDING WT.	1750					
EMPTY WEIGHT	1062	1390	1348	1413	1610	1935
USEFUL LOAD	688	942	1099	1145	1401	1680
WING AREA ft^2	178.5	170	170	170	170	178.3
WING LOAD lb/ft^2	9.8	13.7	14.4	15	17.6	20.2
SPAN ft.	35.3	35	35	35	35.4	36.2
LENGTH/WIDTH ft.	22.5/6.9	23.8	23.8/7.3	23.8/7.3	24.7/7.2	27.7/8.2
CABIN L/W/H in.		98/41.25/44.25	8/41.25/44.25	98/41.75/45	98/41.75/44.75	124.25/49/42
FUEL usable gal.	35.8	48	48	48	77	102
SPEED maximum kts.	113	121	127	129	148	152
economy kts.	100	110	118	125	139	146
RANGE hi speed nm		490	525	520	650	745
economy nm	400	530	553	565	710	805
RATE OF CLIMB fpm	960	670	644	735	1110	990
STALL clean kts.		50	50	53	65	62
dirty kts.	37	44	44	47	56	58
TAKEOFF ground run ft	200	950	1050	870	886	1183
50 ft obst ft	500	1500	1650	1660	1216	1759
LANDING ground run ft	350	590	625	925	640	732
50 ft obst ft	885	1050	1160	1390	1530	1612
PRICE 1989 $s	$45,995	57,495 VFR	67,900	73.300	$103,900	133,300
		66,495 IFR				

PROPELLER: Manufacturer number of blades/diameter
WEIGHTS: All weights in pounds
CABIN: Length/Width/Height in inches
SERVICE CEILING: Feet

Piper Cherokee Warrior.

Piper Aircraft Corporation

Piper Single-Engine Retractable-Gear Aircraft

	SARATOGA SP	SARATOGA SP TURBO	ARROW	ARROW IV	MALIBU MIRAGE
ENGINE	Lycoming	Lycoming	Lycoming	Continental	Lycoming
MODEL	IO-540-K1G5D	TIO-540-S1AD	IO-360-CIC6	TSIO-360-FB	TIO-540-AE2A
RATING hp	300 @ 2700 rpm	300 @ 2700 rpm	200 @ 2700 rpm	200 @ 2575 rpm	350 @ 2500 rpm
	294 @ 2600 rpm	294 @ 2575 rpm	196 @ 2650 rpm	200 @ 2575 rpm	
TBO (hours)	2000	1800	1600	1800	2000
PROPELLER	Hartzell 2/80	Hartzell 2/80	McCauley 2/76	Hartzell 2/76	Hartzell 2/80
RAMP WEIGHT	3615	3617	2760	912	4318
TAKEOFF WT.	3600	3600	2750	2900	4300
EMPTY WEIGHT	1999	2078	1612	1692	2626
USEFUL LOAD	1616	1539	1148	1220	1692
ZERO FUEL WEIGHT					4100
WING AREA ft^2	178.3	178.3	170	170	175
WING LOAD lb/ft^2	20.2	20.2	16.2	17	24.6
SPAN ft.	36.2	36.2	35.4	35.4	43
LENGTH/HEIGHT ft.	27.7/8.5	28.2/8.5	24.7/7.9	7.3/8.3	28.6/11.5
CABIN L/W/H in.	124.25/48.75/42	124.25/48.75/42	93.25/41.75/44.75	93.25/41.75/44.75	148/49.6/47
FUEL usable gal	102	102	72	72	120
SPEED maximum	164 kts	195 kts	152 kts	178 kts	237 kts
economy	153 kts	166 kts	138 kts	167 kts	215 kts
RANGE hi speed nm	784	730	725	695	1018
economy nm	828	790	770	775	1084
RATE OF CLIMB	1010 fpm	1120 fpm	831 fpm	940 fpm	1218 fpm
STALL clean kts	60	61	60	66	72
dirty kts	57	56	55	61	60
SERVICE CEILING	16,700	20,000*	16,200	20,000*	25,000*
TAKEOFF					
ground run ft	1183	1110	1025	1110	1450
50 ft obst ft	1759	1590	1600	1620	2550
LANDING					
ground run ft	732	732	615	645	932
50 ft obst ft	1612	1725	1525	1560	1952
PRICE 1989 $s	158,900	n/a	114,300	120,300	369,900

PROPELLER: Manufacturer number of blades/diameter
WEIGHTS: All weights in pounds
CABIN: Length/Width/Height in inches
SERVICE CEILING: Feet

* Maximum approved altitude

Piper Aircraft Corporation

Piper Cheyenne IIXL.

Piper Piston Twin

SENECA III

ENGINE	Continental
MODEL	TSIO-360 KB & LTSIO-360 KB
RATING hp	220 @ 2800
	200 @ 2600
TBO	1800
PROPELLERS	Hartzell 2/76 constant speed
RAMP WEIGHT	4773
TAKEOFF WEIGHT	4750
LANDING WEIGHT	4513
EMPTY WEIGHT	2852
USEFUL LOAD	1921
ZERO FUEL WEIGHT	4470
WING AREA ft^2	208.7
WING LOAD lb/ft^2	22.8
WING SPAN ft	38.9
LENGTH	28.6
HEIGHT	9.9
CABIN length in.	124.25
width in.	42
height in.	38/35.75/34.5
FUEL usable gal.	93/123
SPEED max kts	196
75% kts	193
65% kts	191
45% kts	168
RANGE 75% nm	665
65% nm	758
45% nm	990
RATE OF CLIMB fpm	1300 2 engines
	200 1 engine
STALL clean kts	67
dirty kts	64
SERVICE CEILING ft	25,000 2 engines[*]
	12,000 1 engine
TAKEOFF ground run ft	920
50 ft.obst.	1210
LANDING ground run ft	1400
50 ft.obst.	2160
ACCELERATE/STOP ft	2400
PRICE 1989 $s	224,500

[*] maximum approved altitude

Piper Turboprop Aircraft

		CHEYENNE I	CHEYENNE II	CHEYENNE IIIA	CHEYENNE 400
ENGINE	manufacturer	Pratt & Whitney	Pratt & Whitney	Pratt & Whitney	Garrett
	model	PT6A-11 (2)	PT6A-28 (2)	PT6A-61 (2)	TPE 331-14 (2)
	shp (flat rated)	500	620	720	1000
WEIGHTS lbs	ramp	8750	9050	11,285	12,135
	takeoff	8700	9000	11,200	12,050
	landing	8700	9000	10,330	11,100
	empty	n/a	n/a	6,837	7,565
	useful load	3850	4074	4,448	4,750
	zero fuel	7200	7200	9,350	10,000
WING	area ft^2	229	229	293	293
	loading lb/ft^2	38	39.3	38.22	41.1
	span ft	40.67	42.68	47.67	47.7
DIMENSION ft	length	34.67	34.67	43.39	43.4
	height	12.75	12.75	14.75	17.0
CABIN inches	length	101.04	101.04	275	275
	width	50.04	50.04	51	51
	height	51.48	51.48	52	56
FUEL gal	usable	300	365.5	560	570
SPEEDS kts	V_{ne}	249	283	305	n/a
	cruise @ 22,000 ft			305	
	cruise @ 24,000 ft				351
	cruise @ 25,000 ft			302	346
	cruise @ 29,000 ft				293
	cruise @ 31,000 ft			293	
	cruise @ 35,000 ft			282	294
RANGE nm	max	940	900	2055	1821
	economy speed	1260	1510	2270	2176
RATE OF CLIMB	2 engines fpm	1750	2800	3220	4110
	1 engine fpm	413	660	1075	1450
STALL	clean kts	84	86	102	93
	dirty kts	72	75	89	84
SERVICE CEILING ft	2 engines	28,200	31,600	35,840	41,000
	1 engine	12,500	14,600	26,300	30,500
TAKEOFF	ground run ft	1712	1410	1465	1425
	50 ft.obst. ft	2541	1980	2280	2325
LANDING	ground roll ft	1695	1430	1914	1090
	w.prop reverse	1193	995	1457	820
	50 ft.obst. ft	2548	2480	3043	2317
	w.prop.reverse	2131	18650	2586	2038

Piper Aircraft Corporation

Piper Cheyenne IIIA.

Piper Cheyenne 400.

pitch   The attitude or movement of an aircraft with reference to or around its lateral axis; in other words, the position of the nose of the aircraft or its movement up or down. Also the blade angle of a propeller.

pitch angle   Propeller blade angle.

pitch axis   Lateral axis.

pitch-out   A sudden sharp turn away from the direction of flight, usually, but not necessarily, downward.

pitot   A term associated with the airspeed measuring systems. Named after Henry Pitot, a French physicist.

pitot-heater   A means of heating the pitot tube to avoid ice accumulation that would cause it to malfunction.

pitot pressure   The pressure produced by an aircraft moving through the air. It increases with airspeed and is the basis for airspeed measurement. Also called ram or impact air pressure.

pitot-static system   A device that compares pitot pressure with static or atmospheric pressure and presents the result in the cockpit terms of indicated airspeed, altitude, and vertical speed. It consists of a pitot tube mounted on the frontal surface of the aircraft or wing and static vents placed flush into the wall of the fuselage. Both parts are needed to operate the airspeed indicator, and the static vents control the altimeter and the vertical speed indicator.

pitot tube   A tube exposed to the airstream, designed to measure the pressure with which an aircraft meets the static air. It must keep clear of obstructions and should be covered when the aircraft is not in use, as insects like to nest in it. Also called pitot-static head.

Pitts Special A high-performance aerobatic biplane, now being manufactured by Christen Industries, Inc.

placard Any sign or message, usually prominently displayed in the cockpit, to remind or warn the pilot to stay within certain performance parameters. An aircraft may be said to be *placarded* against intentional spins.

planning chart An aeronautical planning chart used prior to but normally not during a flight. A VFR planning chart, covering the conterminous 48 states, is available from the NOAA (or through the chart services of the AOPA. Also IFR (radio facility) planning charts are available from the same sources or from Jeppesen-Sanderson, Inc.

PLD Payload.

P-line Pole line.

plotter A combination ruler and protractor, marking nm and sm scales, and used to determine or draw projected courses on charts.

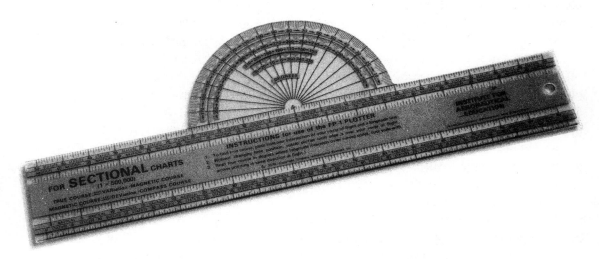

Plotter.

plumbing In relation to aircraft, the term usually refers to the hydraulic system. In hot-air ballooning it refers to the propane tanks and the system of pipes and valves that deliver the propane to the burner.

PNR Point of no return.

pod Nacelle.

point of descent The point at which descent to the destination is initiated. For the formula to determine the most efficient point of descent, *see* EN ROUTE DESCENT.

point of no return The position along a line of flight, having passed beyond which the pilot cannot return to his point of departure on the amount of fuel remaining on board.

polar air mass A cold air mass, continental or maritime, that originated in the polar regions.

polar easterlies The general circulation pattern of easterly winds between 60 degrees north latitude and the north pole.

polar front A frontal zone between cold polar and warm tropical air masses, generally occurring in the middle latitudes.

polar navigation Navigating becomes difficult in the polar regions because of the convergence of the meridians and the proximity of the magnetic north pole. Charts must be used with a so-called grid overlay in order to permit the pilot to fly a straight line from departure to destination. This system translates the rapidly changing true course measurements to a constant grid course.

pop Slang for papa, the phonetic term for P.

portable transceiver A communication transmitter/receiver that operates on batteries, independent of the aircraft, but using aviation com frequencies.

position lights Navigation lights.

position report Reports relating to an aircraft's progress given to ATC by the pilot when passing a geographical or navaid fix. It should include aircraft identification, time over the fix, and altitude. It must also include the ETA for the next fix when the aircraft is not in radar contact.

position symbol A symbol generated by a computer and displayed on the radar screen at ATC facilities to indicate the tracking mode being used.

position control The term means that all traffic, IFR and VFR, is being controlled by and must maintain contact with ATC.

positive control area Airspace from 18,000 feet msl up to and including FL 600 (60,000 feet msl) above the 48 contiguous states and most of Alaska. In parts of Alaska the base is at 24,000 feet.

power Thrust produced by means other than gravity.

power approach An approach using partial power, resulting in a flatter angle of glide and better control over the aircraft than is possible in a power-off approach.

power dive A dive, at a steep angle, with power on.

power glide A gradual descent with power on.

power landing A landing at which partial power is used during final flare and until actual touchdown. It is used primarily by high-performance aircraft to improve control and ensure an easier go-around if such should suddenly become necessary.

power loading The ratio of the certificated gross weight or the gross weight at any given time to the rated horsepower of the engine(s).

power-off glide A glide with the engine at idle.

power-off stalling speed The speed at which the aircraft will stall with its power off. These speeds vary with flap setting and gear position.

power-on stalling speed   The speed at which the aircraft will stall, using partial or full power, by increasing the angle-of-attack beyond the point at which it maintains adequate lift generation. The speeds vary with gear position and flap settings, if any.

powerplant   Engine(s).

power settling   A phenomenon that can occur when a helicopter descends into its own downwash, effectively stalling part or all of the rotor.

pph   Pounds per hour. Used in measuring fuel flow.

Pratt & Whitney Canada   A subsidiary of United Technologies Corporation, is a leading manufacturer of gas turbine engines for general aviation and regional transport aircraft. Currently (1989) in production are the PT6 family of turboprop/turboshaft engines powering a large number of turbine helicopters including the Sikorsky S-76B and fixed-wing turboprop aircraft such as the Beech King Airs, the Starship 1, and the Cessna Caravan I and II, the JT15D family of turbofan engines powering the Beechjet and the Citation II and V among others, the PW100 turboprop engine used in, among others, the Boeing of Canada deHavilland Dash 8, and the PW901A auxiliary power unit. The advanced technology 578-DX ultra high-bypass turbofan engine is produced in a joint venture with Allison Gas Turbine Division. (1000 Marie-Victorin, Longueuil, Quebec J4G 1A1, Canada. (514) 677-9411.)

precession   The tendency of a gyroscope to gradually become unreliable, primarily due to friction. Usually used with reference to the directional gyro, which tends to wander from the heading to which it has been set and must periodically be adjusted in accordance with the magnetic compass.

precipitation   Visible moisture in the atmosphere, condensed to a point at which it will fall in the form of rain, drizzle, snow, hail, etc.

precision approach   An instrument approach using ground-based electronic glide slope guidance. An ILS or PAR approach.

precision approach radar   A radar designed to enable the ground controller to provide the pilot with precise range, azimuth, and altitude information throughout the final approach. (Page 352)

precision turn   A turn made to a specific heading or covering a predetermined number of degrees while maintaining altitude. A training maneuver.

preferential routes   The term refers to a route structure entered into computer memories at various ARTCCs in order to expedite handoffs from one sector or ARTCC to another. They are divided into preferential departure routes (PDR), preferential arrival routes (PAR), and preferential departure and arrival routes (PDAR). In many (though not all) instances PDRs are included in SIDs, PARs, and STARs.

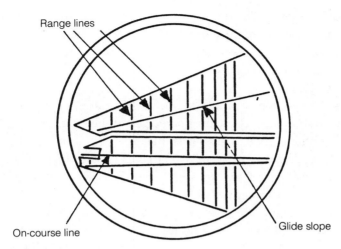

Precision approach radarscope.

preferred IFR routes A route system established in heavy traffic areas designed to increase the efficiency and capacity of the ATC system. They might extend through one or several ARTCC areas. Preferred IFR routes are listed in AIM Part 3, and are coordinated with SIDs and STARs. Pilots are urged to file preferred IFR routes and, barring weather avoidance procedures or other considerations,

Preferred Routes (sample)

from:	NEW ORLEANS METRO AREA	
to:	ATLANTA	PCU V70 MVC V20 TYRONE L17 L18 L20
to:	BIRMINGHAM	PCU V455 MEI V154 V209 BWA DRCT BHM/LOM L17 L18 L14
to:	DALLAS	WALKER V114N AEX V114 GGG V94 V477E FORNEY L17 L13
to:	DULLES INT'L	PCU V70 MVC V20 SBV V39 GVE V39E BRANDY L17 L18 L20 L22
to:	HOUSTON	TBD V20S LFT V20 LCH V222N MONUMENT L17
to:	KENNEDY INT'L	PCU V70 MVC V20 V213 ENO V44 BEECHWOOD L17 L18 L20 L22 L24
to:	MEMPHIS	PCU V9E MCB V9 GRW V9E INDEPENDENCE L14
to:	NEWARK	PCU V70 MVC V20 V213 ENO V29 V433 ROCKY HILL L17 L18 L20 L22 L24
to:	WASHINGTON	PCU V70 MVC V20 SBV V39 GVE V16 IRONSIDES L17 L18 L20 L22

ATC will issue clearances based on this route structure. A pilot may refuse acceptance of such a clearance if he deems it unsafe or uneconomical.

preferred routes   Preferred IFR routes.

preflight   Used as a verb it means to conduct a preflight inspection or to prepare the aircraft for flight.

preflight inspection   A visual inspection of the aircraft before flight intended to discover anything that might result in problems during the flight. It should always include an oil check and a visual check of the fuel level. During winter months it should include the removal of frozen moisture from the airfoils and snow or ice accumulations in the gear assemblies, wheel wells, etc.

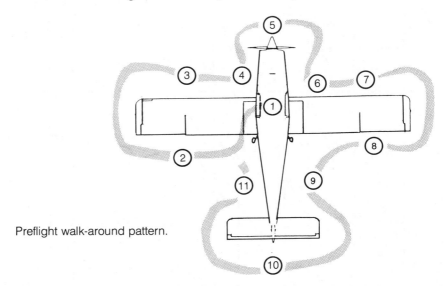

Preflight walk-around pattern.

preignition   The burning of the fuel-air mixture in the combustion chamber before the spark plugs have had an opportunity to fire. It is caused by a hot spot in the engine such as overheated carbon deposits. It usually follows excessive overheating of the engine and results in erratic power output, increased overheating, and, in extreme cases, severe damage to the engine.

pressure altitude   The indicated altitude when the altimeter is set to 29.92 in. Hg. It is equal to the true altitude under standard pressure and temperature conditions and is used to calculate true altitude and density altitude. It is always used when flying at 18,000 feet msl or above.

pressure gradient   The decrease in atmospheric pressure per unit of horizontal distance in the direction in which the pressure decreases most rapidly. It is perpendicular to isobars.

pressure pattern flying   Flying an apparently circuitous route to take advantage of favorable winds resulting from prevailing pressure patterns.

pressure relief valve A valve that is part of the propane tank system on hot-air balloons, designed to open when pressure increases to the danger point, closing again automatically when normal pressure has been restored.

pressure suit A suit used by pilots, usually military, designed to counteract the effects of excessive G loadings.

pressurization A system of maintaining given degrees of atmospheric pressure in the cabin of an aircraft. Pressurization amounts are measured in psi, and a given number of psi will maintain sea level pressure to a given altitude. In pressurized piston-engine aircraft the pressurization is produced by a turbocharger. In turbine aircraft special pressurization equipment must be installed.

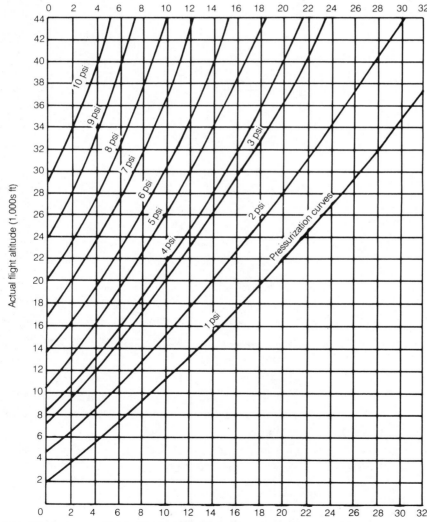

Cabin altitude versus flight altitude with different rates of pressurization.

pressurization system   The equipment on an aircraft to maintain reasonable pressure levels at high altitudes.

pressurized aircraft   An aircraft equipped to maintain a pressure differential between the cabin and the outside.

Pressurized Centurion   A high-performance single-engine aircraft manufactured by Cessna but no longer in production.

Pressurized Centurion.

Pressurized Navajo   A cabin size piston twin manufactured by Piper Aircraft Corporation but no longer in production.

Pressurized Skymaster   A push-pull piston twin manufactured by Cessna but no longer in production.

prevailing visibility   The visibility in terms of distance at a given time and place.

prevailing westerlies   The circulation pattern of the predominantly westerly winds between 30 and 60 degrees north latitude.

prevailing wind   The wind direction most frequently observed at a given area. Runways are usually aligned to take advantage of the prevailing winds.

preventive maintenance   Simple maintenance, repair, and cleaning operations, or replacement of standard parts not involving major disassembly and assembly operations.

primary radar   Radar that transmits a pulsed signal, which is reflected from objects and received back at the ground station without the reflecting objects being in any way involved in augmenting or retransmitting the signal.

primary target   A radar return from an aircraft that is not transponder equipped. Usually weak, the return tends to get lost among the transponder-augmented returns.

primer   A plunger-type cockpit control that releases fuel directly into the cylinders, improving smooth starts especially under cold weather conditions.

private license   A pilot's license that permits the pilot to carry passengers, but not for remuneration.

private pilot   A pilot who has been issued a private license by the FAA. He must be 17 years old to be rated to fly powered aircraft (16 years for gliders), must speak, read, and understand English, must have at least a third-class medical certificate, and must have accumulated a given amount of flight time (solo and dual), must have passed a written examination and practical flight test with an authorized examiner and have demonstrated his flying and navigating capability.

procedure turn   A turn at a definite fix, at or above a definite altitude and within a defined amount of airspace, usually a part of an instrument approach for the purpose of maneuvering the aircraft into the right position, heading, and altitude for the final approach. A procedure turn consists of a 45-degree turn to the left (occasionally right) followed by a 225-degree turn to the right (left), which should terminate at the same place at which the first turn was started.

procedure turn inbound   That point at which the procedure turn maneuver has been completed and the aircraft should be established on the final (or intermediate) segment of the approach. The phrase "procedure turn inbound" may be used by the pilot when reporting his position to ATC, or by ATC for separation purposes.

profile descent   A procedure affecting primarily jet aircraft, designed to minimize noise as well as fuel consumption during the descent and approach portion of the flight. While different descent profiles have been established by the FAA for different airports, the basic principle involves keeping the aircraft above FL 200 (20,000 feet msl) as long as possible (especially when delays are anticipated) and then to execute the entire descent at idle thrust all the way down to the final approach path. Airspeed assignments to speeds below 210 knots are to be minimized, and traffic flow regulated to avoid delaying maneuvers at low altitudes and speeds.

PROG   Prognosis.

PROG   Progress.

prognostic chart   Surface weather forecast chart.

progress report   Position report.

prohibited area   Airspace within certain geographic limits within which civil flight is prohibited. Prohibited areas may be used by the military for purposes that could endanger aircraft in the area or they may simply be portions of airspace above which aircraft flight is undesirable. The White House and any permanent or temporary residence of the president are prohibited areas, as is, for instance, the area covering the White Sands Proving Grounds and Los Alamos Scientific Laboratory in New Mexico.

ProLine   A family of sophisticated avionics designed for large high-performance aircraft and manufactured by Collins.

Promavia S.A.   Developer and manufacturer of the Squalus side-by-side two-seat twin-jet training aircraft. (181, Chaussee de Fleurus, B-6200 Gosselies Airport, Belgium. Phone: 071 350829.)

			SQUALUS
Promavia Jet Trainer	ENGINE	manufacturer	Garret (2)
		model	TFE109-1
		rating	1,330 pound thrust
	WEIGHTS lbs	takeoff	5,290
		landing	5,290
	FUEL gal	usable	190
	LOAD FACTOR	g	+ 7.0/- 3.5
	SPEEDS	V_d knots	380
		V_{ne} knots	345
		M_{ne} Mach	0.7
		V_{no} knots	300
		V_a knots	210
		Stall knots	67
	RATE OF CLIMB	fpm	3,200
	SERVICE CEILING ft		37,000
	TAKEOFF	run ft	1,200
	LANDING	roll ft	1,100
	RANGE	ferry,max fuel	1,000 nm

prop   Propeller.

prop   Used as a verb it means starting an aircraft by manually swinging the propeller.

propane   Liquefied petroleum gas (LPG), the fuel used to heat the air in hot-air balloons.

propeller   A device consisting of two or more airfoil-shaped blades that is designed to convert the turning force of the engine into thrust. Propellers may be fixed-pitch, meaning that the pitch of the blades cannot be varied; or variable pitch (also known as constant speed) in which case the pitch of the blades can be varied by the pilot in flight. Variable-pitch propellers are more efficient. The rotation speed of a propeller is limited to the speed at which the propeller blade tips approach the speed of sound.

propeller reverse   The ability to reverse the blade pitch of a propeller, resulting in negative thrust. Usually available only on turboprop aircraft.

propeller spinner   The central shaft of a propeller to which the blades are attached. It is usually covered by a streamlined cone and this cone itself is often referred to as the spinner.

propeller wash   The fast moving disturbed airstream caused by a rotating propeller. It tends to pick up and blow back sand and small rocks that could damage aircraft or vehicles located behind an airplane with a fast turning propeller.

propping an airplane   Starting the engine by manually swinging the propeller. The
only means of starting an airplane with no electrical system or one in which the
battery is dead. In cold weather the propeller should be swung manually a few
times (with the ignition system turned off) in order to loosen the oil in the engine.

propulsion   The action or process of propelling. Thrust.

ProStar   A computer/calculator designed specifically for experienced and professional pilots. Manufactured by Jeppesen Sanderson.

ProStar computer/calculator.

PRST   Persist.

PSBL   Possible.

PSBT   Pilot self-briefing terminal.

PSG   Passing; passage.

psi   Pounds per square inch. A measure of pressure.

PSN   Position.

PSR   Packed snow on runway.

PST   Pacific standard time.

psychrometer   A hygrometer used for calculating relative humidity by comparing
temperatures on a dry bulb thermometer and a wet bulb thermometer (one covered with a wet cloth), indicating rate of evaporation.

PT Procedure turn.

PTLY Partly.

PTN Position.

published With reference to aircraft maneuvers, procedures that have been established and published by ATC.

published approach Standard instrument approach at any given location.

published route A route for which an IFR altitude has been established and published, such as federal airways, jet routes, etc.

pulse instruments Electronic instruments that emit pulsed (intermittent) transmissions. Radar is a pulse instrument, as are DMEs and radar altimeters.

Puma A 16-place twin-turbine helicopter manufactured by Aerospatiale in France.

pure jet A turbojet engine or aircraft, not equipped with a fan or bypass function. Pure jets are noisier than fan-jets.

PVL Prevail.

PVT Private.

PWI Proximity warning indicator.

PWR Power.

pylon Any prominent mark or feature on the ground used as a fix in executing precision maneuvers.

pylon eight A training maneuver in which the aircraft describes a symmetrical figure-eight path over the ground, using two selected points (pylons) as the hub of each turn. It requires careful control of airspeed, rate of bank and turn, and correction for wind drift.

pylon race An air race using two pylons as the turning points in a racetrack-shaped flight path.

Q Quebec (phonetic alphabet).

Q Squall (in sequence reports).

Q altimeter setting Several different kinds of altimeter settings, such as QFE and QNH. (The Q is an abbreviation left over from years-ago use with Morse code.)

QB Quiet Birdmen, a primarily social organization of pilots.

Q-code The code used in NOTAMs, always preceded by the letter Q.

QFE An altimeter setting in which the altimeter is set in such a way that it will read zero altitude upon touchdown at the selected airport. It reduces the need for complicated arithmetic in the cockpit during an instrument approach and is in common use by some U.S. and by many European airlines. When a QFE altimeter setting is used, a second altimeter must be in the aircraft, set to the conventional setting based on barometric pressure.

QFLOW Quota flow control.

QNH The conventional altimeter setting based on the prevailing barometric pressure and reading altitude in feet msl.

QT Quart.

QUAD Quadrant.

quadrant One quarter of a circle. Also an instrument for measuring altitudes, commonly consisting of a graduated arc of 90 degrees with an index or vernier, usually having a plumb line or spirit level for fixing the vertical or horizontal direction. It is part of the instrumentation used in celestial navigation.

quebec In aviation radio phraseology the term used for the letter Q. (Pronounced kebeck.)

Queen Air A cabin-class piston-engine twin aircraft, once manufactured by Beech Aircraft Corporation. No longer in production.

quick drain valve A valve installed on the outside of the aircraft and connected to a fuel tank or fuel strainer through which water and sediment is collected and can be emptied during the preflight inspection.

quick look A feature of the ATC radar system which permits the controller to briefly display full data blocks of tracked aircraft from other control positions.

quota flow control   An ATC procedure that limits the number of aircraft that may approach or enter a certain (terminal) area, designed to minimize congestion or saturation of that area or sector.

R Ceiling measured by radar (in sequence reports).

R Rain (in sequence reports).

R Romeo (phonetic alphabet).

RAD Radial.

RADAR Radio detection and ranging.

radar A family of electronic devices that use the interval between the time a radio signal is transmitted and the time the same signal, reflected off an object, is received back, to locate that reflecting object. The reflecting object can be an aircraft, precipitation, a ground-based feature, etc. By using combinations of special use antennas, computers, different types of receivers, and transmitters, radar echoes are transformed into useful information for pilots and ATC controllers.

radar advisory Advice or information based on radar observations.

radar air traffic control facility (RATCF) An ATC facility at a Navy or Marine Air Station, using PAR in combination with communication equipment to provide approach control service to aircraft operating in its area of jurisdiction.

radar altimeter An altimeter using radar technology to accurately measure the distance between the aircraft and the ground. Usually usable only up to a distance of 2,500 feet. Also called radio altimeter. (Page 364)

radar approach An instrument using ASR or PAR radar.

radar approach control (RAPCON) *See* RADAR AIR TRAFFIC CONTROL FACILITY.

radar arrival An aircraft is being vectored to the final approach course or to the traffic pattern for a visual approach. *See* VISUAL APPROACH.

radar beacon The signal emitted by a secondary radar answered by a transponder or altitude encoder in an aircraft.

radar contact An ATC phrase to inform the pilot that the controller has him identified on radar.

radar contact lost An ATC phrase to notify the pilot that radar identification has been lost (at least temporarily).

radar environment That portion of the airspace in which radar service is being provided.

Radar Altimeters

MANUFACTURER	MODEL	PRICE	DC	AC	C	P	P	D	L	O	FEET	+/- *	PD	RL	SIG V	SIG A	W	U	lbs	REMARKS
Bendix/King	KRA 10A	4,635 4,807	28 14					¤			20-2,500	5ft 5%			¤	¤		3	3.8	*5 ft to 100 ft,5% above 14V needs KA 133 conv'ter
Bendix/King	KRA 405	11,490	28					¤			20-2,000	5ft 7%			¤	¤		4	10.7	*5 ft to 500 ft,7% above
Bendix/King	KRA 405	11,745	28					¤			20-2,000	5ft 7%			¤	¤		4	10.7	same as above, but for use on helicopters
Collins	ALT55B	n/a	28		¤					*	0-2,500	5ft 7%			¤	¤		2	6.5	*digital displays ProLine II
Terra	TRA 3000 TRI 20	n/a	10 33		¤		¤	¤			40-2,500	5ft 5% 7%			¤	¤		2	2.1	
Terra	TRA 3000 TRI 30	n/a	28		¤		¤	¤			40-2,500	5ft 5% 7%			¤	¤		2	2.5	
Terra	TRA 3000 TRI 40	n/a	28		¤		¤	¤			40-2,500	5ft 5% 7%			¤	¤	¤	2	2.25	
Terra	TRA 3500 TRI 40	n/a	28		¤		¤	¤			0-2,500	5ft 5% 7%			¤	¤	¤	2	4	

PRICE:		uninstalled	O:	logarithmic
VOLT	DC:	DC input voltage	+/-:	accuracy +/- percent
	AC:	AC 400 Hz input voltage	PD:	pitch degrees +/-
TYP	C:	continuous wave	RL:	roll limit degrees +/-
	P:	pulse	SIG V:	visual DH signal
DISPLAY	P:	pointer	A:	audio DH signal
	D:	dial	W:	wheels-up warning
	L:	linear	U:	number of units

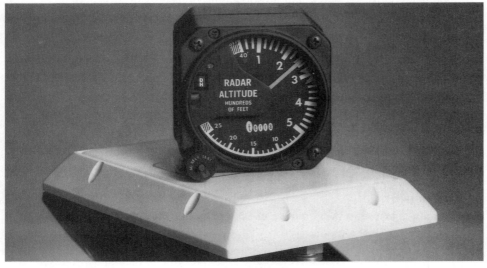

Analog radar altimeter.

Terra Radio

radar flight following The tracking of an aircraft that has been identified on radar, along its route of flight.

radar identification The process of identifying a specific radar return as being generated by a specific aircraft. If the aircraft is transponder equipped the controller can effect identification by asking the pilot to "squawk ident," which causes the radar return to brighten on the radar display. In order to positively identify an aircraft that is not transponder equipped, the controller will usually ask the pilot to execute a number of turns that show up on the radar display.

radar identified aircraft An aircraft that has been positively identified on radar and the position of which is therefore known to the controller.

radar monitoring Providing radar service.

radar navigation guidance Providing radar service.

radar point out A phrase used among controllers in instances when one controller hands an aircraft over to another but intends to continue communication with that aircraft for coordination purposes.

radar report (RAREP) Hourly reports from a weather bureau radar station covering storms and precipitation within approximately 100 miles of that station.

radar route A route flown by an aircraft being vectored. Navigational guidance and required altitudes are provided by ATC.

radar safety advisory Advisories issued by ATC to aircraft that, in the opinion of the controller, are getting dangerously close to the terrain or some sort of obstruction, or to advise pilots of a potential traffic conflict. Once having been advised by the pilot that he has taken corrective action or has the source of the danger in sight, such advisories are discontinued. Issuing such advisories is contingent on the ability of the controller to be aware of the potential danger, and once such an advisory has been issued it is the responsibility of the pilot(s) and not the controller to take the appropriate evasive action.

radar separation Separation of IFR aircraft based on radar observations.

radar service An all encompassing term covering all services provided by ATC to pilots, using radar.

radar service terminated An ATC phrase used to inform the pilot that no further radar service is being provided to that particular aircraft.

radar surveillance Radar observations of a specific geographical area.

radar traffic information service *See* RADAR ADVISORIES.

radar vector Using radar to give navigational information and instructions to an aircraft.

radial Any of the 360 magnetic courses from a VOR, VORTAC, or TACAN station, starting with zero at the magnetic north and increasing clockwise (90 degrees = east; 180 degrees = south; 270 degrees = west; 360 or zero degrees = north.)

radial engine   A reciprocating engine in which the cylinders are arranged in a circle around a central crankshaft. Usually more cylinders are employed than in horizontally-opposed engines, providing an increase in power output. Radial engines are no longer used in modern light aircraft.

radio altimeter   Radar altimeter.

radio beacon   *See* NONDIRECTIONAL BEACON (NDB).

radio direction finding   *See* DIRECTION FINDING (DF).

radio facility   Any electronic navaid.

radio facilities chart   An aeronautical chart used primarily in IFR operations and showing all electronic navaids, airways, distances between fixes and a world of other information, but no terrain features. Produced by NOAA and by Jeppesen Sanderson, Inc.

radio fix   A position determined by the intersecting point of two or more radials from navaids.

radio frequencies   All electromagnetic frequencies between 10 kHz and 300 MHz.

radio magnetic indicator (RMI)   A combination gyro compass (usually slaved) and VOR or ADF display. The compass card rotates to show the current heading of the aircraft; the VOR needle indicates the position of the aircraft relative to a selected radial or bearing FROM or TO a given station; the ADF needle shows the position of the nose of the aircraft relative to the selected station.

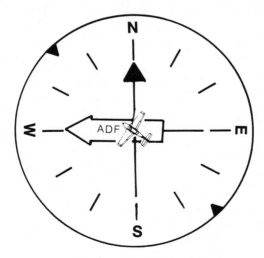

Typical components of a radio-magnetic indicator display.

radio range   LF/MF radio range; a now largely obsolete aid to navigation.

radiosonde   A balloon carrying electronic equipment to measure and transmit data about the upper air. It can be traced to measure the velocity and direction of upper winds.

radio station   Standard broadcast station.

radio station license   The license an aircraft owner must obtain from the FCC in order to legally operate the radio equipment aboard his aircraft.

radius   One half of the diameter of a circle.

radome   A plastic cover for the antenna of airborne weather radar. Usually painted black and installed in the nose of multi-engine aircraft.

RAF   Royal Air Force.

RAIL   Runway alignment indicator lights.

rain   Precipitation in the form of water droplets larger than those referred to as drizzle. The sequence report symbol is R.

Raisbeck Engineering   Designer and manufacturer of a variety of performance enhancing modifications for the family of Beech King Air turboprops. According to the company, the modifications involve changes to the wings and propellers, among other things, and produce considerable fuel savings, horsepower increases, engine overhaul cost reductions, greater climb rates, higher engine flat rating, increased cruise speed, greatly reduced interior noise levels, and a lower engine ITT. Also achieved are a 35 percent reduction in the FAA certified takeoff distance, a 50 percent reduction in the FAA certified accelerate-go distance and a 50 percent reduction in max-reverse stopping distance. The wing modifications result in increased fatigue life, a reduction in stall speeds and typical approach speeds at under 90 knots. (Boeing Field International, Seattle, WA 98108. (206) 763-2000 and (800) 537-7277.)

Rallye   A family of single-engine aircraft manufactured by Aerospatiale in France.

ram air   Air being forced into an orifice at a speed resulting from the motion of a vehicle. Mooney aircraft are equipped with a ram air inlet to be used at the pilot's discretion when the air appears to be free of polluting particles. It produces a slight increase in engine power output.

ram air pressure   Pitot pressure.

ramp   The parking apron and adjacent areas on an airport, used for loading, unloading, tiedown.

range   The distance an aircraft can travel on the available fuel. IFR range implies a 45-minute fuel reserve. No-reserve range refers to the distance it is possible to fly until the tank(s) run dry. To figure the no-reserve range: Divide the fuel on board by the fuel flow and multiply the result by the ground speed. To figure the IFR range take the result of the above and deduct from it: the fuel flow multiplied by 0.75 multiplied by the ground speed. *See* CONVERSION TABLES.

range   A radio or beacon system, as in VFR omni range.

Rangemaster   A high-performance single-engine aircraft produced by Navion. No longer in production.

Ranger   A high-performance single-engine aircraft once manufactured by Mooney Aircraft Corporation.

RAPCON   Radar approach control.

RAREP   Radar report.

RATCC   Radar air traffic control center.

RATCF   Radar air traffic control facility.

rate climb   A climb made at a constant rate requiring power or airspeed adjustments in order to maintain a constant fpm figure.

rated horsepower   The maximum horsepower for which an engine has been certificated.

rate of climb   The vertical distance traveled in terms of minutes, shown as fpm on the vertical speed indicator (VSI). To figure the rate of climb (or descent) if the VSI is inoperative: Divide the horizontal distance traveled in nautical miles by the ground speed. Then multiply the result by 60. Then divide the altitude change in feet by the result of the above to arrive at the correct fpm figures. *See also* CONVERSION TABLES.

rate of climb indicator   Vertical speed indicator (VSI).

rate of descent   Opposite of rate of climb.

rate of descent indicator   Vertical speed indicator (VSI).

rating   A qualification of a pilot to fly a particular type of aircraft (jet rated) or to fly IFR (instrument rated).

Raven Industries   *See* AEROSTAR INTERNATIONAL, INC.

RBN   Radio beacon.

RCAG   Remote communication air/ground facility.

RCC   Rescue coordination center.

RCH   Reach.

RCLM   Runway centerline marking.

RCLS   Runway centerline light system.

RCO   Remote communication outlet.

RCR   Runway condition reading.

RCV   Receive.

RCVG   Receiving.

RCVR   Receiver.

RDG Ridge.

RDO Radio.

read Phrase used in aviation radio phraseology to mean "hear." Such as in "I read you."

read back A request by ATC asking the pilot to repeat a clearance or instruction.

Reading Air Show In its day officially known as the National Maintenance and Operations Meeting, it was for many years one of the biggest and most important annual general aviation events in the U.S. It usually took place in the last week of May or the first week of June, attracting thousands of visitors and was frequently used by manufacturers to introduce new aircraft, avionics, and other products. The event was discontinued in the early 1980s but revived in the late 1980s. *See* AIR SHOWS.

ready for takeoff Phrase used by pilots to inform the tower that they are ready to accept takeoff clearance.

ready to copy Phrase used by pilots in talking either to ground control or clearance delivery, to inform ATC that they are ready to listen to (and actually copy in writing, though this is not mandatory) the clearance for their IFR flight, the flight plan for which has been previously filed with ATC.

ready to taxi Phrase used by pilots to inform ground control that they are ready to leave the ramp or parking area in order to taxi out for takeoff. Often followed by a description of the type of flight: Ready to taxi VFR Dallas, or ready to taxi IFR Albuquerque.

receiver A radio instrument designed to receive either com or nav transmissions.

receiving controller Controller receiving the control over an IFR aircraft from another controller or facility.

receiving facility ATC facility receiving control over an IFR aircraft from another facility or controller.

reciprocal The exact opposite bearing or radial, course or heading, by 180 degrees. To arrive at the correct reciprocal number of degrees, either add or deduct 180, depending on which results in a number of 360 degrees or less. (The reciprocal of 193 is 013; of 289 it is 109.)

reciprocating engine An engine that converts energy from fuel to mechanical motion by driving pistons back and forth. It primarily consists of cylinders, pistons, connecting rod, and crankshaft, operating in a continuous four-stroke cycle.

RECONSTR Reconstruction.

recorder (flight data and/or cockpit voice) (FDR or CVR) Hermetically sealed recorders designed to keep a record of changes in aircraft attitude, control inputs and other flight data; or of what is being said in the cockpit by members of the crew. Usually installed in the tail of the aircraft, it is built to survive a crash and thus to serve investigators by giving them information as to the possible cause of an accident.

recover To return to normal flight after an intentional or unintentional spin or other unusual maneuver.

recover Replacing the fabric on a fabric-covered aircraft or section of an aircraft.

Rediffusion Simulation, Inc. *See* HUGHES TRAINING SYSTEMS, INC.

redline speed Never exceed speed.

redline temperature Never exceed air temperature in a hot-air balloon.

Reduce speed to (knots) ATC request for a pilot to slow to a given speed, usually for purposes of separation.

region (FAA) The FAA is divided into seven regions: Eastern (Hq: Kennedy International Airport, Jamaica, N.Y.), Southern (Hq: Atlanta, GA), Central (Hq: Kansas City, MO), Southwest (Hq: Fort Worth, TX), Western (Hq: Los Angeles, CA), Alaska (Hq: Anchorage, AK), Hawaii (Hq: Honolulu, HI). *See also* GENERAL AVIATION DISTRICT OFFICES.

regional forecast A weather forecast of large-scale phenomena covering several states, good for the next 24 hours.

Regional Jet A greatly stretched version of the Canadair Challenger designed for use as a regional airliner or large corporate jet.

registration certificate A certificate issued by the FAA, registering an aircraft to its owner. It must be carried aboard the aircraft at all times.

registration mark The national identification numbers and letters assigned to all civil aircraft.

registration number Registration mark.

regulations FARs.

REIL Runway end identification lights.

relative bearing Bearing relative to a given fix.

relative humidity The ratio of the amount of water vapor present in the air to the maximum amount it could hold at the prevailing temperature and at the same altitude. It is measured in percent.

relative wind The movement of air relative to the movement of an airfoil. It is parallel to and in the opposite direction of the flight path of the airplane. (Page 371)

release A mechanical means installed in gliders and sailplanes to permit the soaring pilot to release the tow rope that attaches his aircraft to the towing vehicle or mechanism.

release time A departure time slot issued by ATC to a pilot under conditions of congestion, when it becomes necessary in order to separate him from other departing or arriving traffic.

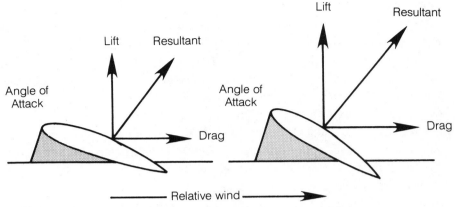

Relative wind.

relief   The contour and topography of the ground, shown on aeronautical charts in terms of variations in color and numbers giving the elevations in feet msl at given points.

relief tube   A rather primitive excuse for a urinal, installed in some aircraft.

remote communication air/ground facility (RCAG)   An unmanned communications receiver/transmitter operating usually on VHF and UHF frequencies and designed to expand the receiving/transmitting range of ARTCCs.

remote mounted   Refers to avionics and other equipment, the major portions of which are mounted somewhere other than behind the instrument panel. *See also* PANEL MOUNTED.

Reno Air Races   Annual air races, usually involving unlimited-class aircraft, T-6s, midget racers, and aerobatic pilots in competition. Normally held some time in September.

repeat   In aviation radio phraseology a phrase preceding a second (or third) transmission of the same message. An alternate phrase is: I say again.

report   Phrase used by ATC to ask pilots to give specific information; such as: Report passing Anton Chico VOR.

reporting point   An exact fix over which a position report is made. For IFR aircraft not in radar contact, some such reporting points are mandatory.

request full route clearance   A phrase used by pilots asking ATC to read the entire route of flight into the flight plan clearance. It should always be used when an already filed flight plan has been subsequently amended for one reason or another by the pilot, in order to avoid any possible misunderstanding or confusion.

rescue coordination center (RCC)   RCCs are operated by the Coast Guard or the Air Force and are designed and equipped to coordinate search and rescue operations.

RESTR Restrict.

restraint systems Seatbelts and shoulder harnesses.

restricted area Airspace above a specific geographical location within which flight of civil aircraft is not prohibited, but is limited at the discretion of the controlling agency. Permission to use such airspace should always be obtained in advance by contacting the controlling agency or the appropriate FSS.

restricted landing area Private airport, not for public use.

resume normal navigation Phrase used by ATC after vectoring an aircraft or when losing radar contact while vectoring an aircraft, to inform the pilot to navigate on his own without further assistance from ATC.

retractable gear Retractable landing gear.

retractable landing gear Landing gear that, after takeoff, can be retracted into wheelwells or other housings in order to reduce drag. On most such aircraft all wheels retract fully. On some only the main gear retracts and on some (the Bellanca Vikings) gears retract only partially.

retreating blade stall The stalling of a helicopter blade when the angle-of-attack of the retreating blade becomes too steep to generate lift. It tends to occur at high forward speeds.

reverse thrust Thrust in the opposite direction as that needed to propel the aircraft. Available primarily only on turbine-powered aircraft and used to reduce the landing roll. Extremely useful on icy runways when normal braking action becomes ineffective.

Reynolds number Named after the English engineer Osborne Reynolds, it is an arbitrary number that relates to the flow of air over an airfoil (laminar or turbulent) and the point at which one turns into the other. The typical Reynolds number for a light aircraft is 3,000,000.

RGD Ragged.

RGN Region.

RGT Right.

RHP Rated horsepower.

rhumbline A line on the surface of the earth that intersects all meridians at equal oblique angles. It is a spiral coiling around the poles but never reaching them.

ribs Stiffeners inside wings and other aircraft components, fastened perpendicular to the surface of the skin.

rich With reference to engine operation, meaning a high percentage of fuel with relation to the amount of air. Rich mixture causes the engine to run cooler, uses an increased amount of fuel per hour, and tends to increase the chance of spark plug fouling.

ridge An elongated area of high atmospheric pressure with the highest pressure along the centerline of the ridge.

ridge soaring Using the lift created by winds blowing at more or less right angles toward a mountain ridge to maintain altitude in a sailplane.

rig To modify or adjust control surfaces or trim tabs on the ground so the airplane will have more stable characteristics in the air. Generally done to reduce or eliminate tendencies for yaw or roll.

right of way When two aircraft are approaching head on, each shall alter its heading to the right. Or when two aircraft are converging at approximately the same altitude, the aircraft approaching from the right of the second aircraft has the right of way. The exceptions to these rules are: airships, gliders, and balloons have the right of way over heavier-than-air powered aircraft; balloons also have the right of way over gliders and, in fact, over all other aircraft including those having declared an emergency. Power driven aircraft towing other aircraft or any other object have the right of way over all manner of power driven aircraft.

right traffic A traffic pattern in which all turns are to the right, often established for certain airports or runways for purposes of noise abatement or to avoid higher terrain or obstacles. The existence of right or left traffic patterns at uncontrolled airports can be determined from the air by overflying and observing the segmented circle.

rigid rotor Helicopter rotors with non-flexing blades, permitting flight at higher than normal forward speeds. Still primarily experimental, though tried by Lockheed in its military Cheyenne helicopter.

rime ice Ice that forms as granular translucent or opaque chunks from the rapid freezing of supercooled water. It is softer and lighter than clear ice and gathers particularly on the leading edges of airfoils, causing deformation and increase in stall speed.

rip panel In balloons, a panel that can rapidly be opened to spill out hot air or gas, usually used at the moment of landing to reduce the chance of the balloon being dragged along by the wind.

rivets The customary means of bonding metal in aircraft construction. Rivets come in a wide variety of sizes and other characteristics. The three basic types are standard rivets with a rounded head, flush rivets that leave no protrusion on the surface of the metal being joined, and pop rivets, used primarily by homebuilders. Pop rivets do not require the use of a rivet gun.

RLA Restricted landing area.

RMI Radio magnetic indicator.

RMN Remain.

RNAV Area navigation.

RNAV approach An instrument approach which requires area navigation instrumentation in the aircraft for navigational guidance.

RNG Range.

RNWY Runway.

Robinson Helicopter Company, Inc. Manufacturer of the two-place R22 Beta piston-powered helicopter. (24747 Crenshaw Blvd., Torrance, CA 90505. (213) 539-0508.)

Robinson Helicopter

	R22 Beta
ENGINE, manufacturer	Lycoming
model	O-320
hp	131
TBO	2,000 hours
WEIGHT, gross, pounds	1,370
empty, pounds	826
ROTOR radius, inches	151
HEIGHT, inches	107
FUEL, standard, gallons	19.2
w. aux tank, gallons	29.7
SPEED, maximum, knots	102.6
economy, knots	96
RANGE, max, no reserve, nm	174+
RATE OF CLIMB at gross weight	1,000 fpm
HOVER IGE	6,970 ft.
OGE	5,200 ft.
STANDARD AVIONICS:	King KY 197 transceiver
EQUIPPED PRICE (1989 $s)	$96,850

Robinson Helicopter Company Incorporated

Robinson helicopter.

Rockwell International Corporation Formerly manufacturer of an extensive line of general aviation aircraft, today manufactures military aircraft exclusively. It is the prime contractor for the B-1B long-range strategic bomber, the AC-130U gunship, and the OV-10D Bravo twin-engine twin-tail turboprop. In different stages of development are the X-31 supersonic fighter aircraft, which is a joint venture with Germany's Messerschmitt-Bolkow-Blohm, leading toward the actual production of two demonstrator aircraft; and the X-30 National AeroSpace Plane (NASP), a hydrogen-powered aircraft that is supposed to be able to use standard runways for takeoff and landing, but will accelerate to 25 times the speed of sound while operating in low earth orbit. First flight of the aircraft is envisioned to take place in the mid or late 1990s with operational vehicles to be ready by the year 2000. (P.O. Box 92098, Los Angeles, CA 90009.)

Rockwell single-engine aircraft. The rights to manufacture the single-engine line were acquired by Commander Aircraft Company.

rods   The sensitive receiving instruments in the human eye, placed around the cones. Rods are color blind, but are able to adapt to very low light conditions and provide us with night vision. Rods cannot see objects straight ahead.

roger   In aviation radio phraseology the term used to imply that the last transmission has been received and understood.

Rogerson Hiller Corporation   Manufacturer of Hiller UH12E and RH-1100 series helicopters. (P.O. Box 1425, 2140 West 18th Street, Port Angeles, WA 98362. (206) 452-6891.) (Page 376)

rogue pilot   A pilot who ignores the regulations. Especially, a pilot who flies IFR without maintaining contact with ATC when operating in controlled airspace.

Roll   Movement of the aircraft around its longitudinal axis. *Also see* BANK.

Roll axis   Longitudinal axis.

Roll out   The completion of a turn and the return to level flight.

Rollout RVR   RVR measured by equipment located near the rollout end of the runway.

Rolls Royce   Manufacturers of a wide variety of turbine engines. These include six turbofans, two turbojets, two turboprops, two turboshafts, and a number of

Rogerson-Hiller agricultural helicopter.

industrial and marine engines. Under development are a 25,000-pound-thrust turbofan destined for the Airbus 320, a 12,000- to 15,000-pound-thrust turbofan for the Fokker 100 and Gulfstream IV and the re-engining program for the BAC 111, and a 2,100 shp turboshaft aimed at the Agusta A129 Mangusta and the European Helicopter Industries EH101, as well as the Sikorsky Black Hawk.

In a joint venture with British Aerospace the company is involved in a project feasibility study, investigating the development of a trans-atmospheric aircraft that would use conventional runways for takeoff and landing. Known as HOTOL (*HO*rizontal *Take*Off and *L*anding), it would be used to launch satellites into orbit.

(Rolls-Royce plc, 65 Buckingham Gate, London SW1E 6AT, England. Phone: 01 222-9020. U.S. offices: Rolls-Royce, Inc. 475 Steamboat Road, Box 2525, Greenwich, CT 06836. (203) 625-8513. 430 Park Avenue, New York, NY 10022. (212) 935-9400.)

romeo   In aviation radio phraseology the term used for the letter R.

RON   Rest over night. Remain over night.

rotary-wing aircraft   Helicopter, gyrocopter; gyroglider.

rotate   The moment prior to actual liftoff when the nosewheel is raised off the ground, but the mainwheels are still in contact with the runway surface.

Rotating beacon   The green and white rotating beacon denoting an airport, always operating after dark and usually when the airport is IFR. Also the red rotating beacon on the aircraft.

rotor   The horizontally rotating air circulation under a mountain wave. Generally an area of severe turbulence.

Rotorway Aircraft, Inc.   Manufacturers of Rotorway Executive helicopter kits including components, engines, training, and plans. (7411 West Galveston, Chandler, AZ 85226. (602) 961-1001.)

round-robin   A cross-country flight in which the aircraft returns to its airport of departure without landing elsewhere in between.

route   A defined path consisting of one or more courses flown in a horizontal plane.

route segment   A definite portion of a route, identified by geographic or navaid fixes.

route structure   Airway structure.

RPD   Rapid.

rpm   Revolutions per minute.

RPT   Repeat.

RR   LF/MF radio range.

RR   Railroad.

RSG   Rising.

RTE   Route.

RTRD   Retard.

RTRN   Return.

rudder   The primary control surface attached to the vertical stabilizer, movement of which causes the tail of the aircraft to swing right or left. It controls yaw; movement around the vertical axis.

rudder pedal   The foot operated pedals that operate the rudder; also used to steer tricycle gear aircraft on the ground. Most rudder pedals include the brake mechanism, which is activated by depressing the toes and thus the top part of the pedals.

RUF   Rough.

run-up   A pretakeoff check of the performance of the engine and, in aircraft with controllable pitch props, the operation of the propeller. The engine is run up to a given rpm and the pilot then switches from one set of magnetos to the other to make sure that each set works satisfactorily independent of the other. To exercise the propeller, he retracts the rpm knob or lever several times.

runway   The portion of an airport designed for takeoffs and landings.

runway condition reading (RCR)   Determining the braking action under prevailing runway surface conditions. *Also see* BRAKING ACTION.

runway gradient   The difference in elevation between two ends or different portions of one and the same runway; measured in percent.

runway in use   Active runway.

runway lights   Lights used to define the side limits of a runway, usually spaced 200 feet apart.

runway markings Centerlines, threshold markings, and other painted signs designed to aid pilots in landing under VFR or IFR conditions.

runway number Each runway has a number rounded off to the nearest 10 degrees. Thus Runway 30 has a 300-degree alignment. Usually these numbers are painted on the approach end of the runway surface, but not always. *See also* PARALLEL RUNWAYS.

runway visibility The horizontal distance at which a stationary observer near the end of the runway can see an ordinary light at night, or a dark object against the horizon or sky in the daytime. It is normally measured by a transmissometer and reported in statute miles or fractions thereof.

runway visual range (RVR) The horizontal distance measured by a transmissometer and reported in hundreds of feet, representing the distance a pilot can see down the runway under low visibility conditions. Different types of instrument approach categories require different RVR minimums. *See* CATEGORY I, II, III APPROACH.

Rutan Aircraft Factory Here Burt Rutan produced the family of canard pusher aircraft kits for homebuilders. The models included the VariViggen, VariEze, Quickie, Defiant, LongEZ, Amsoil Racer, Grizzly, NGT Jet, Voyager, and Solitaire. All of these have been out of production since the start of Burt's work on the Beech Starship. At this writing (spring 1989) he is in the process of developing a new corporate jet. (Building 13, Mojave Airport, Mojave, CA 93501. (805) 824-2645.) (Page 379)

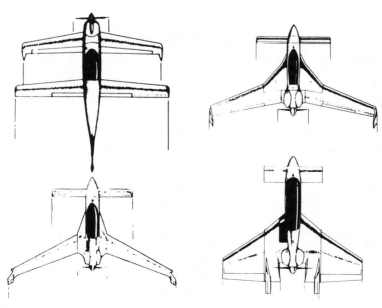

Rutan kit aircraft.

The Voyager designed by Burt Rutan and flown non-stop around the globe by Dick Rutan and Jeana Yeager.

RVR Runway visual range.

RVV Runway visibility value.

RW Rain showers (in sequence reports).

S Sierra (phonetic alphabet).

S Snow (in sequence reports).

S South.

S Special sequence report.

S Straight-in (instrument approach charts).

Saab Scania AB, Saab Aircraft Division Manufacturer of airline aircraft, such as the Saab 340 and the new stretched 50-passenger Saab 2000, powered by either a General Electric GE-38 or a Pratt & Whitney PW 300 turboshaft engine, flat rated at 2,800 shp. Several of these aircraft have been operated as corporate aircraft. (S-581 88 Linköping, Sweden. Phone: + 46 13 18 00 00.)

Sabre A family of corporate jet aircraft (based on the design of the military Sabrejet), once produced by the Sabreliner Division of Rockwell International. It is no longer in production and the company, Sabreliner Corporation, located on Lambert Field in St. Louis, performs FBO functions. It continues to provide support for corporate Sabreliners still in operation.

Sabreliner Corporation Formerly manufacturer of the Sabreliner business jet. Performs aircraft modifications, avionics systems integration, gas turbine maintenance, and overhaul. Component overhaul, repair, and parts manufacturing. It operates an Excalibur program under which Sabreliners with 10,000 flying hours are being rejuvenated into 40EX and 60EX models, adding an additional 5,000 flying hours, or approximately 15 years of operation. (6161 Aviation Drive, St. Louis, MO 63134. (314) 731-2260.)

Sabreliner Corporation

Sabre 40.

SAC   Strategic Air Command.

SAE   Society of Automative Engineers. *See* AVIATION ORGANIZATIONS.

Safe Flight Instrument Corporation   Manufacturer of angle-of-attach indicators, stall warning devices, speed and attitude command systems, performance computers, airborne wind shear warning, and recovery guidance systems, autothrottle and thrust management systems. (P.O. Box 550, White Plains, NY 10602. (914) 946-9500.)

safety factor   The safe limit of load in an airplane.

safety factor   Any design component or procedure that assures a reasonable margin of safety.

safety line   The drop line on a hot-air or gas balloon or a blimp or dirigible.

Saft America, Inc.   Manufacturer of nickel-cadmium batteries for aircraft and space vehicles. (711 Industrial Blvd., Valdosta, GA 31601. (912) 247-2331.)

sailplane   A high-performance glider.

Sailplanes on the ground.

SALS   Short approach light system.

SAP   Soon as possible.

SAR   Search and rescue.

Saratoga, Turbo Saratoga SP   A family of high-performance single-engine piston aircraft manufactured by Piper Aircraft Corporation. (Page 383)

SAS   Stability augmentation system.

saturated air   Air that contains all the water vapor it can at a given pressure and temperature. Equal to 100 percent humidity.

Turbo Saratoga.

SAVASI Simplified abbreviated visual approach slope indicator.

Say again In aviation radio phraseology the term used to mean, please repeat your last transmission.

Say altitude ATC term requesting the pilot to state his current altitude.

Say heading ATC term requesting the pilot to report the actual heading of the aircraft.

scattered clouds Sky cover indicating that clouds cover between 10 and 60 percent of the sky.

Scheibe Aircraft Construction GmbH Manufacturer of high-performance sailplanes and powered sailplanes. (August-Pfaltz Strasse 23, D-8060 Dachau bei München, West Germany. Phone: 08131 72083.)

Alexander Schleicher Glider Construction GmbH Manufacturer of high-performance sailplanes. (P.O. Box 60, D-6416 Poppenhausen/Wasserkuppe, West Germany. U.S. office: P.O. Box 118, Port Matilda, PA 16870. (814) 237-7996.)

Schweizer Aircraft Corporation Manufacturer of sailplanes, motor gliders, special purpose aircraft, agricultural aircraft, and helicopters. In production are the 300C piston helicopter, the 330 turbine helicopter, the Ag-Cat agricultural aircraft, the 2-37A reconnaissance aircraft, and the 2-37 motor glider. (P.O. Box 147, Elmira, NY 14902. (607) 739-3821.) (Pages 384-386)

scope The face of the cathode-ray tube displaying radar returns.

Scott Aviation Manufacturer of oxygen equipment for aviation. (225 Erie Street, Lancaster, NY 14086. (716) 683-5100.)

SCTD Scattered.

SCTR Sector.

Schweizer Fixed-Wing Aircraft

		2-37 motor glider	2-37A reconnaissance	Ag-Cat Super B	Ag-Cat Turbine	Ag-Cat 450B
ENGINE	manufacturer	Lycoming	Lycoming	Pratt&Whitney	Pratt&Whitney	Pratt&Whitney
	model	O-235-L2C	IO-540-W3A5D	R-1340	PT6-11AG	R-985
	power	112 hp	235 hp	600 hp	500 hp	450 hp
	model (optional)	O-320-E26			PT6-15AG	
	power	150 hp			680 hp	
	model (optional)	O-360-A			PT6-34AG	
	power	180 hp			750 hp	
PROPELLER	manufacturer (optional) (optional)	Sensenich McCauley f.p. Hoffman c.s.	McCauley			
	number of blades	2	3	2	2	2
WING	span ft.	59.5	61.5	42.5	42.5	42.5
	area sq.ft.	195.7	199.4	392	392	392
FUSELAGE	length ft.	27.4	27.4	24.5	33.08	24.16
	height	7.79	7.79	11.5	12.08	11.5
WEIGHTS lbs	max gross	1,850	n/a	5,200	5,200	5,200
	empty	1,260	n/a	3,650	3,870	3,395
	max takeoff	1,850	n/a	7,020	7,020	7,020
FUEL CAPACITY	U.S. gallons	14.2	n/a	80	80	64
	(optional)	31				
SPEEDS	V_{ne} knots	116	159			
	V_{stall} knots	42	56			
	$V_{working}$ knots			100	113	100
PERFORMANCE ft.	Takeoff run	500	1,270			
	50-ft.obst.	1,018	2,010	1,050	900	1,300
	Landing „	1,266	2,230			

Schweizer Rotary-Wing Aircraft

		300C	330
ENGINE	manufacturer	Lycoming	Allison
	Type	H10-360-D1A	225-C10A
	rating (derated)	190 hp	200 hp
WEIGHTS lbs	max gross	2,050	2,050
	w. external load	2,150	2,150
	empty	1,100	1,050
	useful load, normal	950	1,000
	w.external load	1,050	
MAIN ROTOR	diameter ft.	26.83	26.83
	number of blades	3	3
TAIL ROTOR	diameter ft.	4.25	4.25
	number of blades	2	2
FUEL CAPACITY	U.S. gallons	30	60
	optional	49	
PERFORMANCE	max cruise knots	89	100
	normal cruise knots	n/a	91
	range nm	224	252
HOVER	IGE ft.	10,800	21,000
	OGE ft.	8,600	17,500

Schweizer 2-37A motorglider.

Schweizer 300C helicopter.

Schweizer 330 turbine helicopter.

scud   Small, low, wind-driven clouds.

SDF   Simplified directional facility.

sea breeze   The movement of air from sea to land during the day. The opposite of the land breeze at night.

sea breeze front   The line of convergence between warm inland air and the moist cool air from the ocean.

Seagil Software Company   Developers of software systems for business aircraft operations including record keeping, performance analysis, scheduling, maintenance, and inventory control. (P.O. Box 720593, Atlanta, GA 30358. (404) 843-8998.)

sea level conditions   Conditions affected by altitude and adjusted to sea level.

seaplane   An aircraft with floats instead of wheels or a boat like hull, operating to and from water.

search and rescue   A service providing all needed functions and aid to locate missing aircraft and assist downed aircraft. It involves cooperation between the FAA, Air Force, Coast Guard, Civil Air Patrol, and various state and local agencies.

seat-of-the-pants   Flying by reference to the kinesthetic sense, which is unreliable and potentially dangerous under instrument conditions when visual reference to the ground or horizon is lost.

SEC   Second.

SEC   Section.

SEC   Sectional.

second   One 60th of a minute of a circle. The symbol for a second is ".

secondary radar   Radar that involves both ground interrogator and airborne transponder signals. It is the type used in ATC radar beacons.

sectional chart   An aeronautical chart of a section of the U.S. at a scale of 1:500,000 or approximately seven nm per inch. A total of 37 sectional charts cover the contiguous 48 states.

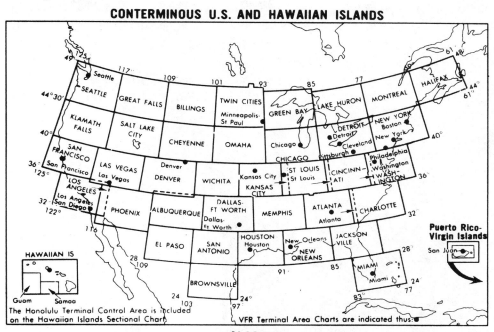

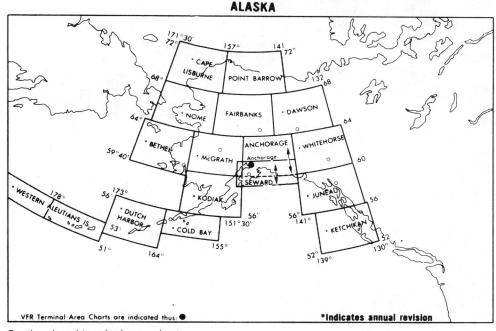

Sectional and terminal area charts.

sector   A portion of the total airspace controlled by a given ARTCC. Each sector has its own discrete frequency for communication between pilot and controller.

sector frequency   The frequency assigned to a sector of an ARTCC.

Securaplane   Manufacturer of aircraft security systems. The System 500 consists of sensors placed in strategic locations on and about the aircraft, a control display unit, rotating beacons and sirens, an antenna, and a portable transceiver. The system informs FBOs and the aircraft crew, when away from the aircraft or airport, when entry to any portion of the aircraft is attempted by unauthorized persons. (3710 East 43rd Place, Suite 101, Tucson, AZ 85713. (602) 571-1502.)

Aircraft security system.

see and avoid   See and be seen.

see and be seen   The concept of avoiding midair collisions by placing the responsibility for maintaining safe separation on the pilot. In VFR conditions, pilots, regardless whether flying VFR or IFR, are responsible for maintaining a visual alertness for other traffic.

segmented circle   A visual indication at uncontrolled airports showing the pattern direction for each runway. Usually associated with a windsock or tetrahedron.

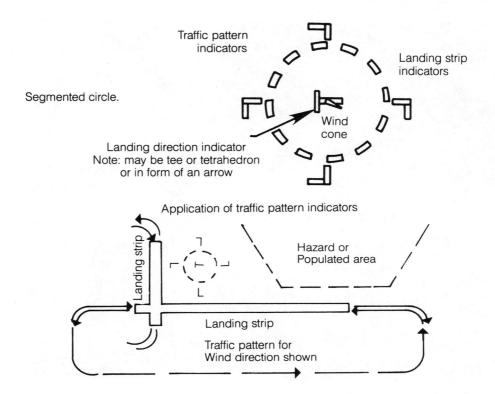

Segmented circle.

Traffic pattern indicators

Landing strip indicators

Wind cone

Landing direction indicator
Note: may be tee or tetrahedron or in form of an arrow

Application of traffic pattern indicators

Landing strip

Hazard or Populated area

Landing strip

Traffic pattern for Wind direction shown

segments of an instrument approach procedure   Instrument approach procedures are divided into the initial approach segment, the intermediate approach segment, the final approach and the missed approach procedure.

SEL   Single-engine land. A pilot rating.

self-launched glider   A hang glider capable of being launched by the pilot using his legs.

self-launched sailplane   Motorglider. A glider or sailplane equipped with an engine of some kind.

Semco Balloon, Inc.   Manufacturers of hot-air balloons. (Rte. 3, Box 514, Aerodrome Way, Griffin, GA 30223.)

Seminole   A four-place twin-engine piston aircraft that has been produced intermittently by Piper Aircraft Corporation. It is powered by a pair of counter-rotating Lycoming 180-hp O-360-A engines and has an IFR range of 910 nm. For performance specifications, *See* PIPER AIRCRAFT CORPORATION. (Page 390)

semi-rigid rotor   A helicopter rotor blade assembly in which flexible blades are rigidly connected to the rotor hub.

Seminole.

Seneca   A six-place twin-engine turbocharged piston aircraft that has evolved
through several stages, the latest being the Seneca III. It cruises at 193 knots and
has an IFR range of 1,140 nm. For performance specifications, *see* PIPER AIR-
CRAFT CORPORATION.

Seneca III.

Sensor Systems Manufacturer of a full line of aircraft antenna systems for VHF, UHF, TV, AM/FM, UHF L-Band, MLS, GPS, C/S band, C-band, X-band, conical spiral, glide slope, marker beacon, VOR/LOC, localizer, altimeter, ADF, duplexer, and power divider equipment. (8929 Fullbright Avenue, Chatsworth, CA 91311. (818) 341-5366.)

separation Spacing of aircraft to achieve safe and orderly movement.

separation minimums The minimum distances in the longitudinal, lateral and vertical dimensions by which aircraft are spaced when operating under ATC control in IFR conditions.

sequence report An hourly report of observed, measured, or estimated weather conditions transmitted over the national teletype system with coded information in a specific sequence and with all reporting stations in a given sequence. Portions of it are broadcast by FSSs at 15 minutes past the hour. When drastic changes in weather conditions occur, special reports are issued as needed (labeled S).

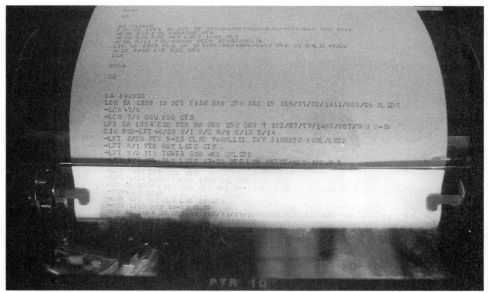

Sequence report coming off the teletype machine in an FSS. (Archaic, now via computer.)

service ceiling The highest altitude at which a given aircraft can continue to climb at 100 fpm.

SES Single-engine sea. A pilot rating.

servo mechanism A mechanism that operates automatically when activated by some other mechanism or electronic signal.

servo motor The small electric motors that operate the control surfaces of an aircraft when they are activated by the autopilot.

severe weather avoidance plan (SWAP)   An ATC procedure in the New York area, designed to move traffic with minimum delays and detours when large portions of the airspace are unusable due to thunderstorms or other severe weather.

sextant   An instrument for measuring angular distances used in navigation to ascertain latitude and longitude by reference to celestial bodies.

SFA   Single frequency approach.

SFC   Surface.

SFENA Corporation   (Societé Francaise d'Equipements pour la Navigation Aerienne) Manufacturers of light control and management systems, digital automatic flight controls, laser gyro inertial guidance systems. (Aerodrome de Villacoublay, F-78141 Velizy-Villacoublay Cedex, France. Phone: 1 463-02385. U.S. address: 2617 Aviation Parkway, Grand Prairie, TX 75051. (214) 988-8000.)

SFIM (Societé de Fabrication d'Instruments de Mesure)   Manufacturers of navigation instrumentation, stabilization and flight control systems. (13 Av. Marcel Ramolfo-Garnier, Massy, Essonne, France. Mail address: SFIM, F 91344 Massy Cedex, France. Telephone: 33 (1) 69 20 88 90.)

shaft horsepower   The amount of horsepower delivered by the engine to the propeller or rotor shaft.

Shark   A piston helicopter manufactured by Enstrom Helicopter Corporation.

shear   Wind shear.

shear line   The line between air masses moving in different directions or at different speeds.

SHF   Super high frequency.

SHFT   Shift.

SHLW   Shallow.

shock strut   Oleo strut.

shoran   Stands for short-range navigation. An electronic position-fixing system in which an airborne pulse transmitter triggers responses from two transponders of known location, providing a means of triangulation.

Short Brothers PLC   Manufacturer of the 330 and 360 commuter aircraft and various utility transport aircraft. (Headquarters: Box 241, Airport Road, BT3 9DZ Belfast, Northern Ireland. U.S. office: Short Brothers (USA), Inc. 2011 Crystal Drive #713, Arlington, VA 22202. (703) 769-8700.) (Pages 393 and 394)

short-field landing   A landing designed to result in the shortest possible landing roll. It is usually made with full flaps and considerable power, holding the nose higher than usual and arriving over the threshold barely above stall.

short-field takeoff   A takeoff designed to get the aircraft airborne in the shortest possible distance. Normal technique calls for running the engine at full power while holding the aircraft in place with hard braking. Then let go of the brakes and feed in partial flaps, using whatever backpressure is needed to achieve liftoff

Short Brothers' Aircraft

		SHORTS 360-300	SHORTS SHERPA	SHORTS TUCANO
ENGINE	manufacturer	Pratt & Whitney (2)	Pratt & Whitney (2)	Garrett (1)
	model	PT6A-67R	PT6-65AR	TPE331-12B
	rating shp	1,424	1,424	1,100
PROPELLER	manufacturer	Hartzell	Hartzell	n/a
	blades	6	5	n/a
	diameter	n/a	9.25 ft	n/a
WEIGHTS lbs	ramp	27,200	25,100	5,997
	takeoff	27,100	25,000	5,952
	landing	26,500	24,500	5,952
	basic operating	17,350	n/a	n/a
	payload	8,300	7,500	n/a
FUEL lbs	max	3,840	4,480	1,224
DIMENSIONS	length	70'10"	58.04 ft	32.35 ft
	height	23'10"	16.41 ft	11.15 ft
	span	74'10"	74.84 ft	37 ft
CABIN	volume ft^3	1,450	1,426.1	n/a
SPEED kts	cruise	216	n/a	215
RATE OF CLIMB	fpm	952	n/a	3,500
TAKEOFF	50 ft. obst. ft	4,280	2,349	1,720
LANDING	50 ft. obst. ft	4,000	1,811	1,880
RANGE	nm	636	n/a	940

Short Brothers (USA) Incorporated

Shorts Tucano single-turboprop training aircraft.

at minimum flying speed. The aircraft, especially low-wing aircraft, might lift off at a speed slightly below normal stalling speed because of ground effect. Assuming no obstacle is in the way, the pilot should hold the aircraft in ground effect until sufficient speed has been gained to permit climbout.

Shorts 360-300 wide-body 36-seat twin-turboprop aircraft.

Shorts Skyvan STOL twin-turboprop aircraft.

short range clearance   A clearance issued to an IFR flight that temporarily terminates at a fix short of the destination while ATC coordinates traffic and obtains
the complete clearance.

short takeoff and landing aircraft (STOL)   Aircraft equipped with special high-lift
devices that permit reduction in takeoff and landing roll.

shower   Precipitation of short duration and limited in area with less wind gustiness
than would be associated with a squall.

shp   Shaft horsepower.

Shrike Commander   One of the Commander family of piston twins, manufactured
by the General Aviation Division of Rockwell International. The aircraft is no
longer in production.

SHWR   Shower.

SID   Standard instrument departure.

side load   The lateral loads exerted on the aircraft and especially the landing gear when the aircraft touches down in a slightly sideways direction, usually the result of crosswind.

sideslip   Yaw.

sidestep maneuver   A visual maneuver executed by a pilot at the end of a straight-in instrument approach, permitting him to land on a parallel runway. The distance between the two runways may not exceed 1,200 feet.

Sierra   In aviation radio phraseology the term used for the letter S.

Sierra   A light single-engine retractable-gear aircraft once manufactured by Beech Aircraft Corporation. No longer in production.

SIFR   Special IFR. Also S/IFR.

SIGMET   Stands for significant meteorology. An in-flight weather advisory covering weather phenomena of importance to all aircraft, such as lines of thunderstorms, tornadoes, large hail, severe turbulence, heavy icing, and widespread dust or sand storms that reduce visibility to less than two miles.

signals   A variety of standard visual signals have been established, some used by line personnel in directing aircraft on the ground, others by the crews of downed aircraft to give information to overflying search aircraft. *(See ILLUSTRATION UNDER* EMERGENCY *AND UNDER* HAND SIGNALS.)

Sigtronics Corporation   Manufacturer of intercom systems, headsets, digital EGTs, and volt meters. (822 North Dodsworth Avenue, Covina, CA 91724. (818) 915-1993.)

Sikorsky Aircraft Division of United Technologies Corp.   Manufacturer of the S-76 family of corporate turbine helicopters and military helicopters. (North Main Street, Hartford, CT 06601. (203) 386-4000.) (Page 396)

Sikorsky Aircraft

Sikorsky S-76B.

Sikorsky S-76A + .

Sikorsky Helicopters

		S-76A	S-76A+	S-76B
ENGINE	manufacturer	Allison	Turbomeca Ariel	Pratt & Whitney Canada
	type	250-C30	1S turboshaft	PT6B-36
	rating $2^1/_2$ min. OEI	700 shp	720 shp	
	30 minutes OEI	630 shp		1,033 shp
	takeoff	650 shp	701 shp	981 shp
	continuous	650 shp	701 shp	676
DIMENSIONS				
FUSELAGE	length	43'4.4"	43'4.4"	44'0.8"
	width	7'	7'	7'
	length incl. rotors	52'6"	52'6"	52'6"
MAIN ROTOR	diameter	44'	44'	44'
	number of blades	4	4	4
TAIL ROTOR	diameter	8'	8'	8'
	number of blades	4	4	4
CABIN	length	8'1"	8'1"	8'1"
	width	6'4"	6'4"	6'4"
	height	4'5"	4'5"	4'5"
	area sq.ft.	45	45	45
	volume cu.ft.	204	204	204
PASSENGERS	capacity	12-13	12-13	12-13
CREW	required	1-2	1-2	1-2
PERFORMANCE	max speed, kts.	155	155	155
	cruise speed kts.	145	145	145
	rate of climb fpm	1,650	1,650	1,650
	hover OGE ft.	1,200	1,850	3,750
	service ceiling 2 eng.	14,167	14,167	15,000 *
	service ceiling 1 eng.	4,300	4,500	6,500
	range @ 135 kts no res	472nm	465nm	358nm
	fuel flow @ 135 kts	534pph	542pph	n/a
PRICE	1988 $s	$2,550,000	$2,900,000	$3,240,000

* Maximum operating altitude

Silver Instruments, Inc. Manufacturer of electronic fuel-management systems. (16100 S.W. 72nd Avenue, Portland, OR 97224. (503) 896-8799.)

simplified directional facility (SDF) A nonprecision-approach navaid similar to a localizer, except that it might be offset up to three degrees from the runway. It is often wider than a localizer and therefore less accurate.

SimuFlite Training International Division A division of The Singer Company, it is an advanced flight training operation using a number of sophisticated motion simulators with computer-generated visuals. The aircraft for which the company operates simulators are: Astra, BAe 800, Challenger, Citation I/II, S/II, III, Falcon 10/100, 20, 50, 200, 900, Gulfstream II/IIB, III, IV, HS 125-1A through 700 series, King Air series, Learjet 24/25, 35/36, 55 Sabreliner, Westwind I/II with the major training subjects including advanced airmanship, flight deck management, international procedures. The simulators are provided by Link-Miles and are equipped with IMAGE III™ full color daylight visual systems. The company also operates a commercial flight training center in Totowa, New Jersey, training Boeing 727, 737, and 747 pilots. At Continental Airlines in Houston, Texas, the company operates a Phase III MD-82 simulator and in Marietta, Georgia, it operates a L-100 Hercules simulator. In addition, the company has a contract with the U.S. Air Force for a variety of training activities. (P.O. Box 619119, D/FW Airport, TX 75261. (214) 456-8000 and (800) 527-2463.) (Page 398)

SimuFlite Training International

Gulfstream G-III simulator with visual system.

Learjet 35/36 simulator on three-axis motion base.

simulated flameout (SFO) A practice approach for jet aircraft executed at idle thrust all the way to the runway. Primarily a military training maneuver.

simulator Any device that simulates actual conditions, used for training purposes. Normally used with reference to simulated aircraft in which a pilot can execute virtually any maneuver that could be flown in a real airplane. Such flight simulators range from simple desktop models, costing from $1,000 on up, to highly sophisticated machines with built-in motion and simulated pictorial displays representing the airport, runway, or other scenes under all imaginable weather conditions. Prices run up into many millions.

single direction route Preferred IFR routes that are normally used only in one direction.

single-engine aircraft An aircraft propelled by a single powerplant. It can be a piston-engine, a turboprop, or a jet.

single frequency approach (SFA) An approach available primarily to single-piloted military jets, in which the pilot can stay on one frequency throughout the approach.

single-piloted aircraft An aircraft with only one set of controls. Usually military.

sink Rate of descent. Used primarily in ballooning.

sink With reference to soaring, descending air in which the glider or sailplane loses more altitude than it would in still air.

SIR Snow and ice on runway.

SKED Schedule(d).

skid Lateral movement of an airplane toward the outside of a turn, caused by incorrect use of the rudder.

skin The outer covering of the airframe. It can be aluminum, fabric, wood, or fiberglass.

skin friction Parasite drag resulting from the contact of the air with the skin (and its imperfections) of the airplane.

skiplane Airplane equipped with skis for operation to and from snow or ice.

Skipper A light single-engine fixed-gear training aircraft once manufactured by Beech Aircraft Corporation. No longer in production.

Beechcraft Skipper.

sky cover The amount of sky obscured by clouds or other phenomena. Generally described as clear, scattered, broken, overcast, obscured.

Skyhawk A single-engine four-seat high-wing piston-powered aircraft that was manufactured by Cessna Aircraft Company. It was the most popular personal aircraft ever manufactured. No longer in production. (Page 400)

Skyhawk.

Skylane   A single-engine four-seat high-wing piston-powered aircraft that was manufactured by Cessna Aircraft Company. It was one of the most popular personal aircraft ever manufactured. No longer in production.

Skylane.

Sky Ox, Ltd.   Manufacturer of portable oxygen systems with adjustable flow regulators and up to 46 man-hours capacity. (P.O. Box 500, St. Joseph, MI 49085. (616) 925-8931.)

Sky-Ox Oxygen Systems

MODEL NUMBER	OXYMIZER DURATION MAN HOURS @15,000 ft.	CYLINDER CAPACITY - TYPE	DURATION WITH MASK OR CANNULA MAN HOURS @12,000 ft.	MAN HOURS @15,000 ft.	MAN HOURS @20,000 ft.	SIZE D x L	WEIGHT lbs.	PRICE 1989 $s
SK 12-15 ADJ	13:48 hrs	15 cu.ft. Aluminum	5:32 hrs	4:36 hrs	3:27 hrs	5x22"	11	723.48 *
SK 11-20	17:33 hrs	20 cu.ft. Steel	7:00 hrs	5:51 hrs	4:23 hrs	5x17"	15	615.12 *
SK 12-24 ADJ	22:42 hrs	24 cu.ft. Aluminum	9:05 hrs	7:34 hrs	5:41 hrs	5x31"	14	800.48
SK 11-40	39:27 hrs	40 cu.ft. Steel	15:47 hrs	13:09 hrs	9:52 hrs	6x22"	28	691.12
SK 11-50	46:21 hrs	50 cu.ft. Steel	18:32 hrs	15:27 hrs	11:35 hrs	8x27"	36	776.92

* with padded carrying bag

The Oxymizer is designed to give controlled flow to the nostrils instead of constant flow, typical of other types.

Skymaster A push-pull twin-engine aircraft once manufactured by Cessna Aircraft Company. No longer in production.

Skyrocket A high-performance single-engine aircraft that was developed by Bellanca Aircraft Engineering (not Bellanca Aircraft Corporation), but was never put into production.

Bellanca Skyrocket. Not in production.

Skytrader Corporation Manufacturers of the Skytrader Scout, a utility STOL turboprop high-wing aircraft, powered by two Turbomeca Astazou XIV engines. Originally the aircraft was powered by two Lycoming IO-720 piston engines. (Richards-Gebaur Airport, 15900 Kensington, Kansas City, MO 64147. (8-16) 322-2811.)

Skywagon A fixed-gear single-engine six-to-eight place aircraft that was once manufactured by Cessna Aircraft Company. No longer in production.

slant range The distance from an aircraft in flight to an object on the ground. For instance, the slant range of an aircraft would be nearly seven miles when positioned five miles horizontally from a VORTAC and 10,000 feet above the elevation of that VORTAC. When used with reference to visibility, the slant range visibility frequently differs markedly from ground visibility. The algorithm to figure slant range:

A = Altitude in feet of aircraft above ground station

B = Horizontal distance in nautical miles from ground station

C = B multiplied by 6,076

S = Slant range in nautical miles

(continued)

The formula:

S = A² + C²

Slant range = Square root of S divided by 6.076

slash   A radar beacon reply represented on the scope by an elongated target.

SLD   Solid.

SLGT   Slight.

sling load   A load carried by a helicopter underneath the aircraft.

Slip   The tendency of an aircraft to lose altitude toward the center of a turn when not enough rudder or deliberate cross-control rudder is used for the degree of bank.

Slipstream   Propwash.

SLMM   Simultaneous compass locator at the middle marker.

SLO   Slow.

SLOM   Simultaneous compass locator at the outer marker.

Slow flight   Level flight just above stalling speed.

Slow roll   An aerobatic maneuver in which the aircraft, starting in level flight, rotates smoothly 360 degrees around its longitudinal axis and returns to level flight.

SLP   Slope.

SLR   Slush on runway.

SLS   Side lobe suppression.

SLT   Sleet.

sm   Statute mile.

Small aircraft   Light aircraft.

Smith (Ted) Aerostar Corporation   Developer and manufacturer of the Aerostar family of high-performance piston twins. The company is no longer. Piper produced the airplane for a short time.

Smiths Industries, Inc., Civil Systems Division   Manufacturer of air data and flight performance instrumentation. (255 Great Valley Parkway, Malvern, PA 19355. (215) 296-5000.)

SMK   Smoke.

SML   Small.

Smoke   Carbon particles suspended in the air resulting from fire. It tends to restrict flight as well as slant range visibility. The sequence report symbol is K.

SMTH   Smooth.

SMWHT   Somewhat.

SN   Snow grains (in sequence reports).

Snap roll   An aerobatic maneuver that is started at a speed approximately 30 knots above stalling speed. To induce a snap roll, bring the stick full back and simultaneously use aileron and full rudder in the desired direction of the roll. The nose comes up sharply and the roll takes place with great suddeness.

snow Precipitation in the form of ice crystals. In sequence reports the symbol is S.

SNRS Sunrise.

SNST Sunset.

SNW Snow.

soaring Flying a glider or sailplane.

Soaring Society of America (SSA) *See* AVIATION ORGANIZATIONS.

SOB Souls on board.

Society of Automotive Engineers (SAE) *See* AVIATION ORGANIZATIONS.

socked in Expression used when grounded by weather, especially fog.

solar still A primitive means of producing small amounts of drinkable water by using the heat from the sun. Dig a funnel-shaped hole in the ground, place a receptacle at its bottom, then cover the sides with plastic (if no plastic is available, most airplane seats are covered with non-porous material, which can be used for the purpose). The heat of the sun will cause moisture to be drawn from even the driest ground. It will collect on the underside of the plastic covering and drip into the receptacle.

Solitaire One of the MU-2 family of twin turboprop corporate aircraft, manufactured by Mitsubishi Aircraft International and Mitsubishi Heavy Industries in Japan. No longer being manufactured.

solo A flight during which the pilot is the only person in the aircraft. To solo usually refers to the first time the instructor leaves the aircraft and permits the student to take it up alone.

Soloy Conversions, Ltd. A company that specializes in converting piston powered fixed- and rotary-wing aircraft to turbine powered aircraft, using Allison turboshaft engines. (1769 Bishop Road, P.O. Box 60, Chehalis, WA 98532. (206) 748-0067.) (Pages 403-405)

sonic boom Two loud bangs occurring in quick succession, produced by the leading and trailing edges of the wings of aircraft flying at supersonic speeds. Severity depends on atmospheric conditions.

SOP Standard operating procedure.

sound barrier A severe shock wave created by the airfoil as the aircraft passes from Mach.95 to Mach 1.05. It produces fluctuations in the airspeed indicator for a few seconds and simultaneously rapid changes in the altimeter reading as the shock wave passes the static vents. As the speed increases, everything returns more or less to normal.

sound, speed of Mach 1. Approximately 600 mph under standard atmospheric conditions at sea level. *See* MACH.

soup Slang for clouds or fog surrounding the aircraft in flight. Flying in the soup.

Soloy Fixed-Wing Conversions

		BONANZA PROP-JET	CESSNA 206 TURBO-PROP	CESSNA 207 TURBO-PROP
ENGINE	manufacturer	Allison	Allison	Allison
	model	250-B17C	250-C20S	250-C20S
	rating hp	420	420	420
PROPELLER	manufacturer	Hartzell	Hartzell	Hartzell
	type	full feather	full feather	full feather
	diameter in.	90	95	95
WEIGHTS lbs	max ramp	3849	3600	4000
	takeoff	3833	3600	4000
	landing	3650	3600	4000
	empty, wheels	2400	1908	2175
	" seaplane	n/a	2248	2545
	" amphibious	n/a	2538	2860
SEATS	standard	6	6	8
FUEL gal	usable	112	88	73
	w.aux tanks	n/a	140	125
SPEEDS kts	max	210	n/a	n/a
	cruise,wheels	208	163	160
	floats	n/a	150	140
STALL	clean	65		
	dirty	57	52	58
RATE OF CLIMB fpm,	wheels	1900	1950	1640
	floats	n/a	1800	1570
SERVICE CEILING ft		25,000	20,000	25,000
TAKEOFF	ground roll	580	570	736
	50 ft.obst.	800	1063	1370
LANDING	ground run	325	553	714
	50 ft.obst.	525	1094	1412

Floats for the Cessna 206: Edo Seaplane, Edo Amphibious
PK Seaplane, PK Amphibious
Wipline Seaplane, Wipline Amphibious
Floats for the Cessna 207: PK Seaplane, PK Amphibious

Soloy Rotary-Wing Conversions

		BELL 47 600 Series Transmission	BELL 47 900 Series Transmission	HILLER UH-12D/E 3 Place	HILLER UH-12D/E 3 Place*	HILLER UH-12E 4 Place	HILLER UH-12E 4 Place*
ENGINE	mfr.	Allison	Allison	Allison	Allison	Allison	Allison
	model	250-C20B	250-C20B	250-C20B	250-C20B	250-C20B	250-C20B
RATING	shp	420	420	420	420	420	420
	derated shp	261	270	301	301	301	301
WEIGHTS lb	empty	1650	1650	1640	1640	1640	1640
	max gross	2950	3200	3100	3100	3100	3100
	useful load	1300	1550	1460	1460	1460	1460
SERVICE CEILING ft		16,000	16,000	12,000	14,000	12,000	14,000
HOVER**	IGE	16,000	16,000	8500	8600	8500	8600
	OGE	13,800	13,800	3500	5600	3500	5600
RATE OF CLIMB max fpm		1250	1250	1518	1518	1518	1518
	vertical	970	970	967	967	967	967
SPEEDS	V_{ne} kts	91	91	83.5	83.5	83.5	83.5
	cruise kts	87	87	78.3	78.3	78.3	78.3
FUEL	standrd gal	57	57	46	46	46	46
	w.aux gal	96	96	85	85	85	85
RANGE nm	stand.fuel	186	186	149.5	149.5	149.5	149.5
	w.aux fuel	313	313	277.4	277.4	277.4	277.4

* with 53200-03 M/R Blades
** HIGE and HOGE for the Bell 47s @ 2950 lbs
HIGE and HOGE for the Hiller UHs @ 3100 lbs

Soloy conversion: turbine-powered Cessna 206.

SP   Snow pellets (in sequence reports).

span   The distance from wing tip to wing tip.

spar   The principal load-carrying beam running lengthwise in an airfoil. In many aircraft the main spar also runs through the fuselage.

sparker   An instrument carried aboard hot-air balloons for the purpose of igniting the pilot light on the burner.

spark plug   Inserted into the combustion chamber, the spark plug uses electric current from a magneto to create an electric spark that ignites the fuel-and-air mixture. All piston engines certificated for use in aircraft have two spark plugs for each cylinder.

spark plug fouling   Deterioration of the ability of the spark plug to function properly, due to carbon deposits or burned tips, usually caused by operating with too rich or too lean a mixture.

spats   Pants.

Speak slower   A pilot request to the controller to speak more slowly.

special IFR   Aircraft that operate under a waiver or letter of agreement in control zones or terminal control areas. The pilots must be IFR rated and the aircraft IFR equipped.

special use area   An area either on the surface or in the air or both, used for special (usually military) operations, such as jet training and missile firings. Flight through such areas may be prohibited or restricted, or pilots may be warned to be extra cautious.

special VFR (SVFR or S/VFR)   A rule that permits pilots to take off or land at controlled airports or fly through a control zone when conditions are below VFR minimums.

special VFR conditions   Except at certain high density airports where special VFR operations are not permitted, pilots may request special VFR clearances for takeoff, landing, or flight through the control zone if the visibility is at least one mile. There are no ceiling restrictions. The pilot must be in communication with the tower, follow the details of the clearance issued by the tower, but it is his responsibility to remain clear of clouds. Special VFR is never offered by ATC. It must be requested by the pilot and approved by ATC.

special VFR operations   *See* SPECIAL VFR CONDITIONS.

speed adjustment   An ATC request to ask pilots to change the speed of their aircraft to a given higher or lower figure. It may be expressed as *increase speed to* (speed), or *reduce speed to* (speed), or *if feasible reduce (increase) speed to* (speed).

speed brakes   Dive brakes.

speed of sound   *See* MACH.

Sperry Flight Systems   The company was merged with Honeywell to form a new company. *See* HONEYWELL SPERRY COMMERCIAL FLIGHT SYSTEMS GROUP.

spin   An intentional or unintentional maneuver in which the airplane, after stalling, descends nearly vertically, nose low, with the tail revolving around the near vertical axis of descent. Most modern light aircraft are placarded against intentional spins.

spin recovery   Push the stick forward and apply rudder in the direction opposite to that of the spin. *See* STALL-SPIN ACCIDENT.

spiral   A climb or descent in a constant turn of 360 degrees or more.

split S   The maneuver following a half roll. It returns the aircraft from the inverted back to the normal attitude. Not to be attempted except at a safe altitude.

spoilers   Flat vertical surfaces which can be raised out of the upper surface of the wing at the pilot's discretion. They spoil the airflow over the wing and cause it to lose lift and therefore drop. Spoilers might be constructed to be deployed simultaneously in both wings, or individually in one wing or the other. All gliders and sailplanes are equipped with simultaneously deploying spoilers to facilitate an increase in the rate of descent without an increase in speed, necessary in order to assure landing at the desired spot. Among powered aircraft, the MU-2 family of corporate turboprops uses individually deployable spoilers in the place of ailerons.

Sport   A two-place single-engine fixed-gear training aircraft once manufactured by Beech Aircraft Corporation. No longer in production.

spot landing   Accuracy landing.

SPRD   Spread.

SQAL   Squall.

SQLN   Squall line.

squall   A strong local wind that starts and stops suddenly and lasts only a short time.

squall   A severe local storm with attendant gustiness and intense precipitation.

squall line   A line or band of active connected thunderstorms, not associated with a front.

squawk Expression used to mean activating the transponder.

squawk ident Activate the transponder and push the ident button. An ATC phrase.

squelch A means of adjusting a radio receiver to eliminate background noise and static from the selected frequency. Most of the more advanced modern com radios have an automatic squelch feature.

SR Sunrise.

SS Sunset.

SSA Soaring Society of America.

SSALR Simplified short approach light system with RAIL.

SSB Single side band.

SST Supersonic transport.

stabilator A horizontal tail surface that moves up or down in its entirety to control pitch movement of the aircraft. It is, in fact, a stabilizer-elevator combination.

stability The ability of an aircraft to remain at a constant heading, altitude, or other condition without being affected by outside forces. A stable aircraft will return to its original attitude after brief disturbance without control input by the pilot. No known aircraft will maintain straight and level flight indefinitely without assistance from the pilot or autopilot. Thus, 100 percent stability has not yet been achieved.

stability augmentation system An automatic autopilot flight control system in helicopters: mandatory for IFR flight.

stabilizer The fixed horizontal or vertical tail surface that gives an aircraft stability.

stable air Air that tends to remain at a fixed altitude. It tends to hold pollution and other obstructions to visibility in place.

Stage I, II, III service *See* TERMINAL RADAR.

stall The inability of an airplane to continue flight due to an excessive angle-of-attack. It will either drop its nose and thus reduce the angle-of-attack and regain flying speed, or, if forced to retain the excessive angle-of-attack and control surfaces are moved, either intentionally or unintentionally, might fall into a spin.

stalling angle-of-attack Burble point.

stalling speed The speed at a given angle-of-attack at which airflow separation begins and a stall occurs. Aircraft can stall at virtually any speed if an acceptable angle-of-attack is exceeded. In normal use the term means the slowest speed at which the aircraft can barely maintain straight and level flight. It varies with different types or aircraft and with flap and gear position.

stall-spin accident A common form of usually fatal accident in which the aircraft is stalled close to the ground and in an effort to avoid hitting the ground the pilot increases backpressure on the yoke and uses ailerons or rudder, causing the aircraft to spin at an altitude from which recovery is not possible.

stall warning A device, usually involving a buzzer, a light or both, that indicates to the pilot that the aircraft is about to stall. It is also the noticeable change in the feel of the controls, indicating that a stall is imminent.

standard atmospheric conditions *See* STANDARD CONDITIONS.

standard broadcast station Any radio station. ADF-equipped aircraft can use standard broadcast stations for VFR navigational guidance. Many such stations are shown on aeronautical charts.

standard class With reference to sailplanes, in U.S. competition soaring, a class of sailplane, the wing span of which may not exceed 15 meters (49 feet 2 inches).

standard conditions (ISA) The abbreviation stands for ICAO Standard Atmosphere. An atmospheric pressure related to the temperature that serves as a basis for comparing actual conditions: A pressure of 29.92 in Hg at sea level with a temperature of 59 degrees F. and a lapse rate of about 5.5 degrees F. per 1,000 feet of altitude.

standard instrument approach procedure *See* INSTRUMENT APPROACH PROCEDURES.

standard instrument departure (SID) A preplanned IFR departure procedure devised by ATC and printed for use by pilots. Use of SIDs reduces the length of IFR clearances and the workload for controllers. In order to accept a clearance involving a SID, the pilot must have the printed instruction with him in the cockpit. (Page 409)

standard rate turn A turn of three degrees per second requiring two minutes for a 360-degree turn.

standard terminal arrival route (STAR) A preplanned IFR arrival procedure devised by ATC and printed for use by pilots. Use of STARs reduces controller workload. In order to accept a clearance involving a STAR, the pilot must have the printed instruction with him in the cockpit.

Stand by In aviation-radio phraseology a request to wait on that frequency for further transmissions.

Stand by one Same as stand by, suggesting that the wait will be short ("one" could mean second or minute or moment).

STAR Standard terminal arrival route. (Page 410)

Starship 1 A twin-turboprop all-composite pusher aircraft designed by Burt Rutan and manufactured by Beech Aircraft Corporation. First customer deliveries were in 1989. (Page 411)

starter Ignition switch and the starter motor that must turn the engine in order to start combustion and ignition.

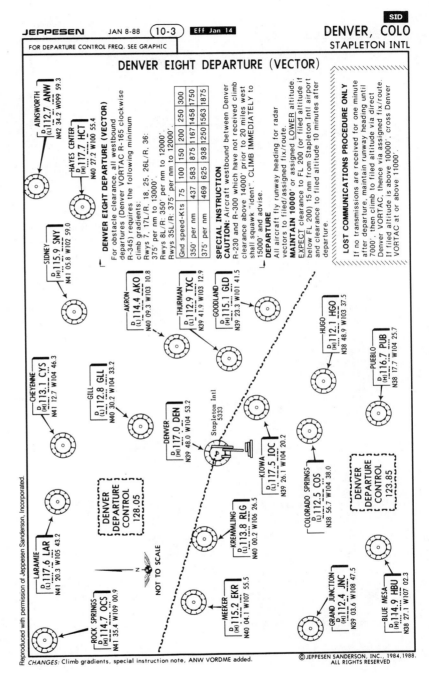

SID chart.

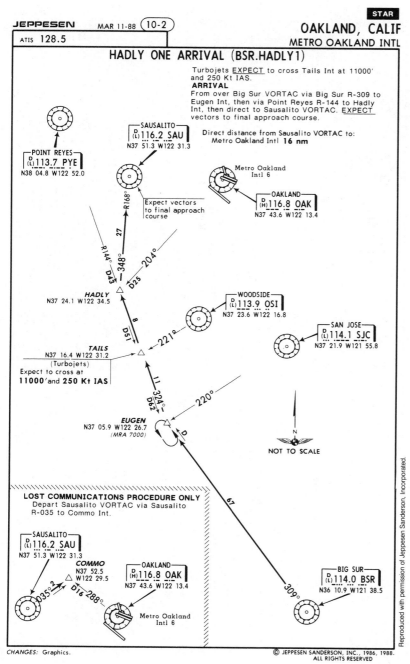

HADLY ONE ARRIVAL (BSR.HADLY1)

Turbojets <u>EXPECT</u> to cross Tails Int at 11000'
and 250 Kt IAS.
ARRIVAL
From over Big Sur VORTAC via Big Sur R-309 to
Eugen Int, then via Point Reyes R-144 to Hadly
Int, then direct to Sausalito VORTAC. <u>EXPECT</u>
vectors to final approach course.

Direct distance from Sausalito VORTAC to:
Metro Oakland Intl **16 nm**

POINT REYES
D
(L) 113.7 PYE
N38 04.8 W122 52.0

SAUSALITO
D
(L) 116.2 SAU
N37 51.3 W122 31.3

Metro Oakland
Intl 6

OAKLAND
D
(H) 116.8 OAK
N37 43.6 W122 13.4

Expect vectors
to final approach
course

R168°

R144°
D43

27

348°

204°

D25

HADLY
N37 24.1 W122 34.5

WOODSIDE
D
(L) 113.9 OSI
N37 23.6 W122 16.8

D51

8

221°

SAN JOSE
D
(L) 114.1 SJC
N37 21.9 W121 55.8

TAILS
N37 16.4 W122 31.2
(Turbojets)
Expect to cross at
11000' and **250 Kt IAS**

11
D62
324°

220°

EUGEN
N37 05.9 W122 26.7
(MRA 7000)

D

N
NOT TO SCALE

67

309°

BIG SUR
D
(L) 114.0 BSR
N36 10.9 W121 38.5

LOST COMMUNICATIONS PROCEDURE ONLY
Depart Sausalito VORTAC via Sausalito
R-035 to Commo Int.

SAUSALITO
D
(L) 116.2 SAU
N37 51.3 W122 31.3

COMMO
N37 52.5
W122 29.5

035°

D16 288°

OAKLAND
D
(H) 116.8 OAK
N37 43.6 W122 13.4

Metro Oakland
Intl 6

CHANGES: Graphics.

STAR chart.

Starship 1.

state aviation departments The departments or agencies of various states, dealing with aviation related matters. They may in no case countermand FAA or ATC regulations.

Alabama Department of Aeronautics
 11 South Union Street, Montgomery, AL 36104
Arizona Department of Aeronautics
 3000 Sky Harbor Blvd., Phoenix, AZ 85034
Arkansas Division of Aeronautics
 1515 Building, Little Rock, AR 72202
California Department of Aeronautics
 Executive Airport, Sacramento, CA 95822
Connecticut Department of Transportation
 24 Wolcott Hill Road, Wethersfield, CT 06109
Delaware Aeronautics Section
 P.O. Box 778, Dover, DE 19901
Florida Department of Transportation
 Tallahassee, FL

Georgia Department of Transportation
  2 Capital Square, Atlanta, GA 30334
Idaho Department of Aeronautics
  3103 Airport Way, Boise, ID 83705
Illinois Department of Aeronautics
  Capital Airport, Springfield, IL 62705
Indiana Aeronautics Commission
  100 North Senate Avenue, Indianapolis, IN 46204
Iowa Aeronautics Commission
  State House, Des Moines, IA 50319
Kansas Department of Economic Development, Aviation Division
  State Office Building, Topeka, KS 66612
Kentucky Department of Aeronautics
  Plaza Tower, Frankfort, KY 40601
Louisiana Dept. of Public Work, Aviation Division
  P.O. Box 44155, Capital Station, Baton Rouge, LA 70804
Maine Department of Aeronautics
  State Airport, Augusta, ME 04330
Maryland State Aviation Administration
  P.O. Box 8755, Baltimore, MD
Massachusetts Aeronautics Commission
  Boston Logan Airport, East Boston, MA 02128
Michigan Aeronautics Commission
  Capital City Airport, Lansing, MI 48906
Minnesota Department of Aeronautics
  Downtown Airport, St. Paul, MN 55107
Mississippi Aeronautics Commission
  P.O. Box 5, Jackson, MS 39205
Missouri Division of Commerce and Industrial Development
  Aviation Section, P.O. Box 118, Jefferson City, MO 65101
Montana Aeronautics Commission
  P.O. Box 1698, Helena, MT 59601
Nebraska Department of Aeronautics
  P.O. Box 82088, Lincoln, NE 68501
Nevada Public Service Commission
  Carson City, NV
New Hampshire Aeronautics Commission
  Municipal Airport, Concord, NH 03301
New Jersey Department of Transportation
  1035 Parkway Avenue, Trenton, NJ 08625

New Mexico Department of Aviation
   P.O. Box 579, Santa Fe, NM 87501
New York State Department of Transportation
   1220 Washington Avenue, Albany, NY
North Carolina Department of National and Economic Resources
   P.O. Box 27687, Raleigh, NC 27611
North Dakota Aeronautics Commission
   Municipal Airport, Box U, Bismarck, ND 58501
Ohio Department of Commerce
   3130 Case Road, Columbus, OH 43220
Oklahoma Aeronautics Commission
   5900 Mosteller Drive, Oklahoma City, OK 73112
Oregon State Board of Aeronautics
   Salem, OR 97310
Pennsylvania Department of Transportation, Bur. of Aviation
   Capital City Airport, New Cumberland, PA 17070
Rhode Island Department of Transportation
   Green State Airport, Warwick, RI 02886
South Carolina Aeronautics Commission
   P.O. Box 88, West Columbia, SC 29169
South Dakota Aeronautics Commission
   Pierre, SD 57501
Tennessee Department of Transportation
   P.O. Box 17326, Nashville, TN 37217
Texas Aeronautics Commission
   P.O. Box 12607, Austin, TX 78711
Utah Division of Aeronautics
   International Airport, Salt Lake City, UT 84116
Vermont Aeronautics Board
   State House, Montpelier, VT 05602
Virginia State Corporation Commission, Div. of Aeronautics
   P.O. Box 7716, Richmond, VA 23231
Washington State Aeronautics Commission
   8600 Perimeter Road, Seattle, WA 98108
West Virginia State Aeronautics Commission
   Kanawha Airport, Charleston, WV 25311
Wisconsin Department of Transportation
   951 Hill Farms Office Bldg., Madison, WI 53702
Wyoming Aeronautics Commission
   P.O. Box 2194, Cheyenne, WY 82001

static   Radio-reception interference resulting in noise.

static pressure   Undisturbed atmospheric pressure as received by the static vents in an aircraft.

static vent   A hole, usually located in the side of the fuselage, that provides air at atmospheric pressure to operate the pitot-static system. There are usually two such vents, one in each side, connected by a Y-shaped tube from which the pitot-static instruments obtain their reading. The dual installation prevents sideways movement from affecting the accuracy of the readout.

Stationair   A six-to-eight place single-engine fixed-gear aircraft once manufactured by Cessna Aircraft Company. No longer in production.

stationary front   A weather front that has stopped moving or at least is moving at less than five mph, or has matching temperatures on each side. The weather associated with stationary fronts tends to spread and remain for several days. The weather chart identification is a line with pointed marks on one side and rounded marks on the other.

stationary reservations   Altitude reservations related to military operations.

station passage   The time at which an aircraft passes over a fix.

station report   A group of symbols on a weather chart showing conditions at a specific weather reporting station. Conditions reported include wind force equal to Beaufort scale number, wind direction, cloud type and altitude, sea-level pressure, barometric tendency and precipitation occurring since the previous report. Reports are issued every six hours.

statute mile (sm)   5,280 feet; .87 of a nautical mile.

STBL   Stable.

STC   Supplemental type certificate.

STDY   Steady.

Stearman   A high-performance single-engine biplane, often used in agricultural operations.

S – Tec Corporation   Manufacturer of autopilots, flight directors, and stabilization systems. (Rt. 4, Bldg. 946, Wolters Industrial Complex, Mineral Wells, TX 76067. (800) 433-5748.)

steep turn   Generally any turn involving a bank in excess of 30 degrees.

STG   Strong.

stick   Control wheel, yoke.

stick pusher   A system built into certain jet aircraft that automatically forces the control wheel forward when the aircraft approaches a stall.

stick shaker   A system built into certain jet and turboprop aircraft that shakes the control wheel quite violently in order to alert the pilot that he is on the edge of a stall.

stiffeners   Members attached to the inside of the skin of an aircraft to help resist the effects of compression or bending loads.

STM   Storm.

STN   Station.

STOL   Short takeoff and landing (aircraft)

STOL aircraft, the Christen Husky.

Stop altitude squawk   An ATC phrase to ask the pilot to turn off his altitude encoder.

stop and go   A landing in which the aircraft comes to a full stop and then takes off again without returning first to the takeoff position on the runway.

stopover flight plan   A single flight plan that includes one or more stops between departure airport and the final destination.

stop squawk   An ATC phrase to ask the pilot to turn off his transponder.

stopway   A continuation of the takeoff runway. It can support an aircraft during an aborted takeoff without causing structural damage. Also known as overrun.

Stormscope   A cockpit instrument that detects lightning strikes and displays their location, relative to the aircraft, on a cathode-ray tube display in order to make it easier for the pilot to avoid areas of heavy thunderstorm activity and the related turbulence. *See* 3M CORPORATION. (Page 416)

Stormscope Lightning Detector

.MODEL	.PRICE	. VIEWING MODE	. CHECKLISTS	. DISPLAY	. RANGES	. TIMER	. VOLTS	. WEIGHT	. REMARKS
WX-1000+	9,995.00	360°/120° fwrd	6 programmable	monochrome*	25,50,100.200	yes	10.5 -32	10.95	* gyro-stabilized
WX-1000	8,995.00	360°/120° fwrd	6 programmable	monochrome	25,50,100,200	yes	10.5 -32	10.95	
WX-8	3,975.00	135° forward	yes	3-color	30 to 100		10/16 24/32	4	
WX-12	11,975.00	360° or radar+	yes	3-color	30 to 100	yes		9.2	+ intrface Sperry rdr

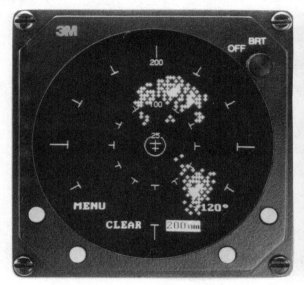 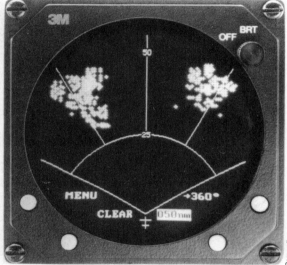

Stormscope displays in two viewing modes.

straight-and-level flight   Flight along a straight course without changes in altitude or airspeed.

straight-in approach   A landing made without first flying a landing pattern. At controlled airports the tower will clear the pilot for a straight-in approach if traffic conditions permit and it reduces the time aloft for the pilot. At uncontrolled airports straight-in approaches are not advisable.

straight-in approach IFR   An instrument approach in which the final approach segment is begun without first making a procedure turn. It does not necessarily have to culminate in a straight-in approach.

straight-in landing   A landing made on a runway that is aligned within 30 degrees of the direction of the final approach course, at the completion of an instrument approach.

Strangle your parrot   Slang for shut off your transponder.

stratiform Clouds occurring in horizontal layers without much vertical development. They are the result of cooling layers in stable air and might occur in small or large patches or might cover the whole sky.

stratocumulus Low clouds with stratiform and cumuliform characteristics; most often forming below an inversion.

stratosphere The layer of the atmosphere above the troposphere and reaching to an altitude of about 30 miles. It is a region of fairly constant temperatures.

stratus Low stratiform cloud, usually found at the level of a temperature inversion.

streamlining Term used for eliminating the maximum number of causes of parasite drag.

stress Resistance of a body to an opposing force.

stress A consideration in the design of an aircraft, aimed toward construction that can withstand all loads exerted upon it.

stress analysis The science of analyzing the amount of stress resistance that must be built into an aircraft.

strobe A light that emits flashes of high intensity in rapid succession.

strut A rigid brace designed to support a given load. Wing struts, for instance, support the wing in terms of compression as well as tension loads.

student pilot A person receiving primary flight instruction.

student pilot certificate An authorization by the FAA, based upon recommendations by a flight instructor, permitting the student pilot to fly an aircraft solo within certain distance limitations. A student pilot certificate does expressly prohibit the student from carrying passengers. In order for a student pilot certificate to be effective, the student must have passed a third-class medical examination within the preceding 24 months.

s-turn An S-shaped path flown on final approach in order to either lose altitude by increasing the distance, or to avoid overtaking a slower aircraft on final for landing.

s-turn A coordination maneuver in which an S-shaped path is flown over reference points on the ground, allowing for wind drift.

SubLOGIC Corporation The company that markets the various versions of the *Flight Simulator* computer game. (713 Egdebrook Drive, Champaign, IL 61820. (217) 359-8482.)

subsonic Any speed below the speed of sound.

substitute route A route assigned to pilots on IFR flight plans when an airway or a portion thereof is unusable because of navaid outages.

sucker hole Slang for something that looks like a safe clear path through a thunderstorm or a layer of clouds, but which can easily actually lead into areas of considerable turbulence or solid clouds.

suction gauge   A cockpit instrument indicating the amount of suction produced by the vacuum pump. It should normally stay at about four inches Hg to keep gyro instruments operating satisfactorily.

Sunair Electronics, Inc.   Manufacturers of airborne and ground single-sideband high-frequency communications equipment. (3101 S.W. Third Avenue, Ft. Lauderdale, FL 33315. (305) 525-1505.)

Sundowner   A four-seat single-engine fixed-gear aircraft once manufactured by Beech Aircraft Corporation. No longer in production.

Beechcraft Sierra and Sundowner.

supercharger   Turbocharger.

supercritical wing   A term used for an airfoil design created by NASA with the help of computers. It has low drag and high lift characteristics and results in a reduction in fuel consumption and an increase in range.

Super Cub   A two-place tandem configuration, high-wing fabric covered tailwheel piston airplane powered by a 150 hp Lycoming 0-320-A2B engine, manufactured by Piper Aircraft Corporation. For a long time the aircraft was out of production, but is, by popular demand being once more manufactured and offered as a complete aircraft or a home assembly package that can be certified in the normal category after inspection by a Piper representative.

Super Cub.

supersonic   Speeds above the speed of sound (Mach 1 and up).

Super Viking   A high-performance single-engine aircraft that was manufactured by Bellanca Aircraft Corporation. The aircraft is no longer in production but many remain in the fleet and are cherished by their owners for, among other features, their exceptional maneuverability and handling characteristics.

supplemental type certificate (STC)   A certificate issued by the FAA approving an addition to, or modification of, a certificated aircraft.

surface forecast map   A weather chart of the earth's surface showing the positions that fronts, isobars, and pressure centers are expected to reach at a specific time.

surface visibility   Ground visibility.

surface wind   The wind blowing near the surface, of importance during approaches, takeoffs, and landings. It is more likely to fluctuate than winds aloft.

surveillance radar   Terminal radar without the capability of determining altitude.

surveillance radar approach (ASR)   A ground controlled instrument approach during which the controller gives vectoring information to the pilot and, during the final phase, reads off altitudes below which the pilot should not descend. It is a nonprecision approach.

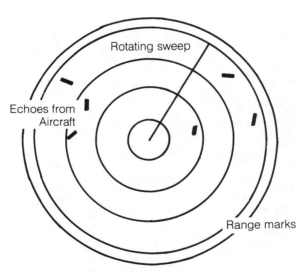

Surveillance approach radar.

SVFR   Special VFR.

S/VFR   Special VFR.

SVR   Severe.

SVRL   Several.

SW   Snow showers (in sequence reports).

SWAP   Severe weather avoidance plan.

swash plate The device in a helicopter that transmits control inputs to the rotor assembly.

Swearingen Aviation Corporation Previously manufactured the Merlin and Metro turboprop aircraft.

Swearingen Engineering and Technology, Inc. Developer of the SA-30 FanJet, expected to be priced under $2 million in 1989 dollars. (1234 99th Street, San Antonio, TX 78214. (512) 921-0055.)

Swearingen Twin-Turboprop Aircraft

		MERLIN IIIB	MERLIN IVA	METRO II
ENGINES	manufacturer	Garrett (2)	Garrett (2)	Garrett (2)
	type	TPE 331-IOU-501G	TPE 331-3U-304G	TPE 331-3UW-304G
	shp each	900	840	840 dry, 940 wet
	TBO hours	3,000	3,000	3,000 (6,000 commuter service)
WEIGHTS lbs	ramp	12,600	12,600	12,600
	takeoff	12,500	12,500	12,500
	landing	11,500	12,500	12,500
	zero fuel	10,000	12,500	12,500
	empty	7,800	8,200	n/a
	useful load	4,700	4,300	4,300
DIMENSIONS ft	length	42.16	59.34	59.34
	height	16.82	16.7	16.76
	span	46.25	46.26	46.25
CABIN ft		17.4	33.1	33.1
	height	4.75	4.75	4.5
	width	5.17	5.17	5.17
PRESSURIZATION	psi	7	7	7
WINGS	area ft^2	277.5	277.5	277.5
	loading lb/ft^2	45	45	45
	max payload	2,000	4,100	4,300
FUEL lbs	usable	4,342	3,712	4,342
	with max payload	2,500	n/a	n/a
FUEL FLOW pph	per engine, hi speed	317	313	349
	economy	230	212	254
TAKEOFF ft	accelerate/stop	n/a	3,450	4,075
	short field	n/a	3,200	3,100
	ground run	n/a	1,600	1,925
	short field	n/a	1,350	1,350
	50 ft.obstacle	3,219	2,620	2,620
	short field	n/a	2,050	2,050
LANDING ft	50 ft.obstacle	3,227	3,550	3,550
RATE OF CLIMB fpm	2 engines	2,782	2,400	2,400
	1 engine	723	650	650
SERVICE CEILING ft	2 engines	31,400	26,600	27,000
	1 engine	16,500	14,700	14,700
SPEEDS knots	V_{xse} CAS	119	126	126
	V_{yse} CAS	138	133	133
	V_{mca} CAS	107	91	91
	V_{ne}	309	269	255
	high speed cruise	300	263	255
	economy	272	244	246
RANGE nm	max	2,278	1,822	2,139
STANDARD EQUIPMENT	de-icing	¤	¤	¤
	propeller synchrophase	¤	¤	¤
	galley	¤		
	toilet	¤	¤	

Swearingen SA-30 FanJet

ENGINES (2)	manufacturer	Williams International
	model	FJ44
	takeoff thrust	1,800 lbs each
WEIGHTS lbs	ramp	9,300
	max takeoff	9,250
	max landing	9,000
	zero fuel	9,250
	empty, equipped	5,200
FUEL lbs	usable	3,350
DIMENSIONS ft	length	41.89
	height	12.92
	span	36.33
	wing area ft^2	165
CABIN ft	length	11.2
	width	4.7
	height	4.3
SPEEDS	max cruise	.78 Mach
	long-range cruise	.72 Mach
	M_{mo}	.82 Mach
	V_{ref}	104 kts
	stall (max landing weight)	80 kts
RANGE nm	VFR (NBAA reserves)	2,170 @ .72 Mach
	IFR (NBAA reserves)	1,830 @ .72 Mach
RATE OF CLIMB fpm	2 engines (max takeoff wt)	9,250
CEILING	max operating altitude ft	41,000
PRESSURIZATION	psi	10.0
TAKEOFF	balanced field length ft	3,270
LANDING	distance ft	2,405
PRICE	1989 $s	under $2,000,000

Swearingen Engineering

Swearingen S-30 FanJet.

swept-back wing A wing on which both the leading and trailing edges are swept back from the lateral axis.

swinging the compass Calibrating the compass, generally accomplished by comparing compass readings with a large compass rose painted permanently on the ramp at an airport. It must be done with the aircraft in flight attitude and with engines running and radios turned on.

symbolic display Pictorial display.

sympathetic resonance A vibration that develops when the frequency of vibration in one mechanism is in phase with that of another. It tends to increase and can become destructive unless checked. It has been a serious problem in helicopters, but has been successfully eliminated by controlling the designs of gear boxes and related mechanisms.

synoptic chart Surface weather map.

SYS System.

T Takeoff (on instrument approach charts).

T Tango (phonetic alphabet)

T Thunderstorm (in sequence reports).

T Tropical air mass.

T True (after bearing).

tab Trim tab.

TAC Tactical Air Command.

TACAN Stands for tactical air navigation. A navigation system that was originally developed for the military. It gives distance and bearing information on UHF frequencies. It is slightly more accurate with reference to bearing information than a VOR and less subject to interference. Today, most TACANs are combined with VORs and called VORTACs, and any aircraft equipped with VOR plus DME or TACAN equipment can use the navaids to receive distance and bearing information.

tachometer An engine instrument that displays the engine rpm (usually in 100s). It also includes a counter showing engine time based on average rpm and a colored line or bar shows the normal operating range(s).

tactical air navigation *See* TACAN.

TADS Target acquisition and detection system.

tail assembly Empennage.

taildragger Popular phrase for tailwheel aircraft.

tail heavy The tendency of an airplane to fly tail low and nose high which requires above normal elevator control or nose down trim. Usually caused by exceeding the rearward limits of the CG.

tail low A flight attitude resulting from a tail heavy condition of the aircraft. It is also the usual flight attitude during slow flight and during the flare just before touchdown.

tailwheel gear Landing gear with the third wheel under the tail and the main gear ahead of the CG. Also called *conventional gear.* (Page 424)

tailwind Wind blowing in more or less the same direction as the line of flight.

Tailwheel aircraft.

tailwind component   The amount of favorable effect on the ground speed resulting from tailwinds. For the formula to determine the tailwind component, *see* CONVERSION TABLES.

takeoff   The phase of flight starting with the aircraft in position on the runway, but not yet moving, and ending at the moment of liftoff.

takeoff distance   The length of runway needed to accelerate to liftoff speed. Ground run.

takeoff distance chart   Charts in aircraft flight manuals showing the takeoff distance under various conditions of airport elevation, wind, etc. Usually given for full-gross-weight conditions.

takeoff horsepower   Maximum permissible horsepower.

takeoff leg   Ground run.

takeoff power   The brake horsepower developed under standard conditions with the engine running at full rpm and the manifold pressure at the maximum allowable setting.

takeoff run   Ground run.

takeoff speed   The airspeed necessary to develop sufficient lift to permit liftoff under prevailing density altitude and aircraft weight conditions.

takeoff weight   The maximum permissible weight of the aircraft for takeoff. It usually coincides with maximum gross weight, but on certain larger aircraft it is slightly below the maximum weight permissible for taxi.

tandem airplane   A two-seat aircraft with dual controls one behind the other.

tandem seating   Two single seats, one behind the other.

tango   In aviation radio phraseology the term used for the letter T.

target   The blip on a radar scope resulting from a primary radar return.

target symbol   A computer-generated symbol resulting from a primary radar beacon return.

TAS   True airspeed.

task   In ballooning, any type of competition.

taxi   To move the airplane on the ground or on water under it own power.

taxi patterns   Patterns established by ATC to expedite traffic on the ground at busy airports.

taxiway   Surfaces designed for the ground movement of aircraft. Their load bearing capability is usually less than that of runways.

TBO   Time between overhauls. TBOs are established for engines and engine related systems by the manufacturer, based on past experience with and performance of the engine or system. It is not an absolute guarantee that the engine will perform satisfactorily for the full TBO hours. Conversely, exceeding the TBO, though not good operating practice, is not illegal.

TC   True course.

TCA   Terminal control area.

TCH   Threshold crossing height.

TDA   Today.

TDZE   Touchdown zone elevation.

TDZL   Touchdown zone lights.

teardrop entry   One of three recommended (but not mandatory) means of entering a holding pattern. After crossing the holding fix the aircraft proceeds outbound on a track of 30 degrees or less to the holding course and then turns right, approximately 210 degrees, to intercept the holding course.

TEC   Tower en route control.

TECA   Tower en route control area.

technical standard order (TSO)   A specific standard of quality established by the FAA with reference to avionics, instruments and equipment. TSOd products are usually somewhat more expensive than non-TSOd products.

Teledyne Avionics   Manufacturer of angle-of-attack indicators and sensors, indicators for TCAS II systems, power, and engine analyzer and recorder computer systems. (Charlottesville/Albermarle Airport, Charlottesville, VA 22906. (804) 973-3311.)

Teledyne Continental Motors, Aircraft Products Division   Manufacturer of air and liquid cooled piston engines for general aviation. Continental produced the engines used on the Voyager on its globe girdling flight. (P.O. Box 90, Mobile, AL 36601. (205) 438-3411.) (Pages 426-427)

telephone, airborne   *See* AIRBORNE TELEPHONES.

Telex Communications, Inc.   Manufacturer of a wide selection of headphones, microphones, and aircraft intercoms. (9600 Aldrich Avenue South, Minneapolis, MN 55420. (612) 887-5510.)

TEMP   Temperature.

tension stress   Stress resulting from pull.

Teledyne Continental Piston Engines

MODEL	CYL	HP/RPM	in²	lbs	DRIVE	FUEL	COMP	REMARKS
O-200	4	100/2750	200	188	direct	80/87	7.0:1	Taylorcraft
O-300 A, C	6	145/2700	300	270	direct	80/87	7.0:1	
O-300 D	6	145/2700	300	272	direct	80/87	7.0:1	
OI-360	6	210/2800	360	294	direct	100/100LL	8.5:1	Cessna 337 Skymaster (2)
IO-360 J, JB	6	195/2600	360	294	direct	100/100LL	8.5:1	Cessna Hawk XP
IO-360 K, KB	6	195/2600	360	294	direct	100/100LL	8.5:1	
TSIO-360 A	6	210/2800	360	300	direct	100/100LL	7.5:1	
TSIO-360 C, CB	6	225/2800	360	300	direct	100/100LL	7.5:1	
TSIO-360 D, DB	6	225/2800	360	278	direct	100/100LL	7.5:1	
TSIO-360 E, EB	6	200/2575	360	352	direct	100/100LL	7.5:1	
TSIO-360 F, FB	6	200/2527	360	359	direct	100/100LL	7.5:1	Piper Turbo Arrow IV
TSIO-360 G, GB	6	210/2700	360	354	direct	100/100LL	7.5:1	Mooney Turbo 231
TSIO-360 MB	6	210/2700	360	412	direct	100/100LL	7.5:1	Mooney Turbo 252
TSIO-360 H, HB	6	210/2800	360	313	direct	100/100LL	7.5:1	
TSIO-360 K, KB	6	220/2800	360	359	direct	100/100LL	7.5:1	Piper Seneca III (2)
O-470 G	6	240/2600	470	431	direct	91/96	8.0:1	
O-470 J	6	225/2550	470	380	direct	80/87	7.0:1	
O-470 K, L	6	230/2600	470	404	direct	80/87	7.0:1	
O-470 M	6	240/2600	470	409	direct	91/96	8.0:1	
O-470 R	6	230/2600	470	401	direct	80/87	7.0:1	
O-470 S	6	230/2600	470	412	direct	100/100LL	7.0:1	
O-470 U	6	230/2400	470	412	direct	100/100LL	8.6:1	Cessna Skylane, Skywagon
IO-470 C	6	250/2600	470	431	direct	91/96	8.0:1	
IO-470 D, E	6	260/2625	470	426	direct	100/100LL	8.6:1	
IO-470 F	6	260/2625	470	426	direct	100/100LL	8.6:1	
IO-470 H	6	260/2625	470	431	direct	100/100LL	8.6:1	
IO-470 J, K	6	225/2600	470	401	direct	80/87	7.0:1	
IO-470 L	6	260/2625	470	430	direct	100/100LL	8.6:1	Beech Baron B55 (2)
IO-470 M	6	260/2625	470	430	direct	100/100LL	8.6:1	
IO-470 N	6	260/2625	470	433	direct	100/100LL	8.6:1	
IO-470 S	6	260/2625	470	426	direct	100/100LL	8.6:1	
IO-470 U	6	260/2625	470	423	direct	100/100LL	8.6:1	
IO-470 V, VO	6	260/2625	470	423	direct	100/100LL	8.6:1	
TSIO-470 B,C,D	6	260/2600	470	423	direct	100/100LL	7.5:1	
IO-520 A, J	6	285/2700	520	431	direct	100/100LL	8.5:1	
IO-520 B,BA,BB	6	285/2700	520	422	direct	100/100LL	8.5:1	Beech Bonanza F33A, V35B, A36
IO-520 C, CB	6	285/2700	520	415	direct	100/100LL	8.5:1	Beech Baron E55, 58
IO-520 D	6	285/2700	520	430	direct	100/100LL	8.5:1	
IO-520 E	6	285/2700	520	427	direct	100/100LL	8.5:1	
IO-520 F	6	285/2700	520	430	direct	100/100LL	8.5:1	Cessna Stationair
IO-520 K	6	285/2700	520	428	direct	100/100LL	8.5:1	
IO-520 L	6	285/2700	520	431	direct	100/100LL	8.5:1	Cessna 210N Centurion
IO-520 M, MB	6	285/2700	520	413	direct	100/100LL	8.5:1	Cessna Turbo Stationair
IO-550 B	6	300/2700	550	422	direct	100/100LL	8.5:1	Beech Bonanza A36
IO-550 C	6	300/2700	550	433	direct	100/100LL	8.5:1	Beech Baron 58 (2)
TSIO-520 B, BB	6	285/2700	520	423	direct	100/100LL	7.5:1	
TSIO-520 C, H	6	285/2700	520	433	direct	100/100LL	7.5:1	
TSIO-520 D, DB	6	285/2700	520	423	direct	100/100LL	7.5:1	
TSIO-520 E, EB	6	300/2700	520	421	direct	100/100LL	7.5:1	
TSIO-520 G	6	285/2600	520	433	direct	100/100LL	7.5:1	
TSIO-520 J,N	6	310/2700	520	412	direct	100/100LL	7.5:1	
TSIO-520 K, KB	6	285/2700	520	412	direct	100/100LL	7.5:1	
TSIO-520 L, LB	6	310/2700	520	514	direct	100/100LL	7.5:1	
TSIO-520 M, P	6	285/2600	520	436	direct	100/100LL	7.5:1	
TSIO-520 R	6	285/2600	520	436	direct	100/100LL	7.5:1	Cessna T210 Turbo Centurion
TSIO-520 T	6	310/2700	520	426	direct	100/100LL	7.5:1	
TSIO-520 U, UB	6	300/2700	520	536	direct	100/100LL	7.5:1	Beech Bonanza B36TC
TSIO-520 V, VB	6	325/2700	520	456	direct	100/100LL	7.5:1	Cessna 402C
TSIO-520 W, WB	6	325/2700	520	539	direct	100/100LL	7.5:1	Beech Baron 58TC, 58P
TSIO-520 AF	6	285/2600	520	418	direct	100/100LL	7.5:1	
TSIO-520 BE	6	310/2600	520	566	direct	100/100LL	7.5:1	Piper Malibu
TSIO-520 CE	6	325/2700	520	527	direct	100/100LL	7.5:1	Cessna P210N Pressurized Centurion
GTSIO-520 C	6	340/3200	520	481	geared	100/100LL	7.5:1	
GTSIO-520 D, H	6	375/3400	520	508	geared	100/100LL	7.5:1	
GTSIO-520 K	6	435/3400	520	600	geared	100/100LL	7.5:1	
GTSIO-520 L,N	6	375/3350	520	557	geared	100/100LL	7.5:1	Cessna 421C Golden Eagle (2)
GTSIO-520 M	6	375/3350	520	507	geared	100/100LL	7.5:1	Cessna 404 Titan
Tiara 6-285	6	285/4000	406	382	geared	100/100LL	9.0:1	

Teledyne Continental turbocharged piston engine TSIO-360 MB.

terminal area A loose term for the airspace in which approach control service or terminal control service is provided.

terminal area facility The ATC facility providing terminal, approach and departure control services.

terminal control area (TCA) Positive control airspace established around certain high traffic airports. Shaped more or less like an inverted wedding cake, it extends in the center from the ground to a given altitude, and on the outer portions from a given floor to the same altitude. Within TCAs all aircraft, whether IFR or VFR, must maintain contact with ACT and operate in accordance with ATC instructions. (Page 428)

Group 1 TCAs	**Group 2 TCAs**	
Atlanta	Cleveland	Minneapolis-St. Paul
Boston	Denver	New Orleans
Chicago	Detroit	Philadelphia
Dallas/Ft. Worth	Honolulu	Pittsburgh
Los Angeles	Houston	St. Louis
Miami	Kansas City	San Diego
New York	Las Vegas, NV	Seattle
San Francisco		
Washington, DC		

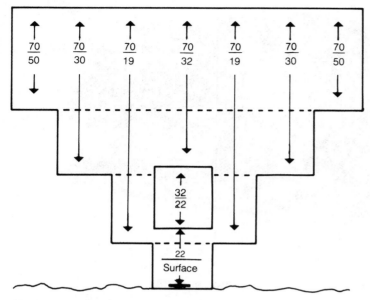

TCA cross section.

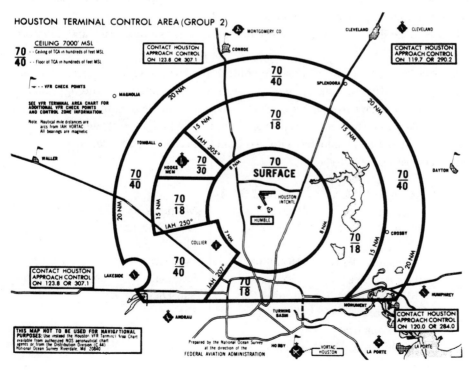

A typical TCA.

terminal forecast   A weather forecast covering expected conditions at a given airport. It is prepared every six hours and refers to weather conditions expected within the following 12 hours. It uses sequence report symbols and is issued for over 400 locations. In addition, 24 hour forecasts are available for about 130 major terminals.

terminal instrument procedures (TERPS)   Standard instrument procedures established for specific terminals, such as SIDs and STARs.

terminal radar approach control (TRACON)   A facility providing approach control service for one or more airports using the same radar system.

terminal radar program   A program in operation at certain airports that extends IFR type separation service to VFR aircraft. Participation by VFR aircraft is optional. It is divided into Stage I: Traffic information and limited vectoring of VFR aircraft on a workload permitting basis. Stage II: The same as Stage I, but on a full-time basis. Stage III: The same as Stage II, plus IFR type separation between all participating aircraft. In view of the fact that VFR pilots may refuse to participate in the service, all aircraft in the area must maintain visual watch for other aircraft.

terminal radar service area (TRSA)   The airspace in which Stage I, II, or III terminal radar service is provided.

terminal VOR (TVOR)   A low power VOR located on an airport and used as a navaid.

TERPS   Terminal instrument procedures.

Terra Corporation   Manufacturer of air/ground telephones, airborne FM communications, intercoms, selective calling systems, and decoders. (3520 Pan American Freeway N.E., Albuquerque, NM 87107. (505) 684-2321.)

terrain clearance   The vertical distance between an aircraft in flight and the highest nearby point or object on the ground.

TET   Tetrahedron.

tetrahedron   A rotating device on the ground, sometimes wedge shaped and sometimes in the shape of an airplane, showing the direction of the wind. At some locations tetrahedrons are equipped with flashing lights which are turned on when the visibility is less than three miles. In addition, most are illuminated at night.

Textron Lycoming   *See* LYCOMING.

TFC   Traffic.

TH   True heading.

T-hangar   A long, narrow hangar building containing T-shaped spaces into which aircraft are pulled tail first from either side. It is ideal for hangaring large numbers of light aircraft in a minimum amount of space.

That is correct   Aviation radio phrase for: you have understood me correctly.

THDR   Thunder.

thermal   A prolonged updraft; especially important to glider pilots.

thermaling   In soaring, using one or any number of thermals to gain and maintain altitude.

thermal runaway   A phenomenon occuring with nickel-cadmium batteries, consisting of continuous and excessive increases in heat during charging. If left unchecked it can result in an explosion of the battery.

THK   Thick.

THN   Thin.

3M Aviation Safety Systems   Manufacturer of the Stormscope that displays lightning strikes on a cockpit instrument. *See* STORMSCOPE. (6530 Singletree Drive, Columbus, OH 43229. (614) 885-3310.)

three-point landing   A landing of a tailwheel aircraft in which the aircraft is stalled a few inches above the runway surface and all three wheels touch the ground at the same time.

threshold   A line perpendicular to the centerline of the runway, indicating the beginning of the portion of the runway that is usable for landing.

threshold crossing height (TCH)   The height of the glide slope at the point where it crosses the threshold.

threshold lights   A line of green lights across the runway at the threshold.

THRFTR   Thereafter.

throttle   The knob or lever on the instrument panel or pedestal with which the pilot controls the quantity of fuel-air mixture fed to the engine.

throttle   The valve that controls the amount of fuel-air mixture being fed to the engine.

THRU   Through.

thrust   The forward force, pushing or pulling, exerted by the engine or, in the case of gliders, by gravity. It opposes and must overcome drag.

thrust horsepower   The actual horsepower delivered by the engine.

thrust reverser   A clamshell type of arrangement that, when deployed, reverses the direction of thrust from a jet engine. It reduces ground run and the need for excessive braking. Popularly called tubs or buckets.

THRUT   Throughout.

THSD   Thousand.

thunderhead   A cumulonimbus cloud.

Thunder Pacific   U.S. Distributor of Thunder Balloons manufactured in England. (114 Sandalwood Court, Santa Rosa, CA 95401.)

thunderstorm   A storm produced by cumulonimbus clouds accompanied by lightning, thunder, strong winds, turbulence, heavy rain, and often hail. The vertical winds inside a thunderstorm are known to reach velocities of 100 mph and the associated turbulence is sufficient to tear an airplane apart.

TIAS   True indicated airspeed.

tiedown   Securing the aircraft with ropes or chains anchored to the ground in the tiedown area of an airport.

Tiger   A single-engine piston aircraft manufactured by Gulfstream American Corporation. No longer in production.

TIL   Until.

time en route   The time the aircraft has been airborne from liftoff until the present moment. There are two ways to figure time en route, one is: distance divided by ground speed and the other is: fuel burned divided by fuel flow. *See* CONVERSION TABLES.

time group   A group of four digits representing the hours and minutes (0342 = 3:42 a.m.). Unless accompanied by a time zone indicator, it is understood to represent Greenwich Mean Time, or more recently Coordinated Universal Time (UTC).

timers   *See* CLOCKS.

time to climb/descend   The time in minutes that is required to cover a given change in altitude at a steady rate of climb or descent. To figure the time required: Divide the altitude change in feet by the rate of climb/descent in feet per minute (fpm). *See also* CONVERSION TABLES.

time zones   The various zones within which local time is different from one another. Time zones covering the U.S. are: (Page 432)

Eastern Standard = GMT minus five hours
Eastern Daylight = GMT minus four hours

Central Standard = GMT minus six hours
Central Daylight = GMT minus five hours

Mountain Standard = GMT minus seven hours
Mountain Daylight = GMT minus six hours

Pacific Standard = GMT minus eight hours
Pacific Daylight = GMT minus seven hours

Yukon Standard = GMT minus nine hours
Alaska/Hawaii Standard = GMT minus 10 hours

Tip stall   A stall occurring at the wingtip area. Tip stalls can result from turns at slow speed when the wingtip pointing to the center of the turn moves too slowly to generate lift.

TIT   Turbine inlet temperature.

Titan   A twin-turboprop 10-seat aircraft, once manufactured by Cessna Aircraft Company. No longer in production.

TKOF   Takeoff.

Time Zones Worldwide

When the time in New York City is **12:00 noon**

the time in the following cities and countries is:

U.S. City	Time	Difference
Albuquerque	10:00 A.M.	- 2:00
Anchorage	7:00 A.M.	- 5:00
Atlanta	12:00 noon	0:00
Boston	12:00 noon	0:00
Chicago	11:00 A.M.	- 1:00
Cincinnati	12:00 noon	0:00
Cleveland	12:00 noon	0:00
Dallas	11:00 A.M.	- 1:00
Denver	10:00 A.M.	- 2:00
El Paso	10:00 A.M.	- 2:00
Honolulu	7:00 A.M.	- 5:00
Houston	11:00 A.M.	- 1:00
Los Angeles	9:00 A.M.	- 3:00
Miami	12:00 noon	0:00
New Orleans	11:00 A.M.	- 1:00
Philadelphia	12:00 noon	0:00
Phoenix	10:00 A.M.	- 2:00
Portland, OR	9:00 A.M.	- 3:00
San Francisco	9:00 A.M.	- 3:00
Seattle	9:00 A.M.	- 3:00
Washington, DC	12:00 noon	0:00

Country	Time	Difference
Argentina	2:00 P.M.	+ 2:00
Brazil	2:00 P.M.	+ 2:00
China	1:00 A.M. next day	+13:00
England	5:00 P.M.	+ 5:00
Egypt	7:00 P.M.	+ 7:00
France	6:00 P.M.	+ 6:00
Germany	6:00 P.M.	+ 6:00
Greece	6:00 P.M.	+ 6:00
India	10:30 P.M.	+10:30
Ireland	6:00 P.M.	+ 6:00
Israel	8:00 P.M.	+ 8:00
Italy	7:00 P.M.	+ 7:00
Japan	2:00 A.M. next day	+14:00
Kenya	8:00 P.M.	+ 8:00
Philippines	3:00 A.M. next day	+15:00
Portugal	5:00 P.M.	+ 5:00
Russia (Moscow area)	8:00 P.M.	+ 8:00
South Africa	6:00 P.M.	+ 6:00
Spain	6:00 P.M.	+ 6:00
Turkey	7:00 P.M.	+ 7:00
Greenwich Mean Time	5:00 P.M.	+ 5:00

(All times based on Standard Time)

TMPRY   Temporary.

TMW   Tomorrow.

TNDCY   Tendency.

TNGT   Tonight.

TO-FROM indicator   The portion of an OBI that shows whether the selected setting is a radial *from* the station or a bearing *to* the station (ambiguity meter.)

TOHP   Takeoff horsepower.

Tomahawk   A two-seat single-piston-engine training aircraft manufactured by Piper Aircraft Corporation. No longer in production.

torching   The burning of fuel in the exhaust outlet. It results from using an excessively rich mixture.

tornado   A violently rotating column of air producing a funnel-shaped cloud which usually tips from a cumulonimbus cloud. It may touch ground leaving a path of destruction from a few feet to a mile wide. It tends to occur in the Midwestern states during late spring and early summer.

torque   The normal tendency of an aircraft to rotate to the left in reaction to the right-hand rotation of the propeller. It alters with changes in power.

total energy variometer   A variometer (vertical speed indicator used in gliders and sailplanes) that has been compensated so as to respond only to changes in the total energy of the sailplane.

touch-and-go landing   A landing in which the aircraft does not come to a complete stop before starting another takeoff run. A popular but not terribly useful training exercise.

touchdown   The point in the landing at which the gear of the aircraft first makes contact with ground or water.

touchdown RVR   The runway visual range measured by equipment located near the touchdown zone of the runway.

touchdown zone   The first 3,000 feet of the runway, beginning at the threshold.

touchdown zone elevation (TDZE)   The highest point in the touchdown zone; used to compute MDA or DH for instrument approaches.

TOVC   Top of the overcast.

tower   Airport traffic control tower.

tower controller   ATC controllers responsible for handling takeoffs and landing at a controlled airport.

tower en route control   The control of IFR traffic between adjacent approach-control areas, eliminating the need to involve ARTCC. It expedites traffic handling and reduces the need for frequency changes.

tower en route control area   The area in which tower en route control service is provided.

tower frequency   The frequency or frequencies used by the control tower for air-to-ground communication. Also called local control frequency.

TPA   Traffic pattern altitude at uncontrolled airports.

TPG   Topping.

TPX 42   Numeric beacon decoder equipment providing rapid target identification, strengthening of the target return, and altitude information from aircraft equipped with Mode C capability.

track   The imaginary line that the flight path of an airplane makes over the earth.

tracking   Flying along a radio beam and, in the process, correcting for wind drift. Also following a certain ground feature, such as tracking a river.

TRACON   Terminal radar approach control.

Tracor Aerospace, Inc.   Manufacturer of long-range navigation systems, global positioning systems, radio management systems, static inverters, computer emulations, and telecommunications. Of primary interest to corporate aircraft operators are the TA 7880 Omega/VLF system base priced at $28,333, the TA 7900 ARINC 599 compatible Omega/VLF and GPS navigation system, base priced at $47,167. (6500 Tracor Lane, Austin, TX 78725-2070. (512) 926-2800.)

trade winds   The general circulation pattern of easterly winds lying in two belts around the globe and divided by the doldrums. Extending to about 30 degrees north and south.

traffic   Aircraft in flight.

traffic advisories   Advisories given by ATC to IFR and often VFR aircraft with reference to other aircraft in such proximity or flying along a path that might result in a conflict.

traffic information   Traffic advisories.

traffic pattern   The pattern, consisting of downwind, base leg, and final approach, that should always be flown by aircraft intending to land at an uncontrolled airport; also at controlled airports unless otherwise cleared by ATC.

traffic in sight   Phrase used by pilots when sighting an aircraft mentioned by ATC in a traffic advisory.

trailing edge   The usually sharp edge at the rear of any airfoil.

trailing vortex   The vortex formed by air moving off the trailing edge of the wings.

TRANS   Transcribed.

transceiver   A combination radio capable of transmitting and receiving.

transcribed weather broadcast (TWEB)   A continuous broadcast of transcribed meteorological information, available on LF/MF and some VOR facilities.

transfer of control   Handoff.

transferring controller   An ATC controller transferring control of a given aircraft to another controller.

transferring facility An ATC facility transferring control of a given aircraft to another facility when that aircraft leaves the airspace under its jurisdiction.

transition A change from one phase of flight to another (climbout to cruise). Also SIDs and STARs that are designed as standard transitions between the en route portion of the flight and the approach or takeoff phases.

transition area The airspace, usually between 700 and 1,200 feet agl, used in conjunction with instrument approach procedures at an airport.

transition zone The region of changing weather conditions occupied by a front. It can vary greatly in width.

translation lift In helicopter flight the additional lift that develops with forward speed and increases with increased forward speed.

transmissometer A device used to measure horizontal visibility.

transmitter The portion of a com radio which transmits. Usually combined with a receiver in one unit.

transmitting (in the) blind Transmitting under circumstances where two-way communication cannot be or has not been established, but where the person transmitting believes that his transmission is being received.

transponder An airborne radar beacon transceiver that automatically transmits responses to interrogation by ground-based transmitters. (Page 436)

Transponders

MANUFACTURER	MODEL	PRICE	VOLTS DC.AC	OUT	A	B	C	D	DIM A	DIM M	R	U	lbs	REMARKS
Bendix/King	KT 76A	1,225	14 28	250	¤		¤		¤			1	3.1	Silver Crown 28V adapter kit $30.00
Bendix/King	KT 79	3,315	14 28	250	¤		¤		¤			1	3.4	Silver Crown
Bendix/King	KXP 756	6,975	14 28	250	¤	¤	¤		¤	¤		3	4.71	Gold Crown
Bendix/King	TRS 42	10,125	28	325	¤	¤	¤		¤			2	8.17	Series III
Aire-Siences	RT-887	1,795	14* 28				¤		¤			1	n/a	Mount in 3-inch round hole, * opt.,need conv.
Aire-Sciences	RT-787	1,495	14* 28				¤		¤			1	n/a	Flat pack. * optional, needs converter
Terra	TRT 250	n/a	14 28	200	¤		¤		¤			1	1.7	Flat pack or 3-inch round hole version
Collins	TDR-950	n/a	14* 28	250	¤	¤+	¤		¤	¤		1	2	+ optional * optional, needs converter
Collins	TDR-90	n/a	28	500	¤		¤	¤				2	3.5	ProLine
Collins	TDR-94	n/a	28	500	¤		¤	¤				2	n/a	also Mode S. ProLine
Collins	TDR-94D	n/a	28	500	¤		¤	¤				2	n/a	also Mode S. ProLine

PRICE:		uninstalled		C:		mode C
VOLTS	DC:	DC input voltage		D:		mode D
	AC:	AC 400 Hz input voltage	DIM	A:		automatic reply-light dimmer
OUT:		output in watts		M:		manual reply-light dimmer
MODES	A:	mode A	R:			remote ident available
	B:	mode B	U:			number of units

Collins Micro Line TDR-950 transponder.

Traveler   A single-engine piston aircraft manufactured by Grumman American Corporation and no longer in production.

triangulation   A method of plotting the position of an aircraft at the intersection of two bearing lines to two known points, usually two VORs. While it can be accomplished with one nav receiver, it is easier and more accurate with two.

tricycle landing gear   A three-wheel landing gear with the two main wheels located aft of the CG and the third wheel under the nose of the airplane.

triggering time and temperature   In soaring, the time and temperature at which usable thermals begin to form.

trim   Adjustment of the pitch attitude of an aircraft to achieve the desired attitude without added elevator input.

trim tab   A small airfoil attached to a control surface, primarily the elevator, which makes minor adjustments in the position of that control surface under varying flight conditions. It may be fixed or hinged. Hinged trim tabs can be adjusted by the pilot in flight. Fixed tabs are installed to correct permanent stability problems in the airplane design.

TRML   Terminal.

TRNG   Training.

TROF   Trough.

tropical air mass   A warm air mass originating in the tropical regions. It might be continental or maritime.

tropopause   The region at the top of the troposphere.

troposphere   The portion of the atmosphere that is below the stratosphere. It extends outward seven to 10 miles from the earth's surface and within it temperature decreases rapidly with altitude, clouds form and convection is active. It is the portion of the atmosphere in which most aircraft operate.

trough   An elongated area of low atmospheric pressure with the lowest pressure at the centerline of the trough.

TRRN   Terrain.

TRSA   Terminal radar service area.

true airspeed (TAS) The actual airspeed of an aircraft relative to the air through which it is moving. It is calibrated airspeed adjusted for actual air density and altitude. It can be calculated from indicated airspeed by using the correction scale of a flight computer.

true altitude Actual height above sea level, expressed in feet msl.

true course (TC) The intended flight path expressed as the angle in degrees between a meridian near the middle of the flight path, and the flight path itself.

true heading (TH) The true course with a wind correction angle added or subtracted as needed.

true indicated airspeed Calibrated airspeed.

true north The geographic (not magnetic) north. The direction of the north pole from any point on the globe.

TSHWR Thundershower.

TSMT Transmit.

TSMTG Transmitting.

TSMTR Transmitter.

TSO Technical standard order.

TSO Time since overhaul.

TSTM Thunderstorm.

tubs Slang for thrust reversers.

tumble To fall out of operating position, such as a gyro or compass. Most gyro compasses will tumble after a 55-degree bank and must then be reset with the caging mechanism.

TURBC Turbulence.

turbine Jet engine.

turbocharger A turbine driven by the exhaust gases that compresses air and thus increases the amount of fuel-air mixture available to the engine. Turbocharged light aircraft usually use either of two types of installations. One type employs a second throttle to activate the turbocharger when the aircraft has reached an altitude at which power begins to decrease because of decreasing atmospheric pressure. The other type of installation is fully automatic and requires no special attention from the pilot.

turbocharging Increasing the pressure of the air that determines the amount of air used in the fuel-air mixture to exceed the prevailing atmospheric pressure at the higher altitudes. Turbocharging provides the pilot with vastly greater power at much higher altitudes. Turbocharged aircraft should be equipped with auxiliary oxygen for the pilot because of the high altitude potential.

turbofan A high-bypass jet engine equipped with a multi-blade fan that acts more or less like a shrouded propeller and delivers a considerable percentage of the total thrust. Fan-jets are quieter and more economical in terms of fuel flow than pure jets, but they lose some of their effectiveness at altitudes above 35,000 feet or so.

turbojet   A pure jet engine.

Turbomeca   Manufacturer of a family of turbine aircraft engines including the Astazou, Artouste, Turmo, Makila, and Arriel, used in many popular helicopters, such as the Aerospatiale Lama, Alouette III, Gazelle, Ecureuil, Dauphin, Puma, and Super Puma, the Agusta 109K, and also the Sikorsky S-76A+. (Bordes 64320 Bizanos, France. Tel: (33) 59 32 84 37.)

turboprop   An aircraft powered by jet engines that drive propellers. More economical to operate than pure jets or fan-jets, they are somewhat slower and the best operating altitudes are usually below 30,000 feet.

turboshaft   A jet-engine installation in a helicopter in which the engine drives the shaft that supports the rotorblades.

turbulence   A disturbance or irregularity in the movement of the air. It can be caused by friction when the air moves over an uneven surface, or by the mixing of several currents of air with differing velocities. Turbulence is described as light, moderate, severe, or extreme. Light turbulence is uncomfortable but has no serious effect on the pilot, or on objects carried in the airplane. Moderate turbulence may cause unsecured objects to tumble or even fly around in the cockpit. Severe turbulence results in considerable fluctuations in airspeed and occupants of the aircraft are forced violently against their seatbelts. The airplane might occasionally seem to be out of control as roll and pitch movement are briefly greater than can be counteracted by the controls. Extreme turbulence means that the airplane is virtually uncontrollable and is simply being tossed about. Since different aircraft and different pilots react differently to the varying degrees of turbulence, turbulence reports tend to be unreliable. Such reports always include the types of aircraft from which the report originated, but a 5,000-hour pilot flying a heavy twin might report a turbulent condition as light while a 200-hour pilot flying a Skyhawk might call the same condition moderate or even severe.

turn-and-bank indicator   A gyroscopic flight instrument that displays the rate of turn and shows whether the turn is properly coordinated. It usually consists of a needle showing the rate of turn and a ball that will remain centered in a slightly curved glass tube, if the turn is properly coordinated. If the ball moves to either side, it indicates the need for increased rudder pressure on the side to which the ball is moving.

turnaround   A semicircular taxiway adjacent to the ends of a runway, usually found at small airports where the runway is used for taxiing as well as takeoffs and landings. It permits the airplane to turn around or to get out of the way of other traffic using the runway.

turn coordinator   Turn-and-bank indicator.

turning radius   An aircraft making the tightest possible self-powered turn either on the ground or in the air describes a circle. The turning radius is, in fact, the distance from the center of that circle to the circle itself. While this is technically correct, the diameter of the circle is often described (incorrectly) as the turning radius.

TV   Television.

TVOR   Terminal VOR.

TWD   Toward.

TWEB   Transcribed weather broadcast.

twenty-four-hour clock (time)   The time used in aviation radio communication (as well as by the military and by several European countries). It consists of four digits (time group), the first two representing the hours from 01 to 24, and the second two representing the minutes from 00 to 59. In spoken communication "zero four five one" would indicate 4:51 a.m. and "two one zero six" would indicate 9:06 p.m.

twin-engine aircraft   An aircraft powered by two engines. Usually used with relation to piston engines. Aircraft powered by turbine engines are referred to as twin-jet, twin-turboprop, or twin-turbine helicopter.

Twin Otter   A twin-turboprop aircraft with exceptional STOL capabilities, manufactured by deHavilland in Canada (now Boeing of Canada).

Boeing Canada

deHavilland Twin Otter.

TwinStar   A twin-turbine helicopter manufactured by Aerospatiale in France.

two-minute turn   A standard-rate turn, requiring two minutes to complete 360 degrees of turn.

II Morrow, Inc.   Manufacturer of a family of Loran-C navigation systems. (P.O. Box 13549, Salem, OR 97309. (800) 742-0077.) (Page 440)

II Morrow Apollo 618 Loran-C system.

two-way radio communication failure   A situation for which, if it occurs in IFR flight, certain specific procedures have been developed. The transponder code to alert ATC to the fact that communication capability has been lost in 7600.

TWR   Tower.

TXWY   Taxiway.

type certificate   The certificate issued by the FAA for a particular type of aircraft, certifying its airworthiness, and stating operational limitations.

typhoon   A Pacific hurricane or tropical cyclone.

U Intensity unknown (in sequence reports).

U Uniform (phonetic alphabet).

U-1 Unicom at uncontrolled airport.

U-2 Unicom at controlled airport.

UDF UHF direction finder.

UFN Until further notice.

UFO Unidentified Flying Object.

UHF Ultra high frequency.

ultimate load The load required to cause a structure to fail.

ultra high frequency (UHF) The band of electromagnetic frequencies from 300 to 3,000 MHz.

ultralight aircraft A lightweight aircraft having a wing loading of less than three pounds per square foot.

unable Aviation radio term stating that the pilot is unable to comply with an instruction or clearance or that a controller cannot approve a route or altitude request.

UNAVBL Unavailable.

UNCLTD Uncontrolled.

uncontrolled airport An airport without an operating control tower. Airports with part-time control towers are uncontrolled during the hours when the tower is not in operation.

uncontrolled airspace Airspace in which an appropriately rated pilot may operate IFR without being in contact with ATC. Airspace over which ATC has no jurisdiction.

undershoot To touch down short of the intended point of landing.

under the hood The pilot is wearing a hood that restricts his visibility to the instrument panel. Used during flight instruction for an instrument rating. An appropriately rated pilot must occupy the other seat and maintain a watch for other traffic.

unicom The radio frequencies assigned to aeronautical advisory stations for communication with aircraft. Unicoms are usually manned by FBOs or airport personnel and provide pilots with such information as the active runway, wind direction and velocity and other conditions of importance to the pilot. Unicoms are not authorized to give takeoff, landing or other clearances, though they might, at times, be utilized by ATC to relay clearance, in which case the transmission must be preceded by *"ATC clears."*

uniform In aviation radio phraseology the term used for the letter U.

United Instruments Manufacturer of aircraft instruments, encoding altimeters, etc. (3625 Comotara Avenue, Wichita, KS 67226. (316) 685-9203.)

United States The 50 states, District of Columbia, Puerto Rico, all possessions including territorial waters and the airspace above.

United States Parachute Association *See* AVIATION ORGANIZATIONS.

Universal Navigation Corporation Manufacturer of Loran-C, VLF/Omega, VOR/DME/TACAN navigation systems and integrated flight management systems. (3260 East Laredo Road, Tucson, AZ 85706. (602) 741-2300 and (800) 321-5253.)

Universal Navigation UNS-1A long-range navigation management system.

UNLGTD Unlighted.

unlimited ceiling A sky cover report indicating that the sky is clear or has scattered clouds, as observed from the ground. The sequence report symbol is W.

unlimited class In U.S. competition soaring, a class of aircraft without specific requirements or restrictions. In air racing any piston-engine aircraft without limit to the horsepower.

unlimited visibility Horizontal visibility in excess of 15 miles.

UNMRKD Unmarked.

unpublished route A route for which no minimum altitude has been established. It might be a direct route between two navaids, a radar vector, a radial from a navaid or portions of an approach beyond the limits of the published instrument approach procedure.

UNRSTD Unrestricted.

unstable air Turbulent or gusty air that tends to move easily and continues to do so when displaced.

UNSTBL Unstable.

unusable fuel Fuel in the tanks of aircraft that might not be able to reach the fuel lines at all or only when the aircraft is in steady straight and level flight. It is subtracted when calculating the range available with the amount of fuel on board. It is included in the empty weight of an aircraft.

unusual attitudes Any attitude in terms of pitch or roll that is beyond the normal operating attitude. Recovery from unusual attitudes by reference to instruments alone is an integral part of flight training for an instrument rating.

updraft A convection current moving upward. A thermal.

upper winds Winds aloft.

UPR Upper.

UPSLP Upslope.

upwind Into the wind.

upwind leg The flight path parallel to the landing runway and in the same direction as the intended landing.

upwind side The side of a mountain or other terrain or man-made feature toward which the wind is blowing.

URD Utterance recognition device.

US United States.

usable fuel The portion of fuel in the tanks that can be drawn into the fuel lines in all usual flight attitudes. It is included in the useful load figure.

USAF United States Air Force.

USB Upper side band.

USCG United States Coast Guard.

useful load The weight that can be carried in an aircraft in addition to the empty weight and without exceeding the maximum gross weight. It differs from payload in that useful load includes useable fuel and the professional crew and its baggage (in aircraft flown by a professional crew), while the payload includes neither.

USMC United States Marine Corps.

USN United States Navy.

utility category aircraft Light aircraft that will safely withstand 4.4 times its design gross weight in specific flying conditions, while aircraft licensed in the normal category require only 3.8 load limit factor.

UVDF Direction finder operating in UHF and VHF frequencies.

V Variable (in sequence reports).

V Variation.

V Victor (phonetic alphabet).

V Symbol for speed. *See* V-SPEEDS.

vapor lock Vaporization of fuel in the fuel lines that blocks the flow of fuel to the carburetor or injection system.

vapor trail Condensation trail.

VAR Variation.

variable-pitch propeller A propeller the blade angle of which can be adjusted in flight or on the ground.

variation (V or VAR) The angle between true north and magnetic north. It varies at different points on the globe because of local magnetic disturbances. It is shown on aeronautical charts as isogonic lines in degrees east or west and must be subtracted (east) or added (west) to the true course to get the magnetic course.

variometer A sensitive rapidly responding instrument showing the rate of climb or descent. A type of vertical-speed indicator used primarily in gliders and sailplanes.

VASI Visual approach slope indicator.

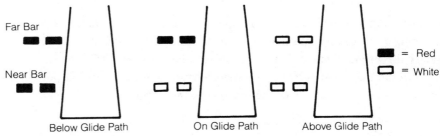

The effect of using VASI during approach.

VCNTY Vicinity.

VDF Direction finder using VHF frequencies.

vector   A heading given to a pilot by a ground-based ATC radar facility.

vector   The product of a combination of speed and direction or other forces.

veering   Wind shifting in a clockwise direction, to the right of the direction from which it is blowing before. The opposite of backing.

velocity   Speed (in a given direction). Most frequently used in relation to wind speeds.

ventral fin   A fin shaped vertical stabilizer located either on top or at the bottom of the fuselage.

venturi   A tube that is narrower in the middle than at either end. When air is forced through a venturi, it results in suction that can be used to drive gyro instruments on aircraft without vacuum pumps.

venturi effect   The increase in wind velocity when wind blows down a valley or through a mountain pass.

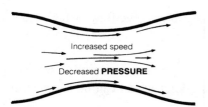

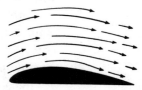

Bernoulli's principle, which explains how lift is created by an airplane wing, is depicted in these diagrams. A fluid traveling through a constriction in a pipe speeds up, and at the same time the pressure it exerts on the pipe decreases.

The constricted airflow shown there, formed by two opposed airplane wings, is analgous to the pinched-pipe situation at left: air moving between the wings accelerates, and this increase in speed results in lower pressure between the curved surfaces.

The same principle applies when the air is disburbed by a single wing. The acceleration airflow over the top surface exerts less pressure than the airflow across the bottom. It is this continuing difference in pressure that creates and sustains lift.

Venturi effect.

verify   In radio communication a request to check the information against the original source of that information to make sure it is correct.

verify direction of takeoff (of flight after takeoff)   An ATC request used when an aircraft makes an instrument departure from an uncontrolled airport. It is usually relayed through a FSS or the unicom on the airport.

vertical axis   The imaginary line running vertically through the fuselage at the CG. Also called yaw axis.

vertical development   Cumulus clouds in the stage of building.

vertical instruments   Engine and other instruments with a narrow vertical instead of a round display.

vertical roll   An aileron roll executed while in vertical climb or descent.

vertical separation   Separation of IFR traffic by altitude.

vertical-speed indicator (VSI)   An instrument, part of the pitot-static system, that indicates the rate of climb or descent in terms of fpm. It is usually calibrated in units of 100 fpm.

vertical stabilizer   The fixed vertical airfoil on the empennage to which the rudder is attached.

vertical stall   Whip stall or hammerhead stall. In a whip stall, the aircraft, having lost flying speed in a near vertical attitude, slides briefly backwards, then pitches violently forward and down. In a hammerhead stall the pilot applies full rudder at the moment the airplane has lost upward momentum. The airplane turns sharply to the right (or left) and continues nose down.

vertical takeoff and landing aircraft   Aircraft capable of liftoff without prior take-off run. Primarily, helicopters.

very high frequency (VHF)   A band of electromagnetic frequencies between 30 MHz and 300 MHz.

very high frequency omnidirectional radio range   VOR.

very high frequency omnirange   VOR.

very high frequency omni test   VOR test facility.

very low frequency   Electromagnetic frequencies below 30 kHz.

vestibular sense   The function of the inner ear that provides a sense of balance. Unreliable under IFR conditions.

VFR   Visual flight rules.

VFR advisory service   Radar service available to VFR aircraft by numerous approach control facilities when the aircraft intends to land at the airport served by the facility.

VFR aircraft   An aircraft operating VFR, or an aircraft not equipped to operate IFR.

VFR conditions   Weather conditions at or above the minimums required by the FARs for VFR operations.

VFR conditions on top   An IFR en route clearance that allows the pilot to fly his aircraft at any appropriate VFR altitude above MEA that is at least 1,000 feet above cloud tops or obscuration.

VFR corridor   A corridor through some TCAs designed to permit VFR traffic to transmit the TCA without contacting ATC.

VFR flight   Flight conducted under visual flight rules in VFR weather conditions.

VFR flight plan   Filing a VFR flight plan assures the pilot that search and rescue operations will be activated automatically if he fails to reach his destination and the flight plan is not closed within 30 minutes of his ETA.

VFR low altitude training routes   Routes flown by military aircraft at or below 1,500 feet agl and at speeds exceeding 250 knots. They are flown only when ceilings are at least 3,000 feet and visibility is better than five miles. *See* OLIVE BRANCH ROUTES, OIL BURNER ROUTES.

VFR on top   VFR flight conducted in VFR conditions above the tops of the overcast.

VFR over the top   VFR on top.

VFR tower   A control tower not equipped to provide approach control services.

VHF   Very high frequency.

VHF omnidirectional radio range   VOR.

victor   In aviation radio phraseology the term used for the letter V.

victor airway   A low altitude airway between VORs. Victor airways are designated by the letter V followed by a number on the radio facility charts.

video map   An electronically displayed map, showing a wide variety of information of importance to the ATC controller. It can be called up on the radarscope by the controller.

Viking   A family of high-performance single-engine aircraft that were manufactured by Bellanca Aircraft Corporation. The aircraft are no longer in production but many remain in the fleet and are cherished by their owners for, among other features, their exceptional maneuverability and handling characteristics.

VIP   Very important person.

visibility   The greatest horizontal distance at which an observer can identify prominent objects with the naked eye. Always reported in statute miles except when referring to RVR in which case it is reported in feet.

visual approach   An approach by an aircraft on an IFR flight plan, made by visual reference to the ground. It may be flown only if the conditions are VFR, and it must be authorized by the ATC.

visual approach slope indicator (VASI)   A two-color light system giving a clear indication to the pilot whether he is on, above, or below the proper glide slope. When above the glide slope he sees only white lights. When on the glide slope he sees red light on the top and white light on the bottom. When below the glide slope he sees only red lights.

visual flight rules   Minimum ceiling and visibility standards established by the FAA under which an aircraft may be operated by visual reference to the ground; plus all rules and regulations affecting VFR operation of an aircraft.

visual holding   Holding an aircraft at an easily recognized geographical fix.

visual meteorological conditions Established minimums in terms of visibility, ceiling, and distance from clouds.

visual separation A means of separating IFR aircraft in terminal areas. Either the controller sees the aircraft in question and issues instructions accordingly, or the pilot sees the other aircraft and, when cleared to do so by ATC, maintains his own separation.

VLF Very low frequency.

VLF/Omega A system of long-range (worldwide) area navigation, using a limited number of VLF transmitters to obtain position information.

VLY Valley.

VNAV Vertical navigation. A type of area navigation equipment that includes a means of flying a controlled descent at a desired rate where no ground-based glide slope information is available.

VOR Very high frequency omnidirectional radio range. A navaid consisting of two transmitters, one of which transmits a constant phase signal through 360 degrees of azimuth while the other rotates at 1,800 rpm and transmits a signal that varies with the constant-phase signal at a constant rate throughout the 360 degrees. This results in an infinite number of radials from the station (or bearings to the station) that are received by the nav receiver in the aircraft and displayed on the OBI. VOR frequencies range from 108.0 MHz to 117.95 MHz (not including the ILS localizer frequencies that are the odd-tenth decimal frequencies between 108.1 and 111.9 MHz). VORs are also referred to as *omni stations*.

VOR approach A nonprecision approach using one or several VORs as navigational reference.

VOR/DME A combination of VOR and DME in one ground station.

VOR station Usually a round flat roofed structure with a cone shaped antenna sticking up in the center. Always painted white.

VOR test facility (VOT) A ground transmitter that is designed to check the accuracy and proper functioning of the on-board VOR receiver while the aircraft is on the ground.

VORTAC A combination VOR and TACAN at the same location, transmitting VOR and DME information.

vortex A rotating air mass created by the movement of an airfoil through the air; especially the trailing vortices which form aft of each wing tip from the tendency of high-pressure air below the wing to flow into the low-pressure area above the wing. *See also* WAKE TURBULENCE.

VOT VOR testing facility.

Voyager A multiengine push-pull aircraft designed by Burt Rutan for the expressed purpose of flying around the world non-stop without refueling. The actual flight was made successfully in December of 1986 with Dick Rutan (Burt's brother) and

Jeana Yeager as the crew. The pertinent data for the flight are:

Takeoff from Edwards Air Force Base: 7:59:38 a.m. on Sunday, December 14, 1986.

Landing at Edwards Air Force Base: 8:05:28 a.m. on Tuesday, December 23, 1986.

Total flight time: 9 days, 3 minutes, 44 seconds.

Total distance covered: 21,712.818 nautical miles.

Average altitude: 9,063 feet msl.

Fuel used: 1,171.8 gallons.

Takeoff weight: 9,694.5 pounds (empty aircraft weight: 2,250 pounds).

Landing weight: 2,699.1 pounds.

Average true airspeed: 97.517 knots.

Average ground speed: 106.011 knots.

(Jeana Yeager, Voyager, 614 Sandydale Road, Nipomo, CA 93444. (805) 929-6345. Dick Rutan, Voyager Aircraft, Inc., Hangar 77, Mojave, CA 93501.)

The Voyager designed by Burt Rutan and flown non-stop around the globe by Dick Rutan and Jeana Yeager.

VR Veering.

VRBL Variable.

VSBY Visibility.

VSI Vertical-speed indicator.

V speeds Designations for certain speeds:

V_a = design maneuvering speed
V_b = design speed for maximum gust intensity
V_c = design cruising speed
V_d = design diving speed

V_{df} = demonstrated flight diving speed (M_{df} same in Mach)

V_f = design flap speed

V_{fc} = maximum speed for stability characteristics (M_{fc} = same in Mach)

V_{fe} = maximum flap-extended speed

V_h = maximum speed in level flight with maximum continuous power

V_{le} = maximum landing-gear-extended speed

V_{lo} = maximum landing-gear-operating speed

V_{lof} = lift-off speed

V_{mc} = minimum control speed with the critical engine inoperative

V_{me} = maximum endurance speed

V_{mo} = maximum operating speed limit (M_{mo} = same in Mach)

V_{mu} = minimum unstick speed

V_{ne} = never-exceed speed

V_r = rotation speed

V_s = stalling speed or the minimum steady flight speed at which the aircraft is controllable

V_{so} = stalling speed or minimum steady flight speed in the landing configuration

V_{xse} = best single-engine angle-of-climb speed

V_y = best rate-of-climb speed

V_{yse} = best single-engine rate-of-climb speed

V_1 = critical engine-failure speed

V_2 = takeoff safety speed

V_{2min} = minimum takeoff speed

VTOL Vertical takeoff and landing (aircraft)

W Indefinite ceiling (in sequence reports).

w Warm (description of an air mass).

W West.

W Whiskey (phonetic alphabet).

WAC World aeronautical chart.

WAD *See* WORLD AVIATION DIRECTORY.

wake turbulence Turbulence created by the movement of an aircraft through the air. Primarily, the trailing wing-tip vortices that develop in the wake of heavy aircraft. Resembling a pair of counter-rotating horizontal tornadoes, they are at their worst behind a slow-moving heavy aircraft just after takeoff and just prior to touchdown. They tend to remain violent for several minutes, capable of throwing a smaller aircraft out of control. To avoid being caught in wake turbulence, liftoff should be accomplished before reaching the point of liftoff of the heavy aircraft, and should be followed by a steeper climb angle, preferably on the upwind side of the climb path of the heavy aircraft. During landing the light aircraft should stay above the flight path of the heavy aircraft (and, if possible, on the upwind side), and should touch down past the point at which the heavy aircraft touched down. The generation of wake turbulence ceases at the moment of touchdown of the heavy aircraft. (Page 454)

walkaround Preflight inspection.

warm air mass A mass of stable air warmer than the surface over which it is moving. It tends to cool as it moves, becoming even more stable, but reducing visibility.

warm front A usually deep front formed by a mass of warm, low-pressure air which is replacing a cold air mass. It is characterized by a sloping bank of clouds, steady precipitation, low ceiling and visibility and, in the winter, danger of icing in clouds. It is shown on weather charts as a line with rounded marks pointing in the direction of movement.

warmup Letting the engine run at idle power until oil temperature and pressure are shown to be in the green.

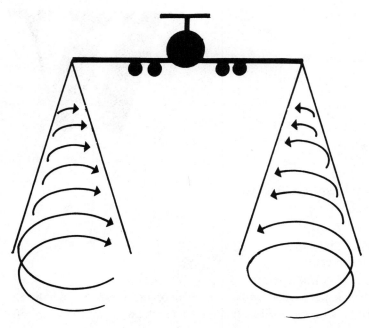

Wake turbulence is produced by slow flying heavy jets.

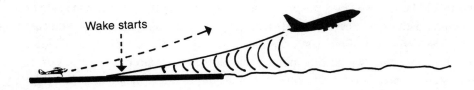

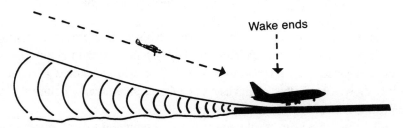

When taking off, lift off ahead of the point of the heavy jet's rotation. When landing, stay above the flight path of the heavy jet and land long.

warning area A special use area off the coast of the U.S. and over international waters. Identified on charts by a W.

washout A decrease in the angle of incidence built into the tip areas of the wings to cause wing tips to fly at a lower angle-of-attack than wing roots. This prevents the tips from stalling during slow flight maneuvers, and assures effective aileron control at low speeds.

water vapor Water in gaseous form in the atmosphere, primarily below 30,000 feet. When condensing it produces rain, snow, fog, dew, etc.

WAVE Wind, altimeter voice equipment.

wave-off Being told not to land by someone stationed on the ground using visual signals. Primarily in the context of landing on an aircraft carrier.

waypoint (WP) A navigational fix used in area navigation, created by electronically relocating a VORTAC from its actual position to a position desired by the pilot.

WBAS Weather bureau airport station.

WCA Wind correction angle.

WDLY Widely.

WEA Weather.

weak link A weak spot in the tow rope used in towing gliders into the air. Its breaking strength is specified by the FAA as a safety feature.

weather advisory Report of hazardous weather conditions not included in previous forecasts. *See also* AIRMET AND SIGMET.

weather broadcast Aviation weather reported by FSSs for areas within approximately 150 miles of the station. It is broadcast hourly at 15 minutes past the hour.

weather charts The different types of charts produced by the National Weather Service and available for inspection at flight service stations. (Pages 456-458)

weathercock The tendency of an aircraft to align itself lengthwise with the direction of the wind.

weather minimums The lowest amount of visibility and the lowest ceiling under which takeoff, landing, or flight is allowed. Weather minimums vary between VFR and IFR, controlled and uncontrolled airspace, type of instrument approach and type of aircraft flying the approach.

weather radar Airborne radar that depicts areas of precipitation on the scope. Its most important feature is its ability to display areas within thunderstorms with the heaviest precipitation, areas that are likely to be those with the greatest turbulence, thus permitting the pilot to plot a reasonably safe path through the storm. Since the introduction of electronic flight instrument systems (EFIS), most new weather radars are equipped with computer-generated graphic displays that can be programmed to display flight paths, checklists, and a number of other features in addition to or in place of the precipitation data. *See also* EFIS.

Explanation of weather station model and symbols

At Weather Bureau offices, maps showing conditions at the earth's surface are drawn 4 times daily or oftener. The location of the reporting station is printed on the map as a small circle. A definite arrangement of the data around the station circle, called the station model, is used. The station model is based on international agreements. Thru such standardized use of numerals and symbols, a meteorologist of one country can use the weather maps of another country even though he does not understand the language. An abridged description of the symbols is presented below.

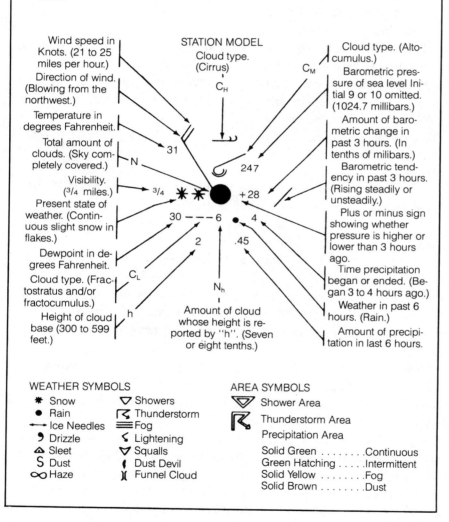

STATION MODEL

Wind speed in Knots. (21 to 25 miles per hour.)

Direction of wind. (Blowing from the northwest.)

Temperature in degrees Fahrenheit.

Total amount of clouds. (Sky completely covered.)

Visibility. (³/₄ miles.)

Present state of weather. (Continuous slight snow in flakes.)

Dewpoint in degrees Fahrenheit.

Cloud type. (Fractostratus and/or fractocumulus.)

Height of cloud base (300 to 599 feet.)

Cloud type. (Cirrus)

Cloud type. (Altocumulus.)

Barometric pressure of sea level Initial 9 or 10 omitted. (1024.7 millibars.)

Amount of barometric change in past 3 hours. (In tenths of milibars.)

Barometric tendency in past 3 hours. (Rising steadily or unsteadily.)

Plus or minus sign showing whether pressure is higher or lower than 3 hours ago.

Time precipitation began or ended. (Began 3 to 4 hours ago.)

Weather in past 6 hours. (Rain.)

Amount of precipitation in last 6 hours.

Amount of cloud whose height is reported by "h". (Seven or eight tenths.)

WEATHER SYMBOLS

* Snow
● Rain
← Ice Needles
🌢 Drizzle
⌂ Sleet
S Dust
∞ Haze

▽ Showers
⌐ Thunderstorm
≡ Fog
⟨ Lightening
▽ Squalls
⟨ Dust Devil
)(Funnel Cloud

AREA SYMBOLS

▽ Shower Area
Ⓡ Thunderstorm Area
Precipitation Area

Solid Green . . . . .Continuous
Green Hatching . . . . .Intermittent
Solid Yellow . . . . .Fog
Solid Brown . . . . .Dust

Weather chart symbols.

Many of the elements in the STATION MODEL are entered in values which can be intrepreted directly. Some, however, require reference to coded tables and these STATION MODEL entries are described in this tables below:

C_L	Description (Abridged From W.M.O. Code)	C_M	Description (Abridged From W.M.O. Code)	C_H	Description (Abridged From W.M.O. Code)
	Cu of fair weather, little vertical development and seemingly flattened.		Thin As (most of cloud layer semi-transparent).		Filaments of Ci, or "mares tails", scattered and not increasing.
	Cu of considerable development, generally towering, with or without other Cu of Sc bases all at same level.		Thick As, greater part sufficiently dense to hide sun (or moon), or Ns.		Dense Ci in patches or twisted sheaves, usually not increasing, sometimes like remains of Cb; or towers of tufts.
	Cb with tops lacking clear-cut outlines, but distinctly not cirriform or anvil-shaped; with or without Cu, Sc, or St.		Thin Ac, mostly semi-transparent; cloud elements not changing much and at a single level.		Dense Ci, often anvil-shaped, derived from or associated with Cb.
	Sc formed by spreading out of Cu, Cu often present also.		Thin Ac in patches; cloud elements continually changing and/or occurring at more than one level.		Ci, often hook-shaped, gradually spreading over the sky and usually thickening as a whole.
	Sc not formed by spreading out of Cu.		Thin Ac in bands or in a layer gradually spreading over sky and usually thickening as a whole.		Ci and Cs, often in converging bands, or Cs alone; generally overspreading and growing denser; the continuous layer not reaching 45° altitude.
	St or Fs or both, but no Fs of bad weather.		Ac formed by the spreading out of Cu.		Ci and Cs, often in converging bands, or Cs alone; generally overspreading and growing denser; the continuous layer exceeding 45° altitude.
	Fs and/or Fc of bad weather (scud).		Double-layered Ac, or a thick layer of Ac, not increasing; or Ac with As and/or Ns.		Veil of Cs covering the entire sky.
	Cu and Sc (not formed by spreading out of Cu) with bases at different levels.		Ac in the form of Cu-shaped tufts or Ac with turrets.		Cs not increasing and not covering entire sky.
	Cb having a clearly fibrous (cirriform) top, often anvil-shaped, with or without Cu, Sc, St, or scud.		Ac of a chaotic sky, usually at different levels; patches of dense Ci are usually present also.		Cc alone of Cc with some Ci or Cs, but the Cc being the main cirriform cloud.

Cloud Abbreviation	R_t	Time of Precipitation	h	Height in Feet (Rounded Off)	N	N_h	Sky Coverage
St or Fs - Stratus or Fractostratus	0	No Precipitation	0	0-149		0	No clouds
Ci-Cirrus	1	Less than 1 hour ago	1	150-299		1	Less than one-tenth or one tenth
Cs-Cirrostratus	2	1 to 2 hours ago	2	300-599		2	Two and three-tenths
Cc-Cirrocumulus	3	2 to 3 hours ago	3	600-999		3	Four-tenths
Ac-Altocumulus	4	3 to 4 hours ago	4	1,000-1,999		4	Five-tenths
As-Altostratus	5	4 to 5 hours ago	5	2,000-3,499		5	Six tenths
Sc-Stratocumulus	6	5 to 6 hours ago	6	3,500-4,999		6	Seven and eight-tenths
Ns-Nimbostratus	7	6 to 12 hours ago	7	5,000-7,999		7	Nine-tenths or over-overcast with openings.
Cu or Fc-Cumulus or Fractocumulus	8	More than 12 hours ago	8	6,500,-7,999		8	Completely overcast
Cb-Cumulonimbus	9	Unknown	9	At or above 8,000, or no clouds		9	Sky obsured

Station model weather symbols

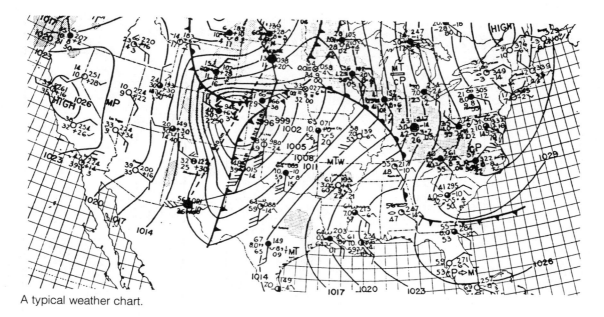

A typical weather chart.

weather station   A service, usually at an airport and often co-located with an FSS, which collects weather information, and conducts pilot weather briefings.

weathervane   The tendency of an aircraft on the ground to face into the wind, resulting from the wind hitting the vertical stabilizer.

weight   The force of gravity that pulls an object to the center of the earth. It must be overcome by lift to achieve flight.

weight and balance   The calculations necessary to determine whether or not the aircraft is loaded within acceptable limits. The numbers involved vary greatly among the different types of aircraft. Large corporate aircraft have to deal with weight limits for different weight conditions:

Zero fuel weight—The weight of the loaded aircraft minus usable fuel.

Ramp weight—The weight of the loaded aircraft including the usable fuel.

Takeoff weight—The weight of the loaded aircraft minus the fuel burned off during taxi and holding for takeoff.

Landing weight—The weight of the aircraft minus fuel burned during the flight.

In addition to the different maximum weight limits, each location of the aircraft where loads might be added or removed involves a different moment arm. There might be moment arms for a nose baggage compartment, an aft cabin baggage compartment, and a rear bay baggage area. Then there are different moment arms for each seat row, and for the fuel tanks. In each instance the moment is calculated by multiplying the moment arm by the weight. Then all moments are added and the total is divided by the takeoff weight to determine the center of gravity (CG). It must be within the limits that are listed in the owner's manual. Also listed in all owner's manuals are the calculations that must be performed for the aircraft in question in order to determine the weight-and-balance condition with reference to a given flight.

Westland Helicopters Ltd. Manufacturer of a wide variety of civilian and military helicopters. (Yeovil, Som, England BA20 2YB. Phone: 0935 75222.)

Westland Helicopters

		W30-100-60	W30-300-60
ENGINES	manufacturer	Rolls-Royce (2)	General Electric (2)
	model	Gem 60-3 MK 530	CT7-2B
	installed hp	2562	3230
	takeoff hp	2450	2750
	max continuous hp	2226	2750
WEIGHTS lbs	gross	12,800	16,000
	external	12,800	16,000
	empty	8,186	8,253
	useful load	4,614	7,747
DIMENSIONS ft	total length	52.2	52.2
	fuselage length	45	45
	height	13.3	13.3
	width	10.2	10.2
MAIN ROTOR	diameter ft	43.7	43.7
	number of blades	4	4
FUEL gal	usable, standard	345	345
	aux.	200	180
SPEEDS knots	V_{ne}	135	150
	max cruise	120	n/a
	economy cruise	120	140
SERVICE CEILING	ft	10,000	15,000
HOVER	IGE	2,600	6,500
	OGE	2,300	4,400

Westwind A corporate twin-engine fan-jet that was developed and manufactured by Israel Aircraft Industries as Westwind I and Westwind II. For performance specifications, *See* ISRAEL AIRCRAFT INDUSTRIES.

whip stall *See* VERTICAL STALL.

whirly bird Slang for helicopter.

Whirly Girls, Inc. *See* AVIATION ORGANIZATIONS.

whiskey In aviation radio phraseology the term used for the letter W.

whiteout The inability to distinguish ground from horizon and sky. A phenomenon occurring when flying over flat, featureless, snow covered terrain when the sky is the same color as the ground.

wicker basket   A gondola for ballooning, made of wicker.

wilco   A phrase used in radio communication, meaning that the message has been received and will be complied with.

Williams International   Manufacturer of the F107-WR-400 and -101 and the FJ44 turbofan engines, the WTS34-16 turboshaft engines, the WTS34 family of small gas turbines, the WR27 auxiliary turbine power unit, and the X-Jet propelling a one-person pod in vertical takeoff. The SA-30 FanJet under development by Swearingen Engineering and Technology will be powered by Williams engines. (2280 West Maple Road, Box 200, Walled Lake, MI 48088. (313) 624-5200.)

winch launch   A means of launching a glider by using a ground-based winch rather than a towplane or automobile.

wind   Air in horizontal motion caused by pressure or temperature differences in the atmosphere.

wind, altimeter voice equipment   An automatic device that reports weather conditions with a computer-generated voice.

wind arrow   A symbol used on weather maps to show wind direction and velocity. The shaft of the arrow shows the direction and each "feather" indicates 10 knots, each half "feather" five knots.

wind chill factor   The still air temperature that would have the same cooling effect on exposed human flesh as a given combination of temperature and wind velocity.

wind correction angle   The number of degrees divergent from the compass course that the pilot must steer in order to compensate for crosswind components. To determine crosswind components, use the algorithm shown under CONVERSION TALBES.

wind drift   The movement of an airplane to the left or right of its line of flight, resulting from the force of the wind.

windmilling propeller   In the event of engine stoppage, the tendency of the propeller to continue to turn because of the airstream moving across the blades. A windmilling propeller produces drag rather than thrust.

winds aloft   Winds at altitudes above 1,500 feet agl. They are measured every six hours by radiosondes and reported in groups of figures representing true heading and velocity in knots. Winds aloft are not usually included in weather broadcasts, but pilots can request the information for whatever altitudes are of interest.

winds aloft chart   A weather map showing wind speed and direction (with wind arrows) at selected altitudes.

windscreen   Windshield.

wind shadow   An expression used primarily in soaring. It denotes an area of calm in the lee of windbreaks such as hills, buildings, trees. When it is sunny they are likely sources of thermals on a windy day.

wind shear   An abrupt change in wind direction or velocity.

wind shift   The veering or backing of the wind.

windsock   A coneshaped cloth sleeve, usually orange or yellow, that catches the wind and points away from the direction from which it is blowing. Usually located on one or several prominent positions on the airport.

wind tee   Tetrahedron.

wind triangle   The basic concept of dead reckoning, involving true heading, airspeed, ground speed and wind direction and velocity. The calculations necessary to arrive at the ground speed and heading to make good the desired course can easily be accomplished with the slide rule portion of a flight computer.

wind velocity gradient   The horizontal wind shear close to the ground caused by the frictional effect of the terrain.

wing   The primary airfoil of an airplane, developing most of the needed lift.

wing loading   The total forces exerted on a wing in flight, expressed in pounds per square foot of wing area. All aircraft have maximum wing loading capability as part of the design concept.

wingtip vortices   *See* WAKE TURBULENCE.

WIP   Work in progress.

WK   Weak.

WKN   Weaken.

WND   Wind.

wobble pump   An emergency fuel pump operated by manually pushing a handle back and forth.

words twice   When used as a request it means that the communication is difficult to understand. Therefore, please say each phrase twice. Or it may be used to inform the listener that each phrase in the message will be spoken twice because of communication difficulties.

World Aeronautical Chart   An aeronautical chart in a scale of 1:1,000,000, or approximately 13.7 nm to the inch.

World Aviation Directory   A collection of all data concerning all companies that are involved in aviation and space related activities. (McGraw-Hill, Inc. 1221 Avenue of the Americas, New York, NY 10020. (212) 512-2528. Editorial offices: 1156 15th Street N.W., Washington, DC 20005. (202) 822-4600. Published in March and September.)

WP   Waypoint.

WR   Wet runway.

WRM   Warm.

WSI Corporation   The company offers a service called NOWrad that produces real time radar weather charts that can be called up with any IBM PC or compatible personal computer with or without color monitor. Such computers can be found in most of the better FBO facilities. Available are national and regional radar images. Additional services include a comprehensive weather information data-base, color satellite images from GOES METEOSAT and GMS, worldwide flight planning including computer flight planning with FAA, ARINC, SITA, AFTN, or TELEX transmission of flight plans to any place on earth, SLOT reservations for ORD, DCA, LGA, and JFK, and several other specialized services, all on a 24-hour a day 365-days-a-year basis. (41 North Road, Bedford, MA 01730. (617) 275-5300.)

WSR   Wet snow on runway.

WT   Weight.

Wulfsberg Electronics   The company was merged with Global Navigation Systems.
   See GLOBAL WULFSBERG SYSTEMS.

WV   Wave.

WX   Weather.

X   Symbol for total obscuration (in sequence reports).

X   Xray (exray) (phonetic alphabet).

XCVR   Transceiver.

XMTR   Transmitter.

XPDR   Transponder.

Xray   In aviation radio phraseology the term used for the letter X.

Y   Yankee (phonetic alphabet).

Y   Yukon standard time.

Y-2   A 17-seat twin-turboprop aircraft developed and manufactured in the Peoples Republic of China. It is expected to be FAA certificated and will be exported to the west, selling at an anticipated price of $1.7 million fully IFR equipped.

yankee   In aviation radio phraseology the term used for the letter Y.

yaw   The movement of the aircraft to either side, turning around its vertical axis (without banking).

yaw axis   The vertical axis through the CG of the aircraft.

yaw damper   A single-axis autopilot that automatically counteracts the tendency of some aircraft to yaw in flight.

yaw string   A few inches of yarn attached inside the cockpit of gliders in view of the pilot. When it leans to one side or the other in flight, it indicates a slip or a skid and the need for correcting the degree of rudder pressure.

yoke   Control wheel; stick.

Z Greenwich mean time.

Z Zulu (phonetic alphabet).

zero fuel weight Some larger aircraft are limited for structural reasons in the amount of weight that can safely be carried when there is a minimum amount of fuel in the wing tanks. Because aircraft are likely to be low on fuel prior to landing, the zero fuel weight must be considered when loading passengers and freight.

zero-zero Phrase used to indicate that both ceiling and visibility are zero.

zinc chromate primer A primer used on bare aluminum and magnesium to prevent corrosion.

ZL Freezing drizzle (in sequence reports).

ZM Z-marker.

Z-marker A VHF radio beacon broadcasting straight up at a frequency of 75 MHz. It is used to obtained position information.

zoom A means of gaining altitude by increasing airspeed and then pulling back on the control wheel and climbing sharply until the excessive momentum is lost and the aircraft approaches stall.

ZR Freezing rain (in sequence reports).

Zulu In aviation-radio phraseology the term used for the letter Z.

Zulu Time Greenwich Mean Time. Coordinated Universal Time.

Other Bestsellers of Related Interest

STANDARD AIRCRAFT HANDBOOK—Enlarge 4th Edition—Larry Reithmaier.

"This updated edition of an important handbook is an excellent guide for the aviation and student mechanic engaged in building, maintaining, overhauling and repairing all-metal aircraft" (NYPL **New Technical Books**). 240 pages, 239 illustrations. Book No. 28512,

FAR 1989—TAB/AERO

Fully updated for 1989,this is the best possible source for information on the portions of the FARs of interest to private pilots, owners, and flight instructors. 192 pages. Book No. 25744,

THE BLOND KNIGHT OF GERMANY—Raymond F. Toliver.

The fascinating story of Luftwaffe ace Erich Hartman: "one of the best aviation biographies to appear for a long time" **Springfield [Mass.] Morning Union**) 384 pages, Illustrated. Book No. 24189, $16.95 paperback only

MESSERSCHMITT: ACES—Walter A. Musciano

Traces the history of the Jagdwaffe—the German Luftwaffe's fighter force—describing its greatest WWII pilots, the battles they fought, and the plane they flew: the legendary Messerschmitt Me 109, includes many never-before-published photographs. 304 pages, 287 illustrations. Book No. 22379, $17.95 paperback only

AIM 1989—TAB/AERO Staff.

An essential manual for every pilot, this ;meticulously indexed guide includes complete reprints of the U.S. government's AIM sections on navigational aids, aeronautical lighting and airport markings, ATC procedures, and more. 272 pages, 74 illustrations, Book No. 21369, $6.95 paperback only

THE ILLUSTRATED BUYER'S GUIDE TO USED AIRPLANES—2nd Edition—Bill Clarke

Raves for the 1st Edition: *'A wealth of information on 'pre-flown' small aircraft . . .'*' (Cessna Owner Magazine-.For those learning toward, or definitely contemplating the purchase of an aircraft, Clarke's volume contains specific, detailed help" *(Raviation Newsletter).* 320 pages, 145 illustrations. Book No. 2462. $18.95 paperback, $27.95 hardcover

THE PIPER CLASSICS—Joe Christy.

A buyer's guide, owner's maintenance manual, and dealer's reference to the fabric-covered Pipers now sought after on the used plane market ". . . easy, interesting reading and good accurate data for reference use—all in one book that ought to be in the library of every Piper owner and/or enthusiast" *(Pipers Magazine).* 160 pages, 94 illustrations. Book No. 2457, $13.95 paperback only

THE CESSNA 172—Bill Clarke

Prospective buyers of this economical, easy-to-fly, and popular small plane will turn to this factual guide for tips on getting the best value for their dollar. ". . . an understandable, accurate, quick reference to C172s" *(Cessna Magazine)* 304 pages, 110 illustrations. Book No. 2412, $13.95 paperback only

THE ILLUSTRATED GUIDE TO AERODYNAMICS—Hubert "Skip" Smith

Explains why and how airplanes fly. An excellent introductory text for aeronautical engineering students, student pilots, or any interested layman. 240 pages, 234 illustrations. Book No. 2390, $15.95 paperback only

HOW TO FLY HELICOPTERS—2nd Edition—Larry Collier, Revised by Kas Thomas

A nontechnical guide that effectively conveys what it really feels like to be in the cockpit. 240 pages, 81 illustrations. Book No. 2386, $13.95 paperback only

THE LUFTWAFFE: A PHOTOGRAPHIC RECORD 1919-1945—Karl Ries

"A wonderful record of the Luftwaffe from the end of WWI through WWII. An excellent book for the library of airplane buffs as well as military history or air operations students" *(Reference & Research Book News).* "A noteworthy contribution to aviation history . . . that deserves to stay in print for years to come. Outstanding" *(Coast Book Review Service).* 236 pages, 450 illustrations. Book No. 22384, $24.95 hardcover only

ENCYCLOPAEDIA OF MILITARY MODELS 1/71—Claude Boileau, Huynth-Dinh Knuong, and Thomas A. Young.

A complete and up-to-date guide to all the 1/72nd scale plastic military models EVER produced worldwide. Color photos show the kits and kitboxes in detail, and an extensive listing of model manufacturers is includes. 204 pages, Illustrated. Book No. 22383, $19.95 paperback, $28.95 hardcover

STEALTH TECHNOLOGY: THE ART OF BLACK MAGIC—J. Jones, Edited by Matt Thurber

A well-researched account of stealth technology and its application around the world. Covers the B-2 and the F-19A, as well as helicopters, unmanned craft, and missiles. Illustrated in color and black-and-white. 160 pages, 103 illustrations. Book No. 22381, $14.95 paperback, $22.95 hardcover

THE MCDONNELL DOUGLAS APACHE (Aero Series, Vol. 33)—Frank Colucci

A concise, illustrated look at the history, design, and mission of the world's most advanced attack helicopter. "I believe this book will give . . . a full appreciation of the Apache program—how it evolved, what it is today and the difference it will make should we have to go to war in the future" (Major General Edward M. Browne, USA [Ret'd], Manager of the Apache Program, 4/76-12/82). 112 pages, 104 illustrations. Book No. 20614, $10.95 paperback only

YOUR PILOT'S LICENSE—4th Edition—Joe Christy

"A valuable reference manual during training" *(ALA Booklist)*. "A book you should not only read but have as a permanent part of your bookshelf" *(Colorado CAP Flyer)*. 176 pages, 73 illustrations. Book No. 2477, $12.95 paperback only

THE PIPER INDIANS—Bill Clarke

"Clarke analyzes in depth the various models of Piper aircrart, their eccentricities, their virtues . . . if you own a Piper, ever thought about owing one, just love Piper aircraft or need an accurate, easy-to-use reference . . . you shouldn't be without The Piper Indians" *(Pipers Magazine)*. 288 pages, 112 illustrations, Book No. 2432, $16.95 paperback, $24.95 hardcover

ABCS OF SAFE FLYING—2nd Edition—David Frazier

"Sound advice for licensed as well as student pilots" *(Private Pilot)* ". . . a carefully written review of the essentials every pilot ought to know" *(Kitplanes)*. 208 pages, 69 illustrations. Book No. 2430, $12.95 paperback only

---

Look for These and Other TAB Books at Your Local BOOKSTORE

To Order Call Toll Free 1-800-822-8158

(in PA and AK call 717-794-2191)

or write to TAB BOOKS Inc., Blue Ridge Summit, PA 17294-0840.

Title	Product No.	Quantity	Price

Subtotal	$ _____
Postage and Handling ($3.00 in U.S., $5.00 outside U.S.)	$ _____
In PA, NY, & ME add applicable sales tax	$ _____
TOTAL	$ _____

☐ Check or money order made payable to TAB BOOKS Inc.

Charge my ☐ VISA ☐ MasterCard ☐ American Express

Acct. No. _____ Exp. _____

Signature: _____

Name: _____

City: _____

State: _____ Zip: _____

TAB BOOKS catalog free with purchase; otherwise send $1.00 in check or money order and receive a $1.00 credit on your next purchase.

Orders outside U.S. must pay with international money order in U.S. dollars.

TAB Guarantee: If for any reason you are not satisfied with the book(s) you order, simply return it (them) within 15 days and receive a full refund.   **BC**